Reading After
FOUCAULT

KRITIK: GERMAN LITERARY THEORY AND CULTURAL STUDIES

LILIANE WEISSBERG, EDITOR

Books in the Series

Walter Benjamin: An Intellectual Biography, by Bernd Witte, trans. by James Rolleston, 1991

The Violent Eye: Ernst Jünger's Visions and Revisions on the European Right, by Marcus Paul Bullock, 1991

Fatherland: Novalis, Freud, and the Discipline of Romance, by Kenneth S. Calhoon, 1992

Metaphors of Knowledge: Language and Thought in Mauthner's Critique, by Elizabeth Bredeck, 1992

Laocoon's Body and the Aesthetics of Pain: Winckelmann, Lessing, Herder, Moritz, Goethe, by Simon Richter, 1992

The Critical Turn: Studies in Kant, Herder, Wittgenstein, and Contemporary Theory, by Michael Morton, 1993

Reading After Foucault: Institutions, Disciplines, and Technologies of the Self in Germany, 1750–1830, edited by Robert S. Leventhal, 1994

Reading After FOUCAULT

Institutions, Disciplines, and Technologies of the Self in Germany, 1750–1830

Edited by ROBERT S. LEVENTHAL

Wayne State University Press   Detroit

Copyright © 1994 by Wayne State University Press, Detroit, Michigan 48202. All rights are reserved. No part of this book may be reproduced without formal permission. Manufactured in the United States of America.
99 98 97 96 95 94   5 4 3 2 1

Library of Congress Cataloging-in-Publication Data

Reading after Foucault : institutions, disciplines, and technologies
  of the self in Germany, 1750–1830 / edited by Robert S. Leventhal.
    p. cm. — (Kritik)
  Includes bibliographical references and index.
  ISBN 0-8143-2510-6 (alk. paper)
  1. German literature—18th century—History and criticism.
  2. German literature—19th century—History and criticism.
  3. Foucault, Michel—Views on literature.   4. Foucault, Michel-
  -Influence.   I. Leventhal, Robert Scott.   II. Series.
  PT285.R38   1994
  830.9′006—dc20   94-16730

Designer: Mark C. Howell

CONTENTS

Preface **vii**

Introduction: Reading after Foucault *Robert S. Leventhal* **1**

I: Institutions and Institutionalization **29**

How, Why, When, and Where Did Language Go Public?
Ian Hacking **31**

Johann Carl Wezel's *Herrmann und Ulrike* (1780) or The Origin of the Good *Franz Futterknecht* **51**

From the Recreation of Scholars to the Labor of the Concept
Friedrich Kittler **65**

Reciprocal Influence *Robert S. Leventhal* **75**

II: Disciplines and Disciplinarity **91**

The Spectacle of Maria Stuart's Imprisonment
Dorothea E. von Mücke **93**

Kleist's *The Broken Jug*: The Play of Sexual Difference
David E. Wellbery **117**

The Enigma of Hermeneutics: The Case of Kaspar Hauser
Gerd Gemünden **127**

CONTENTS

III: Technologies of the Self 151

'Die Erhaltung des Gleichgewichts': Defining and Prescribing a Technology of Self *Courtney Federle* 153

Concerning Several Formulae of Communication in Hölderlin *Rüdiger Campe* 169

Autobiographical Hyperbole: Schiller's *Naive and Sentimental Poetry* *Linda M. Brooks* 193

The Romantic Archaeology of the Psyche: Novalis's *Heinrich von Ofterdingen* *Kenneth Calhoon* 211

Writing after Murder (and before Suicide): The Confessions of Werther and Rivière *Joel Black* 233

Notes on the Contributors 261

Index 265

PREFACE

The task of a volume of Foucauldian readings of German literature, letters, and culture in the period 1750–1830 is less to apply what Foucault wrote to a given body of texts than to carry his research into the power relations of modernity further and reexamine the canon and the institutions that subtend it and make it possible. If the notion of the text has assumed a privileged status in our readings, it is only because Foucault insisted that we return, again and again, to the actual sentences of texts, to what is actually *stated*. This approach to the eighteenth century delivers a very different cultural system than the one typically found in literary histories. It is a cultural epoch at odds with itself, in strife, full of contradictions and discontinuities. As such, it fails to offer an alternative periodization, but rather asks us to examine the structures that persist at the axiomatic level of the cultural production.

Reading after Foucault displays the fourfold force of the term 'after' inherent in the German term *nach*: not only do we read in his wake, having absorbed some of the shocks he offered and translating them into new readings of texts, we also have read 'according to' Foucault in the sense that we have subjected ourselves in part to his discipline and regime of analysis. In addition, we have—to the extent that it is possible—tried to work through the reverberations and distortions of the supplementarity these readings bring to the fore, their *Nachträglichkeit* in the sense in which Freud used the term. Finally, and perhaps most importantly, we are directed towards his researches, in yet another sense of the German *nach*, and 'after' two central objectives he himself stated were of primary importance in writing an archaeology of modernity: a history of the present and a critical ontology of ourselves.

I would like to thank the Associate Provost for Research at the University of Virginia for two Faculty Research Grants between 1990 and 1993, and the Center for Advanced Studies at the University of Virginia for a Sesquicentennial Fellowship during the fall semester of 1992. I would also like to thank those individuals who provided much needed support and encouragment throughout the preparation of the manuscript: Liliane Weissberg, who was unremitting in both her enthusiasm and critical appraisals; Lorna Martens, who gave me precise and insightful readings of the introduction and my contribution; Benjamin Bennett, for the lively discussions we had in his seminar on the eighteenth century. Richard Rorty generously provided me with a draft of his essay on Foucault "Moral Identity and Private Auton-

PREFACE

omy" prior to its publication in the volume *Michel Foucault: Philosopher* (New York: Routledge, 1992), pp. 328–36. I also want to thank the readers at Wayne State, who made careful suggestions for the final version. Arthur Evans gave me extremely useful guidance throughout. Brenda Sprouse and Melody Aylor assisted in the preparation of the final manuscript. Without the decisive input of these individuals, the volume would not have been possible. I would also like to thank the contributors, who answered my call and patiently went through the long and difficult task of editing with me. My good friends gave me support and encouragement, in ways they perhaps are unaware of: Michael Prince, Joel Black, Robert Sackett, Jeffrey Bokor, Volker Kaiser, Joachim Gessinger. Finally, a special thanks to Chelsea and Alethea Leventhal and Miran Dalley for their ability to bring joy into my life, and Janet Warren for her support, care and loving friendship through the period of the volume's emergence. Without their unerring presence, I would never have been able to complete this project.

Robert S. Leventhal

Introduction: Reading After Foucault

ROBERT S. LEVENTHAL

Wenn ich jemand[em] vorlese, ist es denn nicht, als wenn ich ihm mündlich etwas vortrüge? Das Geschriebene, das Gedruckte tritt an die Stelle meines eigenen Sinnes, meines eigenen Herzens. . . . Wenn mir jemand ins Buch sieht, so ist mir immer, als wenn ich in zwei Stücke gerissen würde.

When I read aloud to someone, is it not as if I were presenting something orally to that person? That which is written, the printed matter takes the place of my own sense, my own heart. . . . Whenever someone looks over my shoulder into my book, it is always as if I were being torn in two.

—Goethe, *Die Wahlverwandtschaften* (1809)

The colonization and dismemberment of the individual by the text is of quite recent origin. Divided up as it is between reading individuals and texts that threaten to dissolve such individuality, Goethe's novel *Elective Affinities*, published in 1809, brings to a specific articulation the rupture, underway since the third quarter of the eighteenth century, in the discourse of and on literature, a break or breaking-point that discerns the late eighteenth century and early nineteenth century from what Foucault termed the "classical" semiotic system characteristic of the Enlightenment. In numerous texts around 1800, the sign severed its systematic position in the symbolic order and became an opaque, material, autonomous power.[1] No longer a transparent medium for the transmission of ideas or concepts, the sign began to refer to its own enigmatic texture. Within this new semiology, reading something written to someone within the discursive system of text is precisely *not* the same as communicating something to someone orally. The written text (*das Geschriebene, das Gedruckte* in Goethe's text) breaks the supposedly immediate, reciprocal, and spontaneous relation between the sign and its referent, between the material signifier and the signified idea, a relation taken for granted until about 1770 in German literature, when the letter—the concrete, sensuous and fixed *Buchstabe*—takes the place of one's own self-presence, the immediacy and transparency of the idea and the book.[2] This is the historical-cultural process, the production, one could say, of substitution, replacement, effacement that Goethe's novel enacts: one only need recall how often the process of substitution and replacement, designated by the locution "an die Stelle treten" (literally to "take the place of"), occurs in the novel. Takes the place—"an die Stelle treten"—only in the sense that it cannot properly take the place, for that place was precisely the imaginary, precisely merely the image or *Bild* and not the real presence of literary 'communication': the dream of an absolute understanding or comprehension, one which would settle, once and for all, the meaning of the meaning of text. And in the place of one's own sense—Goethe writes "an die Stelle meines eigenen Sinnes"—we are left with only remnants, the traces or residues of thought: we are left precisely with text, with writing, with *Schrift*. This is the discursive situation beginning circa 1770, the textual condition we refer to as modernity.[3] At this juncture, the institution of literature emerges, not in the abstract sense of a 'school,' 'tendency,' or 'sphere,' but rather as a site of discursive, often embattled interaction between poets, critics, and philosophers. Fundamentally, at this historic juncture, this institution governs the production of a reading and a writing that is forever attempting to establish complete communication, reciprocity, community, mutuality, while at the same time positing the signified—the object of desire—as something distant, inaccessible, incomprehensible. While 'literature' endlessly sought to erase its emergence both in writing and as a culture of the written text—think of the entwinement of idealism and infantilism we call Romanticism, which made the world a "corollary of the subject,"[4]—it cannot belie its origin in the radical finitude of text and the historical culture that produces text. The object of this culture of text is called literature. It marks the final word of Friedrich Schlegel's *Gespräch über die Poesie* and formulates the question of Schlegel's notebooks *Zur Philologie* (1797): "Was ist Litteratur?"[5]

I.

To ask the question of the institution of literature is to embark on terrain that was staked out in a particularly new way in 1966 with the publication of Michel Foucault's *Les mots et les choses*.[6] In this text, Foucault articulated the field of literature as an essentially independent form of language use in which writing is folded back on its own enigmatic character. Literature, in a word, was the discipline devoted to the discipline of language. The move from General Grammar to philology described a "demotion of language" according to which language no longer functioned as a neutral semiotic system, with supposedly equal access and participation for all, as it had functioned within Enlightenment culture. Since the end of the eighteenth century, literature in the sense in which I will refer to it became a kind of licensed deviance or disciplined aberration—precisely a 'discipline' in Foucault's sense of 'normalization'—for which there is no ultimate interlocutor, no final 'word', and no archimedean point outside of literature from which to adjudicate its difficulties. In this discursive structure, writing as

INTRODUCTION

deviant object resists precisely the technique of disclosure that it brings forth: interpretation or *hermeneutics*.

To specify the significance of Foucault's reading of this turn, I will examine the crucial passage in *The Order of Things* where Foucault discusses the advent of 'literature.'

> Finally, the last of the compensations for the demotion of language, the most important, and also the most unexpected, is the appearance of literature, of literature as such—for there has of course existed in the Western world, since Dante, since Homer, a form of language we now call 'literature.' But the word is of recent date, as is also, in our culture, the isolation of a particular language whose particular mode of being is 'literary.' This is because at the beginning of the nineteenth century, at a time when language was burying itself within its own density as an object and allowing itself to be traversed, through and through, by knowledge, it was also reconstituting itself elsewhere, in an independent form, difficult of access, folded back upon the enigma of its own origin and existing wholly in reference to the pure act of writing. Literature is the contestation of philology (of which it is nevertheless the twin figure); it leads language back from Grammar to the naked power of speech, and there it encounters the untamed, imperious being of words. . . . [L]iterature becomes progressively more differentiated from the discourse of ideas, and encloses itself within a radical intransitivity; it becomes detached from all the values that were able to keep it in general circulation during the Classical age (taste, pleasure, naturalness, truth), and creates within its own space everything that will ensure a ludic denial of them (the scandalous, the ugly, the impossible) . . . it addresses itself to itself as a writing subjectivity . . . and thus all its threads converge upon the finest of points—singular, instantaneous, and yet absolutely universal—upon the simple act of writing. At the moment when language, as spoken and scattered words, becomes an object of knowledge, we see it reappearing in a strictly opposite modality: a silent cautious deposition of the words upon the whiteness of a piece of paper, where it can possess neither sound nor interlocuter, where it has nothing to say but itself, nothing to do but shine in the brightness of its being.[7]

INTRODUCTION

For Foucault, the classical system of knowledge or *epistémè* had posited language as the neutral, transparent sign-system in which representations represented nothing other than themselves in their homology and proximity to the representing mind. It was privileged insofar as it was the medium of representation itself, the absolute envelope of representativity. Suddenly, around 1770, Foucault argued, language became just one more positivity among others, one more 'object' on the same level as 'life,' 'value,' 'history.' No longer the exterior and distanced system for the representation of ideas, it folds back on itself, i.e., it becomes its own object. Thus the necessity of exegesis and the reemergence of 'interpretation' at the end of the eighteenth and beginning of the nineteenth century, though this time, in opposition to the Renaissance, it is not a matter of finding the primal words buried in things, but of endlessly glossing and commenting on the words themselves, their density, incomprehensibility, resistance. From Novalis and Hölderlin to Benn and Celan, poetry became an exegesis of its own internal mechanics, a reading of its own syntactic, semantic, and glossematic structure. Thus Novalis's connection of lyric with a form of calculus, a mathematics of what can potentially be expressed in language. The novel—one thinks of the definition formulated by the Romantic Friedrich Schlegel—became the form that endlessly reflected and wrote about its own constitution, and absorbed all other forms within itself in that reflection. And drama did not cease to enact its own dramatic staging, did not cease to play out its own enactment as a split text of text and act in infinite variation. Regarding the *reading* of literature, we can thus see why Foucault asserted that "Philology . . . has become the modern form of criticism."[8] Such a hermeneutic philology does not proceed from language to what language *refers to* or *signifies*, but rather from what is *manifest* in language to what lies hidden in its depths, from the surface to the inner mechanisms of discourse.

Although Foucault referred to his researches at this point as an "archaeology of the human sciences," the import of his text extended well beyond the history of scientific disciplines. It was a devastating assault on the sovereignty of the human sciences, and their most cherished object: 'man.' Foucault was very particular about certain expressions, certain types of sentences. In this case, Kant's fourth question in his *Logik*—"Was ist der Mensch?"—stoked Foucault's imagination. What is, indeed, this object we have called "der Mensch"? How did the human being emerge as an object of knowledge at the end of the eighteenth century? What types of discourses and disciplines encompass this object and seek to 'tame' it? The argument urged nothing less than the rethinking of the foundations of the 'human sciences' in every respect. Foucault began with a critique of the underlying premise of the major theoretical trajectories of the 1950s: existentialism, Marxism and structuralism. Influenced by the psychoanalytic turn of Lacan, the critique of phenomenological subjectivity, Foucault distanced himself from the assumptions of phenomenological thinking: immediacy, immanence, meaning. In the foreword to the English translation of *Les mots et les choses*, Foucault attempted to distinguish his own interests from the interpretation of his work as 'structuralist,' and insisted that he rejected only one approach, that of phenomenology in any of its various forms:

> If there is one approach that I do reject, however, it is that (one might call it, broadly speaking, the phenomenological approach) which gives absolute priority to the observing subject, which attributes a constituent role to an act, which places its own point of view at the origin of all historicity—which, in short, leads to a transcendental consciousness.[9]

If Foucault himself sought to relegate the agency of a sponsoring subjectivity to certain technologies of writing and discourse production, why place the subject "Michel Foucault" in the center of our concerns in a volume that seeks to follow the multifarious strands of his thought and the effects of this thought on German literature 1750–1830? Why should we seek to contextualize Foucault? We do so in order to specify the discursive situation within which Foucault emerged and the discursive formations to which his researches constitute a "response." In the 1950s in France, a critique of three fundamental paradigms of thought surfaced: first, against *humanism*, broadly defined as the belief that there is something 'deep' and 'permanent' about 'man'; secondly, against classical *phenomenology* and the attempt to ground science and praxis in the pure evidence of the 'subject,' against the reliance on the immanent domain of consciousness as a ground for meaning and truth; finally, against a certain reading of *Marxism* as a form of economic determinism obsessed with the power of the state as it is expressed in positive law. Influenced by Heidegger and Kojéve's reading of Hegel—the analysis of Dasein's temporality as a prolegomenon to any possible hermeneutics and the equation of discourse and desire found in Kojéve—Lacan's reinterpretation of Freud provoked a radical critique of the subject as a locus or center of 'meaning.' Although Foucault's relation to psychoanalysis remains ambivalent and often critical, his discussion of psychoanalysis in *The Order of Things* identifies this discipline as one that has, in a very real sense, already taken leave of the primacy of subjective consciousness. Both psychoanalysis and ethnology question the figure of 'man' as a construction of a system or structure yet unthought, that is, not itself a function of intentional consciousness. This critique of phenomenology, at least in its insistence on the constituting power of transcendental subjectivity, remained constant throughout Foucault's career.

However, it is important to note that another tradition runs through Foucault's work: the history of science. Instead of inquiring about intentions and agency, Foucault inaugurated an entirely different set of questions from the ones being asked in other theoretical domains, save some still rather obscure thinking in psychoanalysis and, oddly enough, in the history and philosophy of science:[10] how are scientific objects as objects of rational knowledge constituted? what are the conditions under which a specific scientific discipline or 'field' emerges? what is the 'logic' according to which specific activities, objects, concepts, argumentative strategies, and institutions are rendered scientific and thereby legitimated as such? Although the connection was never made explicit, his writing had some remarkable filiations with (at that time) more radical tendencies of Anglo-American philosophy and history of science ushered in by Thomas Kuhn's *The Structure of Scientific Revolutions*. Although Foucault never mentioned Kuhn's work, he suggested with Kuhn that we should depart from the idea that science is a construction of the observing scientist—the image of the isolated individual sealed in a laboratory—and that we should rather look for regularities and ruptures in the *discourse* of scientific disciplines, to the normative structures that govern a line of questioning, a field of knowledge.[11] With Paul Feyerabend he shared the view that the very idea of a global, transcendent, all-encompassing, ahistorical scientific methodology is absurd, out of touch with the specificity and exigency of scientific discovery, as well as morally and politically indefensible.[12] And finally, with Ian Hacking, he urged that the very objects and instruments of knowledge had shifted, first from what Hacking referred to as the 'heyday of ideas,' roughly from 1650 to 1770, when language went 'public'[13] (according to Hacking, with Hamann in the second half of the eighteenth century), to the 'heyday of meaning' in 1900 (Frege, Husserl, Russell), and finally the most recent move towards a theory of statements: *sentences, statements*, and what is referred to as *discourse*—not 'meanings' (Frege's *Sinn*; Husserl's *Bedeutung*)—have become, in our time, the object of historical-scientific study and philosophical inquiry.[14]

Foucault was concerned with specific techniques of knowledge, the types of subjects engaged in the production, practice, and dissemination of such knowledge, and the institutional loci where such knowledge was applied to human bodies. In his first book—*Madness and Civilization* (1961)—Foucault articulated the fatal rupture in the emergence of mental illness circa 1800 where the institutionalization and codification of such illness become palpable. Foucault's books often begin with stunning before-and-after 'images.' In Sebastian Brant's *Ship of Fools*, the 'fools' or madmen still walk alongside the normal burghers of Europe. What a different picture emerges definitively after 1750. Suddenly, abruptly, there is a massive discourse—institutionalization, codification, specification—of mental illness. In the German sphere, Christian Heinrich Spiess's biographies of the mad and the suicidal attest to the emergence of a 'discourse' concerning the flip side of Enlightenment rationality.[15] The deviant, the aberration, the mutation became privileged subjects of literature. A stunning example of this is to be found in Goethe's book *Die Wahlverwandtschaften*: at the outset, the beggars and indigents roam the estate of the wealthy baron Eduard, living upon the good-will and beneficence of the aristocracy. In the course of the book, a gate is constructed to keep the 'marginal' population at bay, and henceforth they are given a certain amount in a systematic fashion. No longer the subjects of capricious good-will, the social 'case' or the 'marginal' are created as the direct result of the implementation of a bureaucratic rule. The random, asystematic treatment of these people is replaced by a planned and regulated social welfare structure, creating exactly their very 'marginality' in the process.

In the nineteenth century, Foucault sees the emergence of a complex web of clinicians, doctors, nurses, psychologists, sociologists who study precisely the abnormal, that which resists categorization and normalization. Athough he himself subsequently rejected the binary opposition between reason and madness, insisting on a more variegated and differential analysis of the emergence of 'madness,'[16] his argument was that prior to the age of reason—Bacon, Galileo, and Descartes, and the emergence of a *Discourse on Method*—the mentally ill walked side by side with rational burghers in the cities of Europe. Only with the institutionalization of reason as the absolute instance of knowledge is there an exclusionary act of distinguishing out the 'irrational,' the 'mad,' the 'insane.' This distinction—one which had not yet been made when Brant wrote the *Narrenschiff*, for instance—set the stage for the modern institutionalization, codification, classification, and discipline of the 'mentally ill.' In the nineteenth century, this occurred in the form of a radical 'medicalization' of sexuality, madness and delinquency.[17] This medicalization of sexuality and the codification of sexual pathologies reached a new level of scientific legitimation with the publication, in 1886, of *Psychopathia Sexualis* by Baron Richard von Krafft-Ebing, Professor of Psychiatry at the University of Vienna. Although this work provided merely taxonomical descriptions of various symptoms and explained nothing in terms of etiology, it was an important 'manual' for the study of the emergence of the discipline of sexual psychopathology. It was the first classificatory system for the designation of sexual pathologies, and thus launched our modern obsession with the ordering and naming of sexual deviation. As Hacking has pointed out, to this day, one can only go insane in specific ways dictated by the categories of DSM-IIIR.[18]

Similarly, Foucault's *The Birth of the Clinic* (1963) sought to illustrate the rather sudden emergence of modern medical perception. Influenced by the historian of science Georges Canguilhem's *The Normal and the Pathological*,[19] which showed how notions of illness and disease became "pathologized" at the end of the eighteenth and beginning of the nineteenth century, Foucault was interested in the advent of an entire regime of medical perception that transformed observation into a clinical gaze of pathological anatomy. Canguilhem had demonstrated that, until the end of the eighteenth century, illness, disease, and death were conceived as forces that intruded upon the body from without, things of an entirely different order than the "organic," and that only with the works of Bichat and Broussais were disease and death shown to be intrinsic possibilities of bodies, on a spectrum with and related to organic life. Similarly, Foucault taught us how disease and pathology became the object of a scientific perception, a discourse, and an institution that consisted in "leaving to experience its greatest corporeal opacity; the solidity, the obscurity, the density of things closed in upon themselves."[20] The "abyss beneath illness" had emerged into "the light of language."[21]

In *Discipline and Punish* (1975),[22] Foucault attempted to write a history of the modern techniques of discipline, surveillance, and control—in contradistinction to the theory of power as punishment alone—not in terms of 'repression,' not as 'signs' of social structures, but rather as a "political technology of the body," "a microphysics of power" that would ask how the entrance of the 'soul' into punitive practice allowed the 'body' itself to be saturated with a new set of power relations. He wanted to demonstrate this political technology of the body on the premise that a body is only really useful to a society, at least modern societies, if it is at once subjected, disciplined *and* productive, quasi-autonomous, and self-creating. Against the prevailing reading that in the second half of the eighteenth century the brutal display and spectacle of the punished body was replaced by more 'enlightened,' 'humane' procedures of incarceration, exclusion, and a quick and easy death, Foucault inquired as to the possibility of a new system of surveillance and control in which the individual is registered, recorded, monitored with regard to the entire structure of practices, behaviors, desires, tendencies, and propensities of the self.

In *The Order of Things* (1966), Foucault inquired into the emergence of the three central disciplines of the human sciences: life (biology), labor (political economy), and language (philology) as the 'discourse' of these sciences. Here, the question was: how did 'human being' become an object of scientific scrutiny? how was the fourth question in Kant's *Logik*—"Was ist der Mensch?"—at all possible? The argument marked the sudden, abrupt disappearance of what Foucault termed the classical system or *epistémè* and the advent of disciplines involved in the disclosure of structures in which this new scientific object—'human being'—remains captive: what we call the hermeneutic-historical sciences of man. While the classical *epistémè* or order of discourse and its 'disciplines' presupposed the transparency, intelligibility, and homogeneity of the sign—an isomorphism, one could say, between the sign and the signified—modernity introduced the troubling historical opacity and materiality of the object of knowledge, and the simultaneous appearance and erasure of the 'origin':

> Thus, by rediscovering finitude in its interrogation of the origin, modern thought closes the great quadrilateral it began to outline when the Western *epistémè* broke up at the end of the 18th century: the connection of the positivities with finitude, the reduplication of the empirical and the

transcendental, the perpetual relation of the *cogito* to the unthought, the retreat and return of the origin, define for us man's mode of being.[23]

Interestingly, the 1760s and 1770s are concerned precisely with this "origin," which does not designate the *emergence* of an object, but precisely the lack of any carefully defined causal explanation, a literal *Ur-sprung* that traverses the space from nature to culture and language: Rousseau and the *Discourse on the Origin of Inequality* (1754), Herder and his *Treatise on the Origin of Language* (1770) are merely the two most important texts that attempt to trace this movement in the period under consideration. At the end of the book, Foucault speculated that as an object of knowledge, 'human being' would disappear as readily as it had appeared, and he pointed out how specific disciplines—ethnology and psychoanalysis in particular—had already begun to question the centrality and necessity of 'human being' precisely as such a fundamental object of investigation. The emergence of other disciplines that Foucault did not take up explicitly enforces his belief that 'man' is no longer the central object and foundation of inquiry, and that the so-called 'human sciences'—the disciplines that had governed the examination of 'human being'—have been eclipsed by disciplines that indicate the reign of *écriture* in many different forms: information and cybernetics, systems-theory, and media-technologies.[24] As Friedrich Kittler has argued in an important recent work, 'literature' in the 'postmodern' system of information production and dissemination, 'literature' in the era of its own technical self-production and reproducibility, simply doesn't have much more to say: "It ends in cryptograms that resist interpretation and only allow *interception*."[25] No doubt new forms of literature have emerged and will continue to emerge to address precisely the eclipse of the 'human being' and the modern sense of literary discourse.

Foucault's concern was not only the figure of the human being as the object of discipline, but as its most enigmatic subject. As a 'transcendental doublet'[26] since the end of the eighteenth century, 'man' is given *both* as the empirical object and the transcendental condition of the possibility of human scientific knowledge. Kant gave us this bifurcated subject, a subject who is at once subject (autonomous, sovereign) and sub-ject (disciplined, conditioned, heteronomous). In a paper entitled "Making Up People,"[27] Hacking has written:

> I do not believe there is a general story to be told about making up people. Each category has its own history. If we wish to present a partial framework in which to describe such events, we might think of two vectors. One is the vector of labeling from above, from a community of experts who create a "reality" that some people make

> their own. Different from this is the autonomous behavior of the person so labeled, which presses from below, creating a reality every expert must face. (234)

The perception of two 'vectors' mentioned in Hacking's statement derives from two predecessors who might seem at odds with one another. The first is certainly Foucault, who, in his ethics, was in certain ways himself a Kantian.[28] The second, perhaps not so obvious, is Kant himself. For it is precisely the dual description of the modern self formulated in Kant's *Foundations of the Metaphysics of Morals* (1785) that constitutes the subtext of Hacking's, and Foucault's, remarks. In this decisive text, Kant inscribed those two vectors of the modern self or subject: as essentially free from external coercion (*Zwang*), rational and autonomous, the subject legislates for itself. As a being of sense affected by laws external to it, as determinate, material being, as heteronomous, the self becomes sub-ject to laws outside of itself:

> Thus he has two standpoints from which he can consider himself and recognize the laws of the employment of his powers and consequently of all his actions: first, as belonging to the world of sense under laws of nature (heteronomy), and, second, as belonging to the intelligible world under laws which, independent of nature, are not empirical but founded only on reason.[29]

Articulating the breach between the two 'vectors,' the space in which subjectivity becomes palpable, Foucault became increasingly interested in the ways in which individuals constitute themselves and how they thereby contribute to their own discipline and control by ascribing certain features, attributes, dispositions, social 'positionalities' to themselves and others. He began to ask about the function of a radical political and social critique that was not based on the premise of humanism and was therefore not entangled in humanistic ideology, which he thought was suspicious because, in all of its various forms, it held out the dream of a human 'nature' or 'essence' beyond alienation. He began to trace various trajectories of power.

This led Foucault to Nietzsche, and to a strategy that in my view is wholly consistent with the earlier archaeological procedure Foucault utilized in *The Order of Things* and *The Archaeology of Knowledge*. He became involved in genealogy precisely in Nietzsche's sense of a tireless movement through the various strata of specific interpretive constellations. Nietzsche's genealogy demonstrates that all legal and moral systems are struggles for power; that even the most fundamental moral determinations derive from the will to power—which is arguably nothing other than 'interpretation'—and return to it. If Alexander Nehamas is correct that Nietzsche's conception of 'genealogy' is "explicitly modeled on the interpretation of texts,"[30] then we are justified in assigning a specific function to literature in Foucault's writing: the study of 'literature' understood precisely as the place of a heightened, self-reflexive exegesis thematized for Foucault the intersection of the political and the cultural, of power and writing, analogous to the way in which Kant had undertaken to bridge the theoretical and the practical through the aesthetic theory of the Third Critique.[31]

This was not the beginning of Foucault's interest in the possibility of a critique that did not resort to humanistic, historicistic, existential, phenomenological, structuralist, or Marxist forms of explanation, or to the traditional economic, ideological, juridical, and biological categories. In a lecture dated January 14, 1976, Foucault wrote the most succinct formulation of his critical strategy:

> Let us not, therefore, ask why certain people want to dominate, what they seek, what is their overall strategy. Let us ask instead how things work at the ongoing level of subjugation, at the level of those continuous and uninterrupted processes which subject our bodies, govern our gestures, dictate our behaviors, etc. In other words, rather than ask ourselves how the sovereign appears to us in his lofty isolation, we should try to discover how it is that subjects are gradually, progressively, really and materially constituted through a multiplicity of organisms, forces, energies, materials, desires, thoughts, etc. We should try to grasp subjection in its material instance as a constitution of subjects. This would be the exact opposite of Hobbes' project in *Leviathan*.[32]

In the world of Hobbes's *Leviathan*, the individual is given, the sovereign is not; it must be created, it is an artifact. Foucault urged us to turn *Leviathan* upside down; to ask how subjects are constituted and constitute themselves as artifacts; to confront modernity not from the perspective of the master, the sovereign in any of its various masks, but through the production mechanisms of subjection. Rather than focusing on the gaze of the sovereign, the centralized, unified vision of the king (or parliament, or president), Foucault wrote about subjugation: "I believe that we must attempt to study the myriad of bodies which are constituted as peripheral *subjects* as a result of the effects of power."[33]

Some have argued that Foucault did in his written work precisely what he was diagnosing, that he talked of power as others have talked of God, Truth or Being; that 'power' in Foucault is just another 'transcendental signifier.' Richard Rorty in particular has implied that Foucault's notion of 'power' is so vague as to be empty.[34] Foucault considered this objection in volume one of *The History of Sexuality*, where he performed an ironic self-critique: "you keep the essential practical consequence of the principle of power-as-law, namely the fact that there is no escaping from power, that it is always-already present."[35] In response, he distinguished between a 'theory' of power, which would indeed posit 'power' as a represented object of juridical discourse, and his own 'analytics' of power, which struggled against the identification of power with repression and the law and sought instead an articulation of "the specific domain formed by relations of power" and "a determination of the instruments that will make possible its analysis."[36] 'Power' for Foucault is neither a transcendental signifier, nor is it so vague as to be vacuous.[37] Power occurs in direct proportion to the establishment of knowledge, the implementation of reason as a tool of discipline, surveillance, control, and the proliferation of discourses that intensify, specify, and distribute the pleasure that derives from the communication of 'truth.' That power is multiple, diffuse, difficult to analyze does not mean it is ineffable; that it is intrinsic to specific forms and techniques of knowledge does not diminish its distinguishing 'edge.' For we can say that each specific mechanism of power has its specific 'constellation' and 'trajectory.' As Feyerabend argues, one can be a relativist on the global level and still insist on very specific rationalities proper to particular societal or scientific practices. Similarly, we can assert that discourse and power are co-extensive, but qualify that by saying that it is extremely important to distinguish different *types* of power/discourse in different historical cultures, and even more precisely, in specific institutions. In his essay "Nietzsche, Genealogy, History," Foucault wrote:

> Even in the greatly expanded form it assumes today, the will to knowledge does not achieve a universal truth; man is not given an exact and serene mastery of nature. On the contrary, it ceaselessly multiplies the risks, creates dangers in every area; it breaks down illusory defenses; it dissolves the unity of the subject; it releases those elements of itself that are devoted to its subversion and destruction.[38]

Power as the will to knowledge does not permit of a univocal, final determination, but rather splinters and fractures its object and itself in the course of genealogical analysis. In *Discipline and Punish*, he wrote: "Of course, this technology [of the body] is diffuse, rarely formulated in continuous, systematic discourse; it is often made up of bits and pieces; it implements a disparate set of tools or methods."[39] In a word, Foucault sought to outline a noneconomic, nonjuridical analysis of power as a multiplicity whose tentacles spread out in all directions and entwine the subject, producing diverse and ever proliferating mechanisms of autonomy and control, sovereignity

INTRODUCTION

and discipline. In *The History of Sexuality*, Foucault defined power in the following manner:

> [P]ower must be understood in the first instance as the multiplicity of force relations immanent in the sphere in which they operate and which constitute their own organization; as the process which, through ceaseless struggles and confrontations, transforms, strengthens, or reverses them; as the support which these force relations find in one another, thus forming a chain or system, or on the contrary, the disjunctions and contradictions which isolate them from one another; and lastly, as the strategies in which they take effect, whose general design or institutional crystallization is embodied in the state apparatus, in the formulation of the law, in the various social hegemonies.[40]

Foucault shifted the focus of an analysis of power relations from the law and state apparatus to specific techniques practiced in particular institutions—the family, the school, the asylum, the hospital, the prison—and from corporeal punishment to subtle, ongoing methods of subjugation, surveillance, and control.

One of Foucault's most important contributions to the study of historical cultures was his discovery of discipline as the antipode to "the public right of sovereignity"—as the exact opposite, one could say, of the discourse of "law, rule, or sovereign will." Is there, to paraphrase Ian Hacking, a general story to be told about 'discipline'? While there might be an entire *series* of histories of 'discipline' in its many forms, a *genealogy* produced certain strata of ongoing processes of subjection that the excavations of *archaeology* tend to obscure. Foucault sought to theorize 'discipline' negatively as the Other of 'right' and 'law,' two well-known figures from the political discourse of the seventeenth and eighteenth centuries. He understood that the discussion of 'discipline' and 'disciplinarity' is itself fraught with 'discipline,' a dilemma he did not resolve but sought to articulate. Again, I quote from "Two Lectures":

> Hence, these two limits, a right of sovereignty and a mechanism of discipline, which define, I believe, the arena in which power is exercised. But these two limits are so heterogeneous that they cannot possibly be reduced to each other. The powers of modern society are exercised through, on the basis of, and by virtue of, this very heterogeneity between a public right of sovereignty and a poly-

morphous disciplinary mechanism.... Disciplines are the bearers of discourse, but this cannot be the discourse of right. The discourse of discipline has nothing in common with that of law, rule or sovereign will. The disciplines might well be the carriers of a discourse that speaks of a rule, but this is not the juridical rule deriving from sovereignty, but a natural rule, a norm. The code they come to define is not that of law but that of *normalization*.[41]

The condition of the possibility of 'human science' is precisely the juxtaposition of these two 'limits'—"the reorganization of right that reinvests sovereignty and the mechanics of coercive forces whose exercise takes a disciplinary form" (107). While the discourse of 'right' can be traced to the Greek *Polis* and civic humanism in early modern Europe,[42] its most powerful modern political expression emerges in the eighteenth century, in the era of absolutism, where the language of 'rights' and civic 'virtue' is placed over and against the language of 'law,' 'duty,' and 'obedience'; where the discourse of the 'republic' is radically opposed to that of 'monarchy.'

This well-known opposition, however, of the discourse of 'rights' to that of 'law,' the distinction common to Enlightenment discourse between 'morals' and 'politics,' 'freedom' and 'duty', the 'private' and the 'public' tends to obscure Foucault's point. For Foucault, the sovereign takes many forms, and the discourse of 'rights' and institutions such as 'parliament' simply transforms the centralized, unified will of the sovereign into that of the people. For whatever strengths a republic exhibits over a monarchy, modernity over feudalism, the principle of sovereignty is either systematically ignored[43] or remains operative under different names.[44] Rather than remain within the parameters of a discussion of 'rights' versus 'law' and buy into the progressive, liberal narrative of emancipation through self-representation, Foucault wrote about an entirely different *order* of power, another *type* of control that does not speak the language of 'rights' at all. These 'other' forces Foucault spent so much time writing about—"the mechanics of the coercive forces whose exercise takes disciplinary form"—constitute the basis of a more internal, insidious production of power and control. Discipline can therefore not be identified with or reduced to the discourse of 'right,' 'rule,' 'law,' 'representation,' or 'will' inherent in Enlightenment discourse and present today in critical theory.[45] Discipline might be defined as the intersection of a discourse—concepts, enunciative modalities, institutional sites, argumentative strategies—and the specific forms of *normalization, subjection, codification, and organization* it engenders.

II.

The effects of Foucault's theories on literary theory and criticism have been far-reaching.[46] The first, most obvious and perhaps most important departure from traditional literary theory is one mentioned at the outset of this introduction: the implicit rejection of hermeneutics as a reconstitution of textual meaning.[47] Foucault urged that we stop reading for 'ideas' and hidden 'meanings' behind the text and interrogate the text instead at the level of its statements, at what might be called the level of the text as discourse. This strategy that Foucault attempted to theorize in *The Archaeology of Knowledge* forms part of what I might refer to as the *performative* turn in the study of historical discourse, and it interfaces with developments in historical theory going on elsewhere. A first breakthrough in this direction can be found in Quentin Skinner's trailblazing article of 1969 "Meaning and Understanding in the History of Ideas."[48]

This essay appears so frequently in the literature of our various 'disciplines' that one wonders if we have grasped some of the radical implications of its argument for historical studies today. Skinner's title is particularly interesting if one reads him as debunking the very idea of the discipline we have called 'the history of ideas.' This is precisely what Skinner was up to. According to Skinner's argument, 'intellectual history' or the 'history of ideas' and its subdisciplines—the history of historical study, of political thought, of the human sciences—cannot and should not be conducted as a history of *ideas*. For Skinner, the *idea* is simply the wrong unit of inquiry. It is too vague, slippery, indeterminate. Instead, intellectual historians should study historical *languages*, the *function* of specific terms, phrases, and locutions as they are employed by specific historical agents in a specific context with a range of specific purposes. They ought to be interested in what Skinner calls, following Austin and Searle, the *illocutionary act* of the statement, i.e., how the statement is functioning; how it works; how it resists, distributes, or engenders power.

At about the same time that Skinner articulated this theory of the study of historical languages as *performative texts*, Foucault suggested a similar, though not identical, theory of historical *statements*.[49] While Foucault explicitly rejected the identification of 'statement' with 'performative' or 'speech-act'—a statement for Foucault could be a statistical table—both his 'statement' and the 'performative' as utilized by Austin, Searle, and Skinner must be *analyzed* with regard to what we might call systemic function. In the case of speech-act theory, one must articulate the rules that govern the utterance of statements, the positionality of the speaker and the addressee, the institutional conventions that obtain for the successful utterance to achieve its intended object. Following Foucault, the reader must define not only the operative concepts and strategies of the statement, but also the possible *types* of subjects who might utter such statements, and the institutional sites of such utterance. Rather than asking what the 'term,' 'phrase,' 'sentence,' or 'text' *means*, he urged that we ask what it *states*. How is it functioning? Who are its locutors and interlocutors? What purposes does the deployment of the expression serve? What kinds of scientific subjects, objects, strategies does it invoke? How, for example, does it organize and control, centralize and unify the multifarious and heterogeneous instances of writing and reading? Some tend to think that activities like 'reading' and 'writing,' and subjects like 'authors' and 'critics' display a uniform structure across historical and disciplinary boundaries. Foucault thought otherwise. He 'historicized' the subject and the 'statement,' not in the usual sense of placing the subject and text into a social-historical context, but by showing that certain forms of subject can only emerge on certain sites, under the aegis of certain institutions. In historical studies today, the primacy of the rhetoric of the statement is a commonplace: from Koselleck to LaCapra, historians of discourse maintain that social history in and of itself cannot provide a firm basis for the analysis of complex rhetorical writing.[50]

The second aspect of Foucault's impact on literary studies revolves around the notion of the "author." Foucault questioned the notion of the author as a sponsoring, meaning-endowing, transcendental agency and reinscribed the problematics of authorship as an organizational and strategic *function*.[51] He asked how texts are ascribed to certain proper names and what the significance of specific assignments of intentionality, authorship, oeuvre, text, and work are in the context of modernity, where discourse operates in a circuit on which the 'author' maintains a purely derivative position. Concerned with neither the empirical author nor the romantic, intentional subjectivity that forged meaning onto the written page, Foucault was interested in the ways in which words, sentences, statements, and texts are classified, ordered, interpreted, and organized in order to produce the 'author,' a particular genre, an oeuvre and a canon: "the author is not an indefinite source of significations which fill a work; the author does not precede the works, he is a certain functional principle by which, in our culture, one limits, excludes, and chooses."[52] Thus his comment in *The Order of Things* referring to the figure we call 'Kant,' who for Foucault is a kind of shorthand for the form of criticism of the third quarter of the eighteenth century. 'Author-function' designates the historical, social, and ideological construction of authorship as one of authority, as an historical-cultural mechanism of ordering and appropriation, as a textual organizing-principle.

The emergence of the "author" in the German territorial states at the end of the eighteenth century gives us a good example of the uses of discourse analysis for literary history and theory. In the society of orders and privileges, the sovereign guaranteed the possible uses to which the literary 'work' could be put; in modern society, and in the German States after the *Allgemeines Preussisches Landrecht* (Prussian State Law) of 1794, the author is placed in the position of the sovereign and becomes an 'economic subject.'[53] The word becomes a commodity as spiritual 'property' of an author. Thus the entire opposition 'original' vs. 'copy,' the 'auratic work' vs. the 'everyday,' the 'genial' vs. the 'banal' becomes the fulcrum around which 'literature' gravitates. The spiritual 'core' or 'meaning,' which, for Romantic Hermeneutics, is endowed by a transcendental constituting subjectivity, thus stands over and above the actual letters, the physical writing, and inhabits them as a productive force, endows them with a significance that transcends their character as *Schrift*. The author thus repeats the gesture of the sovereign and claims dominion over the word. Literary discourse—a discourse about reading, writing, and speaking about literature—thus guarantees the author as originator of a material reality (writing) accessible to the literate public.

Poets and writers in Germany first begin to demand their rights as 'producers' and 'originators' of 'works' in the 1770s. Is it a mere coincidence that this coincides with the *Sturm und Drang* movement and the theory of 'genius'? Heinrich Bosse, whose work on the history of rhetoric and of the emergence of authorship bears the influence of Foucault, traces the distinction between rhetorical and literary culture in the following manner: "In rhetorical discourse, the 'author' transmits an already established truth—a truth he has picked up or taken from others, as a kind of *distributor*. In written discourse, on the other hand, the author brings forth texts, ideas, formulations, and fictions which function as a kind of truth as a *producer*."[54] In effect, rather than being itself a formative principle, the theory of 'genius' and the notion of Romantic authorship are a production of modern literary discourse, which requires a criterion for the spiritual endowment of the writing subject, an endowment that renders the word a commodity and a property that can be controlled by law. The placement of the force of law with regard to the author and the imposition of the claim of law on the literary text demanded a criteriological instance of originary creation. Romantic subjectivity provided just that.

It is striking that precisely the material element of writing, the scriptural process of encoding and decoding—in itself of no juridical value or meaning according to the theory of 'genius'—comes to occupy such an important position in the discourse of and on literature circa 1800; 'writing,' material 'discourse'—that which cannot be appropriated, which defies interpretation and 'subjective agency'—becomes the function of the production of literature.[55] From Herder's critique of the scholarly world of books, papers, lexica, and journals (written itself in a *Journal*!) to Lichtenberg's *Wörterwelt*, Schlegel's era of the book, and finally, Charlotte's ink mark in Goethe's book, the ink mark that intrudes upon and soils the paper and continues to get worse the more she attempts to elide it—writing as an autonomous power, contingent and transgressive, colonizes literature and subverts the very idea of a controlling agency, whether that agency is that of the 'author,' the 'narrator,' the 'interpreter,' or the 'critic':

> Sie schrieb mit gewandter Feder gefällig und verbindlich, aber doch mit einer Art von Hast, die ihr sonst nicht gewöhnlich war; und was ihr nicht leicht begegnete, sie verunstaltete das Papier zuletzt mit einem Tintenfleck, der sie

ärgerlich machte und nur größer wurde, indem sie ihn wegwischen wollte.[56]

She wrote in pen and ink with experience, agility and with confidence, but with a kind of haste that was not usual for her; and what she encountered and was not easy for her, she messed up the paper with a spot of ink that made her angry and only became larger when she tried to wipe it away.

III.

Michel Foucault's untimely death in 1984 abruptly ended a debate on the Enlightenment—more specifically, how we are to read the call to critical reflection—he was engaged in with the German philosopher Jürgen Habermas. In a posthumously published article entitled "What is Enlightenment?,"[57] Foucault defined Enlightenment not as a doctrine of 'critical rationality,' but as a moral posture toward selfhood, a philosophical stance concerning the reflective process of self-construction in view of the age in which one is situated. This *performative* reading of Enlightenment hinges on the ambiguous status of one of the central terms of Kant's definition: *Ausgang* or "exit." Kant's text does not simply offer a definition. It rather poses a question and installs a difference: "What difference does today introduce with respect to yesterday?"[58] Foucault reads in Kant's text the literal coincidence of two strands of critical reflection: a reflection on history and on the historical moment of this reflection itself. By framing Enlightenment as a theoretical demarkation or as a "critical ontology of ourselves," Foucault places or positions himself on the threshold of a sustained analysis of modernity. To understand Enlightenment not as theory or doctrine but as an *ethos*, a kind of self-interrogation, and as a departure or exit from what has been thought before, as a self-imposed or generated exit or *Ausgang* produces a very interesting reading of Kant. Such a reading calls both the traditional reading (modernity is equated with critical reason) and the Marxist reading (a philosophical apology for instrumental domination, as a text of bourgeois ideology) into question. As an "ethos, a philosophical life in which the critique of what we are is at one and the same time the historical analysis of the limits that are imposed on us *and* an experiment with the possibility of going beyond them,"[59] Enlightenment is not a period or program. It is an historical and philosophical situation in which the modern subject—in the split sense of being subject to a specific historical discourse regime and being a self-fashioning, self-creating individuality—exercises a critical, historical stance as constituted and constituting itself as object of knowledge and power.

The essays in this volume tacitly assert that the discourse of and on 'literature'—in the German-speaking territories especially circa 1800—materializes exactly this type of historical stance, in a way that parallels the vicissitudes of Kant's text and Foucault's reading of Kant. They read for traces of subjection, discipline, normalization, and institutionalization in German culture 1750–1830, technologies of self-fashioning and self-construction, and they demonstrate how the 'institution' of literature becomes both a textbook and an instance of power in that period. The coherence of their procedure and methodology stops there. The essays range from precise semiological arguments on specific texts or passages of texts to analyses of *problematics* across a wide range of texts. Insofar as they do not adopt a singular approach, they approximate the heterogeneity, contingency, and transgressive character of the object they are engaged with: the institution of literature itself. It will be noted that not all of the essays cite Foucault or bear his name, either in the text themselves or in the footnotes. All *assume* Foucault's work, however, and continue his research into the emergence of the institutions of literature and the institutionalized, disciplined individual at the emergence of modernity.

In an essay that creates an alternative reading of the debate concerning eighteenth century theories of language, Ian Hacking attempts to answer the question "How, why, when, and where did language go public?" In his reconstruction, Hacking identifies J. G. Hamann (1730–88) as a discursive point of emergence of language as a public medium. Clearly, this is not to deny that language was circulated and distributed in public and public media before that point, nor to assert that there was no such thing as 'public' discourse before Hamann. Rather, Hacking shows that prior to the third quarter of the eighteenth century, language in the Classical period had always been considered the very 'private' and individualized connection between 'idea' and 'sign' (as it is, for example, in Locke in his *Essay on Human Understanding*). Hamann spelled out a public notion of discourse in which what is thought is always already linguistic, the possession of a community, and operates according to specific conventions and rules in terms of which the individual speaks and writes. His thesis is that language went public circa 1770 in the German States and this institution of public language has been with us ever since. On this view, Wittgenstein's argument against a 'private' language is a latter-day version of certain widely held beliefs in eighteenth-century German theories of language. By playing Chomsky, Berlin, and Aarsleff off each other, Hacking produces a different account of this decisive turn in modern theories of language. Perhaps most importantly, Hacking underscores for us the stark distinction between Hamann's insistence on the public, communal nature of language and Kant's requirement of a very private individuation prior to language: "Hamann did not have Kant's problems. He thought that there is no such thing as a person except what is constituted in a social setting, characterized by a unique historical language. Language is essentially public and shared; it is prior to the individuation of one's self."

INTRODUCTION

In his study of Johann Karl Wezel's novel *Herrmann und Ulrike* (1780), Franz Futterknecht examines the emergence of the new social order that revolves around the nuclear family, and the effects of such a new order: "This new family becomes the 'raison d'être' of the reformed state and enjoys its special protection. Herrmann's educational reforms supply the offspring of the new families with the appropriate schooling to prepare the sons for careers as the new civil servants." Thus instead of reading the liberal reforms of the late eighteenth century as emancipating the individual from the vertical, hierarchical order and producing the autonomous bourgeois subject, Futterknecht shows how the reforms actually institute a new order with its own mechanisms for control and domination: "The new epoch . . . did not end this castration or render the state less mechanical." According to Futterknecht, the new order did not liberate or enslave univocally; it produced loyal male civil servants and lustless, childbearing, homebound mothers.

Friedrich Kittler's contribution traces the institution of individual textual interpretation to the year 1788, when Karl Leonard Reinhold began a lecture series at the University of Jena of a single epic work: C. M. Wieland's *Oberon*. Academic "free time" inaugurates the disease of scholars, the antidote to which, Kittler argues, we still seek today. A by-product of this production of academic free time or recreation is a poetry that occupies reason and the imagination, the "labor of philosophers and the recreation of poets." After 1788, the new reader-interpreter finds his or her recreation not in the leisurely nature walk but between the lines of a poetic book. New career channels open up utilizing this "interpretation of texts" as its dominant modality: "Interpretation as a power-technology of state civil servants took the place of rhetoric as a power-technology of the scholarly servants of sovereigns." Poetry achieves a new status and content. The Hegelian concept and the work of art recognize and determine themselves reciprocally as one and the same. The representation of art itself in the interpretation of poetry performs this task of making the poetic text the making of the institutionalized self.

My contribution on "reciprocal influence" analyzes the vicissitudes of one the most significant rhetorical figures of the second half of the eighteenth century—the notion of mutual or reciprocal influence—in J. G. Herder's prize-essay of 1780 entitled "Concerning the Influence of Governments on the Sciences and the Sciences on the Government." Herder generates an asymmetrical argument in this essay, quoting and placing question marks next to the question of the Berlin Academy. By reading for symptoms of the figure of "the Third"—the figure that disrupts the reciprocal communication of the dialogic—on the surface of Herder's text, we find that writing here introduces an Other into the supposedly reciprocal dialogue between the government and the sciences, and that, in fact, reciprocity is just another maneuver in the struggle of texts. Instead of buying into the metaphor of the "reciprocal," Herder's text endlessly exposes this figure as exactly the central issue in late Enlightenment discourse in the Berlin Academy of Sciences. Instead of mutuality, reciprocity, equal distribution and communication, Herder's text enacts a disruption of such economy and reveals the new, horizontal order as another means of surveillance and discipline.

This leads directly to the thesis of Dorothea von Mücke in her essay on Friedrich Schiller's *Maria Stuart*. Von Mücke analyzes this famous dramatic treatment of human freedom and contends with the series of "closed spaces" in which the text unfolds. She examines the way in which the focus of the play shifts from the spectacle of the execution to the scene of the imprisonment, demonstrating the renewed presence of the spectacle as the ordering principle for the structuring of anxiety and pointing out the significance that this is carried out within the genre of the drama. As von Mücke writes: "If the genres of the bourgeois tragedy and epistolary novel could be characterized as antitheatrical rejections of the spectacle in favor of an internalization and an identification with the fictional events in the mental cinema, Classical German Tragedy gives new value and power to the spectacle. . . . This new spectacle accomplishes a movement of externalization and internalization which can only come into being once the masses have already been disciplined into individuals."

David Wellbery reads Heinrich von Kleist's *Broken Jug* as an enactment of the transgression of the boundaries that define and govern the legal and scientific rational structures of modernity. Delineating the traces of Sophocles' *Oedipus*, Wellbery shows the "double violation" which the breaking of the jug stages: the loss of virginity and the castration of the male body. He is therefore in a position to signify the enigmatic "event" that trips up the characters and makes it impossible to effect a smooth transition from the traumatic dream of the night to the daylight of integrity, *ratio*, and juridical authority. Kleist's *Broken Jug* thus articulates the divided subject of desire and of speech.

Gerd Gemünden has presented the famous case of foundling Kaspar Hauser as the production of the human sciences from the spirit of silence. Hauser's speechlessness and lack of culture call forth an entire battery of human scientific procedures, measures, and writing practices that, in turn, engender and codify the modern "subject." As Gemünden writes: "Romanticism . . . together with its interest in the enigmatic and the impenetrable . . . developed the disciplines to overcome this condition."

Courtney Federle examines the discourse of *Empfindsamkeit*— questions and answers concerning the essence and proper measure of sentiment—as the first modern effort by pedagogues, philosophers, physiologists, and literary critics to define and prescribe a technology of the self appropriate to a utilitarian vision of society. His interpretation of J. H. Campe's exemplary text of enlightened pedagogy shows the "disequilibrium" of reason in the late Enlightenment—that is, how the installment of reason to counteract the dominance of sentiment actually questions the balance and moderation that reason is supposed to engender.

INTRODUCTION

Rüdiger Campe's essay on Hölderlin's 'care' for the speech-act registers the "uneasiness" that inhabits Hölderlin's letters to his mother, a poem, and even the novel *Hyperion*. Through a rhetorical analysis of the disturbances inherent within this practice of writing, Campe argues that in Hölderlin's letters "the relation between *techné* and style is reversed. No longer is style—the name of a certain formal coherence—the result of the application of a literary *techné* (of rules), rather style first makes possible—as image and example of formal coherence—the (calculable) *techné*." By examining the interruption, deferral, incalculable, and irregular rhythm of the mail, and by examining in particular the use of the term *zustellen*— which means in German both to deliver a letter *and* to obstruct or place an obstacle in the way of a process—Campe is able to identify the features of this discursive practice in Hölderlin and on the threshold of modernity. In particular, the linkage between the epistle and the postal system, which forms the institutional framework for the sequencing of communication, allows us to gain insight into the devastating effects of the belief in the unfettered freedom of written exchange. In this analysis, the letter does not merely announce or represent the catastrophe; it actually *performs* it.

Linda Brooks' essay on Friedrich Schiller's *Naive and Sentimental Poetry* illustrates a prime example of self-fashioning in the modern period. Focusing on the specularity of self-writing, Brooks identifies the hyperbolic as one of the dominant modes of dealing with the enclosed specularity which threatens modern consciousness. She shows that the necessity of securing self-definition in the modern period requires and necessitates a movement beyond the human into the sublime, a transgression that must be "bridged" in the aesthetic. The modern idea that the self can only define itself in modernity by exceeding itself, by moving beyond its boundaries, is evident in modern poetry and theory. In her analysis of the hyperbolic tendency of the modern self as it is presented in Schiller's seminal essay, however, Brooks makes the case that this impulse to transgress defines the very project of the aesthetic at its origin.

Ken Calhoon articulates the archive and the library as models of the institutionalization of the psyche in Novalis, one of the central theorists and poets of German Romanticism. By concentrating on metaphors of "surface" and "depth," the excavation or archeology of the mind in Novalis's texts, Calhoon spells out one of the dominant modalities in the encounter with the enigmatic and incomprehensible Other constitutive of the birth of the human sciences in the Romantic period. According to Calhoon, "Romanticism had made the lure of the untranslateable the basis for a quest which is not subordinate to its destination, but exists for the sake of the journey." Drawing connections to Freud and psychoanalysis, Calhoon shows the proximity and difference between the Romantic sense of the enigmatic text and our own; while the enigma in Romanticism resides in a depth behind the text or book, for us—following the reading of Freud—the enigma exists in the text itself.

INTRODUCTION

Joel Black—whose book *The Aesthetics of Murder* explores the relation between murder, the literary text, and media—points out striking differences in the narrative technique of autobiography by contrasting Goethe's *Werther* and Foucault's *I, Pierre Rivière*. Positioned between the servant's murder and his own suicide, Werther's autobiographical text states a direct relation between a phantasized bloodletting (of Charlotte and her husband) and his self-destruction. Black shows how our reading of a text can change according to genre; in this case, how *I, Pierre Rivière* can be read as a memoir or a confession, depending on whether we choose to include the subsequent suicide. Black reads *Rivière* as an "autobiographical confession," and he shows how the insertion of this autobiographical text into the interstice between murder and suicide structures the narrative form and the material outcome. Operating on the boundary between fiction (*Werther*) and non-fiction (*Rivière*), Black indicates how autobiography functions both as a model and a manual in the construction of narrative and real events.

In an interview, Foucault once characterized the contemporary discursive scene as a shift from the centrality of the subject to the dispersion, heterogeneity, and multiplicity of various *systems*. The essays contained in this volume comprise a contribution to the analysis of the modern system of literature—not as ideological reflex, 'medium,' or 'vehicle' for the transmission of 'meaning' or 'ideas,' but as diverse and often paradoxical instantiations of power/knowledge and techniques of self-production. The period between 1750 and 1830 gives us many examples of this: the advent of "extensive" reading; the emergence of the modern university as an institution of research and teaching; the systematic production of bureaucratic subjects then capable of serving the state; the hermeneutics of the text as an agonistic struggle among different "models" of world-experience; the asylum; the examination; the "lesson"; the bourgeois family and its ceaseless creation of future poets, philosophers, and pedagogically-minded mothers. These elements belong to a constellation that requires a specific discursive articulation, a constellation that itself becomes the condition of the possibility of a sentence, written in 1873, that suffers and endures the process of self-formation from the outside: "Sind das noch Menschen, fragt man sich, oder veilleicht nur Denk-, Schreib-, und Redemaschinen" (Are these still human beings, one asks oneself, or perhaps only thought-, writing-, and discourse-machines).[60] In the period between 1750 and 1830, as the human being became, in Nietzsche's words, a "historische Bildungsgebilde"—an historical construct of self-formation, and therefore also literally a mere *Bild* or image—the reader entered into a system of the written text where identity and conduct, act and event operate along a circuit that is already prescribed by the code of the many institutions and disciplines of the word.

NOTES

1. On the collapse of the symbolic order, see David Wellbery, "*Die Wahlverwandtschaften*. Desorganisation symbolischer Ordnungen," in P. M. Lützeler, *Goethes Erzählwerk. Interpretationen* (Stuttgart: Reclam, 1985), pp. 291–318.

2. On the eclipse of the idea and the book, see R. S. Leventhal, "Semiotic Interpretation and Rhetoric in the German Enlightenment," *DVjs* 60/2 (1986), 223–248 and my forthcoming book *The Disciplines of Interpretation: The Emergence of the Hermeneutic Order in Germany, 1750–1800* (Berlin and New York: de Gruyter, 1994).
3. Herder had already grasped this crucial transformation in a series of fragments published in 1768–69 under the title *Über die neuere deutsche Literatur. Fragmente*. There he wrote: "Daher ist auch unsere Zeit um so viel reicher an Journaälen, als sie an Originalwerken arm wird. Der junge Schriftsteller nimmt alten Richtern das Brot vor dem Munde weg, weil er glaubt, urteilen zu können, ohne denken zu dörfen; Arbeiten schätzen zu können, ohne selbst ein Meister zu sein. Der Leser wiederum lieset Advocatenberichte, um nicht selbst richten zu dürfen; Auszüge und Kritiken, um keine Bücher durchzustudieren." (For that reason our era is that much richer with journals as it is poor on original works. The young writer takes bread away from the old critics because he believes to be able to judge without having to think; to be permitted to evaluate works without being a master himself. The reader in turn reads reports of lawyers so as to not have to judge themselves; excerpts and critiques so as not to have to study books through and through). J. G. Herder, *Werke. Frühe Schriften 1764–1772*, ed. U. Gaier (Frankfurt: DKV, 1985), pp. 169–70.
4. Philip Lacoue-Labarthe and Jean-Luc Nancy, *The Literary Absolute: The Theory of Literature in German Romanticism* (Albany: State University of New York Press, 1986), p. 34.
5. Friedrich Schlegel, "Zur Philologie I," in F. Schlegel, *Kritische Friedrich Schlegel Ausgabe*. Edited by Ernst Behler (Paderborn/München/Wien: F. Schöningh, 1981), Vol. XVI, p. 46.
6. Michel Foucault, *Les Mots et les choses* (Paris: Gallimard, 1966); English translation *The Order of Things: An Archeology of the Human Sciences* (New York: Random House, 1970).
7. Foucault, *The Order of Things*, pp. 299–300.
8. Ibid., p. 298.
9. Ibid., p. xiv.
10. I am thinking here of the work of Pierre Duhem, *The Aim and Structure of Physical Theory* (Princeton: Princeton University Press, 1954).
11. Thomas Kuhn, *The Structure of Scientific Revolutions* (Chicago: University of Chicago Press, 1962). Although both Kuhn and Foucault took issue with histories of science that take as given the individual subject as the center for such histories, Kuhn remained a scientific realist, maintaining that despite differences in lexica it is indeed one and the same world scientific theories are about, while Foucault remained agnostic regarding scientific realism.
12. Paul Feyerabend, *Against Method: Outline of an Anarchistic Theory of Knowledge* (London: Verso, 1975).
13. See Ian Hacking, "How, Why, When and Where Language Went Public," *Common Knowledge* 1, No. 2 (1992), 74–91 and in this volume. My thanks to Hacking for sending me the unpublished draft of this paper.
14. See Ian Hacking, *Why Does Language Matter to Philosophy?* (Cambridge: Cambridge University Press, 1975).
15. Christian Heinrich Spiess, *Biographien der Wahnsinnigen*, ed. W. Promies (Darmstadt & Neuwied: Luchterhand, 1976).
16. In the *Archaeology of Knowledge*, Foucault wrote: "We are not trying to reconstitute what madness itself might be, in the form in which it first presented itself to some primitive, fundamental, deaf, scarcely articulated experience, and in the form in which it was later organized (translated, deformed, travestied, perhaps even repressed) by discourses." Foucault, *The Archaeology of Knowledge* (New York: Harper & Row, 1976), p. 47.
17. Michel Foucault, "Two Lectures," in *Power/Knowledge: Selected Interviews and Other Writings 1972–1977*, ed. Colin Gordon (New York: Pantheon, 1977), p. 101.
18. See the articles of Ian Hacking: "Making up people," in T. Heller, M. Sosna, and D.

Wellbery, eds., *Reconstructing Individualism: Autonomy, Individuality and the Self in Western Thought* (Stanford: Stanford University Press, 1986), pp. 222–36; "Biopower and the Avalanche of Printed Numbers," *Humanities in Society* 5 (1982), 279–95.

19. Georges Canguilhem, *The Normal and the Pathological* (New York: Zone, 1991), a translation of *Le normal et le pathologique* (Paris: Presses Universitaires de France, 1966). The first essay was written in 1943.
20. Foucault, *The Birth of the Clinic* (New York: Vintage, 1975), p. xiii.
21. Ibid., p. 195.
22. Michel Foucault, *Discipline and Punish: The Birth of the Prison* (New York: Random House, 1977).
23. Foucault, *The Order of Things*, p. 335.
24. On this new web of knowledge and power, see Jeremy Campbell, *Grammatical Man: Information, Entropy, Language, and Life* (New York: Simon & Schuster, 1982); Friedrich A. Kittler, *Grammaphon, Film, Typewriter* (Berlin: Brinkmann & Bose, 1986).
25. Kittler, *Grammophon, Film, Typewriter*, p. 378.
26. This is the formulation Foucault utilized in *The Order of Things*, Chapter 9, "Man and his Doubles," pp. 303–44.
27. Hacking, "Making Up People," in Heller, Sosna, and Wellbery, eds., *Reconstructing Individualism*, pp. 222–36.
28. See Ian Hacking, "Self-Improvement," in David Couzens Hoy, ed., *Foucault—A Critical Reader* (Oxford: Blackwell, 1986), pp. 235–40.
29. Immanuel Kant, *Foundations of the Metaphysics of Morals*, translated with an introduction by Lewis White Beck (New York, London: Macmillan, 1959), p. 71.
30. Alexander Nehamas, *Nietzsche: Life as Literature* (Cambridge, Mass.: Harvard University Press, 1985), p. 107.
31. In the 'aesthetic' moment, the subject sees itself in the image of the creator, in the *Bild* of something that transcends concepts and itself has no origin or purpose, no *arché* or *telos*. On this, see Lacoue-Labarthe and Nancy, *The Literary Absolute*, p. 31.
32. Michel Foucault, "Two Lectures," in Michel Foucault, *Power/Knowledge. Selected Interviews and Other Writings 1972–77*, ed. Colin Gordon (New York: Pantheon, 1977), p. 97.
33. Foucault, "Two Lectures," p. 98.
34. This is the point of Rorty's critique in *Contingency, Irony and Solidarity* (Cambridge/New York: Cambridge University Press, 1989), and, more specifically, in a recently published paper entitled "Moral Identity and Private Autonomy," in *Michel Foucault. Philosopher* (New York: Routledge, 1992), pp. 328–36. Rorty thinks that "the term 'power' is stretched so far that it loses any contrastive force and becomes vacuous," and that Foucault's work is "pervaded by a crippling ambiguity between 'power' as a pejorative term and as a neutral, descriptive term" (330). I want to thank Richard Rorty for making this paper available to me before its publication in the aforementioned volume.
35. Michel Foucault, *The History of Sexuality. Volume 1: An Introduction* (New York: Vintage, 1980), p. 82.
36. Ibid.
37. See Charles Taylor, "Foucault on Freedom and Truth," in *Philosophy and the Human Sciences: Philosophical Papers 2* (Cambridge: Cambridge University Press, 1985), pp. 152–84.
38. "Nietzsche, Genealogy, History," in Paul Rabinow, ed., *The Foucault Reader* (New York: Pantheon, 1984), pp. 95–96.
39. Foucault, "The Body of the Condemned," in *Discipline and Punish*.
40. Foucault, *The History of Sexuality. Volume I: An Introduction*, pp. 92–93.
41. Foucault, *Power/Knowledge*, pp. 106–7.
42. Both Vico and Montesquieu recognize this tradition of 'virtue' and 'right' in *The New Science* (1725, 1744) and *The Spirit of the Laws* (1725).

43. Cf. the analysis of Carl Schmitt, *Political Theology: Four Chapters on the Concept of Sovereignty* (Cambridge: MIT Press, 1985).
44. Richard Rorty argues that Foucault "still thinks in terms of something deep within human beings, which is deformed by acculturation." Pace Rorty, Foucault is an ironist who wants to avoid being a liberal. I doubt that Foucault thought there was anything deep within human beings, which is then deformed. His researches seem to suggest that 'human being' is just another 'object' for ongoing mechanisms of subjugation. See Richard Rorty, *Contingency, Irony and Solidarity* (New York: Cambridge, 1989), p. 64.
45. Cf. Jürgen Habermas, who complains that Foucault gives us no lever with which we can launch an effective critique of power relations. See Habermas, "Mit dem Pfeil ins Herz der Gegenwart," in J. Habermas, *Die neue Unübersichtlichkeit* (Frankfurt: Suhrkamp, 1985), pp. 126–30.
46. Some of these 'effects' have already been fleshed out on a theoretical level by David Wellbery, "Theory of Events: Foucault and Literary Criticism," *Revue Internationale de Philosophie* 162–63 (1987), 420–32; and "Contingency," in Ann Fehn, Ingeborg Hoesterey and Maria Tatar, eds., *Neverending Stories: Toward a Critical Narratology* (Princeton: Princeton University Press, 1991), pp. 237–57. See also Friedrich Kittler, ed., *Die Austreibung des Geistes aus den Geisteswissenschaften* (Paderborn/München/Wien: F. Schöningh, 1981); and Horst Turk and Friedrich Kittler, eds., *Urszenen: Literaturwissenschaft als Diskursanalyse und Diskurskritik* (Frankfurt: Suhrkamp, 1977), pp. 9–44. For an excellent discussion of the usefulness of Foucault's work for literary history, see Friederike Meyer, "Diskurstheorie und Literaturgeschichte: Eine systematische Reformulierung des Diskursbegriffs von Foucault," in Lutz Danneberg, Friedrich Vollhardt, eds., *Vom Umgang mit Literatur und Literaturgeschichte* (Stuttgart: Metzler, 1992), pp. 389–408. Most recently, Simon During has traced the multiple effects Foucault's work has had on literary studies in *Foucault and Literature: Towards a Genealogy of Writing* (London and New York: Routledge, 1992).
47. On the end of hermeneutics as a methodology of the 'human sciences,' see Friedrich Kittler, "Vergessen," in U. Nassen, ed., *Texthermeneutik: Aktualität, Geschichte, Kritik* (Paderborn/München/Wien: F. Schöningh, 1979).
48. Quentin Skinner, "Meaning and Understanding in the History of Ideas," *History and Theory* VII, No. 1 (1969), 3–53.
49. In *The Archaeology of Knowledge*, Foucault distanced himself from the theory of speech-acts as developed by Austin and Searle. I would maintain, however, that there is a deep-structural alliance between the performative turn in historical studies and Foucault's own project insofar as both ask about the *functioning of statements and texts*, not about 'ideas' and 'meanings' as traditional 'history of ideas' tends to do.
50. Reinhard Koselleck, "Social History and *Begriffsgeschichte*," in Koselleck, *Futures Past: On the Semantics of Historical Time* (Cambridge: MIT Press, 1985), pp. 73–91; Dominick LaCapra, "Rhetoric and Criticism," in LaCapra, *History and Criticism* (Ithaca: Cornell University Press, 1986), pp. 34–44.
51. Michel Foucault, "What is an Author?" in Josué Harari, ed., *Textual Strategies: Perspectives in Post-Structuralist Criticism* (Ithaca: Cornell University Press, 1980), pp. 141–60.
52. Ibid., p. 159.
53. See Heinrich Bosse, *Autorschaft ist Werkherrschaft: Über die Enstehung des Urheberrechts aus dem Geist der Goethezeit* (Paderborn/München/Wien: F. Schöningh, 1981), p. 7.
54. Ibid., p. 14.
55. See Friedrich Schlegel, "On Incomprehensibility," in Kathleen Wheeler, ed., *German Aesthetic and Literary Criticism: The Romantic Ironists and Goethe* (Cambridge/New York/London: Cambridge University Press, 1984), pp. 32–40.
56. J. W. von Goethe, *Die Wahlverwandtschaften* (München: DTV, 1963), p. 18.

57. Michel Foucault, "What is Enlightenment?" in Paul Rabinow, ed., *The Foucault Reader* (New York: Pantheon, 1984).
58. Ibid., p. 34.
59. Ibid., p. 50.
60. Friedrich Nietzsche, *Werke*, ed. K. Schlechta (München: Hanser, 1980), I: 240.

I

Institutions and Institutionalization

How, Why, When, and Where Did Language Go Public?

IAN HACKING

Some time ago I published a small primer about philosophy and language.[1] It blithely skipped along in three parts: a heyday of ideas, a heyday of meanings, and a heyday of sentences. To get a sense of how an analytical philosopher could see things, call that Locke, Frege, and Now. There is a howling gap in there. The hole in time is disgraceful, given that my story was told against Michel Foucault's larger archaeological canvass, but I don't mind that. What's missing is any account of the passage from language as private to language as public. That transition cannot be structured in terms of heydays.[2]

What do I mean by private and public? Hobbes spoke for the era of ideas when he wrote that language is mental discourse.[3] In his opinion, language has two distinct values. First, words, being signs of ideas, serve as memory aids that help us to recall previous thoughts. Secondly, but only secondly, words are wonderfully adapted to communication, so that they enable me to transfer ideas in my mind to yours. Language is essentially private and only accidentally public. Descartes and Hume, Locke and Leibniz, even Kant, were much of the same mind.

Long after ideas had yielded to meanings, some philosophers, like Bertrand Russell, also thought that meanings are as private as Hobbesian ideas. "When one person uses a word, he does not mean by it the same thing as another person means by it."[4] And in our latter-day world of sentences, many theorists, especially the cognitive scientists, continue in that vein. Marvin Minsky writes that "a word can only serve to indicate that someone else may have a valuable idea—that is, some useful structure to be built inside the mind."[5]

Hobbes, then, lives, but since his day there has arisen an entirely different conception of language, as essentially public. Analytic philosophers are the least likely of our contemporaries to break with old ways. Most of their discussions and problems are recreations of Enlightenment models. That was one conclusion of my primer: Structurally identical problems are rephrased, over three centuries, in the successive idioms of ideas, meanings, and sentences. In at least one respect that won't do at all. Even the analytically minded now believe, or write as if they believed, that language is essentially public. They take for granted that, aside from codes and other derivative kinds of record keeping, a strictly private language is impossible. That is hardly their discovery: thinkers in other traditions are astonished at the notion of an essentially private language. Bertrand Russell and cognitive science notwithstanding, language went public. How, why, when, and where did that happen?

A full response to the question of my title would be a prolix analysis of many times and places. A brisk answer whose merit is brevity results from adding a "who?" to my roster of queries. Who was the first unequivocal public linguist? J. G. Hamann (1730–88).[6] I learned that by reading Isaiah Berlin. "Poor Hamann—he really was original—tangled, dark, absurd, but first-hand, he got on to something; but I do not believe that anyone in the English-speaking world, except eccentric truffle-hunters like me, will ever read him."[7]

NOT WITTGENSTEIN

What's wrong with the more straightforward answer that language went public in the 1930s as Wittgenstein's philosophy evolved? Because the event happened long before. Wittgenstein's readers did want a short name for a long stretch of the *Philosophical Investigations*, and they called it the private language argument.[8] The passages in which he presented the argument or arguments are original and profound. Nevertheless the conception of language as essentially public long precedes those thoughts, and runs along quite different lines.

I shall soon turn to Hegel as a public linguist of long ago, but we need not move beyond philosophers favored in the analytic tradition to show that the idea precedes our century. Two of the three nineteenth-century philosophers most respected by analytic philosophers were public linguists. I mean C. S. Peirce and Gottlob Frege, as opposed to J. S. Mill (an inveterate private linguist). In an early essay Peirce astoundingly found it hard to answer the question, "What distinguishes a man from a word?" He held that "the word or sign which man uses is the man himself." The fact "that every thought is an external sign, proves that man is an external sign. That is to say, that the man and the external sign are identical . . . my language is the sum total of myself; for the man is the thought."[9] Peirce is uncommonly hard to understand, but whatever he meant in 1868, he was in a publicizing mood, making consciousness, the self, language, inference, and words not only external but also communal. A couple of pages earlier he had been insisting on COMMUNITY, printed in capital letters.

Frege was equally a public linguist. His core theory about language is one of what he called sense, reference, and associated idea. The third is indeed private, mentioned by Frege deliberately to exclude it from his theory of meaning. To hold that language is essentially public you don't have to deny that words conjure up various thoughts in various minds. You say only, with Frege, that these thoughts are "associated ideas" that are not the sense of what is said. Associated ideas may be private but in Frege's theory the sense of a word "is not a part or a mode of the individual mind." Frege found this obvious even from the fact that "mankind has a common store of thoughts which is transmitted from one generation to another."[10]

HEGEL

Frege and Peirce hardly began publicity. One might guess that Hegel did, in 1807, perhaps, with *The Phenomenology of Spirit*. Time and time again the man will say something like, "Language is self-consciousness existing for others."[11] He spoke of language as an "outer reality that is immediately self-conscious existence." There are problems about Hegel. He was a bit of a backslider, apparently espousing a more private view of language later in life. For example in 1830 he said that language, in one of its aspects, "is a product of intelligence for manifesting its ideas in an external medium."[12] Those are not the words of a convinced public linguist. But let us ask whether this date of 1807, which is not quite arbitrary, makes sense. Is this a reasonable time to think of language going public?

Yes. Should one not expect a change in conceptions of language, given the many changes in the place of Europe in the world, which inevitably affected the way its citizens thought about language? They had access to a large number of new texts in languages they had never known or had forgotten: Sanskrit, Persian, Celtic, Norse. There were many newly-met, nonliterate peoples in Polynesia, the Amazon, aboriginal Australia, the American Midwest. Travel and conquest gave Europe ancient texts of the Indian subcontinent and new speech in the South Pacific. It is inviting to imagine that these two kinds of imperial discovery directly suggested the idea of language as public. Almost the only item that you cannot wrest from another people by barter or victory is language. It cannot be private property, or one could take it. So language is not private. That would seem like a bad pun, were it not that the bourgeois individualism of the seventeenth

Georg Wilhelm Friedrich Hegel, from the Bildabteilung, Deutsches Literaturarchiv of the Schiller Nationalmuseum, Marbach, Germany. Reprinted with permission.

century is (or is often argued to be) an admixture of the self-as-owner-of-its-thoughts and the self-as-owner-of-its-goods.

Yet that won't quite do. European contact with foreigners had always been going on. The founding of colonies was as much an enterprise of earlier years as it was of Hegel's time. Jesuit missionaries had learned the Algonquin languages from Newfoundland to Manitoba, and their adventures were eagerly followed in France, where examples of "Huron" activities, languages, and even games were bandied about. Leibniz was fascinated by Chinese language and writing. New linguistic discoveries and encounters are not sufficient for revolutionary thoughts. They did surprisingly little for Locke. He knew of voyages as well as anyone, but he made only wan observations about differences among languages.[13] If we wish beginnings in Enlightened philosophy of an historical, culture-laden vision of language and its study, we must turn to Leibniz. His most extended discussion of language, Book III of the *New Essays* directed at Locke, lay unpublished for half a century, until 1765. Its readers were of a new generation; one of the first was Hamann, who told Herder about the book's publication.[14] Before thinking about those two, let us examine more closely the period of language study leading up to Hegel.

There are three widely read accounts of a radical transition in the conception of language around that time: by Michel Foucault, Noam Chomsky, and Isaiah Berlin. All three attribute something, in different degrees, to newly circulated ancient texts and encounters with preliterate peoples. Each has cast his own stamp on reports of the transition. I shall also call an expert witness, Hans Aarsleff, an historian of the study of language, for yet another version of events. None of these four men was addressing my question of when language went public. Yet the going-public of language may be the core event that links their otherwise conflicting analyses.

MICHEL FOUCAULT

During the Cartesian or "classical" era, so goes *The Order of Things*, students of language were preoccupied by General Grammar. Words are signs of ideas. General Grammar aimed at understanding how thoughts can be represented by articulated strings of words. Actual languages were studied but with no sense of their particularity. The questions asked were truly general: how do signs work? That exactly parallels the philosophical debate: how do our ideas correspond to the world? Toward the end of the eighteenth century, as colonial advance provided ancient texts and new languages, the study of abstract grammar was replaced by a fascination with the varieties of syntax within linguistic families. Languages became historical entities, fit for empirical investigation. Foucault famously claimed that the emergence of life, labor, and language as objects of study was part of a widespread transformation from representation to history.

Foucault's account is, in its large features, correct, at least for the case of grammar—although I have observed elsewhere that in many points of detail it is not quite right.[15] His is not an unusual version, for it parallels the official history of the emergence of philology in Germany. The philological seminar in Göttingen was founded in 1761. When Prussia restored itself in 1810 after humiliating defeat, Alexander von Humboldt recreated the educational system with philology at its core. His brother, Wilhelm, played a remarkable part in bringing home from the South Pacific new languages to study and new thoughts about how to do it. Philology became the premier academic subject in Germany. Nietzsche may be its most remembered professor, but Foucault's lesson is about Franz Bopp.

Bopp's first major publication was in 1816. General Grammar was dead and philology had replaced it, but Bopp does not help us much with public and private language. He had little to say about meaning, for he wrote of syntax and the historical development of the verb form in comparative grammars of Sanskrit, Persian, Greek, Latin, Lithuanian, Old Church Slavonic, Gothic, and German (I recite from one of his titles). He also wrote on aspects of Malay and Polynesian. Bopp's primarily syntactic concerns are perfectly consistent with a private view of meaning. So none of this explains why language went public, which was, of course, never Foucault's intention. He aimed only at establishing a point at which certain kinds of knowledge became historical. He fixed on Cuvier, palaeontologist; Ricardo, economist; and Bopp, philologist. Bopp was twenty years younger than the other two men, and I want to begin Foucault's philological story long before Bopp.

NOAM CHOMSKY

Cartesian Linguistics is Chomsky's brilliant, brief exposition of his rationalist forebears. He published it soon after he had decisively established transformational grammar as the wave of the future. He was, he implied, restoring to prominence the attitude to knowledge that underlay projects of General Grammar. A single text serves as focal point for both Chomsky and Foucault, namely Port Royal's *Grammaire générale et raisonée* of 1660. Where Foucault had seen a theory about how to represent continuous reality in disjointed words, Chomsky found systematic attention to the creative aspect of language use—our ability to say endlessly many things. The transition from the good, Universal Grammar, to the bad, descriptive philology, was hardly the main point of the book, but Chomsky did find it important to say that Humboldt's *Über die Verschiedenheit des menschlichen Sprachbaus* was the last work in the great tradition of Cartesian linguistics. Humboldt's study of Polynesian languages, combined with much theoretical reflection, published posthumously in 1836, fully reflects the "creative aspect" so emphasized by Chomsky: the idea that language must "make infinite employment of finite means."[16] It also has attractions for an innatist: "Language could not be invented or come upon if its archetype were not already present in the human soul."

Leonard Bloomfield, one of the villains of Chomsky's essay, had claimed *Über die Verschiedenheit* as the first work of modern linguistics, of descriptive philology.[17] It may seem a fine point, to discuss whether a posthumous book was the last work of the old regime or the first of the new. Chomsky knew well that Humboldt held that historical languages serve to define a people, a vision of the world, and constitute an individual within a community. In that respect, Chomsky admitted, Humboldt "departs radically from the framework of Cartesian linguistics."[18]

In Chomsky's version Humboldt retained old truths but promulgated new errors. In Bloomfield's version Humboldt advanced a new vision while cleaving to old mistakes. In fact Humboldt impresses by emphasizing a duality about language, as arising partly from the very nature of human beings (Chomsky), but also as being formed as part of the historical individuality of a community or nation. Humboldt can well serve to represent the battlefront between cognitive science and cultural anthropology in the 1990s.

Bopp's ideas reached maturity just when Humboldt's lifework came to an end. Hegel's *Phenomenology* reminds us that the idea of language as public had been around for some time, and so must precede whatever claim could be made for Bopp or Humboldt. Indeed if Humboldt were understood only as an innatist and the last practitioner of General Grammar we would expect to file him among the private linguists. Hans Aarsleff does exactly that. He argues that Humboldt's philosophy is in part driven by "the radical impossibility that others can have direct access to what goes on in our minds . . . it involves what had long been recognized as the privacy of language."[19] Those are not my perceptions. Humboldt must be understood as part of a different lineage, in the sequence of Isaiah Berlin's favored trio of Hamann, Herder, and Humboldt. If we push back to Hamann we come to a very public conception of language—within which, I venture, the subsequent transformations in the study of language take place.

ISAIAH BERLIN

Philology is only one strand in German Romanticism. An immense literature has been devoted to it, the very literature that Foucault ostentatiously ignored by directing us to the dusty Bopp. I choose to mention only one elegant and rather loving version of a more standard account. Berlin much admires Herder, who taught that there can be no thought without language, that a language characterizes a culture, and that language is the medium in which a human being becomes a person. He distinguishes three doctrines distinctive of Herder's thought. Pluralism, as Berlin calls it, is "the belief not merely in the multiplicity, but in the incommensurability, of the values of different cultures and societies."[20] Populism has to do with the necessity of being part of a group or culture in order to be an individual person. Expressionism is the holistic doctrine that human activity expresses the entire personality of the individual or group, and is intelligible only to the degree that it does so.

Guiding all three of these is the way in which, according to Herder, a language defines or even constitutes a culture, and thereby its people. I have mentioned travel to past times and foreign climes as bringing a new awareness of languages as repositories of a group or civilization. We must not forget the inverse, that in those days, following the lead of Leibniz, German thinkers were trying to forge their own identity by creating and writing in their own tongue. This was a political act. Herder's king, Frederick the Great, read only books in French and spoke German "like a coachman." The Academy in Berlin was filled with Frenchmen of brilliance (Maupertuis was its president), Frenchmen of promise, and Frenchmen—even Frederick's head tax-collectors (Hamann's bosses) were to write memoranda in French. Frederick's contempt for religion was that of the *philosophes*. His "French" sexual preferences were veridical gossip. The new idea that language defines a culture was part of an attempt to define a German culture, something anti-Frederician, unfrench not so much in manners as in speech.

Let us call this family of ideas—Isaiah Berlin's trio of pluralism, populism, and expressionism, plus the emphasis on the language of a people defining that people as a political entity—the "culture-concept." In variant forms it is characteristic of Romanticism, and, notoriously, it can be exploited by master racism. Many agree that Herder was one of the earlier exponents of a generous culture concept. Berlin has a less widely shared affection for Herder's friend Hamann, by fourteen years the senior of the two men:

> Herder had derived from Hamann his notion that words and ideas are one. Men do not think, as it were in thoughts and ideas and then look for words in which to "clothe" them, as one looks for a glove to fit a fully formed hand. Hamann taught that to think was to use symbols, and that to deny this was not so much false as unintelligible.[21]

We are on the verge of the essential publicity of language when we add Hamann's insistence that the symbols are part of an historical and public language. On the one hand, language characterizes a culture and helps define a people as a collectivity: the culture concept. On the other, all thoughts are in symbols located within a culture, so there is no autonomous "private object" for words to denote.

HANS AARSLEFF

Things are never so simple. Hans Aarsleff has been a vociferous opponent of Berlin's version of events.[22] He rightly insists that Berlin's favored German writers learned much from French ones. But he goes further. He gives us the impression that aside from wrong turnings the German writers were unoriginal. There is a certain piquancy to this. Aarsleff himself appears to be a private linguist. Hence he does not want to acknowledge the very concepts that the likes of Herder brought into being.

Just as one of Berlin's more obscure heroes is Hamann, so Condillac (1715–80) is one of Aarsleff's. The French philosopher nicely serves to clarify a difference between public and private language. Aarsleff thinks that you can find in Condillac, for example, the radical thoughts supposedly invented by the Germans. That is because Aarsleff won't acknowledge the existence of the radical thoughts. Condillac was an idéologue, a Lockeite, and a private linguist if ever there was one. We have ideas. Words signify ideas, which are private objects. He did go so far as to say that "it appears that every language expresses the character of the people that speak it."[23] Is that not Herder's culture-concept? No. Condillac was noticing a merely empirical fact on a par with the influence on a people of climate and prosperity. It never occurred to him that a language and a people are co-constitutive.

Condillac agreed to the ancient truism that none of the characteristic features of the mental life of humans is possible without language. We need language in order to sharpen and classify ideas, and to make them determinate and distinct. Those private linguists of today, the cognitive scientists, would agree. The word is the sign of the idea. A private object, an idea, might not have been formed had not humans the power of speech, but it is private all the same. Words signify ideas, their private referents. Condillac did not imagine what (according to Berlin) Herder learned from Hamann, namely that words and ideas are one.

Having separated Herder from the private linguist Condillac, can we say that Herder inaugurated the publicity of language? He is commonly regarded as a progenitor of the great German philological tradition. May he not also have loosed the bonds of the Lockeite idea-ology and its private references of words? Yes, but he was not the first nor did he do it thoroughly. Aarsleff (quoting in part from another scholar) writes of what he calls "Herder's principle that each human being 'in the true metaphysical sense' speaks his own language."[24] Herder may not have learned quite as much from Hamann as Berlin would have wished. Hamann had qualms on this very point. His own published animadversions on Herder's famous prize essay on the origins of language can certainly be read as worries about, among many other things, publicity. Hamann, at any rate, was sure that in the true metaphysical sense no person speaks his or her own language.

ROLE MODELS

Something fundamental happened to the way in which we think about language around 1800, give or take quite a few years. Chomsky thinks it was a bad thing. Berlin thinks it was a good thing. Foucault thought it was a remarkable thing. Aarsleff, the professional, thinks that it did not happen. The history of thinking about language was an enthusiasm of Berlin, Chomsky, and Foucault, but it was incidental to their grander themes and greater enterprises. All three were passionate about a big transition, but totally at odds about its nature. Worse, when we call in an expert, he polemically denies that there was a significant change at all. What is going on?

Aarsleff is partly defending his territory against the incursions of amateurs such as Chomsky and Berlin. The title of his 1970 attack, "The History of Linguistics and Professor Chomsky," does not belie its tone. Chomsky, we are in effect told, made a big mistake. There is no such thing as Cartesian linguistics: there is only a great Lockeite tradition adopted in France. And much later Aarsleff savaged Berlin for failing to understand that the Germans had merely aped the French.

Aarsleff's fierce rebuttals connect him with two of our authors. As for other pairings, I think that Chomsky and Foucault never discussed their opposed views about language, but there was one remarkable confrontation between the two men. The topic was not language but justice and human nature. Each hammed up the role of himself—Foucault as manic post-Maoist, Chomsky as wrathful rationalist republican; Chomsky as *philosophe*, Foucault as terrorist.[25] Although the debate had nothing to do with anything so recondite as the history of language study, it displays the politics that underwrites our authors' analyses of language. For we are not talking here only about language, but about high politics, about the person and the state, about individual rights, about the self, and much else.

Chomsky's role as spokesman for egalitarian rationalism is too well known to need elaboration here. The creative aspect of language use, together with the innate species-specific powers of the human mind have, for him, a deep political significance. To think that something so constitutive of humanity as language is merely embedded in cultures is to encourage illiberalism and perhaps to invite despotism.

Aarsleff and Berlin, both emigrés, are different again. Each, in his view of language, is like Chomsky, expressing his own profoundly held liberalism. For the Danish-born expert, the virtues are those of English tolerance and Locke is the man. For the assimilated German Jew, the virtues are those of reform during the early days of German liberal culture. The golden age of Germany lost so long ago was none other than the period when Hamann, Herder, and Humboldt could flourish. Berlin's Herder is the man who "protests, not without a certain malicious satisfaction (as Hamann also did, with equally ironical pleasure), that the great liberal Kant in his *Anthropologie* emphasized race and color too much."[26] Singing the praises of Herder, Berlin is honoring a larger set of values. So the theme of these diverse stories is less language than a celebration of liberalism, perceived from different quarters. Each of our protagonists save Foucault, no professed liberal, implies, "I am more liberal than you, and my guys are more liberal than your guys."

HAMANN

A standard account of the study of language tells of the Romantic attitude starting with an almost invisible Hamann profoundly influencing the highly visible Herder. This attitude was in turn cast into institutional form through the work of the Humboldts. Aarsleff has rightly insisted that this version of history is manifestly impoverished, if only because of the immense amount that both Herder and Humboldt took from their French predecessors and contemporaries. Hamann is not too promising a figure for those of us who favor clarity of statement over visions, clouds of erudition, and abrupt aphorisms. If you become captured by his more flamboyant prose your own becomes tinctured with it. Yet he had many of the tastes of the rationalist that favor elegance of style and clarity of exposition. After he had read Kant's first *Critique*, he wrote Herder: "Hume is always my man."[27] He translated Hume's *Dialogues Concerning Natural Religion*. His great admirer, Kierkegaard, understated the number of Hamann's preserved words, but the spirit of this comment is exactly right: "Just as Socrates left no books, Ha-

Johann Georg Hamann, from the Bildabteilung, Deutsches Literaturarchiv of the Schiller Nationalmuseum, Marbach, Germany. Reprinted with permission.

mann left only as much as the modern period's rage for writing made relatively necessary, and furthermore only occasional pieces."[28]

The only systematic review of Hamann's work by a first-class mind was written by Hegel in 1828. It accompanied the publication during that decade of Hamann's works, many of which had not been printed earlier.[29] By Hegel's lights, Hamann was too dark, too obscure, despite flashes of brilliance. One can also sense that Hegel felt somewhat threatened by Hamann's words. Those less scared have been, in their own ways, more receptive: not just Berlin but Kierkegaard, or Gershom Scholem commending Hamann and his tradition to Walter Benjamin.[30]

Hamann was a born-again Christian whose practices make little sense in our age, which is so simplistic with regard to religion. Here was a young man who—after low life in London, where he had been sent on a confidential commercial mission by his prospective father-in-law, a powerful Baltic merchant, and where he had taken up with a lute player, found himself betrayed, survived a breakdown by studying the Bible, and experienced an intense conversion to a personal and fundamentalist Lutheranism— proceeded to write his fiancée and her father in quite vivid detail about all that had happened; end of engagement. Shocked by his emotional and religious state and his indifference to the values of reasonable analysis, his best friend Berens (brother of the former fiancée) arranged with Kant to try to restore him to sound principles. The result was a disastrous weekend à trois that left Hamann unmoved. He was involved with God throughout his life. But he would on occasion deny the immortality of the soul. He lived in domestic harmony with his common-law wife, whom he declined to marry and who bore him four children. Ever Lutheran, he spent his last couple of years in the intellectual company of Catholics, and was buried in the Roman churchyard of Münster. He was explicit about physical sex, which he identified with mystical union. Vastly franker in print than his peers, he would yet win no admirers from most sexual revolutionaries of recent times and much contempt from many feminists. It is easy to read him as even more antiSemitic than most of his contemporaries: that is, profoundly absorbed in Hebrew history as revealed in the Bible, well aware of cabalistic and Talmudic writing, but contemptuous of most European Jews in his own time.

KANT

What can we learn from Hamann, the self-styled "Magus of the North," about conceptions of language? It is useful to begin by playing him off against Kant. The two men form a paradoxical contrast of public and private. Kant was a very public personality, but founded his philosophy on privacy. Hamann was a very private man whose world view was founded upon community. Kant was the elder by six years and outlived Hamann by fifteen. They knew each other well, although toward the end Kant distanced himself.

Hamann edited a good number of Kant's occasional pieces, and read the first *Critique* in proof, probably before Kant himself. His short essay about the great book was scathing, yet Hamann retained much respect and affection for Kant, whom he long called the "Prussian Hume." "My poor head is a broken pot compared to Kant's—earthenware against iron."[31] No one will disagree.

Kant was Enlightenment, Hamann its opposite, but it is not the tag that counts. However much we tend to think of Kant as dry, withered, wizened, obsessive, Kant was a truly public man. He attracted large audiences and, in the *Anthropologie* and elsewhere, wrote meticulously about how to arrange the best dinner parties, where all the news of the world would be exchanged before moving to the later stages of frivolity. But Kant's philosophy is founded upon privacy, quite as much as that of Descartes or Locke or Leibniz. A person is an ego with a buzzing sequence of sense impressions and thoughts. Hence arises the challenge of discovering a basis for objectivity. Throughout Kant's final work we find the same solution for the natural and the moral sciences: one's judgment must be the judgment of every rational man, when placed in the same circumstances. In our knowledge of the world, we obtain objectivity because of certain preconditions for experience in space, time, and causality, substance and the like; in the moral realm, we attain objectivity by willing (as noumenal private agents) to will only what we would wish any other like being to will. The voice of reason is the voice of standardization and of public norms. These are required by a self whose essence is private, an essence whose objectivity is assured only by "the transcendental unity of apperception" according to which every thought is accompanied by the thought, "I think this."

Kant's attempts to solve the problem of public objectivity gave him a metaphysics, an epistemology, an ethics, and a theory of the state. Hamann did not have Kant's problems. He thought that there is no such thing as a person except what is constituted in a social setting, characterized by a unique historical language. Language is essentially public and shared; it is prior to the individuation of one's self. For Kant, the "I think" had to accompany every thought in order for there to exist an objective and continuous "I." For Hamann, there is an "I" only in linguistic communities, and as a child becomes formed publicly within a language, so the objective and continuous "I," such as it is, comes into being.

One's self is constituted within a society and a language. Hamann did not infer that there is an unchanging and irrevocable linguistic framework. On the contrary it is Kant who requires the standardized language, for without that, the world dissolves into solipsism. Hamann, who had no problem about intersubjectivity, felt free to reform the language into which he was born. Some of his prose intended for "publication" is as rupturing as Artaud or *Finnegans Wake*. He was one of the earlier expositors of the originality of genius and its responsibility to remold language. That's not to say he wasn't also old-fashioned in his wonderfully quirky way. He wrote a spirited defence of the silent *h* in old German orthography. It indicated a breath (i.e., also *Geist*, spirit). Hamann held that the pedants who were trying to rationalize spelling were also trying to strip language of spirit. Language makes a person possible, but the conscious person should never be constrained by the very forms that made the personality possible. Hamann denied originality in his own propaganda for originality. He owned as his master Edward Young—author of *Conjectures on Original Composition*. Young's own original composition, *Night Thoughts on Life, Death and Immortality in Nine Nights* had won far more fame in the German-speaking lands than it ever knew in England.[32] Hamann did not mind saying that he knew not how much he had learned from Young, perhaps everything.

Kant, whose whole philosophy was founded upon the Classical notion of the private ego, had to construct a theory of shared judgments in order to assure any objectivity for the person at all. Hamann, taking for granted a self that is constituted in the public world of language and social intercourse, was empowered to become a thoroughly private figure. For Kant, the objectivity of the self was always in principle threatened and so required a metaphysical foundation. For Hamann there was no threat and no foundation. He was a person from the very fact that he spoke. He did not need to be obeisant to public guarantees of objectivity because there was no need of guarantee. He could afford to make fun of the public. In 1759 he stated on the title page of his *Socratic Memorabilia* that they are "Compiled for the Boredom of the Public by a Lover of Boredom, with a Double Dedication to Nobody and to Two." The two are Hamann's lifelong friends Berens and Kant, who had tried to restore him to Enlightenment conventions. The work is dedicated as well to the public, i.e., nobody.[33]

FLASH-FORWARD

There is much in common between today's analytic philosophy and the projects of enlightened Europe from the time of Hobbes to that of Kant. I've taken as premise that there is one radical difference. Aside from those influenced by cognitive science, few think that there could be a private language. There may be as many versions of this idea as there are widely read philosophers. That vogue owes nothing to Hamann, Herder, or Humboldt, nor even (despite "the private language argument") to a present enthusiasm for Wittgenstein. It is a common enough complaint "about many contemporary American philosophers that they appear never to have read Wittgenstein."[34]

Language, I claim, went public at the time of Hamann, but the present analytical enthusiasm for the publicity of language may have quite different roots. There may be various ways to go public, one of which stems from Kant. The theory of shared judgments was both essential to and novel in Kant's philosophy of objectivity. That leads to the conception that what is asserted must be public in order to be objective—an idea quite alien to

Hamann. This, perhaps, is the kind of publicity that has been made a commonplace of the analytic philosophers. It follows that answers to the question, "What are the roots of a modern analytic enthusiasm for the publicity of language?" may be entirely different, and vastly more Kantian, than my answer to my title question.

If one were to pursue this thought, one might better understand why the modern analytic "Kantians" are so at odds about what "the private language argument" is. Wittgenstein's argument may lie within a vision of language and the soul that shares much with Hamann. It is preoccupied not with reason, not with objectivity, but, in the end, with what it is to be a person.[35] That is not to deny that Wittgenstein has mattered to the analysts. One effect of his work has been to de-politicize the idea of language as essentially public. Language becomes regarded as an abstract phenomenon. One need not become involved in practical consequences of the idea: hence (perhaps) its background appeal to analytic philosophy. Writing about language as some sort of abstract entity has made it possible to leave aside questions about what it is to be a person in a community. Hence questions about the soul and personal identity have continued to be discussed in very much the manner of the Enlightenment. Analytical philosophy found thereby a protective screening from other strands of contemporary philosophical thought. It is as if Wittgenstein vaccinated analytic philosophy against more radical transformations: by giving us the cow-pox of public language, he left the rest of our constitution intact.

PURE REASON AND ITS CRITIQUE

Hamann wrote several pieces on Kant's first *Critique*. One is a "Metacritique of the Purism of Reason" (1784). This title is typically packed with allusions. The metacritique is not just "about a critique"—in it Hamann used the word "metaschematism" both with reference to Kant's schematism, and with reference to Paul's Epistle (I Corinthians 4:6), a pun that takes several pages to elucidate.[36] The word "purism" in the title is of Hamann's invention (*Purismum*). It has connotations of the purity of reason. But, as he wrote to his friend and Kant's critic, Jacobi, "With me it is not so much the question, What is reason? but rather, What is language?"[37]

It is significant that Hamann begins this piece with a paragraph about Berkeley and Hume. Not any Berkeley, not any Hume. He writes of Berkeley on abstract ideas and of Hume saying that Berkeley's proof, that there are no abstract ideas, is one of the greatest and most valuable discoveries of the day. Assuredly Berkeley and Hume were private linguists, but they abandoned one core tenet of Locke, the private reference of general words to abstract ideas in the mind. There are no abstract ideas to refer to. How then do general words succeed in referring to more than one entity? Well, we so use them. The *third*, chief, and as it were *empirical* purism concerns language, the only, the first, and the last instrument and criterion of reason, with no other credentials but tradition and usage.[38] That doctrine Hamann attributes not to Berkeley or Hume but to the poet Young: "language, the organon and criterion of reason, as Young says. Here is to be found pure reason and its critique."[39] Or, more bluntly with reference to pure reason: "All chatter about reason is pure wind: language is its organ and criterion, as Young says. Tradition is its second element."[40]

Hamann can evidently be made to come out sounding like Wittgenstein, what with language having no credentials but tradition and usage, with "the whole of philosophy is grammar." That way lies anachronism and would betray a complete incomprehension of what Wittgenstein did teach. One nevertheless recognizes a kindred spirit in the matter of writing. We would not be astonished to find in notes for the *Tractatus* Hamann's gentle saying, "the more one considers language the deeper and more inward is one's dumbness and loss of all desire to speak."[41]

Kant provided a critique of pure reason in order to vindicate reason by preserving it against its excesses. Hamann is dismissive of reason, not necessarily because he wants us to be unreasonable, but because all the certainty that's attributed to reason is to be found only in the language used to reason. This applies even to mathematics, which Kant took so seriously and about which Hamann was indifferent. Kant had a brilliant explanation for the mathematical rigor he so much admired. Arithmetic and geometry were not merely the glories of reason but, as the synthetic a priori laws of the pure concepts of space and time, were preconditions for possible knowledge of the world. Hamann? "If mathematics is noble, then it should give way to the *instinct* of insects."[42] So much for the synthetic a priori. He was hardly one to be moved by mathematical argument, but he had a considered view of apodictic certainty and a priori knowledge, and of the experience of discovering geometrical proofs that has so impressed mathematical minds from Plato to the present. Hamann's view anticipates the opinion made popular by the Vienna Circle, largely acquired from Wittgenstein's *Tractatus*: "The whole certainty of mathematics depends upon the nature of its language."[43]

LINGUISTIC IDEALISM

Hamann called himself a philologue and also a verbalist.[44] His philology was not that which was emerging at the famous philological seminar at Göttingen. His was an older sense of the word, that of John the Evangelist. He was a lover of *logos*. Referring once again to the organon and criterion of reason he wrote, "Without words, no reason, no world. Here is the source of all creation and order!"[45] This is a characteristic sentence that looks two ways. I shall try to indicate the directions.

One is what I would call backwards, although another sensibility would take Hamann's words differently. "Speech is translation—out of angel speech, that is thoughts into words—things into names—forms into signs."[46] "This kind of translation is . . . analogous more than anything else to the reverse side of a tapestry ('and shows the stuff but not the workman's skill')."[47] In the celebrated debates on the origin of language, and in particular in criticism of Herder's famous essay on the topic, he held that there is no such thing as a question about how language came into being. Much later Humboldt would rather somberly state that the archetype of language had to be already present in the human soul. That's diluted Hamannism, not innate General Grammar. Hamann more dramatically thought, like the evangelist, of language and the world as coming into being together. The backward-pointing, Renaissance version of this is the idea that God created man and language when the world was created, or shortly thereafter, with the words being true signs both of the things and of Adam's ideas of the things, which are in turn true ideas of God's creation of the things.

The forward-looking version of Hamann (say I with distorting hindsight) was altogether different. It was quite properly called "verbalism" by Hamann himself. There is nothing, neither substance nor form, without language. That is a kind of linguistic idealism that has been common enough in our century.[48] According to Hamann the fable of the first naming is misunderstood. There were not things, to which names were then attached by God or man. Individuated things are there only when there are words to describe them. Moreover, these words are not the private artifact of some Enlightenment Adam, discoursing within his soul. They are the words of what is to be the first human community. "In the language of every people we find the history of the same," not just because there are traces in the language of the history but because there is no people aside from historical language.[49]

In short, language for Hamann is profoundly nonrepresentative. It is the exact opposite to the linguistic theories of the Enlightenment or General Grammar. Language is creative; to it we owe the existences and structures that populate our world-versions. Thanks to language alone do we have the forms and logic that we call reasoning. Moreover, by an apparent circularity that Hamann found totally unproblematic, this language which is creative has its existence and regularity only within tradition and use. The human being who would be an original is not the one who has a great private thought within him that he then makes public. The original is the one who can change the very language that we share, in which we think, and which is our communal version of the world, both inner and outer.

NOTES

1. Ian Hacking, *Why Does Language Matter to Philosophy?* (Cambridge: Cambridge University Press, 1975).
2. The introduction to the Japanese edition of *Why Does Language?* (1988) did address this absence, along the lines of the present essay. To tell history by this method is obviously to make fun of oneself (and of "epistémès"); I am unrepentant about that.

3. Thomas Hobbes, "Concerning Body," *Elements of Philosophy* 1 no. 2 (London, 1656), p. 3.
4. Bertrand Russell, "The Philosophy of Logical Atomism," in *Logic and Knowledge*, ed. R. Marsh (London: Allen and Unwin, 1956), p. 195f.
5. Marvin Minsky, *The Society of Mind* (New York: Simon and Schuster, 1987), p.270; he put this sentence in italics.
6. Johann Georg Hamann, *Sämtliche Werke: Historische-Kritische Ausgabe*, ed. J. Nadler (Vienna: Thomas Morus Presse, 1949–57)(hereafter cited as W); J. G. Hamann, *Briefwechsel*, ed. W. Siesemer and A. Henkel, 5 vols. (Wiesbaden: Insel Verlag, 1955–65) (hereafter cited as B).
7. Quoted with permission from a personal letter dated 14 November 1985. I don't know Berlin personally. Hamann has a substantial following among Christian existentialists, especially in Germany. Since my interests are neither biographical nor exegetical, I shall at my own risk ignore that central aspect of his life and work.
8. Ludwig Wittgenstein, *Philosophical Investigations*, trans. G. E. M. Anscombe (New York: Macmillan, 1953), sec. 243–315. Early readers tended to identify these as self-contained. More recently they have been seen as integral to 139–242, a discussion of following a rule. See the editorial introduction to *Wittgenstein: To Follow a Rule*, ed. S. Holzman and C. Leich (London: Routledge & Kegan Paul, 1981); and Saul Kripke, *Wittgenstein on Rules and Private Language* (Cambridge: Harvard University Press, 1982).
9. C. S. Peirce, "Some Consequences of Four Incapacities" (1868) in vol 2. of *Writings of Charles S. Peirce: A Chronological Edition*, ed. E. C. Moore et al. (Bloomington: Indiana University Press, 1984), pp. 240–41. Author's italics.
10. Peter Geach and Max Black, eds. and trans., "On sense and Reference," in *Translations from the Philosophical Writings of Gottlob Frege* (Oxford: Blackwell, 1952), p.59.
11. G. W. F. Hegel, *Phenomenology of Spirit*, trans. A. V. Miller (Oxford: Clarendon Press, 1977), p.395; cf. 308.
12. G. W. F. Hegel, *Hegel's Philosophy of Mind*, trans. W. Wallace and A.V. Miller (Oxford: Clarendon Press, 1971), p.214.
13. Hans Aarsleff regularly asserts that Locke with his idéologue successors is the source of what he calls "linguistic relativism"; see Hans Aarsleff, *From Locke to Saussure: Essays on the Study of Language and Intellectual History* (Minneapolis: University of Minnesota Press, 1982), pp. 22, 27, 30f., 181, 185f., 189f., 301, 306f., 345–47, 376. I disagree; see my "Locke, Leibniz, Language and Hans Aarsleff," *Synthese* 75 (1988), 135–53.
14. Leibniz's *Nouveaux Essais* was reviewed, with special attention to book III, "On Words," in the *Göttingsche Anzeigen*, 10 January 1765. At that time Herder was in Riga. Hamann wrote him from Königsberg a detailed and unenthusiastic account of the book, 21 January 1765, B. II, 296–303.
15. Ian Hacking, "Night Thoughts on Philology," *History of the Present* 4 (1987), 3–10. Foucault's emphasis on the role of Cuvier for the study of "Life" has been more vigorously challenged in a special issue of *Revue d'histoire des sciences et leurs applications* 23 (1970).
16. W. von Humboldt, *On Language: The Diversity of Human Language Structure and Its Influence on the Mental Development of Mankind*, trans. Peter Heath (Cambridge: Cambridge University Press, 1988), p. 91.
17. L. Bloomfield, *Language* (New York: Holt, Rinehart and Winston, 1933), p.18, "refers to Humboldt's treatise as 'the first great book on general linguistics.' Considered against the background that we are surveying here, it seems to mark the terminal point of Cartesian linguistics rather than the beginning of a new era of linguistic thought"—Noam Chomsky, *Cartesian Linguistics: A Chapter in the History of Rationalist Thought* (New York: Harper and Row, New York, 1966), p. 86, n.36.
18. Chomsky, *Cartesian Linguistics*, p. 21.
19. Hans Aarsleff, "Introduction" to Humboldt, *On Language*, p. xxii.

20. Isaiah Berlin, *Vico and Herder: Two Studies in the History of Ideas* (New York: Random House, 1977), p. 153.
21. Ibid., pp. 165f.
22. See Aarsleff's essay "Vico and Berlin," together with Berlin's rejoinder, in *The London Review of Books* 3, no. 20 (5–18 November 1981), pp. 6–9.
23. E. B. de Condillac, *Essai sur l'origine des connaissances humaines* (*An Essay on the Origin of Human Knowledge*) (1746), II.i.143. (Gainesville, Fla.: Scholars Facsimiles & Reprints, 1971), p. 285.
24. Aarsleff, *From Locke to Saussure*, on p. 344.
25. Chomsky and Foucault met in a debate for Dutch television, transcribed in *Reflexive Waters: The Basic Concerns of Mankind*, ed. Fons Elders (Gateshead, U.K.: Condor, 1974), pp. 133–98.
26. Berlin, *Vico and Herder*, p. 163. It is not literally correct to have Hamann commenting on the Anthropologie, but what Berlin means is right. Cf. pp. 159f. for Berlin's optimistic reading of Herder on Jews. Berlin's continuing faith in Herder was recently stated in "Two Concepts of Nationalism: An Interview with Isaiah Berlin," *The New York Review of Books* 37, no. 19 (21 November 1991).
27. B. VI, p. 187.
28. From a journal note printed in S. Kierkegaard, *The Concept of Irony*, trans. H. V. Hong and E. H. Hong (Princeton: Princeton University Press, 1989), p.435.
29. G. W. F. Hegel, "Ueber Hamann's Schriften," reprinted in *Berliner Schriften*, ed. J. Hoffmeister (Hamburg: Meiner, 1956), pp. 221–94.
30. Walter Benjamin, *Briefe*, ed. G. Scholem and T. Adorno (Frankfurt: Suhrkamp, 1966), vol. 2, p. 526.
31. B. V, p. 108.
32. Cf. J. L. Kind, *Edward Young in Germany* (New York: Macmillan, 1906), esp. pp. 28–40; J. Barnstorff, *Youngs Nachtdenken und ihr Einfluß auf die deutsche Literatur* (Bamberg: C. C. Buchner, 1895).
33. W. II, p. 59; James C. O'Flaherty, *Hamann's Socratic Memorabilia: A Translation and Commentary* (Baltimore: Johns Hopkins University Press, 1967).
34. Michael Dummett, *The Logical Basis of Metaphysics* (Cambridge: Harvard University Press, 1991), p. xi, where Dummett acknowledges that he, too, has long been working contrary to the spirit of Wittgenstein. Nevertheless for Dummett, as for so many other analytic philosophers, the idea of a private language remains unthinkable.
35. This remark was inserted in the light of a letter of 2 October 1991 from Victoria McGeer. She wrote that Kant and Hamman "give me two paradigms for how language can go public, and it seems to me the Kantian one is paramount in contemporary work."
36. Cf. Rudolf Unger, *Hamann und die Aufklärung* (Jena: Eugen Diedrichs, 1911), vol. I, pp. 501–05.
37. B. V, p. 294; translation in Ronald Gregor Smith, *J. G. Hamann, 1730–1788, A Study in Christian Existence, With Selections from His Writings* (London: Collins, 1960), p. 249.
38. W. III, p. 284, original emphasis; Smith, *Hamann*, p. 215, plausibly translates "organon" as "instrument," but Hamann's word is "organon" in all such aphorisms about language.
39. B. V, p. 360.
40. B. V, p. 108.
41. W. III, p. 285; Smith, *Hamann*, p. 216.
42. W. III, p. 285.
43. B. V, p. 360.
44. For a systematic survey of Hamann's relation to the various kinds of philology, see V. Hoffman, *Johann Georg Hamanns Philologie: Hamanns Philologie zwischen enzyklopädischer Mikrologie und Hermeneutik* (Stuttgart: Kohlhammer, 1972).
45. B. V, p. 95.
46. W. II, p. 199.

47. W. III, p. 287.
48. I may have originated the phrase "linguistic idealism" in *Why Does Language Matter to Philosophy?* p. 182. It has since also been used by G. E. M. Anscombe, Hilary Putnam, and a number of others. As I noted then, although the meaning of the phrase is fairly self-evident, at least for philosophers, it is nevertheless a solecism, because "idealism" once meant the doctrine that nothing existed but ideas. I there suggested that the absurd term "lingualism" would be better (p. 174); Hamann's "verbalism" is more apt.
49. B. I, p. 393.

JOHANN CARL WEZEL'S *HERRMANN UND ULRIKE* (1780) OR THE ORIGIN OF THE GOOD

FRANZ FUTTERKNECHT

When Johann Carl Wezel was rediscovered in the sixties and seventies, the academic scene dominated by ideological critics believed they had found one of their intellectual precursors. Wezel was enthusiastically celebrated as a 'poeta politico-philosophicus,' who was radically critical in his analysis of late eighteenth century society and thoroughly negative in his philosophy.[1] Due perhaps to this initial enthusiasm, even the most obvious differences between Wezel and modern critical theories have been virtually ignored. This is especially true with regard to the primary influences on Wezel's thought: the discoveries made about organic matter in the latter half of the eighteenth century,[2] including the theories on the functioning of the nerves and the brain that severely undermined traditional body-soul theories. Although explanations were available neither to explain the functioning of the 'influxus physicus,' nor the interaction between the material brain and the immaterial soul, existing knowledge made it all too evident that the separation of mind and body, the fundamental principle of rational philosophy, was empirically untenable.[3]

In accordance with the latest physiological hypotheses,[4] Wezel believed that human beings are integrated organisms with interactive mental and bodily faculties. In accordance with the philosophy of his time, he assumed that bodily faculties consisted not only of the ability to maintain life, but also to produce a specific kind of knowledge, the 'cognitio sensitiva.' Differing from the 'clear and distinct' perceptions of the mind, this knowledge manifested itself in intuitive judgments and individual preferences, as well as in gut feelings, taste, and sense of beauty. In addition to this, the body was the place where the abstract and general ideas, theories, and concepts of the mind were converted into forms in which they could be applied to concrete and individual situations and lives. Wezel believed that the body's main function in processing knowledge is the conversion of imaginary mental representations into the 'real.' Body and mind, therefore, represent two different, but interdependent systems of knowledge. It is tempting, in fact, to suggest that the 'interface' that organizes the communication between the two systems in Wezel's philosophy is similar to the dispositive that Foucault calls discourse. In Wezel's view it is of utmost importance that the interplay between these two forms of knowledge be based on equality and mutual recognition. However, Wezel recognized that in cultural systems such as the Judeo-Christian tradition or Platonism or the rationalist philosophies of the Enlightenment this cooperation was distorted forever by the successful attempt to change the interface in favor of the mind. This 'takeover' by the abstract mind, which exerted its position as the dominant operating system in the psycho-physical human 'machine,' created, according to Wezel's theory, precisely those conditions that are the object of Foucault's discourse analyses. However, the fact that life and history are consumed in 'discourses' is, for Wezel, not a primary condition, but the effect of the enthronment of the mind as the absolute ruler over a mutilated and imprisoned body which is kept speechless and deprived of its 'senses.'

Wezel's concept of open interplay between the mind, the body and their environment does not assume perpetual harmony among them. Wezel's key term is 'empowerment.' This means that the rules determining the interaction between the systems do not favor any of the three, but provide each with equal status and power. Conflicts between these systems are, in Wezel's view, inevitable, but can and should be resolved without one system being silenced by the other. Wezel rejected those theories claiming the attainability of personal and societal harmony on the basis that they merely mask the domination of one system over another. Although he was anti-utopian on principle, it was Wezel's conviction that the human misery European culture has generated through centuries of setting mind against body, men against women, humankind against nature, God against humankind, and so on, unnecessarily aggravates the ordeal that human life undeniably is. In short: for Wezel most of the central topics that preoccupied the critical intelligentsia in the sixties and seventies are irrelevant. Interested in the functioning of interacting physical and mental systems and in the regulators that determine this interaction, traditionally called "commercium mentis et corporis,"[5] Wezel studied the culturally induced barriers that interfere in this "commercium," the mutilations committed in the process of acculturation that cut off much of the communication between body and mind, as well as systematically distort the modes of mental representations of the external world. Involved in the educational reforms of his time, Wezel knew that mental and psychological characteristics are formed by the manipulation of early childhood experiences that influence the interaction between mind, body, and outside world. Also, he became increasingly aware of the fact that these innovative pedagogical strategies would have unforeseen effects on the very essence of men, women, and children. In view of the fact that Wezel lived and wrote in precisely the period when, according to Foucault[6], the break between Classical and modern discourses occurred, I will argue in this article that—in applying his materialistic anthropology—Wezel was not only aware of the discoursive dimension of the changes occurring, but that his analysis of them can, in many respects, be considered a Foucaultian discourse analysis 'avant la lettre.' In his novel *Herrmann und Ulrike* the author most clearly demonstrates his perception that a complete mutation of human life and society could be expected as a result of nobly motivated contemporary reforms in pedagogy, socialization, and acculturation. Although Wezel conceded the merit of some of the declared goals of reform pedagogy, he was very much aware that the educationally induced inclination for 'good' exacts a very high price: the loss of all vital 'commerce' between body and mind, the transformation of sexuality and reality into the simulated and dead world of ideals, and the loss of any hope for a fulfilling life pursuing intrinsic individual interests and goals.

This lengthy novel is generally considered Wezel's literary masterpiece and an early example of the 'Bildungsroman.'[7] In my view, it is, at most, an 'Anti-Bildungsroman,' for, indeed, its main tenets discredit the Classical understanding of the term 'Bildung.' This term contains the notion of synthesis between nature and culture in individual development and attributes this synthesis to the pedagogical practices introduced in Rousseau's novel *Emile* (1762). In *Herrmann und Ulrike* Wezel demonstrates such disturbing insight into the new pedagogy that it can hardly be classified as a 'Bildungsroman.' The novel reveals that the widely acclaimed achievement of the time, the creation of "der Mensch" (the Man, *l'Homme*) was, at best, a Pyrrhic victory. In fact this ill-conceived undertaking would have been a complete disaster if the state had not been shrewd enough to recognize the value of its victims and put them to good use for its own purposes.

The novel opens with a caricature of that recently evolved and instantly sanctified institution of the period, the bourgeois family. The protagonist, Herrmann, is introduced as a young child of six, playing happily in a public park, absorbed in the gratifying fantasy that he is king. His mother looks on adoringly, holding back the father, who, infuriated by his son's frivolous activities, is about to punish him with his whip. The details of this scene express Wezel's opinion that this new mother- and love-centered early childhood does not, in fact, nurture natural and innocent mental and moral growth, but instead contributes to the creation of a fantasizing, narcissistic ego. In Wezel's pedagogical view, the 'empowerment' of a child means that s/he experiences that her/his needs and desires are taken seriously; however, it also means that children learn to take the needs and desires of others as seriously as they take their own. This is hardly the case in young Herrmann's playing 'king.' Since the new, pedagogical theories are based on rejecting and avoiding social reality in favor of so-called natural development, the child's mind is carefully protected from interaction with the real social world. The result is that the child's mental activities are determined and nourished by the experiences of love and adoration that the young child encounters in an exclusive and illusory world created by maternal love and devotion.

The scene indicates, furthermore, that the new, intensified bonds between mother and child create conjugal tension. The father, previously the center of the family, finds himself competing for the attention of his wife and struggling to maintain his role of paternal authority. Eroded paternal authority is, in Wezel's view, both to the child's advantage and disadvantage. Protected from the father's rod, the child has a chance to become more than the fulfillment of the father's will. On the other hand, whereas in traditional paternal education the father taught and told the child what s/he had to be within the existing social structures, the new pedagogy assigns mothers the role of creating a 'natural' realm for the beloved child in which he is protected from all expectations of society. Early years in this pseudo-paradise raise in the child expectations that the real world can never fulfill. Neither Herrmann's father nor mother offers the child that which, according to Wezel, is crucial for the development and the individualization of the mind: realistic choices or options. These options would prevent the operations of the mind being reduced to a mere 'copy' of the father's. Also, they would enable the mind to leave its purely imaginary mode and link fantasies to concrete situations. Lacking this opportunity, the inherent faculty of the mind to adapt to the structure of a given social environment is not stimulated and, therefore, does not develop. Instead, the product of the new pedagogy recalls the stored, paradise-like childhood experiences and perceives them as evidence of an attainable *ideal*. Thus deprived of a realistic attitude to the world, this 'idealistic' man is acutely aware that the real world is lacking when compared with his ideal. A new mind has been created that, when confronted with reality, has to either avoid or change it.

The conflict between mother and father concerning the upbringing of the son is a central theme in most of the German 'Bildungsromane.' The sympathy of the authors, however, is usually slanted toward the attitudes represented by the mothers. That is certainly not the case in *Herrmann und Ulrike*. Although father Herrmann appears in the end to have lost the battle for control over his son's education, there is no suggestion that his desire to do so was unjustified. The conflict comes to a head in the park scene, when the local count and his wife appear on their walk. Young Herrmann, who has been conditioned by his close, loving relationship with his mother to respond spontaneously to the feelings aroused in him by women and who is caught up in the aura of his aristocratic fantasies, boldly addresses the countess. He declares his love for her, immediately proposes marriage, and then proceeds to insult the count. The countess comments at once that, under the prevailing social laws, Herrmann's apparent psychological disposition predestines him to become either a "great fool" or a "great man" (I, 13). Amused by Herrmann's insulting comments about her boring husband, she feels more than mere sympathy for her childish suitor and decides to take him to the castle as her foster son. The hope of a brilliant future for her son delights the mother as much as it enrages the father, who sees himself deprived of his right to form his son in his own image.

In this sequence of events we can recognize a situation typical of the transition phase between the two discourses toward the end of the eighteenth century. Before the marginalization of the fathers had been institutionalized, and before state reforms provided a suitable environment for, and social integration of, the new 'good men,' their survival depended on a) escaping from authoritarian paternal education and/or b) chance circumstances resulting in close contact with the ruling aristocracy. This is precisely Herrmann's experience. However, the initiation rituals in which he is forced to participate at court leave no doubt about the limitations of his future life. As planned by the count, Herrmann is introduced to his new life on the countess' birthday in an allegorical scene in which he appears as Amor, the boyish god of love, *in a cage*. The clear-sighted countess interprets this allegory with the words: "One might think that this means that Amor and I would best been taken care of if we were imprisoned" (I, 106). And the count agrees. This scene, however, should not be interpreted as a warning from a jealous husband. In fact, the count does not care at all about the tender exchanges between his wife and young Herrmann. As is clearly demonstrated throughout the novel, this ritual in which Herrmann is 'Amor incaged' has the status of a discursive law: it is part of the 'dispositive' that enables the existence of the 'good man.' This discourse fosters early childhood sensuality in order to produce affectionate and appealing children. However, before the onset of puberty this childish drive for affection is systematically immured and its energies redirected toward an asexual, ideal love for humankind in general.

In Herrmann's case this task is to be achieved not by the countess, his foster mother, but by Mr. Schwinger, the tutor responsible for the other adopted child at the court, Baroness Ulrike. It is soon evident that Schwinger has been strongly influenced by Rousseau's pedagogical theories and philosophy. Schwinger's dreams of far-reaching social reforms have ended in his experimenting with new pedagogical strategies. Instead of a new, improved society, he plans now a new, improved human being. In order to achieve this he applies Rousseau's principles of 'negative education.' First he consciously wins the children's friendship. Then, instead of explicitly teaching them the principles governing conduct and behavior in society, he guides them by means of suggestions. He encourages them to develop their own opinions and values on the basis of awarenesses gained in carefully selected and prearranged experiences orchestrated within an artificially 'natural' environment.

Although aware of the emotional needs of his preadolescent pupils, Schwinger does not prohibit contact between Herrmann and Ulrike. When their bodily development reaches the phase in which the young female and male 'discover' each other as an endless source of mutual pleasure, not surprisingly, they fall in love. Ignoring the outrage of the scandalized, class-conscious count and his noble 'entourage,' Schwinger refuses to separate the two young innocents; he intends to elevate their relationship by developing in both a sense of shame, honor, and justice. Using his power as a beloved teacher he encourages Herrmann to read biographies of admired and respected Roman emperors and heroes, and fills his room with plaster statues of famous Roman republicans. They are all stoics, models of chastity, justice, duty, and self-discipline. Before Schwinger's intervention, Herrmann's mind 'read' pleasurable messages from his 'body'; now he must read books instead, which tell him how pleasurable it is to be loved for great political and moral deeds. In this conversion of 'eros,' it is evident that the mind usurps energies that really originate from the body. In the attempt to fulfill the 'script' that replaced his 'body,' Herrmann accepts a 'role' for his 'ego' and a 'mask' for his 'face.' Evidently, he will never perceive the differences. As intended, Herrmann's desire takes a political turn and rekindles his early ambitious fantasies of power. Soon Herrmann's political dreams replace his amorous fantasies, and his preferred toy is now the "plaster senate" (I, 160).

It is noteworthy that the educational function Schwinger assigns to books is the exact opposite of the one Wezel strove for in his own writing. He refused to create plots and figures with which the reader could readily identify. For Wezel literature has to be honest. Simulating human and social reality, it should show its readers what life and society really are. Schwinger's choice of reading material for his charges reveals clearly how the new educators are to proceed: they exploit the child's narcissistic fantasies by substituting the real objects of his desire with their own political and ideological expectations. Far from being an overtly painful act of drills, the suggestive method conditions the child to the intended patterns of thoughts and behavior in a quasi-natural manner. Since fantasies are used to inscribe the will of the pedagogue into his charge's subconscious, this method has a deeper and longer lasting effect than any form of direct teaching. Herrmann will go through life 'hypnotized,' dreaming not his own dreams, but those of his tutor. Although the child offers no resistance, this is by no means an act devoid of violation: the difference between this and authoritarian force is that the new educational strategies give the child no chance to resist. S/he capitulates before the battle has begun. The child, now living in an ideal world of books, is increasingly less at home in the real world. Herrmann is oblivious to and, therefore, unable to defend himself against the intrigues and manipulations of the courtiers. His survival depends on Schwinger's protection. On the one hand, Herrmann is secure from becoming corrupted and vicious; on the other, however, he is rendered vulnerable and kept from acquiring essential social skills and competence.

Ulrike is similarly subjected to subtle pedagogical strategies designed to redirect her childish passion. In addition to her instruction from Schwinger, she is receiving training for her role as a young baroness at court from an aristocratic governess, who, in the traditional French way, teaches her to avoid words which directly express any aspect of love. It is, however, evident that while the words might be prohibited at the court, the actions are most certainly not. Schwinger, motivated by his bourgeois morals, seeks to influence Ulrike, too, through literature and encouragement of her romantic fantasies. For Ulrike he chooses idyllic love poetry in order to awaken in her feelings of chaste and tender womanly love. She easily identifies with this bucolic world, and in her vivid imagination she and Herrmann become the nymphs and shepherds in the stories that she is reading. Soon it is in this dream world, not with Herrmann, that Ulrike's romantic longings are fulfilled. Her resulting psychological state, shared by Herrmann, is referred to by Wezel as "profundity" (I, 201), a pathological sublimation of natural desire. Unaware of how they have been manipulated, they begin to perceive the others as leading superficial, pleasure-oriented lives, whereas they themselves have attained a unique inner depth. Isolated by this uniqueness, Herrmann and Ulrike develop eternal bonds which trivialize the barriers between their two social classes. Deformed as they are by their 'discursive' status, each of them is prevented from entering a relationship with someone else and, at the same time, they are deprived of living in a fulfilling relationship with each other. At best, their relationship is 'meaningful,' but it never makes sense.

The pedagogical manipulation of their love, however, breaks down upon the onset of their puberty. Wezel seems to suggest that culture, no matter how carefully ingrained, is powerless in the face of the first surge of hormones. Herrmann loses interest in the politics of antiquity and becomes an eager reader of mythological stories about free love in the lives of the ancient gods, as well as of the erotic literature he finds in Schwinger's library. Whereas before nothing was meaningful to him that was not related to his political fantasies, now all meaning is related to Ulrike's physical charms. The 'venal drives,' though powerful, cannot, however, completely erase the embedded taboos and values. A struggle begins between the opposing forces of their physical desires and their internalized rejection of them. For many years to come their psycho-structure is one of constant torment and frustration. That Herrmann and Ulrike do not succumb to their 'venal drives' cannot be credited to them. On their ill-conceived escape from the castle, they are surprised by the count and his men just in time to interrupt Herrmann's tentative exploration of his beloved Ulrike.

Separated and expelled from the court, Wezel's heroes, now in Dresden's high society, find themselves for the first time unshielded from the harshness of reality. Landing on a strange planet could not have caused more adversities for them. Exposed to the petty struggles of power, jealousy, envy, and exploitation in bourgeois society, these two lost souls only escape disaster through the generous financial support of Schwinger and the countess. Herrmann and Ulrike's experiences in Dresden, their first encounter with the real world, prove that in no way has their exposure to Schwinger's reformed pedagogical strategies prepared them to successfully process information from the real world. Only their love for one another and their determination to overcome the separation forced upon them keep them alive.

Eventually they are reunited in Prussia's libertine and enlightened capital, Berlin. The conflict that gradually emerges between the couple and their noble Berlin acquaintances appears at first to be another struggle between bourgeois virtue and aristocratic vice, a favorite topic of eighteenth-century bourgeois literature. Unlike Richardson, Lessing, and others, however, Wezel focuses on the fact that the egos involved in this struggle are not the true combatants, since they have no real options. None of them can cease behaving according to a specific circuit of energies embedded in them by nature and socialization. The real combatants are incompatible systems that determine the generation and sequence of thoughts and actions. For Wezel, however, the operational principles that govern the thoughts and behavior of the epicurean nobility—with their orientation to pleasure and power—are much closer to nature than the 'virtuous' principles that guide Herrmann and Ulrike. And although 'human nature,' represented by Madame Vignali and the Prussian aristocracy, produces competition, stress, and enormous hardship, the author avoids directing the reader's sympathy toward the new virtuous man and woman. While the most outstandingly successful specimens produced by the old system were not much more than intelligent vital animals, the products of the new system are little more than beautiful, sick souls.

It is, therefore, understandable that Ulrike and Herrmann are, at first, fascinated and not repelled by the lives of their new Berlin friends. Herrmann, who in the meantime has learned that he is not suited to be a merchant or to serve in subaltern positions, briefly resists the extended welcome into the circles of the local nobility. After his "Adonisation" (II, 411) by tailors and barbers, however, he lets himself be seduced by the refined life-style of his friends. The attractions of their hedonistic pursuits are so irresistible that Herrmann begins to seriously entertain the possibility that the principles inculcated in him so subtly by his tutor have alienated him from real life. The dawning realization that—unlike his aristocratic companions—he cannot even wholeheartedly desire what he is longing for, nor is he the master of his own will, let alone that of others, is a growing source of anger in Herrmann. Unable to experience sensual enjoyment, he laments the limited state of his life and is frustrated by his powerlessness to change it. Bound by a "profundity," which excludes physical fulfillment, Herrmann and Ulrike try to assure each other that their relationship would not survive the consummation of their love. If the episodes in Dresden proved the inability of the new mind to deal with reality, Berlin proves its inability to function according to the pleasure principle. This sets the two young people apart. For the others, they are endless contradictions; for themselves, they decide—in order to give their deficiencies a positive interpretation—that they are morally superior. At first, these two odd newcomers pose little more than bizarre challenges to Berlin's libertine circles. From the moment, however, that Ulrike naively declares their moral superiority to Madame Vignali, a life-and-death struggle begins between the old and the new discourses.

The assaults against the fortress of virtue are masterminded by Madame Vignali, la Grande Dame and most experienced mistress in Herrmann's and Ulrike's circles of Berlin friends. Ulrike, who enjoys being attractive to men, suddenly has to defend her virginity against the violent attacks of men whom she had become accustomed to inviting into her 'boudoir.' Herrmann's virtue is especially challenged, since it is the cunning Madame Vignali who has taken him on personally. Although delighted by the interest she shows in him, Herrmann desperately attempts to resist her charms and advances. The contradictions in Herrmann's behavior reveal to Madame Vignali that he is incapable of acknowledging his sexual desires. An expert in psychology, as befitting all enlightened libertines, she seeks access to Herrmann's real desires through his imagination. After a romantic dinner and several glasses of wine she invites him to visualize and praise her body. Then, during Herrmann's effusions, Madame Vignali suddenly begins disrobing. In regard to maintaining his virtue Herrmann has been fortunate: Madame Vignali has miscalculated slightly, not allowing him sufficient time in his erotic fantasy before making the transition to her very real physical attributes. Herrmann flees in terror. Her second attempt at seduction also fails, although this time by chance, not miscalculation on her part.

Not only do Herrmann and Ulrike survive all their seductors' ambushes. Ulrike's manifestly different attitude toward men arouses thoughts of marriage in her aging, noble employer, who is tired of dealing with excessively stimulating and stressful mistresses. For the first time, the qualities of this new human 'breed' find the interest of people in power, thereby giving hope for their perpetuation. Alarmed by this new development, Madame Vignali revises her strategies. Cognizant of the secret love between Herrmann and Ulrike, she arranges long and private meetings between them in seductive environments. Finally, when thunderstorm and night surprise them on a long walk, forcing them to seek shelter in a small cabin, the inevitable happens. However, this long-desired and hitherto rejected consummation of their feelings is devoid of pleasurable fulfillment; instead it is a tormented fall with devastating psychological effects.

Rejoicing over this defeat of virtue, Madame Vignali generously organizes Herrmann and Ulrike's departure from Berlin, and arranges their wedding in Leipzig. The humiliated lovers, however, avoid each other out of feelings of guilt and shame. Ulrike, like Clarissa after being raped by

Lovelace, literally loses her will to live. She has only one desire: to give birth to the child she is carrying and then to die. Herrmann's reaction is quite different. Considering himself a wastrel and the "murderer" (III, 259) of Ulrike's virtue, he consciously throws himself into the decadent and wanton life of a gambler. This choice is not entirely arbitrary. Herrmann intuitively realizes that for a man who has no place in real life the best place is a gaming table. And Herrmann and gambling seem to be a perfect fit. Although his chosen life of dissolution only temporarily appeases his need to do penance, it produces a considerable benefit: for the first time in his life Herrmann makes a sizable amount of money.

Disgusted by society, the reunited Herrmann and Ulrike use this money to pursue a truly Rousseauian life: they buy a farm. Both, however, are more interested in the aesthetic embellishment of the estate than in successful farming. Here their child is born, but dies soon after his birth. Herrmann swears on his grave to rigorously practice sexual abstinence for at least two years. Their lives have now finally reached the status of pure simulation: they pretend to be lovers and pretend to be farmers, yet they are neither one nor the other. Before the two years are over, the gentleman-farming of the young couple ends in financial disaster. Their lives, which resemble the plots of many books, have taken on the character of an ongoing novel over which they have lost control, both of the plot and of the roles they have assigned themselves. In spite of the "profundity" of their relationship, when poverty sets in, their love cools. This cooling of their passion has, however, a practical result. Herrmann's venal drive is sharply reduced. This leads to an automatic rearrangement of his desires: spiritually reborn, Herrmann discovers the dominant drive in his life is again politics. He wants nothing more than to serve humankind by reforming society. His inability to cope with reality and sexuality has finally transformed him into a political idealist and state reformer, a man on an eternal quest for social improvement. As the product of an ideal childhood, Herrmann now has no choice in life but to pursue the goal of attempting to perfect the world. This is precisely the personality his tutor Schwinger had set out to create.

His search for Ulrike, who was kidnapped by the old count, provides Herrmann with the opportunity to become involved in government affairs. He becomes secretary to the "First Minister" of the state in which Ulrike and he are now living. The prince is greatly impressed by Herrmann's devotion and the speed with which he becomes competent in all administrative matters. His real political breakthrough, however, comes when he uncovers the first minister's fraudulent activities. The prince soon realizes that the state could profit from persons like Herrmann, those who are addicted to serving their country and countrymen. In other words, the prince discovers in Herrmann the born civil servant. At once, he appoints him his counselor with tenure and modest but sufficient pay, supporting all his initiatives for useful state reforms. The beneficiaries of these reforms are the prince, representing the state, and hard-working, bourgeois society. The parasitism of the aristocracy has been eliminated; the libertine and hedonistic philosophy that had dominated society has been replaced. Madame Vignali, who is still up to mischief under the name of Madame Dormer, is banished from the court forever and ends up a bohemian on the margins of society. Under the protection of the state, the new system, represented by Herrmann, is crowned the central new discourse. All the institutions necessary to insure the authority and perpetuation of the new system are soon established. Herrmann and Ulrike can finally found a family. As the mother of several children, Ulrike becomes the undisputed center of family life, providing an ideal childhood for their beloved children and a peaceful haven for her hardworking husband. This new family becomes the 'raison d'etre' of the reformed state and enjoys its special protection. Herrmann's educational reforms supply the offspring of the new families with the appropriate schooling to prepare the sons for careers as the new civil servants.

Wezel's attitude toward the establishment of a new social and cultural order in the late eighteenth century is clearly quite different from that of most writers of his generation. In his well-known essay "Auch eine Philosophie der Geschichte zur Bildung der Menschheit" (1774) Herder, for example, describes this new development in human nature within a philosophy of progressive cultural history. He combines contemporary physiological discoveries on organic evolution with the ideas of modern pedagogical goals and practices, explaining the cultural history of humankind as a natural development along the path of recovering the virtuous, idealistic human being. The consequence of Herder's understanding of nature is to consciously turn away from so-called enlightened society and philosophy and to embrace the new, so-called natural or negative pedagogy as the foundation of a new culture. Wezel, on the other hand, analyzes the ruptures in eighteenth-century cultural, social, and political history as the results of unnatural pedagogical manipulations with unpredictable side-effects. He was not expressly opposed to these measures, for it was evident that this new 'breed,' though reduced and deprived in the area of vital energies, held promise for certain achievements which would benefit society in general. Wezel believed, however, that the moral and intellectual structure of these new 'Herrmanns and Ulrikes' can only be considered human progress by those who live their lives according to the same illusions which determine Herrmann's and Ulrike's existence. Johann Georg Hamann accused the brain-centered Enlightenment of having produced a machine-state and castrating humankind by separating the mind from its body. The new epoch that owes so much to Hamann did not, in Wezel's view, end this castration or render the state less mechanical. Instead of rehabilitating and respecting the harmony and interaction of body and nature in their full vitality, which was the goal of materialist philosophy, the new idealism spiritualized both, cutting the human mind off from the 'real' and from the body in order to implant ideals. For the physiologist Wezel, ideals do not exist in nature. They are no more than enslaving substitutions for the empowering vitality of those who are fit to accept the ordeal of life and dare to follow their inclinations. In fact, the new 'good' human being has neither achieved 'whole personality' nor 'regained humanity' or 'individual autonomy.' Rather, the man has become a loyal civil servant and the woman a lustless, childbearing, homebound mother. In other words, they are nothing more than useful, to some extent glorified, tools of the state. Interpreters who have overlooked this may have neglected to read the subtitle of this novel: *Ein komischer Roman*.

NOTES

All quotations from Wezel's novels are indicated in the text. The following edition has been used: Johann Karl Wezel, *Herrmann und Ulrike. Ein komischer Roman*. Faksimiledruck nach der Ausgabe von 1780. Mit einem Nachwort von Eva D. Becker, 4 vols. (Stuttgart: Metzler, 1971). The roman numerals indicate the volume, the arabic the page. All quotations in the article have been translated by me.

1. In spite of considerable differences, the following can be subsumed under this rubric: Detlef Kremer, *Über die Nachtseite der Aufklärung. Skeptische Lebensphilosophie zwischen Spätaufklärung und Frühromantik* (München: Fink, 1983); Johann V. Müller, "Aufklärung als 'traurige Wissenschaft.' Johann Carl Wezels 'Belphegor oder die wahrscheinlichste Geschichte unter der Sonne,' " in H. J. Pichota, ed., *Reise und Utopie: Zur Literatur der Spätaufklärung* (Frankfurt; Suhrkamp, 1976), pp. 170–221; Günter Strube, *Die Physiognomie der Unvernunft. Zur Rolle der Einbildungskraft im erzählerischen Werk Johann Karl Wezels* (Heidelberg: Carl Winter, 1980); Hans Peter Thurn, *Der Roman der unaufgeklärten Gesellschaft: Untersuchungen zum Prosawerk Johann Karl Wezels* (Stuttgart: Kohlhammer, 1973); Thilo Jörger, *Roman und Emanzipation. Johann Carl Wezels 'Bürgerliche Epopee'* (Stuttgart: Akademischer Verlag, 1981); Philipp McKnight, *The Novels of Johann Karl Wezel. Satire, Realism and Social Criticism in Late eighteenth Century Literature* (Bern, Frankfurt/Main, Las Vegas: Lang, 1981).
2. In his editorial comments to Wezel's novel *Lebensgeschichte Tobias Knauts, des Weisen, sonst der Stammler genannt* (Stuttgart: Metzler, 1971) (Deutsche Neudrucke), Victor Lange gives an excellent summary of the impact of contemporary physiology on Wezel's ideas, as well as a precise survey of Wezel's most important sources. To my knowledge, Wezel research has not made extensive use of this information.
3. Johann Karl Wezel, *Versuch über die Kenntnis des Menschen (1784–1785)* 2 vols. (Frankfurt/Main: Athenaum, 1971) (Athenaum Reprints) pp. 5–12.
4. Wezel, for the most part, refers to authors like Charles Louis de Buffon, Albrecht von Haller, Charles Bonnet, Johann August Unzer, Samuel A. Tissot, and Johann Friedrich Blumenbach, but is also familiar with the materialist and sensualist philosophies of La-Mettrie, Helvetius, and d'Holbach.
5. Rainer Specht, *Commercium mentis et corporis. Über Kausalvorstellungen im Kartesianismus* (Stuttgart: Frommann-Holzboog, 1966).
6. Michel Foucault, *Les mots et les choses* (Paris: Gallimard, 1966).
7. Traditionally, *Herrmann und Ulrike* is situated between two early examples of the 'Bildungsroman,' Wieland's *Agathon* and Goethe's *Wilhelm Meister*. Karl Adel, for instance, writes: "Almost exactly between these two novels, *Agathon* and *Wilhelm Meister*, is the place of *Herrmann und Ulrike*: Guided by destiny, matured by misfortune, Herrmann awakens to active life. The archetypical of human experience are put forward, the main

characters and their fate are enhanced and highlighted by subordinate figures. From bondage to egocentric emotional dreams Herrmann advances into the clarity and self-determination of reason" [*Johann Karl Wezel. Ein Beitrag zur Geistesgeschichte der Goethezeit* (Wien: Notring, 1968), p. 108; my translation].

FROM THE RECREATION OF SCHOLARS TO THE LABOR OF THE CONCEPT[1]

FRIEDRICH KITTLER

For Heinrich Bosse

Lectures and seminars concerning literary studies occur during the week, while literary-scholarly conferences occur preferentially on the weekend. The former are played out in the concrete of the newly built universities, the latter in the castles and cloisters of a by-gone power or in the hotel-fortresses of a present one. In other words: our free time simulates our work and vice versa.

What I would like to narrate in the following is a short story of such rituals. Stated as a thesis, the paradoxical concept of 'academic free time' has only existed since the incisive threshold in our culture that designates the end of rhetoric and the emergence of interpretation.

In the summer semester of 1788, that is, after more than two hundred years of academic studies, the University of Jena witnessed an unheard-of event. On the afternoon of April 26, Karl Leonard Reinhold, professor of philosophy and son-in-law of the writer C. M. Wieland, began his projected two-hour per week lecture entitled "On the Closer Consideration of the Beautiful Elements of an Epic Poem as a Recreation for Scholars and Students" ("Über die nähere Betrachtung der Schönheiten eines epischen Gedichts als Erholung für Gelehrte und Studierende").[2] The epic poem that Reinhold interpreted was the *Oberon* of his father-in-law; the publicistic forum that published the inception of the lecture series was none other than the *Teutsche Merkur* of the same father-in-law. In accordance with the technology of print, everything seemed as if the new conspiracy between poets and thinkers, writers and philosophers should immediately become a public matter. Reinhold's lecture institutionalized a discourse that was to make school or university history: the individual interpretation of so-called 'works' as the central concern of a by now all-too-familiar literary science that simultaneously philosophizes and trains teachers.

But Reinhold did not really want to train teachers of German; rather, his purpose was to create recreation for students and scholars, that is, the auditors and speakers of the lecture themselves, through a consideration of the 'humanities' (*schöne Wissenschaften*)(387). Whether the 26th of April 1788 was a sunny spring day remains unclear; in any case, the professor began with references to "a sunny spring day" that academics could spend together "under a free sky" and misuse by pitying a simple farmer to whom the beauty of the day says nothing. For the indifference of peasants toward the "lovely song of the lark and the nightingale," their blindness regarding all of the "graceful and magnificent scenes" (386) of nature resides in the order of precisely the same nature.

"It is quite a different matter," according to Reinhold, in the case of a scholar or a student, who expects "nothing but work and bread on the fields of science, just as the farmer on bucolic fields," and therefore "in the immeasurable realm of human knowledge does not see anything more than his cultivated land, that he has leased, or thought to lease, in order to serve himself" (287). Such livelihood scholars (*Brotgelehrte*)—as Schiller's Jena inaugural lecture at the University of Jena would baptize them a year later[3] — forget, because of sheer study and service to the prince, that they and *only* they in principle require free time. The scholar and the student, Reinhold the scholar told his students, each

> require[s] a recreation, he needs it for the advantage of his work itself. He requires a recreational activity that is appropriate to his level (*Grade*) and to the quality of his work. . . . Only the body replaces [as in the pitiful case of the peasant] his exhausted powers through rest; the spirit refreshens its powers through a change of pursuit; it cannot be satisfied with the participation that he has in the pleasures of the body that belong more to the instrument (*Werkzeug*) than to himself. . . . Spirit therefore requires all the more nourishment for the imagination, the more his reason is concerned with the analysis of general concepts; . . . it requires, in a word, more of the pleasure that the fields of the humanities offer to such a high degree, the more difficult and complex the works themselves (*Arbeiten*) are that it must complete on the fields of the so-called earnest bread-and-butter sciences and the more significant the success of this work is. (389)

That is plain text. Reinhold's lecture succeeded in producing precisely the recreation with whose concept of nature it began. In juxtaposition to his other lectures, which, as a bread-and-butter exercise for science, had the task of conceptually analyzing philosophical writings, sometimes even Kant, the interpretation of *Oberon* provided the scholars with poetic imagination. In doing that, however, Reinhold's lecture replaced all the infamous pleasures that students were permitted to pursue under the conditions of the old European 'academic freedom.' They learned the concrete act of interpreting as a "skill that is determinant not only for the easy and favorable, but even for the possible success of study," instead of wasting their recreational hours in entertainments "through which one takes on the opposite skills of thoughtlessness, triteness, and stupidity" (400). Precisely these things they gleaned from drinking and fencing, that is, from the diverted masters of their "body-instruments" (*Körper-Werkzeuge*), at the very latest when Reinhold told them that he had displaced his *Oberon* lecture "intentionally" on Saturday as the very afternoon normally destined to be a recreation from their more serious intellectual labor (390). In the same spirit, only much more strategically crafted, Reinhold's colleague Fichte scheduled his lecture concerning *The Science of Knowledge* for the weekend—more specifically, for the oldest, the highest, and the holiest free time: he lectured on philosophy at precisely the hour when the church bells called the professors and students of Jena to the Sunday words of a priest or of God.

This new free time, which is actually not free time at all, but rather, like war in the texts of Clausewitz, a continuation of labor by different means, became an enormous success. With tremendous pride, a footnote in the *Teutscher Merkur* stated that "far more than *four hundred* students were present," that is, about half of the actual student population of Jena at the time. Even Reinhold found it a bit strange (*nicht unmerkwürdig*) that exactly this characteristic of an ever increasing culture distinguished "the current academic citizens of Jena over and against their predecessors" (385).

Indeed. Weekends with cultural-industry or, perhaps more exactly, interpretations of poets would have been unthinkable in the epoch of rhetoric and the republic of scholars. After the work that has been accomplished in the studies and offices of scholars—as Faust's originary tragedy documents and memorializes in such fascinating manner[4]—these old European scholars did not simply fall into pleasures of the body or a mindless stupor; they also still wrote books which identified precisely this desire and stupidity as the single legitimate option of their recreation.

Only twenty years before Reinhold's innovative cultural event, Simon André Tissot—doctor of medicine in Lausanne and the agent of all of the inquisitions against onanism in the eighteenth century—published his treatise *On the Health of Scholars*.[5] That this 'health' existed only on the back of a book and nowhere in empirical reality, Tissot concluded from his own medium of the book. Since about 1700—when, according to Tissot, throughout Europe a mass of presses spewed forth an "enormous amount of books onto the market"—illnesses, and above all nervous disorders had continually increased both according to the frequency of such illnesses and the formation of various symptoms. The so-called School-Teacher (*Schulgelehrte*)—and that means "a *genre* or type of person that was hardly known to the ancients"—became a fakir with the one difference that fakirs "tear themselves to pieces with nails, chains, and whips," while scholars and teachers give themselves an actual death: a death "with books, manuscripts, seals, old inscriptions, unsolvable letters, and most of all with this absolute vegetation of the body, which is the second and unfortunately an all-too-fruitful source for the disease of scholars" (61).

On the bright side, in the active field of writing and studying, the Gutenberg Galaxy produced psychotic scholars, just as on the dark side, in the passive field of reading and enjoyment, "the seemingly infinite accumulation of novels called forth hysterical women" (196). And because the printing of books differentiated the festival of the Middle Ages into the conceptual pairs of body and spirit, sports and literature,[6] every deficit of recreation had to lead to recreational and psychotic simulacra of 'learnedness':

> Even catelepsis, this very rare disease, is a direct result of a very powerful strain of the spirit, and Fernel gives a very strange observation. A man, he says, who spent his days and nights studying and writing was suddenly befallen with this disease; he remained seated, feather in hand, with his eyes glued to the paper, so that an onlooker would believe that the man was involved in his studies until he perceived that, after having called to him and tugged at him, the man had lost all movement and sense. (53)

Cataleptic monuments of learnedness, in which human beings become hardened long before Beckett's Murphy, are not to be cured by a talking cure with themselves through the medium of interpretation of poets. Tissot's suggestions for therapy therefore propagate the exact opposite of a free time that would be true labor of the spirit. His first prophylaxis (*Verwahrung*), that is, "that without which all other medical aids would be useless," simply commanded that "the spirit be allowed to rest" (123). Precisely because almost all scholars "piece together the most familiar things" and "kill themselves" either by "producing the most miserable useless stuff" or by "writing the most tasteless works," the doctor only knew one imperative: "To penetrate into their sphere with force, pull them out of their studies, and compel them to rest and to recreate" (134).

If he succeeded in accomplishing *that*, Tissot would then employ his second means of curing them. According to the motto that "the narrow walls of a study drive learned souls into dire straits," while conversely the "smell of rural nature elevates their spirits," bucolic walks were on the treatment plan. But all remedies were simply that, for Tissot did not see an ideal prescription for the disease of scholars growing anywhere on the earth: "If one could find a remedy that would suspend the power of thought *without danger*"—and that means specifically in emphatic juxtaposition to opium, poppy juice and tobacco (225)—"then that would be the specific medicine for the disease of scholars" (237).

We are still seeking this drug today.

Progress in the development of such a drug, however, could be announced as soon as doctors and patients of the scholarly disease became identical. Because Goethe's Faust was fully trained in both philosophy *and* medicine, he could apply Tissot's therapeutic suggestions on his own case: Faust fled the pile of books in his "damned stifling hole in the wall," celebrated the resurrection of his own and all of nature during a walk at Easter time; indeed, he even considered Tissot's ideal prescription: the "brown liquid" of a flask of opium. But all of these home made recipes had to fail as long as Faust did not cross the epochal threshold from Tissot to Reinhold. That was accorded to him by two modern doctors, who were obviously one: a devil promised "not to hurry and to rest" for Faust; a God places a premium on "striving effort" that remained in service "always," that is, even on weekends and during declarations of love. Faust's scholar-tragedy ended with the identification of the 'lazy bed' and the punishment of hell.

"Only the body," Reinhold had taught, "replaces its exhausted powers through rest; spirit replenishes its powers through a change of occupation or pursuit" (389). This self-enhancement as a historical innovation made Easter walks and walks in general obsolete if the scholar in question did not (like Faust or Reinhold's colleague Schiller) immediately translate his contact with nature into lyric poetry. Why that became necessary is clear from Schiller's review of Bürger's poems:

> Because of the isolation and separated efficacy of our spiritual powers which necessitates an expanded circle of knowledge and a division of labor, it is only poetry that brings the separated powers of the soul together in unity, that occupies head and heart, insight and wit, reason and imagination in a harmonious bond, that produces the total human being once again in us. Poetry alone is in a position to turn away the saddest fate that can confront the philosophical understanding: to lose the price of its attempts over the diligence of research and to die for the joys of the real world in an abstract, remote world of reason.[7]

In the place of Tissot's drug, which would do away with all power of thought immediately and for good, came a poetry which occupied the so-called 'human being' in a double way: as reason and imagination, as the labor of philosophers and the recreation of poets. And in the place of Tissot's landscape came a discourse, that was simultaneously culture and nature and that made the sympathy with peasants superfluous. That the "sun of Homer"[8] even shines for us moderns meant in Schiller's "Spaziergang" and in general: belles-lettres became nature. Under the explicit premise that "one read correctly, a real, visible world unfolded according to the words."[9] As long as scholars stared at 'books' and 'manuscripts', old 'inscriptions'[10] and 'insoluble letters'—as we read in Tissot—this wonder remained absent. "Letters do not appear in free nature."[11] The interpretation of poets simply eliminated what it could not resolve. Reinhold forbade his students to practice any philology that would read 'poetic works' in a 'dead language' without 'danger' of 'being interrupted by a living beauty' simply because it searched for 'treasures' of 'grammatical wisdom' or classical learnedness and in the final analysis with all of that to simply ornament the office of a schoolteacher. To the visitors of his weekend lectures, on the contrary, Reinhold promised all of the happiness that, since 1890, was to come from films and records:

> While music and the plastic arts, due to the nature of their signs, must suffice to show specific objects from a particular point of view, poetry rules with unlimited power as far as the realm of beauty extends. . . . Precisely the condition that is made into a criticism against poetry by so many who do not understand, namely that poetry only only has words, that is, only these sensible signs in her power—precisely this condition, I say, she has to thank for the fact that she is not only bound to what allows itself to be represented in lines, colors and tones, but rather that the entire creative power of fantasy stands at her beck and call without limitation. Equipped with the magical letter of this fairy queen, poetry replaces and indeed surpasses the effect of the sensible impression; allows us not merely to *think*, but to *see* and *hear* what she wants us to see and hear. (Reinhold, 392f.)[12]

In 1788 it became superfluous to listen to the nightingale or to view pleasant scenes on walks in the afternoon: the new interpreters of poets, blind and deaf for letters just as once peasants were for nature, discovered noises and visions even between the lines in the book. Systematic reformulations engendered the phenomenology of ideal readers that wandered from lecture to lecture out of rhetorical strategies as they had once wandered from scribe to scribe. Under the conditions of perfect literacy, the rhetorical nominal value hypotyposis became a real value in the poetics of effect and poetry became the medium of all media. Otherwise Reinhold would never have won half of all the Jena students for that Saturday afternoon.

The question is what the servants of the sovereigns gained from all of this. But aside from, or perhaps exactly *in the center* of this new recreation, Reinhold also promised his students a new profession. Whoever had already learned to jump over Wieland's letters or—as Friedrich Schlegel put it—to distill Lessing's letterless spirit from his writings avoided the risk of old-fashioned learnedness: "Just as so many a scholar among our contemporaries had spent his life with abstractions and syllogisms, with the construction and the demolition of systems without anybody who had taste to lose being able to read or hear him" (402). In other words, only with the emergence of philosophical interpretations of poets did professors produce the quite practical poetic talent of offering the public a 'second nature' with tasteful lectures or writings. They were then able to place learnedness aside and hold lectures according to the terms of their poetic imagination[13] or even—as Hegel—write books whose "speculative thought" came into close proximity with the "poetic fantasy."[14] In this way, the new recreation for scholars and students was transformed into a labor of professors and teachers of German.

According to Klaus Weimar, "German literary science emerges as an applied aesthetics from the Hegelian school."[15] That is valid concerning the institution itself no less than for the contents of that institution. The inversion of the philosophical faculty from a mere propaedeutics to the systematic training of teachers, the officialization of all professors and gymnasium-teachers, the introduction of the *Abitur* and state examinations for teachers, the feedback-mechanism between gymnasium-output and university-input, university-output and gymnasium-teacher input: all of these measures of the era first made our discipline at all possible. Interpretation as a power-technology of state civil servants took the place of rhetoric as a power-technology of scholarly servants of sovereigns.

For Reinhold, the interpretations of poets were the recreation of the spirit, spirit that requires for its recreation not rest, but rather spontaneous self-activity, and therefore *poetry* as a media-less, that is, "immediate effect on the spirit" (392). For Hegel, the labor of the concept designated not merely to express the "life of God" as some recreational play of love with oneself, but even more importantly the seriousness, pain and patience of the Negative.[16] So the Berlin professor of philosophy Hegel sat for two years on a central commission which had the task of examining all of the Prussian candidates who had produced *Abitur* essays consisting of the interpretation of poets with an eye toward their suitability and usefulness as future civil servants. For Reinhold, aesthetics meant to replace the intuition of nature and those peasants who had failed to truly see her by a nature that hallucinates visions and noises in the reading of poets and poetry. For Hegel, aesthetics meant to put "natural beauty aside,"[17] even to "exclude"[18] it, and henceforth to only interpret *media*, "wherein spirit encounters spirit."[19] Poetry achieves, once again, a clear priority among all the artistic media because "she *works (arbeitet)* neither for the sensible intuition as in the plastic arts, nor for the mere ideal sensation as in music, but rather wants to make her significations of the spirit that are structured in her internal workings only for the representation and the intuition of spirit itself."[20]

With that, however, poetry exceeds not only writing and print,[21] but also, from the very beginning *(immer schon)*, the region of aesthetics itself. Her contents, and only her contents, make interpretation possible that—in the words of a title of one of Hegel's students—functions as a "contribution toward a recognition of a philosophical consideration of art."[22] If the labor of the concept had finally shown that the world-historical path of spirit could be interpreted utilizing fictitious heroes of dramas just as well as revolutionary terrorists, fictions as well as real events, then spirit succeeded in moving beyond art in order to achieve its elevated representation; namely, not merely the *substance* that is born out of the self, but rather *to be* this self in its representation as *object*; not merely to give birth to itself out of the concept, but to have its concept itself as its structure so that the concept and the produced work of art recognize and know themselves reciprocally as one and the same.[23]

The true interpretation of art would then be the art of interpretation. In other words, stated with the finale of Hegel's *Aesthetic*, these lectures had "fastened" a "higher, indestructible bond of the Idea of the Beautiful and the True" or between poetry and philosophy.[24] Students of philosophy became the future teachers of German.

NOTES

1. This essay was translated by Robert S. Leventhal.
2. Karl Leonhard Reinhold, "Über die nähere Betrachtung der Schönheiten eines epischen Gedichtes als Erholung für Gelehrte und Studierende," in *Der Teutsche Merkur*, May 1788, pp. 379–404. Hereafter referred by the page number.
3. Friedrich Schiller, "Was heißt und zu welchem Ende studiert man Universalgeschichte? Eine akademische Antrittsrede," in Schiller, *Sämtliche Werke, Säkular-Ausgabe*, edited by Eduard von der Hellen (Stuttgart-Berlin, no year given), vol. XIII, p. 5.
4. Compare Johann Wolfgang von Goethe, *Faust. Der Tragödie erster Teil*, in *Goethes Werke*. Hamburger Ausgabe (Munich, 1976), pp. 20f.
5. Simon André Tissot, *Von der Gesundheit der Gelehrten* (Zürich, 1768). Hereafter referred to utilizing page number.
6. Compare Hans-Ulrich Gumbrecht, "Beginn von 'Literatur'/Abschied vom Körper?" in Gisela Smolka-Koerdt, Peter Spangenberg, Dagmar Tillman-Bartylla, eds., *Der Ursprung von Literatur: Medien, Rollen, Kommunikationssituationen zwischen 1450 und 1650* (Munich, 1988), p. 42.
7. Friedrich Schiller, "Über Witz und Scharfsinn," in *Sämtliche Werke*, vol. XVI, p. 227.
8. Schiller, "Der Spaziergang," in *Sämtliche Werke*, vol. I, p. 140.
9. Friedrich von Hardenberg, *Schriften*, ed. Paul Kluckhohn and Richard Samuel (Stuttgart/Berlin/Köln/Mainz, 1960–75), vol. III, p. 377.
10. Concerning 'inscriptions,' see Jan Assmann, "Schrift, Tod, und Identität. Das Grabmal

als Vorschule der Literatur im alten Ägypten," in *Schrift und Gedächtnis. Archeologie der literarischen Kommunikation I*, ed. Aleida and Jan Assmann, Christof Hardmeier (Munich, 1983), p. 6
11. Sigmund Freud, *Die Traumdeutung*. In Freud, *Gesammelte Schriften*, ed. Anna Freud (London/Frankfurt, 1950), vol. II/III, p. 384.
12. For a similar definition of poetry, compare Friedrich von Hardenberg, *Heinrich von Ofterdingen*, in *Schriften*, vol. I, pp. 209f.
13. Compare J. G. Fichte, *Die Grundlage der gesamten Wissenschaftslehre*, in Fichte, *Gesamtausgabe*, ed. Reinhard Lauth and Hans Jacob (Stuttgart/Bad Canstatt: Friedrich Fromann, 1962f.), vol. I/2, p. 415.
14. G. W. F. Hegel, *Vorlesungen zur Ästhetik*, ed. Friedrich Bassenge, vol. 2, p. 342.
15. Klaus Weimar, "Zur Geschichte der Literaturwissenschaft. Ein Forschungsbericht," *Deutsche Vierteljahrsschrift* 50 (1976), p. 312.
16. G. W. F. Hegel, *Phänomenologie des Geistes*, ed. J. Hoffmeister (Hamburg: Meiner, 1952), p. 20.
17. Hegel, *Ästhetik*, I, 17.
18. Hegel, *Ästhetik*, I, 15.
19. Hegel, *Phänomenologie*, p. 489.
20. Hegel, *Ästhetik*, II, 19.
21. Compare Hegel, *Ästhetik*, II, 399.
22. Hermann Friedrich Wilhelm Hinrichs, *Ästhetische Vorlesungen über Goethes Faust als Beitrag zur Anerkennung wissenschaftlicher Kunstbeurtheilung* (Halle, 1825).
23. Hegel, *Phänomenologie*, p. 492.
24. Hegel, *Ästhetik*, II, 586.

RECIPROCAL INFLUENCE

ROBERT S. LEVENTHAL

"... so daß man das Jahrhundert in der Theorie beinah das ökonomische nennen möchte ..."

... so that one could almost name the century in the realm of theory the economical century ...

—J.G. Herder, *Vom Einfluß der Regierung auf die Wissenschaft und der Wissenschaft auf die Regierung* (1780) (*SW* IX, 356)

With regard to Herder's prize-essay of the Berlin Academy of Sciences in 1780, "On the Influence of Government on Science and Science on Government," we are in the throes of a metaphor: 'reciprocal influence'; *gegenseitiger Einfluß*; 'l'influence réciproque.' It is a central rhetorical figure of the late Englightenment—a period in which, as Reinhart Koselleck has shown, a hierarchical society of vertical orders and *Stände* gives way to a horizontal society of *citizens* who participate in orders or *Stände*.[1] Indeed, the figure commands an entire discursive *system*, an organization of writing; a whole battery of texts of the period 1760–80 bears the mark of reciprocity: Maupertuis, Michaelis, Sulzer, and Herder.[2] This figure is all the more decisive since what is at stake is precisely the 'economy' or 'system' of late Enlightenment discourse itself. If the question of the 'origin' defines the thought and writing system from the 1750s to the 1770s—one thinks of the 'origin' of language and of inequality; of Condillac, Süßmilch, Rousseau, Herder—the discursive network of the 1760s and 1780s is governed by this figure of 'reciprocity.'

I would like to begin with two methodological remarks. First, I translate Herder's term *Wissenschaft* not merely as the traditional 'science,' but equally as 'discourse,' and justify this move by way of Herder's statement, in the *Fragmente* 1767–69, that a language (*Sprache*) constitutes an immeasurable 'field' of actual and possible *Wissenschaften*.[3] These *Wissenschaften* or 'discourses,' on Herder's reading, are not merely 'aspects' or 'regions' of language, but *language itself* applied for a specific purpose. For

Johann Gottfried von Herder, from the Bildabteilung, Deutsches Literaturarchiv of the Schiller Nationalmuseum, Marbach, Germany. Reprinted with permission.

Herder, these particular uses of language or *Wissenschaften* are primary, not secondary or derivative. It is in and through such 'discourses' that a language (*Sprache*) emerges as such. Herder's translation of the Academy's original prize question registers this shift. The question read: "Quelle a eté l'influence du gouvernement sur les lettres chez les nations ou elles ont fleuri? Et quelle a eté l'influence des lettres sur le gouvernement?" This deliberate misreading and response to the question, evident in the replacement of *Wissenschaften* for the term *lettres*—Herder's essay is entitled "Vom Einfluß der Regierungen auf die *Wissenschaften*"—indicates the trajectory of my reading. Herder is writing around, circumventing, misapprehending, and actually misquoting the *Preisfrage* in order to place question marks next to it, and therefore undermine the authority and legitimacy of the question at the very moment it successfully answers it.

Secondly, I shall presuppose a knowledge of Foucault's analysis in *Discipline and Punish*. What I glean from this analysis is this: the 'subject' of the late Enlightenment—a period in which a certain constancy, regularity, universality, and necessity forge a new discourse of the 'humane' and the 'sensible'—far from being a 'subject' of participatory communication, as Habermas argued in *Structural Transformations of the Public Sphere* (1963), is actually being placed in a 'field' of surveillance as the object of information. According to Foucault, it is at this time—at the precise moment of the birth of *Polizeiwissenschaft*, the institutionalized and disciplinary study of the 'science' of the state—that the individual is situated within a network of writing, more precisely into a 'register'[4] in which presence, absence, habits, morality, achievement, failure, lateness, reliablity, performance are duly noted, recorded, and studied as part of an analysis for the regulation and successful ordering of society.[5] This 'society of individuals'—on which most theorists from Koselleck to Foucault agree—is not so much an extension of a mercantile society of contracts and exchange, but rather the production of a specific technology of power and control. From the 'book,' the 'lesson,' 'reading,' the 'mutual improvement school' to the 'examination,' the 'written essay,' the 'seminar,' the 'university,' and the 'prison,' knowledge is both extracted and constituted, the subjects themselves rendered a 'field' of inquiry.

It comes as no surprise that the rhetoric of reciprocity—mutuality, communication, credit and debt, expenditure and conservation, award and punishment—figures in an important way for Foucault's argument. From the 'mutuality' and 'reciprocity' inscribed in elementary pedagogy to the construction of the new prison defined by a strict economy of expenditure and conservation, the society of 'rights,' 'contract,' 'communication,' and 'consensus' enacts a social space of interrogation, accumulation of information, and progressive 'training.' For according to this reading, the process of modernization is not the superimposition of the human sciences on social institutions; rather, the new 'humanism' and enlightened 'rationalism' are coextensive with a process of surveillance, subjugation, control. We move, pace Foucault, from the terror and horror of the 'spectacle' and the 'display' to a micro-economy of perpetual penality, a world of voyeuristic opacity in which a 'seeing' or 'vision' occurs that is itself hidden from the visible field of the monitored subject.

The discourse of reciprocity must be situated in a spatio-temporal academic location: the Berlin Academy of Sciences 1759–80. It was an institution ravaged by difference, disagreement, power struggles, infighting: the strife between Paris and Berlin, between the French influence of Maupertuis and D'Alembert and the German tradition of J. G. Sulzer, Mendelsohn, Lessing, and Herder; and between Berlin and Göttingen, which had emerged as the progressive university circa 1770 and where Heyne was instituting a royally funded philological seminar; finally, the specific *Klassen* or disciplines within the *Akademie* itself vying for power. The academy was a scene of tremendous upheaval, a place of secret wars, a labyrinth of machination. The strife concerning the *Preisfragen* is in itself ample evidence of the instability and disunity of the academy. Herder's *Preisschrift* of 1780 is born of this strife, the offspring of an embattled institution. Herder's stunning essay at once displays, analyzes and, most significantly, *participates in* this discursive struggle, and thus the process of institutionalization within the academy.

On this reading, Herder's textual strategy stages the conflict of the various players, bringing into play another metaphor or trope, one which informs the theory of interpretation at least since Leibniz and prominently in the German *Aufklärung*, namely the 'battle.' It occurs frequently as the figure for the reconciliation of various standpoints or 'points of view,' and is thus a constant participant in the talk about interpretation, reading, appropriate 'discourse.' But instead of displaying the conflict of perspectives, 'representing' the friction, Herder's text is a kind of *enactment*, i.e., it actually *performs* what it is writing about. In so doing, Herder's prize-essay fails to produce a 'critique of ideology'; rather, it doubles back on itself and becomes a text that must be regarded as an *event* or act that, precisely in its execution, deploys the required strategy of an institution in order to expose *itself* as complicitous with such strategy. Maintaining exactly the harmony and balance, the mutuality and reciprocity encoded within the very prize-question itself—something which Herder's text accomplishes on the surface—was surely a problem area for the academy in the literal sense. In this regard, the prize-essay of 1780 offers a vivid, textured account of a complex, academic institution attempting to chart its own staggering path until, after 1810—following the acceptance of Humboldt's plan for the relation between the academy and the University of Berlin—its function is set, its role in the structure of higher education in Prussia defined and implemented. Herder's prize-essay of 1780 simultaneously *interprets* and *carries out* the institutional 'tactics' of the academy.

In the Enlightenment's ideological apparatus of progressive, rational perfectability, there governs a metaphor of economy: moderation (*Maß*), proper balance, symmetry (*Gleichgewicht*), temperance, and toleration, a reservoir of energy that is continually replenished, a rigorous system of credit and debt, the proper organization and relation of the parts of the machine, negentropy, *oikonomia*. This metaphor of economy, the figure that informs the prize-questions of the Berlin Academy from 1759, when Michaelis successfully answered the question with his essay "Über den Einfluß der Meinungen des Volks auf die Sprache und der Sprache auf die Meinungen des Volkes," until 1780, when Herder repaid the debt and won the prize with his essay "Vom Einfluß der Regierung auf die Wissenschaft," is not merely a 'political' discourse derived from mechanics and hydraulics; hermeneutics, the theory of interpretation and of reading, also abides by its law until Lessing and Herder contest its rulership—Lessing in his criticism of allegorical interpretation (*Allegorese*) and Klotz, then in the *Fragmenten-*

streit with Goeze, where what is at stake is precisely the ground rules of reading and discourse. Herder later performed a similar destabilization of the hermeneutic 'code' in a stinging review of A. L. Schlözer's *Universalhistorie*.[6]

We might be inclined to accept the mutuality, closure, systematics, productivity, totality—indeed, the entire model of communication and communicativity between distinct and potentially hostile forces—implied by the economic metaphor of *reciprocal influence*. And yet such a discursive trope or figure must inevitably refer not merely to its Other in the sense of a *second* term that is to be reconciled in its own procedure, which is "only a variety—or a variation—of the Same,"[7] but also the *third*, the figure that renders possible and threatens the system, the figure against which the system struggles, a figure of a different order, one might say, that is prefigured by the second law of thermodynamics and what information theorists call 'noise.'[8] This is a figure which, as Michel Serres notes, "is precisely a rupture of the law of exchange,"[9] a figure which simultaneously holds, maintains, and yet endangers the crypto-egalitarian ideology of mutual power. As Jacques Derrida has stated in an essay entitled "Rhétorique de la drogue" regarding AIDS:

> At the heart of that which would preserve itself as a dual intersubjectivity it inscribes the mortal and indestructible trace of the third—not the third as the condition of the symbolic and the law, but the third as destructuring structuration of the social bond, as social disconnection, and even as the disconnection of the interruption.[10]

The figure of the third—the demon, the noise of *prosopopeia*, the parasite, the intruder, drugs, the interpretant—makes its appearance in Herder's earlier prize-essay, a discourse on the institutionalization of discourse, the "Essay on the Origin of Language": "Denn der Unterschied von Zween läßt sich nur immer durch ein Drittes erkennen"[11] (For the difference between two can only be known through a third). Herder's *Ursprungsschrift* is haunted by this third: the relation between "to know" (*erkennen*), and "getting to know" (*kennenlernen*), between the *Merkmal* and the *Merkwort*, between the internal *naming* of objects and the *communication* between individuals or intersections of power (*Disposition der Kräfte*) that at once requires mediation and is constitutive of language. Herder: "Das erste Merkmal, was ich erfasse, ist Merkwort für mich, und Mitteilungswort für andre!" (43) (The first attribute that I grasp is a catchword for me, and a communicating word for the Other!). While the text urges simultaneity, i.e., that the aspect or characteristic is *at one and the same time* a signifier and signified, the *procedure* of the *Ursprungsschrift* establishes the priority of reflection as the condition of the possibility of communicability. If this grasping, this form of fastening is in fact made possible by recognition or reflection, then we will read this 'reflection' itself as an attempt to erase this figure of the third. The absence, delay, divergence, and deferral constitutive of writing and the text are not accidental characteristics of 'communication'—which always gives the pretense of an undistorted and unobstructed 'transmission'—but rather inhabit it and indeed make the iterability central to writing and the written possible. In Herder's prize-essay of 1780, the third, this intruder from the outside who places question marks next to the equation of reciprocal influence and destabilizes the positionality of the question, is written as the 'misuse of discourse' (*Mißbrauch der Wissenschaft*). It is this 'misuse' that cannot be incorporated into the system of reciprocal influence and is symbolically expelled or purged in the final maneuver of Herder's text.

Difference—and, we might add, precisely that which holds the system in its disequilibrium, its *productive*, energy efficient state of contrast and friction, forestalls *stasis* and creates *homeorrhesis*—must itself be maintained through its relation to this dangerous figure of the third. Thus the system of reciprocity that the prize-question enacts—the academy will be rewarded with cultural capital and knowledge-credit, the recipient with the 'distinction' and booty of the prize—is held in check by something that it is not, something nonreciprocal, something that operates at its margins, intercepting its 'messages' but not *participating* in the game. I would place even further pressure on *reciprocal influence*, under the influence of Serres, Foucault, and Derrida, and say that *reciprocal influence* is a contradiction or, at the very least, an oxymoron. For is it not the entire function of influence to precisely *negate* reciprocity, to gain power over the Other and control it? Is not the very trajectory of influence to negate the influence of the Other? To overcome the attempt of the Other to influence, and thus finally to reign in the knowledge of the Other's dependence, abjection, subjugation? In a word, the pleasure of power? Herder's 'influence' is precisely the achievement of power over something or someone, the very *inequality* in the matrix of forces and counter-forces.

Reading the prize-essay of 1780, we find that a simple identification suggests itself. We have a binary structure, and the 'free' competition, reciprocity, and exchange envisaged by Herder's system might be readily juxtaposed to its supposed Other. The one, unified academy of self-formation (what Herder praises as "die Eine Akademie der Bildung")[12] is placed over and against the *false ordering* of faculties and disciplines (what Herder criticizes as a "falsche Zusammenordnung") (355); the fatherly government (*die väterliche Regierung*) (323) over and against capricious despotism (*der willkührliche Despotismus*) (324); criticism, art, and science (*Kritik, Kunst, Wissenschaft*) over and against mere factionalism and disputes, 'imitation,' and repetitive 'erudition' (*Streitigkeit, Nachahmung, Gelehrsamkeit*). Herder's essay appears to exemplify the structural balance and integrity already inscribed in the very position of the question. We are beckoned along this binary path. It is, at first glance, a perfectly symmetrical argument. And yet for this very reason, such a reading—a reading that would somehow offer us the satisfaction of closure, completion, identity, and order; a reading that would once again clearly and univocally place Herder's text on the side of *freedom* and 'radical democracy' (to use the terms of F. M. Barnard's[13] and Jost Hermand's[14] collections in which this *Preisschrift* is excerpted)—must be rejected. Such a reading cannot hold for three reasons: (i) it would effectively place Herder outside of or 'beyond' the discursive struggle that I would say is the central thematics, the very point of the prize-essay of 1780; (ii) it denies the presence of the *third* referred to above that maintains, holds in check, and endangers the system of 'reciprocal influence.' Such a move would thus buy into or invest in the very positionality of the question; and (iii) it cannot adequately account for the rhetorical complexity of the *Preisschrift*, which, I shall argue, is marked by a striking collusion and complicity with the power and authority of the academy even—or should we say *exactly*?—in its radical critique of the discursive practices and power of the institution.

Is it any coincidence that the *Preisschrift* seems more concerned with the status of discourse, with *Rede* and *Beredsamkeit*, with *Wissenschaft* as a kind of shorthand for discourse/science, with the *history* of the loss of great rhetoric, than it is with the question of the reciprocity of discourse and government proper? Or we might ask: why do eighteenth century tracts on politics—to which the *Preisschrift* belongs—inevitably revolve around questions of *discourse*, while treatises on language—from Rousseau and Condillac to Herder, Schlegel, and Humboldt—gravitate toward theories of polity? One answer might be found in procedures of 'text-coding,' by which I mean genre-motivated and genre-sensitive considerations regarding the limits of expression, the type or *scopus* of the text, and censorship. But this cannot suffice. As Harnack notes in his history of the Berlin Academy,[15] the Prize-question had been reviewed by the king himself, and "keine einzige Schrift brauchte ihres staatsfeindlichen Inhalts wegen zurückgewiesen werden" (not a single entry would be rejected on account of its critical attitude toward the state). Of course not. It was a brilliant method of establishing the enemy itself, a truth-discourse in the literal sense, by which I mean a discourse which, while supposedly aiming at 'truth,' is actually functioning as a form of police, a monitor, a procedure of surveillance, an Enlightenement 'wire,' 'phone tap,' or 'bug.' The prize-essay, a practice of the Berlin Academy since 1744, became a discursive event; for the prize-question of 1780 concerning the deception of the people, there were no less than forty-two entries. The prize-essay is installed as an excellent informant, perhaps even more informative than 'direct' methods of surveillance advanced by the newly established *Polizeiwissenschaft*, the science of the state, of policy, and of the regulation and normalization of individuals.

I shall urge that the thematic intersection, and the generic crossover of discourses or treatises on discourse and government, rhetoric, and the state result from an explicit recognition of the identity of discourse and power, the conformity of, in Herder's terms, *Wissenschaft* and *Einfluß*. Herder's narrative of the influence of *free* governments should not divert us from the fact: discourse is a field, and in the 'literal' military sense; Xenophon and Thucydides, Herder states, were great orators and field marshals, "Staats- oder Kriegsleute, Männer von Geschäften" (327). Discourse is always already inscribed as a match, a duel, war. It should be noted that, prior to the 'humanization' and 'rationalization' of education in the late 1760s, the 'lesson' was always carried out in the framework of the 'dispute,' which is in turn explicitly based on the scene of the 'battle' or the 'war': "The general form was that of war or rivalry; work, apprenticeship and classification were carried out in the form of the joust, through the confrontation of two armies."[16] The strife and struggle entwined in discourse places it in a systematic relation to another key site of polity: the theory of reading. What fuels reciprocity in the *Preisschrift* of 1780 is competition—*Wetteifer*—the *exact* term utilized incessantly in Herder's texts to characterize the process of reading: "lebendiges Lesen" is not, as has often been argued, most recently again by Brian Whitton, a divinatorial entrance "into the life of a culture,"[17] but rather *Wetteifer*, *innere Hevristik*: collision, clash, confrontation. Prior to reciprocity, there is an originary clash of conflicting readings; in a word, interpretation is war by other means.

My interpretive hypothesis is this: Herder's argument is fully circular, relentlessly citational, self-consciously or ironically complicitous, in other words, its very *form* is in *full accordance* with the question itself, the very *Fragestellung*; it conforms and colludes with the question, affirms the very mode of the question, in order to exert force, exercise power, by winning the prize. Herder's textual practice realizes—on the level of statement or *Aussage*—that the text can only gain influence, power, and control, that it can only win the prize and be published, through an affirmation of 'reciprocal influence,' *thus fulfilling the explicit contract* and *conditions* of the system of the question, which is in actuality not a *reciprocal* system, but a duel, a war, a military operation. On this reading, the *Preisschrift* of 1780 is an ironic and deliberate self-negating argument that, precisely by fulfilling the 'conditions' and following the 'directions' of the academy, breaks its influence at the very moment of its complicity, thereby intruding upon and threatening the intended closure of that system, creating an asymmetry or imbalance in the reciprocal-influential machine of discourse and counter-discourse. And insofar as Herder's argument folds back on itself— exploiting *explicandum* as the *explicans*, utilizing what is to be articulated as a term of articulation, reverting the signified back into a signifier—it can be demonstrated how this rhetorical negation disrupts precisely the economy, reciprocity, mutuality that the question was supposed to call forth.

In the historical narrative of the fall of Greek Antiquity, Herder asks how the *Geist* that animated oratory, theory, poetry, theater vanished, 'code' for the central question of the essay itself: how did this *Geist* function to affect talent, discourse, science, art? or how does the form of government influence *Wissenschaft*? The luminous reply: "Ich kann nicht anders sagen, als *durch sich selbst*, dadurch, daß solche Regierungsform, solche Verfassung zu einer solchen Zeit existierte" (I cannot say otherwise than *through itself*, through the fact that such a form of government, such a constitution existed at a particular time)(329). Reciprocally, and running parallel to Herder's writing of the closed 'system' here, a system reflexively shoring up its own closure, we read once again, at the end of the *Preisschrift*, this rhetorical collapse as Herder attempts to repay the debt and settle the account: "Nach so vielen Beispielen der Geschichte laßt uns *allgemeine Summen* ziehen und fragen: *wie* Wissenschaft auf die Regierung würkt? Ich kann simpel antworten: *durch sich selbst*" (After so many examples of history, let us take stock and ask: *how* science/discourse affects government? I can answer simply: *through itself*)(400). So the following phrase brackets Herder's argument: *durch sich selbst*. Through itself. This is not, by any standard, reciprocal influence. Thus, the *reciprocity* of reciprocal influence has been placed under an external influence outside the system, what we might refer to as the reflexive compulsion activated when entropy, equilibrium, stasis threaten the system; it has been placed into the 'place' of the question—the *Fragestellung* of the academy, thereby placing question marks next to the authoritative positionality of the question itself. Herder's response, in other words, is at once an elision *and* a fully rhetorical intensification/augmentation of the question of the loss of rhetoric as strife, struggle, war and the emergence of modern *Wissenschaft* with its claim of polite, reciprocal, mutual influence. In a word, Herder employs rhetoric as an agonistic modality that operates outside of and in opposition to the economy of reciprocity while simultaneously maintaining the rhetoric of reciprocity itself.

A less charitable reading of *Wissenschaft*, according to Herder, would indeed be Nietzsche's, written a century laterexplicated in "Homers Wettkampf,"[18] where Nietzsche will read the discursive scene as a pure agonistics, as a struggle or war concerning *illusion*, where there is no maximum or optimum, and the system is designed to keep precisely the struggle of conflicting agents intact. Nietzsche writes that "Neid, Eifersucht, wettkämpferischen Ehrgeiz" are constitutive of rhetoric, discourse—Herder's *Wissenschaft*. The very object of the *Redner* is precisely not 'consensus' or 'agreement,' what modern hermeneutic theory theorizes as *Gespräch*, a friendly conversation, *Einverständnis*, *Verständigung*. Herder states it: discourse, considered *discursively*, that is, from what one might call its 'operation' or 'function' as opposed to its 'meaning,' is *nothing other than* struggle, strife, conflict, battle—"im Wettkampf . . . mit einander wetteifernd" (330).

Herder's text performs this rhetorically complex procedure of questioning, answering, satirizing, and quoting the *Fragestellung*, or the very positionality (*Stellung*) of the question, while remaining heavily indebted to it, tearing the system of the question—its institution, its network of discipline and influence—apart, while remaining addicted to it in a vicious way.

According to Herder, the 'reciprocal influence' of government and *Wissenschaft* is, strictly speaking, inscrutable. While it might be useful to construct a model of this relation, and while it might be interesting to produce historical narratives on the concrete relation of a particular government to its specific *Wissenschaften*, the world is only accessible to us in its locality, contingency, specificity: "der Welt indessen ist sie [die Wissenschaft, wie die Regierung *in abstracto*, R.L.] immer nur in einzelnen Zügen, nach solchen und solchen Veranlassungen die Entwicklung gewisser Lokalumständen gewesen" (In the meantime, to the world, discourse and government have only been the development of local circumstances, in particular tendencies and according to specific conditions)(371). Herder's historical critique of concepts—one of the accomplishments of *Auch eine Philosophie*[19]—does not permit a general theory of the relation between government and *Wissenschaft*. The relation cannot be theoretically fixed in a general fashion because our concepts—monarchy, republic, philosophy, art, poetry, indeed, rhetoric or discourse itself—radically shift in their empirical content: "der philosophischen Geschichte bleibt nichts übrig, als diese Einzelheiten scharf zu bemerken und anzuwenden" (Nothing remains for philosophical history than to notice these specifics and apply them)(372). By dispensing with the very possibility of abstracting a theory of this relation due to the differing empirical content of concepts, Herder contradicts the question of the academy once again, for even if one were to specify, as the academy was careful to do, "in the time in which they flourished," thereby further disciplining and controlling the possible answers, the discourses or *Wissenschaften* are presumably too disparate to allow for a general theory of the form: "What is the influence of the government on science?" Absolute reciprocity in the form of an *adequate* theory would be either false or trivial, and Herder knows this. At this crucial juncture, Herder states—and this statement brings into play the entire problematics of the *Preisschrift*: "Ich wünschte, wir hätten eine solche Philosophische Geschichte [in caps, with *Sperrdruck*, R. L.] sowohl der Wissenschaften als der Regierung und ihres Einflußes in einander" (I wish we had such a philosophical history of the sciences as of government and their influence upon one another) (372). Herder wishes for, desires such a 'philosophical history'; he has, however, none himself. Indeed, the methodological critique of historical concepts, the stability of which is central to the academy's question, actually preempts and apostrophizes this 'desire' for such a philosophical history in the form of a general theory, leaving only what Herder refers to as "beautiful fragments" (*schöne Bruchstücke*), e.g., the remnants or waste of the system of science/discourse, the traces of media, data of history.[20]

The real question, the question perhaps of the next *Preisfrage* (for we know the production mechanism of the essay, how the *Preisfragen* of the academy were manufactured; one can find the prize-question of the origin of language *word for word* in Michaelis's essay of 1759 on nothing other than "the reciprocal influence of the opinion and languages of peoples")[21] — and Herder already has it in quotations in his text, ready to be distributed for immediate use — is: " 'Wie Wissenschaft in ihren Zweigen und Früchten, allmählich, hie und da, und durch welche Veranlassungen sichtbar geworden' " (How science [discourse, R. L.] in its many branches and with its fruits, gradually, here and there, became visible, and through which causes)(372). The 'tree' of the 'totality' (*Der Baum des Ganzen*), however, is lacking, and this lack or privation is not coincidental, but rather constitutive of Herder's rhetorical project. The question of the academy thus only serves to reproduce the system or structure of the academy itself, as the contemporary academic disciplines or *Klassen* reproduce, in Herder's view, the medieval order of faculties as closed *corpora* in conflict with one another. As a response to the question posed by the academy, Herder's text thus itself poses the question, the question of the possibility of a philosophical history of this question, a question to which Herder's essay, ideally, would have already been the answer. But Herder's text does not, and, according to Herder's argument, in principle *cannot* adequately respond. There exists a breach or privation in the system that, according to Herder's historical critique of the *Begriff*, cannot be healed, thus effectively opening up and interrupting the very closure, system, and totality which the economy of 'reciprocal influence' signifies.

If I am correct that Herder deliberately and discursively circumvents, avoids, misses, and misinterprets the *Preisfrage*, posing in its place the 'real' question as to the possibility of philosophical history, we must state that Herder's text enacts the labor of the Hegelian *Begriff*, the consumptive, devouring movement of notional analysis, without, however, succumbing to the dream of totality or synthesis. On this view, Herder's text performs the identification of science-discourse as power *media*. Universities and academies are *nothing other* than *media* of science-discourse in the hands of the Government: "was sind jetzt solche Universitäten, *als Mittel der Wissenschaft* in den Händen der Regierung betrachtet" (What are universities now other than media of science/discourse in the hands of the government) (344). And yet we know, as Herder himself is fully aware (two hundred years before McCluhan), that the 'medium' is never simply a *medium*, an innocent, transparent corridor or vessel for the transmission of *Wissenschaft*. The *Preisschrift* of 1780 can thus be read as a discourse analysis of its own rhetorical, discursive, and historical situatedness, an articulation of the 'jamming' or 'distortion' of the academy, the discursive *critique* that relentlessly implicates itself in its own material. In the history of this discursive event or constellation, which we might refer to, with Foucault, as the emergence of 'literature,' it is the intervention of the figure of the third in the form of "wealth, medicines, herbs" in Herder's text — capital, pharmaceuticals, drugs — that serves as an ignition for the motor of *Wissenschaft*. In other words, it is precisely that which intrudes from without the closed space of the question and the answer, the *Preisfrage* and the *Preisschrift*, that challenges the discipline of the *Fragestellung* and demands a discursive response. It is the third that breaks the present economy and introduces a new order or circuit. Describing the advent of the modern discursive network, Herder writes: "Der neue Cirkel, in dem alles ging,"—and thereby it becomes evident that the very function of *Wissenschaft qua* 'discourse' can be, for Herder, nothing other than its own overthrow, its own contradiction, which produces nothing other than *a new circle*, a different circuit or economy. And we begin all over again.

At the end of the text, Herder supposedly presents, in the form of six theses, a response to the question: how have the sciences affected the government? It is, rhetorically, a strict repetition of the first pages of the *Preisschrift*. Compare, for instance, this quote from the very outset: "Die ältesten Proben und Keime menschlicher Wissenschaft sind Worte, bedeutende mächtige Sprüche und Sprüchwörter" (The oldest attempts and seeds of human science are words, meaningful, powerful sayings and proverbs) (314) with the following closing statement: "Die ersten Sprüche und Wörter . . . sind von größter Wirkung" (378). Words and sayings are sciences/discourses—*Wissenschaften*—and these are merely words and sayings. Herder running out of things to say? Hardly. This repetition *must* be read ironically. Indeed, the symmetrical structure of the entire argument must be read as a 'quotation' or ironic paraphrase of precisely that structure. Not simply an amplification or elaboration, it is rather 'reciprocal' discourse boomeranging through the text, thereby producing the symmetry, alignment, balance of 'reciprocal influence,' a principle that controls Herder's text on 'reciprocal influence' and governed the very structure of the *Preisfrage* of the Berlin Academy 1780.

However, the circle of Herder's text is closed—if we can even speak of a closure *as such*—not with the gesture of reason and moderation, balance and economy, not with the serene sense of harmony and reconciliation that would befit a *Preisschrift* on the 'reciprocal influence of discourse/science and government,' but rather with a brutal exclusion, an abrupt and violent gesture of discipline. If previously the question of censorship in the text revolved around a possible delimitation of what is said and written, making a fine distinction between *censorship* on the one hand, and *guidance* or *advice* in matters of taste on the other—"Ich glaube also, es sei dem Staat freigelassen, ja nothwendig, gewisse Wissenschaften, so wie Ergötzlichkeiten und Beschäftigungen auszuschliessen, wenn er sie mit seinem Principium der Wirksamkeit nicht binden zu können sich getrauet" (I believe it must be left up to the state, necessarily, to exclude [*ausschliessen*] certain discourses, as well as other frivolities and activities, if it does not believe to be able to integrate these with its principle of effectiveness) (358)—it is, in the end, a desperate struggle, a scene of surveillance of instances of transgression that mocks reciprocity and transforms it into its opposite: univocal control, discipline, punishment:

Stünden junge Leute auf Akademien und ehe sie zu Ämtern gelangen und wenn sie in Ämtern sind, unter Aufsicht; käme in Betracht nicht bloß, wie sie aussehen und was sie etwa wissen, sondern auch, womit sie sich beschäftigen, was sie schreiben; wäre jedweder gehalten, ein Verzeichniß dessen, was er gethan, womit er sich und dem Publikum die Zeit gekürzt, denen, die ihm die Regierung vorsetzt, zu liefern und erginge hiernach Zurücksetzung und Beförderung, Lohn und Strafe; wäre jeder Verleger angehalten, im Fall es erfordert würde, seinen Autor und Kritikus zu nennen oder für das Geschriebene selbst zu haften; müßte insonderheit die Kritik, das eigentliche Afterreden hinter Werken, dabei man selbst nicht würket, nie namenlos erscheinen; geschähe so manchen Übervortheilungen im Handel der Literatur Einhalt—mich dünkt, es würde Mißbräuche der Wissenschaft aufhören, die jetzt den übelsten Erfolg [sprich: Einfluß, R. L.] auf die Köpfe der Leser und Schriftsteller, ja ganzer Stände und Ämter haben. (402)

If young people at the academies, and before they entered office and while in office stood under supervision; if it were to be considered not merely how they look and what they know, but also how they occupy their time, what they write; if everyone were required to keep a register of what he or she did, of how he or she was useful to to him/herself and the public, and deliver this register to their superiors; and if demotion and promotion, reward and punishment were implemented accordingly; if every publisher were required (if it were demanded) to name the critic or be responsible for what is written; if critique itself, which is always a kind of post-discourse 'behind' or 'after' the works themselves, could never appear anonymously; if there weren't so many acts of cheating or fraud in the trade of literature itself—I think misuses of discourse, which now have the most horrible effects on readers and writers, indeed, entire orders, classes, and offices, would cease altogether.

A register. Supervision. Promotion and demotion. Reward and penalty. Names. Proper appearances. Identity cards. Signatures.[22] Abuses of discourse: "Giebt er also dem Fieber seiner Phantasie oder dem Ausbruch seiner Unvernunft Raum; so muß es immer dem Staat frei stehen, ihn als einen Kranken und Irren zu behandeln" (If the individual gives license to the fever of his fantasy or the eruption of unreason; so the state must be allowed to treat him like a sick and insane person) (401). With the introduction of this quote into my discourse, I do not seek to discredit Herder, to expose or reveal him, to give a statement to the effect that we have second-guessed Herder, looked 'behind' his text, that we 'understand' his text better than he himself. Lest one think that I am practicing a hermeneutics of suspicion, I stress that my interest is what the text *states*, not what it means. It is the strength of Herder's text that it does not conceal and indeed fully registers the knowledge-power implied in the figure of 'reciprocal influence.' I leave open the question of how he *intended* this quote; whether we are to read it, *per* his own rhetorical *Anweisung*, as a prescription; or whether it might be read as subterranean contemporary description and *Zeitkritik*, as a subliminal and ironic coupling of 'reciprocity' and 'control,' 'mutual communication' and the police state. On a discursive plane, on the sentential level, Herder's text *connects* the figure of 'reciprocity' as maintenance of the illusion of equal competition with its function or operation as power. This text, then, is itself a *Mißbrauch der Wissenschaft*—a misuse or abuse of discourse that threatens the disciplinary matrix of the question. Herder's prize-essay of 1780 enacts this 'misuse' by allowing the discourse of reciprocity to betray itself as an instance of institutional force.

In 1809, Friedrich Wilhelm III accepted Humboldt's recommendation for the construction of the University of Berlin, the model of the modern university of research and teaching. In that plan—"Antrag auf Errichtung der Universität Berlin" (1809)[23]—the discourse of reciprocity still holds, but the rough edges of Herder's text, the competition, rivalry, clash of Herder's discourse have been eclipsed; all separation of faculties, all rivalry between the disciplines is destructive to the idea and practice of science; the rhetoric of 'organism' and 'community' displaces Herder's 'productive strife' and 'competition.' As the old 'conflict of the faculties,' the strife between the *Klassen*, is being dismantled piece by piece; as we enter into Koselleck's modern society of *citizens*, free and equal, who participate in orders; as we leave the vertical hierarchy of power behind and embrace the egalitarian, reciprocal order, we are simultaneously placed into the 'register'—Herder's *Verzeichniß*—our abuses of discourse registered in the databanks. We wake up into the historical nightmare in which we are 'seen' without ourselves being able to see the multifarious ways in which that seeing occurs. We wake up into a world in which 'reciprocity' and panopticism, discourse and power, *Wissenschaft* and the prison are not two distinct phenomena, but rather, as Foucault conjectured,[24] exactly one and the same, identical historical emergence.

In 1786, Herder became an *auswärtiges Ehrenmitglied* of the Berlin Academy of Sciences. Welcome to the machine.

NOTES

1. Koselleck, "Begriffsgeschichte and Social History," in *Futures Past: On the Semantics of Historical Time* (Cambridge, Mass.: MIT Press, 1985), pp. 73–91.

2. Adolf Harnack, *Geschichte der Königlichen Preußischen Akademie der Wissenschaften zu Berlin* Band I.1 (Hildesheim: Olms, 1970), pp. 403–09.
3. See Benjamin Bennett, *Beyond Theory* (Ithaca: Cornell University Press, 1993), pp. 247–62.
4. Michel Foucault, *Discipline and Punish: The Birth of the Prison* (New York: Vintage, 1975), p. 189.
5. On this, see Thomas Kempf, *Aufklärung als Disziplinierung: Studien zum Diskurs des Wissens in Intelligenzblättern und gelehrten Beilagen der zweiten Hälfte des 18. Jahrhunderts* (München: Iudicium, 1991), pp. 57–90.
6. Cf. my article on Herder's critique of the 'Göttingen' School: "Progression and Particularity: Herder's Critique of Scholözer's *Universalhistorie*," in Wulf Kopeke, ed., *J. G. Herder: Language, History, and the Enlightenment* (South Carolina: Camden House, 1990), pp. 225–47.
7. Michel Serres, *Hermes: Literature, Science, Philosophy* (Baltimore: Johns Hopkins, 1982), pp. 66–67.
8. Campbell, *Grammatical Man: Information, Entropy, Language, and Life* (New York: Simon & Schuster, 1982).
9. Serres, *Hermes*, p. 6.
10. Jacques Derrida, "Rhétorique de la drogue," *Autrement* 106 (April, 1989), 197–214. Cited in Laurence Rickels, *The Case of California* (Baltimore and Lodnon: Johns Hopkins, 1991), p. 288.
11. Herder, *Abhandlung über den Ursprung der Sprache*, ed. H. D. Irmscher (Stuttgart: Reclam, 1970), p. 36. All references to Herder's treatise are from this edition.
12. Herder, "Vom Einfluß der Regierung auf die Wissenschaften und der Wissenschaften auf die Regierung" (1780), in Herder, *SW*, IX.
13. F. M. Barnard, *J. G. Herder on Social and Political Culture* (Cambridge: Cambridge University Press, 1969).
14. Jost Hermand, ed., *Von deutscher Republik: Texte radikaler Demokraten, 1775–1795* (Frankfurt: Suhrkamp, 1975).
15. Harnack, *Geschichte*, p. 419.
16. Foucault, *Discipline and Punish*, p. 146.
17. Brian J. Whitton, "Herder's Critique of the Enlightenment: Cultural Community versus Cosmopolitan Rationalism," *History & Theory* 27 (2), 1988, 154.
18. Nietzsche, "Homers Wettkampf," *Werke*, ed. Karl Schlechta (München: Hanser, 1960), vol. III, pp. 999–1007. See also Samuel Weber, "Blindness and the Seeing Eye," in S. Weber, *Institution and Interpretation* (Minneapolis, Minn.: University of Minnesota Press, 1986).
19. Herder, *Auch eine Philosophie*, ed. H. -G. Gadamer (Frankfurt: Suhrkamp, 1969), p. 40: "übrigens weiß ich es wie du, daß jedes *allgemeine Bild*, jeder *allgemeine Begriff* nur Abstraktion sei."
20. Herder, *Auch eine Philosophie*, p. 38. Herder knows that the loss of the concept or *Begriff* is the emergence of information. He writes: "Allein *Data* ihrer Verfassung und Geschichte müssen entscheiden."
21. Michaelis, *A Dissertation on the Influence of Language on the Opinions of Peoples* (New York: AMS, 1973), p. 76: "How can language be introduced among men, who as yet have no language, and by what means may it attain among them to the perfection in which we see it?"
22. Derrida, "Signature, Event, Context," in Derrida, *Limited inc* (Evanston, Ill.: Northwestern University Press, 1988), pp. 12–23.
23. Humboldt, "Antrag auf Errichtung der Universität Berlin," in Humboldt, *Werke in fünf Bänden* (Stuttgart: J. G. Cotta and Darmstadt: Wiss. Buchgesellschaft, 1960), I, p. 112–16.
24. Foucault, *Discipline and Punish*, p. 23: "Instead of treating the history of penal law and the history of the human sciences as two separate series whose overlapping appears to

have had on one or the other, or perhaps on both, a disturbing effect, according to one's point of view, see whether there is not some common matrix or whether they do not both derive from a single process of 'epistemologico-juridical' formation: in short, make the technology of power the very principle both of the humanization of the penal system and of the knowledge of man."

II

Disciplines and Disciplinarity

THE SPECTACLE OF MARIA STUART'S IMPRISONMENT*

DOROTHEA E. VON MÜCKE

Schiller's *Maria Stuart* (1800) is an extremely carefully crafted artistic construct; indeed, many interpretations of the play have emphasized Schiller's attention to the play's composition, its stylization, and its symmetry.[1] Its symmetrical architecture creates a textbook example for the composition of a five-act classical tragedy. Thus Acts I and V focus on Maria, Acts II and IV on Elisabeth, and Act III on the encounter of the two queens. The characters of the two queens are symmetrically juxtaposed: in Act I Maria is depressed and discouraged, in Act V she returns triumphant; Elisabeth's initial self-assurance in Act II turns into desperation in Act IV. Both women embody fundamental opposites: Catholic versus Protestant, sensuality versus chastity. This opposition is played out in the most basic terms on the axes of apperance and truth and of weakness and strength. Thus Maria's jailor, Paulet, describes her at her first entry in the following terms: "Den Christus in der Hand, / die Hoffart in dem Herzen." ("Christ's image in her hand / Pride, and all worldly lusts within her heart"; I, 1, 142–43; p. 9). As the play progresses, however, it is Elisabeth who increasingly produces a false front, covering up for her true intentions and actions.

These formal qualities clearly distinguish this drama from the bourgeois tragedy and situate it in the context of classicist aesthetics: instead of a familiar, intimate setting, we are presented with public personae; the play's

---

*Reprinted from *Virtue and the Veil of Illusion*, by Dorothea E. von Mücke with the permission of the publisher, Stanford University Press. ©1991 by the Board of Trustees of the Leland Stanford Junior University.

formal rhetoric, verse, and stylization produce an aesthetic distance that prevents an identificatory, emotional engagement by the audience. The foregrounding of the play's artistic features, part of the "disinterested interest" of aesthetic contemplation in German Classicism, has led many critics to speculate about its qualities as a spectacle in terms of religious symbolism and ritual. Thus it has been praised as "religiöses Festspiel" and analyzed in terms of its "theatricality."[2] Indeed, the play's qualities as a spectacle deserve detailed analysis. My reading shows how this play about the execution and transfiguration of Maria Stuart is actually a dramatization of the execution and transfiguration of sovereign power, how as a spectacle the play attempts to "make visible" those powers that can structure and anchor the order of representation. I also demonstrate that this spectacle does not operate like the old-style spectacle of tyrannical power, which is displayed through the sovereign's body in the public theater of royal pomp or through public torture and execution. What distinguishes Schiller's *Maria Stuart* from the old-style spectacle is that it is set in an altogether new situation, one in which the sovereign's absolute power has already vanished.

Thus, the two queens never appear in any scenes of public splendor. Mostly they are shown behind closed doors: Maria is incarcerated; Elisabeth is in her "office," surrounded by "advisors" and scribes. Although one might expect that the play would end with Maria's execution, there are five subsequent scenes all centered around the fate of two secretaries. Maria's scribe, Kurl, becomes insane from guilt for having falsely implicated Maria in a plot to assassinate Elisabeth. Elisabeth's scribe, Davison, is condemned to death. He becomes her scapegoat, for she cannot acknowledge the performative power of her signature on Maria's death sentence. And throughout the play the disinterested, cold voice of the *raison d'état*, Burleigh, argues for Maria's clandestine murder for the sake of England's and Elisabeth's safety; not for his own benefit as the old-style intriguing villain (the figure of the Machiavelli) would have argued. Indeed, the setting of the play can be described in words Schiller used to characterize the modern state: "The palace of kings is closed now; the courts of justice have withdrawn themselves from the gates of cities into the interior of the houses; writing has displaced the living word; the sensuous mass of the populus itself—if it does not rule as brute force—has become the state, an abstract term; the gods have returned to the bosom of man."[3] But how then is this situation to be remedied? What does the play qua spectacle have to offer to counter the effects of the abstract, disembodied state? Schiller does not return to the old-style public spectacle in which the scene of the execution itself becomes the spectacle of truth, power, and justice. We are not shown Maria's execution on stage but perceive it mediated through Leicester, who does not see the scene himself but reacts to hearing it. The focus of the spectacle is shifted from the scene of execution to the one preceding it: not a scene of torture and public confession in which the truth is produced through the body of the accused but a scene of the private confession of guilt, absolution, and communion. Schiller himself called this scene the "keystone" of the play.[4] Furthermore, the meaning of the execution is altogether changed, as compared to its traditional function as a public spectacle: for England, Maria's execution is not an act of revenge or retribution but the removal of a politically dangerous object. Not Maria but Leicester is punished with the execution. For Maria the execution represents the renunciation of her "physical" existence, her sensuality, and her hopes of gaining freedom and being with Leicester—in brief: her sexuality. But before analyzing in further detail the possible redemptive function of these two scenes with regard to an alienated abstract state and the political danger of semantic and social destabilization, I first take a detour beginning with another figure who underwent a transformation, one that consists not of a reformation but of a conversion: Mortimer.

Since Mortimer is not a historical figure but was invented by Schiller, we can assume that this character is quite crucial for understanding the play.[5] Mortimer enters Maria's prison in his uncle Paulet's presence but totally ignores the beautiful queen and pays attention only to his uncle. This apparent rudeness establishes his credibility as Elisabeth's loyal subject and later enables him to see Maria alone. In their first private conversation, he immediately reveals himself as her ardent admirer, who has come from the French Cardinal Guise to free Maria. But before explaining to Maria her imminent fate—Elisabeth's plans to ground her rule in Maria's execution and the Catholic scheme for Maria's rescue—Mortimer narrates in broad detail the history of his conversion. Brought up a Protestant with a strict sense of duty, at the age of twenty he was driven by an ardent desire to leave England for Italy. He was carried along in the stream of pilgrims toward Rome and charmed by the power and magic of the fine arts and music. Exposed to Rome's luxurious display of religious art, music, jewelery, and pomp, he developed a hatred of the "disembodied word" of Protestantism, the "prison" of his own upbringing, which had deprived him of the sensual joys of life.

From Rome he went to Maria's uncle Guise, who became for him the paradigm of masculine power and strength and who sets forth for him the truth of his newly found belief.

> Er zeigte mir, daß grübelnde Vernunft
> Den Menschen ewig in die Irre leitet,
> Daß seine Augen sehen müssen, was
> Das Herz soll glauben, daß ein sichtbar Haupt
> Der Kirche nottut, daß der Geist der Wahrheit
> Geruht hat auf den Sitzungen der Väter.

> He showed me how the glimmering light of reason
> Serves but to lead us to eternal error:
> That what the heart is called to believe

> The eye must see: that he who rules the church
> Must needs be visible; and that the spirit
> Of truth inspired the councils of the fathers.
> (I, 6, 477–82; pp. 19–20)

Mortimer's conversion to and through the senses (the magic charm and palpable splendor of Catholicism) is confirmed and anchored through Guise, who embodies a paternal principle for the young man. Mortimer joins the company of English exiles and Catholics. One day in the bishop's residence, he is struck by the sight of a woman's picture. The bishop tells him that this woman, Maria, is not only the most beautiful of all women but also the most miserable, a true martyr, who instead of being on the English throne is imprisoned by an illegitimate pretender. Upon receiving this knowledge and the news that his uncle Paulet is in charge of Maria, Mortimer decides to rescue her before she is decapitated. He is willing to risk his life for Maria and his own fame.

In the next scene in which Mortimer appears, he is introduced to Elisabeth as her loyal servant, who has come with intelligence from France. Elisabeth tries to recruit him for Maria's clandestine murder; he pretends to agree in order to gain time for her rescue. This private conversation with Elisabeth confirms Mortimer's view of his role vis-à-vis the two queens. He cannot serve this duplicitous queen, head of the abstract state he has learned to hate. Both as woman and as queen, Elisabeth has nothing to promise him. But Mortimer's motives with regard to Maria are not entirely selfless. He wants to free her in order to possess her (see II, 6, 1645–61).

In Mortimer's criticism of abstract, Protestant rule, we can hear an echo of Schiller's own critique of the rigorous moral state of pure law with its administrative apparatus and alienated civil servants articulated in the Letter 6 of the *Aesthetic Education of Man*. But there is a decisive difference: Mortimer's critique is not derived from "man's ideal image"; he is not led to Rome, to his conversion, and to Maria by a "beautiful instinct" or a "a drive to play." Consequently Mortimer's conversion cannot be called an aesthetic education in Schiller's sense. Although Mortimer suddenly learns to love beauty, the arts, and the life of sensuality, his conversion to the aesthetic does not result in the formative stage of distanced aesthetic contemplation. He is not rendered calm and reflective by the object of his sensual attraction but rushes to satisfy his desire. When he returns to Maria to rescue her, he is driven by unmitigated hatred and love.

> Ja glühend, wie sie hassen, lieb ich dich!
> Sie wollen dich enthaupten, diesen Hals,
> Den blendenweißen, mit dem Beil durchschneiden.
> O weihe du dem Lebensgott der Freuden,
> Was du dem Hasse blutig opfern mußt.

> Mit diesen Reizen, die nicht dein mehr sind,
> Beselige den glücklichen Geliebten.
> Die schöne Locke, dieses seidne Haar,
> Verfallen schon den finstern Todesmächten.
> Gebrauchs, den Sklaven ewig zu umflechten.
>
> Yes, glowing as their hatred is my love;
> They would behead thee, they would wound this neck,
> So dazzling white, with the disgraceful axe!
> Oh! offer to the living god of joy
> What thou must sacrifice to bloody hate!
> Inspire thy unhappy lover with those charms
> Which are no more thine own. Those golden locks
> Are forfeit to the dismal powers of death,
> Oh! use them to entwine thy slave forever!
> (III, 6, 2554–63; p. 81)

And indeed, he assaults her and would have raped her were he not interrupted by the turmoil over the failed attempt on Elisabeth's life. Finally, after losing all hope of gaining Maria, he commits suicide. Mortimer's aesthetic education fails to the extent that it represents a mere relapse into what Schiller calls the "physical state," the chaotic state of unrestrained sensual drives.

Triggered by the sight of Maria's image in the bishop's house, Mortimer's aesthetic education ends in his idolatrous love for her.[6] But Mortimer is not the only one influenced by a portrait of Maria. Someone much closer to Elisabeth is also affected by Maria's image. Even as Maria rejects Mortimer's proposal to rescue her and insists that only Elisabeth's free will can liberate her, she appears to place her hopes in a private encounter with Elisabeth, "in opening herself to her equal, the woman and sister."[7] In order to achieve this, she pursues a double strategy: through Paulet she sends a letter to Elisabeth, and through Mortimer she sends her portrait to Leicester. It is in this double strategy that the strength and ultimate weakness of the two queens is revealed. Neither woman can rule over the written word. Maria's strength, however, as has already been demonstrated with regard to Mortimer, consists in exerting a powerful influence through her physical appearance as an erotic object captivating the male gaze.

By sending her portrait to Leicester, Maria indicates to him (her former lover, who rejected her in favor of Elisabeth) that she will be his if he frees her. For Leicester this promise comes at an extremely convenient moment: his long period of hoping to marry Elisabeth has come to an end with Elisabeth's engagement to her French suitor. While his ambitions kept him courting Elisabeth, he had been humiliated and kept captive, a toy of her vanity.[8] Leicester is not able to act openly and assert his masculine strength vis-à-vis Elisabeth, as Mortimer urges him to do.[9] He accuses Mortimer of ignoring England's actual situation, which necessitates duplicity and makes any forthright heroic action impossible.

> Wißt Ihr, wie's steht an diesem Hof, wie eng
> Dies Frauenreich die Geister hat gebunden?
> Sucht nach dem Heldengeist, der ehmals wohl
> In diesem Land sich regte—Unterworfen
> Ist alles, unterm Schlüssel eines Weibes,
> Und jedes Mutes Federn abgespannt.

> Are you acquainted with this court? Know you
> The deeps and shallows of this court? With what
> A potent spell this female scepter binds
> And rules men's spirits round her? 'Tis in vain
> You seek the heroic energy which once
> Was active in this land! it is subdued,
> A woman holds it under lock and key,
> And every spring of courage is relaxed.
> (II, 8, 1933–38; p. 62)

The only action Leicester undertakes on behalf of Maria is to tease Elisabeth into agreeing to a meeting with her opponent. By appealing to her vanity, he presents this meeting to Elisabeth as an occasion to exhibit not only her sovereign power but also the force of her feminine presence and beauty. Elisabeth lets herself be persuaded, to provide Leicester, as it were, with the spectacle of the two women together. The encounter with Maria does not, however, lead to Elisabeth's victory over her opponent but only reinforces their animosity.

Even before the meeting takes place, it is clear that it will be more than a private face-to-face encounter between the two "sisters"—that the two women will encounter each other within a triangular structure, that their speech and actions will be determined by this scene qua spectacle. For it is not only Elisabeth who arranges their meeting in view of another; Maria too, although it had been her hope to achieve a sisterly understanding and reconciliation with her opponent, makes a spectacle of herself as soon as she learns of Elisabeth's imminent coming. When Elisabeth's advisor Shrewsbury announces her arrival to Maria, all of Maria's previous hopes of arousing her opponent's pity vanish. She finds herself moved by violent hatred.

> In blutgem Haß gewendet wider sie,
> Ist mir das Herz, es fliehen alle guten

> Gedanken, und die Schlangenhaare schüttelnd
> Umstehen mich die finstern Höllengeister.
>
> My heart is turned to direst hate against her;
> All gentle thoughts, all sweet forgiving words,
> Are gone, and round me stand with grisly mien,
> The fiends of hell, and shake their snaky locks.
> (III, 3, 2184–87; p. 70)

Nevertheless, she tries to control her passionate impulses and throws herself at Elisabeth's feet. She does so, however, by pronouncing the "stage directions" for her behavior and words, producing and emphasizing the incongruity between her words and her performance.[10]

> Ich will vergessen, wer ich bin, und was
> Ich litt, ich will vor ihr mich niederwerfen,
> Die mich in diese Schmach herunterstieß.
> *(Sie wendet sich gegen die Königin)*
> Der Himmel hat für Euch entschieden, Schwester!
> Gekrönt vom Sieg ist Euer glücklich Haupt,
> Die *Gottheit* bet ich an, die Euch erhöhte!
> *(Sie fällt vor ihr nieder)*
> Doch seid auch *Ihr* nun edelmütig, Schwester!
> Laßt mich nicht schmachvoll liegen, Eure Hand
> Streckt aus, reicht mir die königliche Rechte,
> Mich zu erheben von dem tiefen Fall.
>
> I will forget my dignity, and all
> My sufferings; I will fall before her feet
> Who hath reduced me to this wretchedness.
> *(She turns towards the Queen)*
> The voice of heaven decides for you, my sister.
> Your happy brows are now with triumph crowned,
> I bless the Power Divine which thus hath raised you.
> *(She kneels)*
> But in your turn be merciful, my sister;
> Let me not lie before you thus disgraced;
> Stretch forth your hand, your royal hand, to raise,
> Your sister from the depths of her distress.
> (III, 4, 2247–56; p. 72)

It is exactly the kind of appeal that will not win Elisabeth's mercy, since Maria makes the fact of Elisabeth's rule an act of God's choice between two alternatives, a divine favor bestowed on Elisabeth rather than an unquestionable right she exercises by virtue of her own power. If Elisabeth raised Maria from the ground, she would recognize her as an equal.

Elisabeth must emphasize the difference and distance between herself and Maria. Therefore she cannot let herself be moved by Maria in terms of sympathy, the identification with an other in terms of a relation of similarity. Ironically, however, driven by hatred and pride, the two women begin to resemble each other more and more. Describing Elisabeth's composure as she approaches her, Maria hails Elisabeth as another Medusa: "Wenn ihr mich anschaut mit dem Eisesblick, / Schließt sich das Herz mir schaudernd zu" (If you regard me with those icy looks / My shuddering heart contracts itself; III, 4, 2275–76; p. 73). Elisabeth is indeed not moved to pity; instead she accuses Maria of instigating assassination attempts against her. Elisabeth does not want to hear Maria's defense that she was only a victim of fate. Nor does Elisabeth want to listen to Maria's suggestion that the two could peacefully succeed each other in the rulership of England; to her, Maria would always be an instrument of Catholic politics. As their argument heats up, Elisabeth turns her accusations *ad feminam,* calling Maria a whore. At this point Maria's restraint breaks down, and she returns to her initial state of unrestrained passion and open hatred, invoking the basilisk, the reptile with the deadly glance.

> Zum Himmel fliehe leidende Geduld,
> Spreng endlich deine Bande, tritt hervor
> Aus deiner Höhle, langverhaltner Groll
> Und *du,* der dem gereizten Basilisk
> Den Mordblick gab, leg auf die Zunge mir
> Den giftgen Pfeil.
>
>   farewell
> Lamb-hearted resignation, passive patience,
> Fly to thy native heaven; burst at length
> Thy bonds, come forward from thy dreary cave,
> In all thy fury, long suppressed rancor!
> And thou, who to the angered basilisk
> Impart'st the murderous glance, oh, arm my tongue
> With poisoned darts!
>   (III, 4, 2438–43; p. 77)

Invoking the deadly look of the basilisk, the oriental version of Medusa, Maria unleashes the monster's poisonous words, denying the legitimacy of Elisabeth's rule by calling her the daughter of a whore, a bastard, and a swindler.

At the moment Elisabeth turns the argument *ad feminam,* she addresses Leicester as the onlooker of the scene. Later, Maria similarly asserts that she was strengthened in their fight by his presence. The two women cannot look at each other without setting themselves in a scene perceived from a male angle. The manner in which they can represent themselves to each other is subjected to the male gaze. It is this gaze that reduces Maria to an erotic object; in Elisabeth's words: "Es kostet nichts die *allgemeine* Schönheit / Zu sein, als die *gemeine* sein für alle" (She who to all is common, may with ease / Become the common object of applause; III, 4, 2417–18; p. 77). In response, Maria exposes the feminine sex: she insists that although her own history is marked by a guilty sexuality, she at least did not hide this fact. Then she lifts Elisabeth's robe of honor.

> Das Ärgste weiß die Welt von mir und ich
> Kann sagen, ich bin besser als mein Ruf.
> Weh Euch, wenn sie von Euren Taten einst
> Den Ehrenmantel zieht, womit Ihr gleißend
> Die wilde Glut verstohlner Lüste deckt.
> Nicht Ehrbarkeit habt Ihr von Eurer Mutter
> Geerbt, man weiß, um welcher Tugend willen
> Anna von Boleyn das Schafott bestiegen.
>
> The worst of me is known, and I can say,
> That I am better than the fame I bear.
> Woe to you! when, in time to come, the world
> Shall draw the robe of honor from your deeds,
> With which thy arch-hypocrisy has veiled
> The raging flames of lawless, secret lust.
> Virtue was not your portion from your mother;
> Well know we what it was which brought the head
> Of Anne Boleyn to the fatal block.
> (III, 4, 2425–32; p. 77)

The showdown ends in the two antagonists' mutual display of the feminine sex (to put it crudely, the women end up lifting each other's skirt), which is figured as a sight of violence and horror (Medusa), of the uncontrolled sexuality of an adulterous mother (Anne Boleyn), and of the ultimate destabilization in the realm of representation (the interrupted line of inheritance and the decapitation of the king's wife). Maria reveals Elisabeth's rule as a fraud. From birth on Elisabeth's relation to the realm of representations has been one of compensating for what she has *not*: legitimate birth, masculinity, and control over her sexual desires. Marked by ultimate lack—that is, reduced to a mere woman—Elisabeth is unable to pardon Maria and assert her sovereign presence: a woman cannot exercise the royal prerogative of pardon.

The encounter betweent he queens in Act III, Scene 4, reenacts the dilemma prefigured in all the preceding scenes, which raise the issues of Elisabeth as sovereign and Maria's executioner. The vicissitudes of the modern abstract state (i.e., its inability to exercise its sovereign power in the open, its false relation to the realm of representation) are figured in terms of Elisabeth's fundamental double bind, her role as woman and her role as monarch. And it is this double bind that connects the subplot of Elisabeth's potential engagement with the French prince with her position vis-à-vis Maria.

In Act I, Scene 8, Burleigh suggests to Paulet that if he were a truly loyal servant of the state, he would not take his role as Maria's jailor too literally; he would make it possible that his captive be secretly murdered and thus spare Elisabeth the duty of having to execute Maria. For if Elisabeth were openly to become Maria's executioner, she would draw the public's ire.

> Das Richterschwert, womit der Mann sich ziert,
> Verhaßt ists in der Frauen Hand. Die Welt
> Glaubt nicht an die Gerechtigkeit des Weibes,
> Sobald ein Weib das Opfer wird. Umsonst,
> Daß wir, die Richter, nach Gewissen sprachen!
> Sie hat der Gnade königliches Recht.
> Sie muß es brauchen, unerträglich ists,
> Wenn sie den strengen Lauf läßt dem Gesetze!
>
> The sword of justice, which adorns the man,
> Is hateful in a woman's hand; the world
> Will give no credit to a woman's justice
> If woman be the victim. Vain that we,
> The judges, spoke what conscience dictated;
> She has the royal privilege of mercy;
> She must exert it: 'twere not to be borne,
> Should she let justice take its full career.
> (I, 8, 1018–25; p. 35)

Thus Elisabeth is free neither to exercise the male role of judge and executioner nor to pardon Maria. As a woman she has but one choice: she must pity and forgive the other woman. Maria's pardon can never be seen as Elisabeth's assertion of her royal prerogative. She lacks what Burleigh calls the male's "adornment": the phallic sword of the judge.

Elisabeth's reluctance toward the French suitor also illustrates how her double bind as woman and sovereign marks her ultimate weakenss. On the occasion of the French courtship, Kent recounts to Davison the allegorical "Ritterspiel" about the siege and attack of the chaste fortress; he seems to be saying that once Elisabeth agrees to the marriage, England will be relieved of the fear of a return to Catholic rule. If Elisabeth produces an heir, Maria can no longer threaten the Protestant succession to the throne; Elisabeth's acquiescence to the engagement would therefore make Maria's pardon possible. Elisabeth's view of the situation, however, is altogether different. For her, the engagement means degradation from sovereign to mere "housewife" (Bürgersweib).[11] She conceives of her "highest good," her chastity, as the sign of her sovereign freedom, as the compensation for her femininity and lack, a sign she would lose in marriage.[12] Elisabeth acknowledges the "natural" law of woman's subjection to man, but she claims that her relentless work in the service of her country should exempt her from this natural purpose, which "subjects one half of the human race to the other."[13] Thus when the French, after Elisabeth's tentative acceptance of the engagement, plead for Maria, this demand in the name of "Menschlichkeit" (being humane) only reinforces her desire to assert her sovereign power: "Frankreich erfüllt die Freundespflicht, mir wird / Verstattet sein, als Königin zu handeln" (France has discharged her duties as a friend, / I will fulfill my own as England's queen; II, 2, 1243–44; p. 41).

Elisabeth's resistance to feeling pity for Maria is progressively overcoded as both unnatural and inhuman. Unnatural, in the sense that she attempts to act like a man and does not accept her natural position as woman; inhuman, in the sense that she blocks the human sensibility toward a suffering fellow being. Elisabeth's severance from "nature" is also shown in her relation to writing and reading, which again places her on the side of false appearance and clandestine actions (witness her inability to assume responsibility for her signature).

When Elisabeth reads Maria's letter in the assembly of her advisors, she is moved to tears. However, this letter does not move Elisabeth to feel *Mitleid à la* Lessing; she does not see Maria in terms of similarity. Rather, she reads the letter allegorically and is moved by the instability of human destiny, shocked by the recognition of her own potential weakness.

>—verzeiht, Mylords, es schneidet mir ins Herz,
>Wehmut ergreift mich und die Seele blutet,
>Daß Irdisches nicht fester steht, das Schicksal
>Der Menschheit, das entsetzliche, so nahe
>An meinem eignen Haupt vorüberzieht.

>Forgive me, lords, my heart is cleft in twain,
>Anguish possesses me, and my soul bleeds
>To think that earthly goods are so unstable,
>And that the dreadful fate which rules mankind
>Should threaten mine own house, and scowl so near me.
>(II, 4, 1538–42; p. 51)

Shrewsbury, the gentle father figure, who could have been borrowed from a bourgeois tragedy, appeals to her feminine duty to exercise her royal prerogative of pardon.

> Nicht Strenge legte Gott ins weiche Herz
> Des Weibes—Und die Stifter dieses Reichs,
> Die auch dem Weib die Herrscherzügel gaben,
> Sie zeigten an, daß Strenge nicht die Tugend
> Der Könige soll sein in diesem Lande.
>
> God hath not planted rigor in the frame
> Of woman; and the founders of this realm,
> Who to the female hand have not denied
> The reign of government, intend by this
> To show that mercy, not severity,
> Is the best virtue to adorn the crown.
> (II, 3, 1343–47; p. 45)

Of course, Shrewsbury's argument has to be ineffective. When he attempts to excite Elisabeth's pity by recounting the circumstances of Maria's upbringing and explains Maria's shortcomings as feminine weaknesses, he only hardens Elisabeth's determination not to identify with the weak sex.

> Wo sie, die Schwache, sich umrungen sah
> Von heftigdringenden Vasallen, sich
> Dem Mutvollstärksten in die Arme warf
> Wer weiß, durch welcher Künster Macht besiegt?
> Denn ein gebrechlich Wesen ist das Weib.
> ELISABETH. Das Weib ist nicht schwach. Es gibt starke
>   Seelen
> In dem Geschlecht—Ich will in meinem Beisein
> Nichts von der Schwäche des Geschlechtes hören.
>
> When she, a woman, helpless and hemmed in
> By a rude crowd of rebel vassals, sought
> Protection in a powerful chieftain's arms.
> God knows what arts were used to overcome her!
> For woman is a weak and fragile thing.
> ELIZABETH. Woman's not weak; there are heroic souls
> Among the sex; and, in my presence, sir,
> I do forbid to speak of woman's weakness.
> (II, 3, 1369–76; p. 46)

Right after this meeting with her advisors, she tries to persuade Mortimer to murder Maria.

Despite Elisabeth's refusal to acknowledge her feminine weakness, the play makes her feminine weakness increasingly obvious. Her lack of control over the realm of representations becomes increasingly apparent through her attachment and dependence on Leicester. It is he who appeals to her *Weiblichkeit* and persuades her to meet Maria. And in Act IV, even after she has discovered Maria's letter to him, Elisabeth cannot maintain her decision to ban Leicester from her presence and to try him for treason; he quickly deceives her by misrepresenting the events. In her soliloguy preceding the signing of the death sentence, she finally acknowledges the end of sovereign power. She cannot exercise the old-style tyrannical power of the monarch, who determines Truth, Right, and Justice; rather, she has to acknowledge her dependence on the opinion of the crowd.

> Die Meinung muß ich ehren, um das Lob
> Der Menge buhlen, einem Pöbel muß ichs
> Recht machen, dem der Gaukler nur gefällt.
> O der ist noch nicht König, der der Welt
> Gefallen muß! Nur der ists, der bei seinem Tun
> Nach keines Menschen Beifall braucht zu fragen.

> I must respect the people's voice, and strive
> To win the favor of the multitude,
> And please the fancies of a mob, whom naught
> But jugglers' tricks delight. O call not him
> A king who needs must please the world: 'tis he
> Alone, who in his actions does not heed
> The fickle approbation of mankind.
> (IV, 10, 3194–99; p. 102)

As a powerless woman, she has no control over representations and public opinion. Ultimately she blames Maria for depriving her of the laboriously constructed front that was supposed to hide her lack of legitimacy and her stained birth, a situation she condenses in the image of her father's incestuous rape:

> Ein wehrlos Weib! Mit hohen Tugenden
> Muß ich *die Blöße meines Rechts* bedecken,
> Den Flecken meiner fürstlichen Geburt,
> Wodurch der eigne Vater mich geschändet.
> Umsonst bedeck ich ihn—Der Gegener Haß
> Hat ihn *entblößt,* und stellt mir diese Stuart,
> Ein ewig drohendes Gespenst entgegen.

> A poor defenceless woman: I must seek
> To veil the spot in my imperial birth,
> By which my father cast disgrace upon me:
> In vain with princely virtues would I hide it;
> The envious hatred of my enemies
> *Uncovers* it, and places Mary Stuart,
> A threatening fiend, before me ever more!
> (IV, 10, 3221-27; p. 103; my italics)

She kills Maria (she refers to her as a "specter," a double), who has exposed her sex ("entblößt" means literally: "to strip naked") and her impotence and threatened to take away her lover. Ultimately Elisabeth's execution of Maria becomes—thought planned as the final assertion of her sovereign power—an admission of her feminine weakness. Shrewsbury resigns his office, remarking that although he rescued her from the assassination attempt, he has been unable to save her "better half" (V, 15, 4028-29). When she summons Leicester, she learns that he has fled to France. By exposing Elisabeth's rule as ultimately grounded in feminine weakness, Schiller has thoroughly recoded the vicissitudes of sovereign power in terms of gender polarities. And if one considers the powerful mise-en-scène of Maria's execution, it becomes clear that both women work in tandem to assert sovereign power as "true" masculinity. Although in terms of plot the drama appears to be a "conflict" between Maria and Elisabeth, on the discursive level of the text the conflicting parties share a common function. They participate equally in the construction of a specific form of masculine subjectivity.

How does the execution figure with regard to Maria? If Elisabeth is ultimately morally condemned, how does Maria achieve her moral victory? What is the nature of Maria's reformation? Although my reading attributes to the encounter between the queens a crucial function for the play's closure and overall cathartic effect, it certainly does not locate in this scene the origin of Maria's reformation.[14] Instead, I suggest that the main key to her reformation can be found in her incarceration.

This drama about freedom is set in enclosed spaces, and the main character is detained in prison. Mortimer refers to his English upbringing as "imprisonment," and Leicester describes his relationship to Elisabeth as being held "in chains." It is through Maria's changes, however, that the true meaning of "prison" is established. The traditional function of the prison was to detain the body of the accused until the trial, which would produce the truth of the crime and display this truth in conjunction with the sovereign's power in the spectacle of a public punishment. Traditionally only debtors' prisons held the bodies of the accused after their guilt had been established. During the late eighteenth century, however, the function and architecture of prisons were radically altered. From a place of confinement, the prison became an institution of examination and reform: the individual's isolation was intended to establish the truth of the individual "case" and aid the process of investigation; once this knowledge had been established, the incarceration replaced corporeal punishment as a place where the individual's soul and body were disciplined and reprogrammed.[15]

It is curious that Schiller, in criticizing the abstract modern state in which kings, gods, and courts are no longer visible, produces a play that echoes this critique of an abstract state apparatus but does not revert to the old-style spectacle and instead produces a new spectacle, one that puts on stage the modern penal institution.[16] As early as Act I, we see Maria as somebody who, in her isolation from worldly splendor, has learned to reflect on her history. She internalizes Paulet's reproach that she has seduced too many men (I, 4, 264–67). In her first appearance on stage, on the anniversary of her husband's murder, she utters words of remorse and acknowledges that she is pursued by the specter of this crime. Despite her Catholicism, she seems unable to assuage her guilt by the absolution for her crime she has obtained from the church. Nor is her conscience calmed by her servant Kennedy, who depicts her crime as a sin of her distant youth and suggests that she was seduced by some supernatural power and magic potions. Rejecting all possible excuses, she takes full responsibility for her history and guilt, which she attributes to her feminine weakness alone: "Seine Künste waren keine andre, / Als seine Männerkraft und meine Schwachheit" (All the arts he used / Were man's superior strength and woman's weakness; I, 4, 331–32; p. 15).

Although historically Mary's complicity in Darnley's murder has never been established, Schiller's play passes unequivocal judgment on the character.[17] Maria's anamnesis and remorse focus on the murder of her husband, an altogether different crime from the one of treason against Elisabeth of which the court has found her guilty. Thus, the play juxtaposes external and internal guilt, a true and a false crime. At the end of the play, the incarcerated Kurl becomes insane when he learns of Maria's execution. His overwhelming guilt because of his false testimony reinforces the function of the prison as the institution that can produce the truth of the individual. The prison becomes the place for the "construction" of the individual in terms of an inquiry into all the specific circumstances as well as the personal motives that led to the crime, that is, into the particular "case."[18] The findings of the court ("guilty" or "not guilty" of an external crime) are discredited and opposed to the truth-producing power of the prison.

If the modern penal institution and its associated techniques of examination were invoked merely to establish whether the accused committed the crime, the play could be over in the first act. But this is not the focus of the play; as Schiller wrote in a letter to Goethe dated April 26, 1799: "It [the material of Maria Stuart] seems particularly qualified for the Euripidean method, for this method consists of the complete representation of the situation. For I can see the possibility of laying aside the entire court procedure together with all the politics."[19] Since Schiller's interest lies with "the complete representation of the situation," the play, like the prison, has the function of disclosing why and how the crime was committed in the first place: What was behind Maria's murder of Darnley?

In Act I, Scene 4, Maria attributes her crime to female weakness, but only in the confession scene prior to her execution does she formulate her "gravest guilt" in its entirety. Although from the beginning she sees herself as a weak and sensual woman, she still hopes for her release from prison and places her hopes in her physical beauty when she sends her portrait to Leicester. Thus, in the scene just before her encounter with Elisabeth, she finds herself suddenly released from prison to walk in a castle park; she rejoices at the sight of open nature, and a small boat kindles her hope she might be able to bribe the boatsman to take her to France. When her servant, Hannah Kennedy, directs her attention to the hidden guards and warns her not to cherish false hopes, she insists that her freedom is imminent.

> Nein, gute Hanna. Glaub mir, nicht umsonst
> Ist meines Kerkers Tor geöffnet worden.
> Die kleine Gunst ist mir des größen Glücks
> Verkünderin. Ich irre nicht. Es ist
> Der Liebe tätge Hand, der ich sie danke.
> Lord Leicesters mächtgen Arm erkenn ich drin.
> Allmählich will man mein Gefängnis weiten,
> Durch Kleineres zum Größern mich gewöhnen,
> Bis ich das Antlitz dessen endlich schaue,
> Der mir die Bande löst auf immerdar.

> No, gentle Hannah! Trust me, not in vain
> My prison gates are opened. This small grace
> Is harbinger of greater happiness.
> No! I mistake not; 'tis the active hand
> Of love to which I owe this kind indulgence.
> I recognize in this the mighty arm
> Of Leicester. They will by degrees expand
> My prison; will accustom me, through small
> To greater liberty, until at last
> I shall behold the face of him whose hand
> Will dash my fetters off, and that forever.
> (III, 1, 2119–28; p. 68)

In spite of hymnic overtones of this passage, the savior she imagines is Leicester, the freedom she anticipates a life with her lover in France.

In the scene immediately after the disillusioning encounter with Elisabeth, however, Mortimer approaches her, not to bring her any message from Leicester, but on his own behalf. He announces that the conspiracy for her rescue is under way and that he is willing to risk his life and even kill his own uncle in order to free her. Maria is shocked and tries to withdraw from this fanatic release of violent impulses. But for Mortimer the violent act of freeing her is intimately linked with his desire to possess her, and at this point he harasses her and attempts to rape her. Maria is saved from her "savior" only because of the turmoil over the assassination attempt on Elisabeth.

This scene forces Maria to recognize that as long as she conceives of her freedom in physical terms, as a release from the incarceration at Fotheringhay, she will remain the erotic object of men, unleashing their violent passions of love and hatred. She cannot be physically free as a sensual, beautiful woman if her alternative is death or rape. She is forced to reinterpret her prison and her freedom. Thus, in the scene before her execution, the transfigured Maria admonishes her weeping attendants:

> Was klagt ihr? Warum weint ihr? Freuen solltet
> Ihr Euch mit mir, daß meiner Leiden Ziel
> Nun endlich naht, daß meine Bande fallen,
> Mein Kerker aufgeht, und die frohe Seele sich
> Auf Engelsflügeln schwingt zur ewgen Freiheit.

> Why these complaints? Why weep ye? Ye should rather
> Rejoice with me, that now at length the end
> Of my long woe approaches; that my shackles
> Fall off, my prison opens, and my soul
> Delighted mounts on seraph's wings, and seeks
> The land of everlasting liberty.
> (V, 6, 3479-83; p. 112)

In this passage she takes up her previous image of liberation (the loosening of the bonds and the release from prison), except that here she refers no longer to her escape to France with her lover but to her apotheosis. Her true prison is her own body, and the freedom to which she aspires is that of pure spirituality, her beautiful soul released from the prison of her body.[20]

When Melvil administers communion and hears her last confession, she confesses that she has been driven by hatred toward her opponent and that she still feels guilt for the murder of her husband. But her gravest sin she formulates in the following words:

> Ach, nicht durch *Haß* allein, durch sündge *Liebe*
> Noch mehr hab ich das höchste Gut beleidigt.
> Das eitle Herz ward zu dem Mann gezogen,
> Der treulos mich verlassen und betrogen!

MELVIL. Bereuest du die Schuld, und hat dein Herz
Vom eitlen Abgott sich zu Gott gewendet?
MARIA. Es war der schwerste Kampf, den ich bestand,
Zerissen ist das letzte irdsche Band.

Ah! not alone through hate; through lawless love
Have I still more abused the sovereign god.
My heart was vainly turned towards the man
Who left me in misfortune, who deceived me.
MELVIL. Repentest thou of the sin? And hast thou turned
Thy heart, from this idolatry, to God?
MARY. It was the hardest trial I have passed;
This last of earthly bonds is torn asunder.
    (V, 7, 3684–91; p. 118)

The true transformation of Maria consists in her acknowledgment of her "sinful love," her sexuality as her crime, and in the renunciation of her body. Only once she abandons her body can she be transformed from a beautiful woman, defined in terms of physical appearance, into a beautiful soul. She abandons her idolatrous love of Leicester and turns to God. The transfigured Maria turns away from the gaze of men and subjects herself entirely to the gaze of God.

  Leicester, until this moment the fraudulent stand-in for the (male) gaze, is left in despair. He is unable to carry on his deceit; that is, he is unable to attend Maria's execution and thereby free himself from the suspicion of having been her lover. Against the threat of "melting away in womanly compassion" (in zartem Mitleid weibisch hinzuschmelzen; V, 10, 3853), he appeals to the reassuring stiffness granted by the sight of horror:

Verstumme Mitleid, Augen, werdet Stein,
Ich seh sie fallen, ich will Zeuge sein.
*(Er geht mit entschloßnem Schritt der Türe zu, durch
 welche*
Maria gegangen, bleibt auf der Mitte des Weges stehen)
Umsonst! Umsonst! Mich faßt der Hölle Grauen,
Ich kann, ich kann das Schreckliche nicht schauen,
Kann sie nicht sterben sehen—

Pity be dumb; mine eyes be petrified!
I'll see—I will be witness of her fall.
*(He advances with resolute steps towards the door through
which* MARY *passed; but stops suddenly half way.)*
No! No! The terrors of all hell possess me.

> I cannot look upon the dreadful deed;
> I cannot see her die!
> (V, 10, 3859–63; p. 124)

He is not turned into stone, but his power vanishes and he is unable voluntarily to witness Maria's decapitation. Nevertheless he has to hear the event and hallucinate the scene of horror step by step.[21]

> Nur schluchzen hör ich, und die Weiber weinen—
> Sie wird entkleidet—Horch! Der Schemel wird
> Gerückt—Sie kniet aufs Kissen—legt das Haupt
> *(Nachdem er die letzten Worte mit steigender Angst gesprochen, und eine Weile inne gehalten, sieht man ihn plötzlich mit einer zuckenden Bewegung zusammenfallen, und ohnmächtig niedersinken, zugleich erschallt von unten herauf ein dumpfes Getöse von Stimmen, welches lange forthallt.)*
>
> And sobs and women's moans are all I hear.
> Now, they undress her; they remove the stool;
> She kneels upon the cushion; lays her head
> *(Having spoken these last words, and paused awhile, he is seen with a convulsive motion suddenly to shrink and faint away; a confused hum of voices is heard at the same moment from below, and continues for some time.)*
> (V, 10, 3873–75; pp. 124–25)

Castration and decapitation are intimately linked in the perception of the audience: they see Leicester's inability to move to the scene of execution, his "melting away in female pity" and his final collapse on stage, and this collapse is accompanied by the sound track of Maria's decapitation. Leicester, the fraudulent lover and stand-in for the male gaze, is punished with the hallucinated vision of the decapitated woman. The scene of horror, the female sex, which he had already once provoked, this time exercises its annihilating power on him. When "he is seen with a convulsive motion suddenly to shrink and faint away," his castration on stage is substituted for the decapitation of Maria. The hallucinated spectacle of the execution is turned into a powerful image of deterrence.[22]

In terms of the succession of scenes toward the end of the play, between Maria's transfiguration into a beautiful soul, her exit in order to leave the prison of her body, and the play's last four scenes in Elisabeth's office, in which the results of the administrative apparatus reveal their course, the play focuses on Leicester's gaze and collapse. Through the character of Leicester, this scene is connected back to the encounter between the queens.[23] In Act III, Scene 4, the course of history is rendered graphic in terms of the ultimately destabilizing force of female sexuality; in Act V, Scene 10, this "visibility" is recalled as the ultimate threat to the unity and stability of the male ego. The function of the second scene consists in the mobilization of the audience's defense mechanisms. For the audience the sight of horror is both explicitly invoked in all its terror and at the same time kept at a safe distance through the mediation of Leicester. The figure of Medusa is restored to her full ambiguity: terrifying but also reasssuring to the extent that it structures anxiety and links it with a perception.[24]

If the genres of the bourgeois tragedy and epistolary novel could be characterized as anti-theatrical rejections of the spectacle in favor of an internalization and an identification with the fictional events in the mental cinema, Classical German tragedy gives new value and power to the spectacle. This new spectacle is, however, not one of amusement and distraction such as, say, the display of freaks or acrobats in a fair, nor is it one of torture or execution, or of a royal procession, in which an exceptional body displays its power over the undisciplined, anonymous masses. The concrete body of the actor in this new spectacle is of no interest. The spectacle itself addresses not the crowd but each individual member of the audience as a representative of mankind. The new spectacle accomplishes a movement of externalization and internalization that can only come into being once the masses have already been disciplined into individuals.

This analysis of Schiller's *Maria Stuart* as an example of classical tragedy has also addressed the position of the ideal woman with regard to ritual and spectacle and thereby examined those representational strategies that serve to discipline male subjects for the state. In this regard, Weimar Classicism seems to pose a certain paradox: on the one hand, by the last decade of the eighteenth century the ideology of a fundamental gender polarity pervades discourse on language and the arts to an unprecedented degree while, on the other hand, the literature of Weimar Classicism furnishes numerous "strong" female figures (or even amazons) who do not share the virtues of feminine passivity and receptivity celebrated in aesthetic theory.[25] Yet my reading has demonstrated how this seeming contradiction is resolved through the polarized representation of femininity as (1) a threatening corporeality and sexuality (Medusa) and (2) the ideal of a harmonious autonomous appearance (beautiful soul). Both aspects serve to organize male subjectivity vis-à-vis representations: the former prevents identification with the theatrical illusion; the latter provides a model for a unified self.

NOTES

1. In my reading of *Maria Stuart*, I refer to relatively few of the interpretations of the play, since a fairly recent survey of the major interpretations can be found in Gert Sautermeis-

ter's "Maria Stuart," in Walter Hinderer, ed., *Schillers Dramen: Neue Interpretationen* (Stuttgart: Reclam, 1979), pp. 174–216.

2. See Benno von Wiese, *Friedrich Schiller* (Stuttgat: Metzler, 1959), pp. 721, 727–28. For an excellent study of late eighteenth-century relations between Enlightenment rationality, aesthetics, and religion, see Heinz-Otto Burger, " 'Eine Idee, die noch in keines Menschen Sinn gekommen ist': Ästhetische Religion in deutscher Klassik und Romantik," in Albert Fuchs and Helmut Motekat, eds., *Stoffe, Formen, Strukturen: Studien zur deutschen Literatur*. Festschrift for Hans Heinrich Borcherdt (Munich: Hueber, 1962), pp. 1–20.

3. "Über den Gebrauch des Chors in der Tragödie," preface to *Die Braut von Messina*, in Schiller, *Sämtliche Werke* (Munich: Hanser, 1984), 2: 820. Dieter Borchmeyer sets out from the same problem in *Tragödie und Öffentlichkeit: Schillers Dramaturgie im Zusammenhang seiner ästhetisch-politischen Theorie und der rhetorischen Tradition* (Munich: Fink, 1973), pp. 198–209. He likewise takes Schiller's preface to *Die Braut von Messina* as the crucial link between the *Aesthetic Education* and Schiller's dramatic praxis.

4. Helmut Koopmann, *Friedrich Schiller, II: 1794–1805* (Stuttgart: Metzler, 1977), p. 61.

5. Roger Ayrault, "La figure de Mortimer dans *Marie Stuart* et la conception du drame historique chez Schiller," *Etudes Germaniques* 14 (1959), 313–24, reads Mortimer as representing a mistaken, idolatrous Catholicism, a contrasting foil that Schiller needed to prevent a confounding of Maria's spiritualized, "true" religiosity with Catholicism per se.

6. See Mortimer's response to the meeting of the two queens, which he hallucinates seeing: "Ich hörte alles. / Du hast gesiegt! Du tratst sie in den Staub, / Du warst die Königin, sie der Verbrecher. / Ich bin entzückt von deinem Mut, ich bete / Dich an, wie eine Göttin groß und herrlich / Erscheinst Du mir in diesem Augenblick" (I heard all— / Thine is the palm; —thou trod'st her to the dust!— / Though wast the queen, she was the malefactor;— / I am transported with thy noble courage;— / Yes! I adore thee; like a Deity, / My sense is dazzled by thy heavenly beams; III, 6, 2469–73, p. 79 in *Historical Dramas by Friedrich Schiller*, trans. Samuel Taylor Coleridge, E. A. Aytoun, and A. J. Morrison [London, New York, Chicago: Anthropological Society, 1901]). All references to the English translation are to this edition.

7. See Maria Stuart's words when she hands Paulet her letter for Elisabeth: "Man hat mich / Vor ein Gericht von Männern vorgefordert, / Die ich als meinesgleichen nicht erkenne, / Zu denen ich kein Herz mir fassen kann. / Elisabeth ist meines Stammes, meines / Geschlechts und Ranges—Ihr allein, der Schwester, / Der Königin, der Frau kann ich mich öffnen" (I have been summoned / Before a court of men, whom I can ne'er / Acknowledge as my peers—of men to whom / My heart denies its confidence. The queen / Is of my family, my rank, my sex; / To her alone—a sister, queen, and woman— / Can I unfold my heart; I, 2, 170–76, p. 10).

8. See II, 8, 1779–93: "Man preist mich glücklich—wüßte man, was es / Für Ketten sind, um die man mich beneidet— / Nachdem ich zehen bittre Jahre lang / Dem Götzen ihrer Eitelkeit geopfert, / Mich jedem Wechsel ihrer Sultanslaunen / Mit Sklavendemut unterwarf, das Spielzeug / Des kleinen grillenhaften Eigensinns, / Geliebkost jetzt von ihrer Zärtlichkeit, / Und jetzt mit sprödem Stolz zurückgestoßen, / Wie ein Gefangener vom Argusblick / Der Eifersucht gehütet, ins Verhör / Genommen wie ein Knabe, wie ein Diener / Gescholten—O die Sprache hat kein Wort / Für diese Hölle!" (They call me happy! did they only know / What the chains are, for which they envy me! / When I had sacrificed ten bitter years / To the proud idol of her vanity; / Submitted with slave's humility? To every change of her despotic fancies. / The plaything of each little wayward whim. / At times by seeming tenderness caressed, / as oft repulsed with proud and cold disdain; / Alike tormented by her grace and rigor; / Watched like a prisoner by the Argus eyes / Of jealousy; examined like a schoolboy, / And railed at like a servant. Oh, no tongue / Can paint this hell; pp. 58–59).

9. See II, 8, 1923–20: "Weg mit der Verstellung! Handelt öffentlich! / Verteidigt als ein

Ritter die Geliebte, / Kämpft einen edeln Kampf um sie. Ihr seid / Herr ihrer Schlösser, / Sie ist euch oft dahin gefolgt. Dort zeigt ihr / Den Mann! Sprecht als ihr Gebieter! haltet sie / Verwahrt, bis sie die Stuart freigegeben!'' (Away with feigning—act an open part, / And, like a loyal knight, protect your fair; / Fight a good fight for her! You know you are / Lord over the person of the queen of England, / Oft hath she thither followed you—then show / That you're a man; then speak as master; keep her / Confined till she release the Queen of Scots; p. 62).

10. Peter Utz, "Auge, Ohr, Herz: Schillers Dramaturgie der Sinne im Jahrhundert der Aufklärung,'' *Jahrbuch der deutschen Schillergesellschaft* 22 (1978), 62–97 interprets the dynamics of the gaze as the dichtotomy between the look and speech of the encounter of the queens in the following terms: "Because Maria wants to understand her subjection to Elisabeth merely as a political act she prematurely elevates what she sees onto the level of political speech and simultaneously denies that Elisabeth has a 'heart.' . . . Speech becomes a barrier between eye and heart and turns the eye into a cold mirror that merely reflects the public sphere of the court and its moral values. Only the silent spectator can escape this pragmatic paradox. But neither Maria nor Elisabeth is forced to legitimate herself. In the escalation of the 'affect' in the dispute, the gaze is charged with the dominant morality in the same degree as the dispute is shifted from the political to the moral level, where finally the erotic competition of the women erupts'' (pp. 85–86).

11. See II, 2, 1207–11: "Hat die Königin doch nichts / Voraus vor dem gemeinen Bürgerweibe! / das gleiche Zeichen weist auf gleiche Pflicht, / Auf gleiche Dienstbarkeit—der Ring macht Ehen, / Und Ringe sinds, die eine Kette machen'' (In this a queen has not / One privilege above all other women. / This common token marks one common duty, / One common servitude; the ring denotes / Marriage, and 'tis of rings a chain is formed.; p. 40).

12. See II, 2, 1166–71: "Auch meine jungfräuliche Freiheit soll ich, / Mein höchstes Gut, hingeben für mein Volk, / Und der Gebieter wird mir aufgedrungen. / Er zeigt mir dadurch an, daß ich ihm nur / Ein Weib bin, und ich meinte doch, regiert / Zu haben, wie ein Mann und wie ein König'' (And I must offer up my liberty, my greatest good, / To satisfy my people. Thus they'd force / A lord and master on me. 'Tis by this / I see that I am nothing but a woman / In their regard; and yet methought that I / Had governed like a man, and like a king; p. 39). For a study of the historical Elisabeth I, see Louis Adrian Montrose, "The Elisabethan Subject and the Spenserian Text,'' in Patricia Parker and David Quint, eds., *Literary Theory/Renaissance Texts* (Baltimore: Johns Hopkins University Press, 1986), pp. 303–40.

13. The phrasing of these lines is quite interesting if one considers that King Friedrich II of Prussia (r. 1740–86) is famous for referring to himself as the first servant of the state: "Doch eine Königin, die ihre Tage / Nicht ungenützt in müßiger Beschauung / Verbringt, die unverdrossen, unermüdet, / Die schwerste aller Pflichten übt, die sollte / Von dem Naturzweck ausgenommen sein, / Der eine Hälfte des Geschlechts der Menschen / Der andern unterwürfig macht—'' (But yet a queen who hath not spent her days / In fruitless, idle contemplation; who, / Without murmur, indefatigably / Performs the hardest of all duties; she / Should be exempted from the natural law / Which doth ordain one half of human kind / Shall ever be subservient to the other; II, 2, 1178–84, pp. 39–40). See also Rudolf Vierhaus, "Politisches Bewußtsein in Deutschland vor 1789,'' in Jürgen Bolten, ed., *Schillers Briefe über die Ästhetische Erziehung* (Frankfurt: Suhrkamp, 1984), pp. 135–60: "A remarkable phenomenon: In his two political wills from 1752 and 1768 the Prussian Monarch claims to have pursued the 'first' duty of a citizen (*citoyen*) to serve his fatherland (*patrie*) and to be useful to his fellow citizens (*concitoyens*)'' (p. 142).

14. Sautermeister ("Maria Stuart,'' cf. fn. 1) argues that Maria's turning point in becoming a "beautiful soul'' lies in the acknowledgment and liberation of her repressed affects: "The liberation from noble morality is here the liberation from self-imposed servitude. In this play Schiller's pyschology explodes the classical mean, demystifies the ethics of self-discipline, of the acceptance of suffering and all-forgiving humanism, and reveals in

this a good portion of self-enslavement and self-deception; finally he exposes the dregs of anger and vengefulness that can accumulate behind exaggerated tolerance and heroic love for one's fellow human beings. . . . When Maria finally acknowledges her aggressions, she points at the origin of injustice and suppression and transforms a suffering self-oppression into an active presentation of self'' (p. 194).

15. See Michel Foucault, *Discipline and Punish: The Birth of the Prison*, trans. Alan Sheridan (New York: Random House, 1979).
16. For an excellent historical survey of the eighteenth-century homologies between the aesthetic/poetological and juridical arguments about the spectacle of deterrence, see Carsten Zelle, "Strafen und Schrecken," *Jahrbuch der deutschen Schillergesellschaft* 28 (1984), 76–103.
17. See note in *Sämtliche Werke*, vol. 2, p. 1262.
18. See Foucault, *Discipline and Punish*, pp. 225–28.
19. Quoted in *Sämtliche Werke*, vol. 2, p. 1259.
20. See Foucault, *Discipline and Punish*, p. 29: "If the surplus power possessed by the king gives rise to the duplication of the body, has not the surplus power exercised on the subjected body of the condemned man given rise to another type of duplication? That of a 'non-corporal,' a 'soul,' as Malby called it. The history of this 'micro-physics' of punitive power would then be a genealogy or an element in a genealogy of the modern 'soul.' Rather than seeing this soul as the reactivated remnants of an ideology, one would see it as the present correlative of a certain technology of power over the body. It would be wrong to say that the soul is an illusion, or an ideological effect. On the contrary, it exists, it has a reality, it is produced permanently around, on, within the body by the functioning of a power that is exercised on those punished—and, in a more general way, on those one supervises, trains and corrects, over madmen, children at home and at school, the colonized, over those who are stuck at a machine and supervised for the rest of their lives. This is the historical reality of this soul, which, unlike the soul represented by Christian theology, is not born in sin and subjected to punishment, but is rather born out of methods of punishment, supervision and constraint."
21. Two recent interpretations of *Maria Stuart* also focus on this scene: Benjamin Bennett, *Modern Drama and German Classicism* (Ithaca: Cornell University Press, 1986) sees in Leicester's hallucination of Maria's decapitation the representation of modern consciousness and an instance in which the play becomes self-reflective and appeals to the audience's constructive participation in establishing its "wholeness" and "identity": "The locked room in which he [Leicester] is compelled to experience Mary's execution (V.10) is an example of what I have called phrenographic theater; it represents his entrapment within himself, his inability to undertake any outward-directed action and so escape from the self-conscious circle of his own thoughts. And that it is this scene by which the execution is represented on stage indicates that we are meant to think of Mary's death, at least in one aspect, as an event within Leicester's mind, as the disaster of self-consciousness, as the final collapse into utter dispair of a fruitlessly self-preoccupied mental attitude'' (p. 200). Peter Utz's interpretation of *Maria Stuart* in his article "Auge, Ohr und Herz" (fn. 10) likewise locates in this scene the cathartic effect and political message for the audience. He claims that the eye is devalorized as the instrument of a cold state rationality and that it is through the ear that finally Leicester's heart is struck (see p. 87). In that sense Leicester's collapse has to be seen in contrast to Elisabeth's composure; it indicates that the realm of political power is always closed to the "heart." For the audience this scene is supposed to bring together the dissociated visual and auditory realms and lead the spectator to a critical weighing of both (p. 84).
22. See Foucault, "Generalized Punishment," in *Discipline and Punish*, pp. 73–103; and for Germany, see Gerd Kleinheyer, "Wandlungen des Deliquentenbildes in den Strafrechtsordnungen des 18. Jahrhunderts," in Bernhard Fabian, Wilhelm Schmidt-Biggemann, Rudolf Vierhaus, eds., *Deutschlands kulturelle Entfaltung: Die Neubestimmung des Menschen* (Munich: Kraus International Publications, 1980), pp. 227–46.

23. Dieter Borchmeyer ("Die theatralische Sichtbarkeit der Staatsaktion in *Maria Stuart*," in *Tragödie und Öffentlichkeit*, cf. fn. 3) concludes that Schiller attempts to render the machinations of the abstract state apparatus "visible" through the psychological analysis of the two women, mainly as their pysches are exposed in the encounter of the two queens: "In the fight of the two queens that Schiller as the 'decisive hour' (line 2176) of the action had placed exactly into the middle of the play the political tension of lengthy historical events is heightened and indistinguishably fused with human conflicts and thus assumes extreme theatrical efficacy. The political contrast is simultaneously revealed as female rivalry, the public is connected with the most intimate sphere. Schiller has succeeded in 'spinning the cold, sterile action of the state out of the human heart and thereby binding it back to the human heart,' as he had set himself the task in the preface to *Fiesco*. In *Maria Stuart* he conjures up a state of the world in which individual passion still entails worldly, historical relevance and the gravest political implications" (p. 206). Although my reading of the play agrees with Borchneyer's description of the function of the scene, i.e., of "rendering visible" invisible political forces and threats, I do not see Schiller's solution as a flight into a distanced past, in which the great individual could wield power and mark the course of history. Rather, I would read this scene as a topical response to his contemporary situation, a situation of an expanding state apparatus, on the one hand, and the threat of public violence on the other, which was encoded in terms of late eighteenth-century gender ideology: a situation of social peace is portrayed in terms of a blissful domesticity based on gender polarity, one of political upheaval and unrest in terms of women invading the public realm, turning into beasts and assuming the threatening aspects of a castrating Medusa or the Thracian maenads dismembering Orpheus. One example would be Schiller's poem about the French Revolution, "Die Glocke," which refers to the revolutionary violence in the passage: "Da werden Weiber werden zu Hyänen / Und treiben mit Entsetzen Scherz, / Noch zuckend, mit des Panthers Zähnen, / Zerreißen sie des Feindes Herz" (And women become hyenas / And jokingly provoke horror, / Still twiching with the panther's teeth / They tear apart the enemy's heart; *Sämtliche Werke* I, p. 440).
24. For a brilliant study of the function of the sight of the Medusa in the French Revolution and in 1848, see Neil Hertz, "Medusa's Head: Male Hysteria under Political Pressure," in Hertz, *The End of the Line: Essays on Psychoanalysis and the Sublime* (New York: Columbia University Press, 1985), pp. 161–93.
25. A prime example of this seeming contradiction is Goethe's Dorothea (in the epic *Hermann und Dorothea*), who represents the modern housewife seeking fulfillment in unpaid domestic labor, but who also—otherwise she would not have been worthy of becoming a literary character according to Goethe—committed the heroic (for Wilhelm von Humboldt "appalling") act of killing a soldier in defense of her female companions. For an extensive historical study of late eighteenth-century gender polarization, see Karin Hausen, "Die Polarisierung der 'Geschlechtscharaktere: Eine Spiegelung der Dissoziation von Erwerbs- und Familienleben," in Werner Conze, ed., *Sozialgeschichte der Familie in der Neuzeit Europas* (Stuttgart: Klett, 1976), pp. 363–93. For the role of women in the administrative reforms of an expanding state apparatus in the late eighteenth century with its fundamental changes in the educational system, see Friedrich Kittler, "Mütterlichkeit und Beamtentum," in Kittler, *Aufschreibesysteme, 1800/1900* (Munich: Fink, 1985), pp. 59–75.

KLEIST'S *THE BROKEN JUG:* THE PLAY OF SEXUAL DIFFERENCE

DAVID E. WELLBERY

A border—thin, wavering, porous, and uncertain—divides our lives: the limit between waking and sleep, between reality and dream. Every account of our accountability, every attribution of responsibility, every justice and judgment, let us say, keeping in mind the juridical dimension of the drama under discussion here, requires that this limit be clearly marked, that the distinction between waking and consciousness be rigorously made and maintained. Thus, it is precisely at this limit that the modern philosophy of the subject—the philosophy of responsible rational agency—establishes its bastion: Descartes, in the *Discourse on Method* and the *Meditations*, grants everything to the world of dream that could possible be granted in order, by virtue of this enormous con—cession, to demarcate the line across which dream cannot pass, the line circumscribing the wakefulness of the *ego cogito*. Some hundred and seventy years later Fichte, in his *Vocation of Man*, pursues the same strategy, allowing that all my knowledge might be dream in order to disclose that which can't be dreamt and which every dream presupposes, the self-creating I. For modernity, everything depends on being able to say: I am wakeful. I am wakeful, therefore I am.

    This, however, is the statement that literature subverts with the subterfuge of fiction. With only slight exaggeration one could say that literature, at least since Romanticism, constitutes itself by disturbing the distinction between consciousness and dream, by crossing the limit, passing from one side of the line to the other. This passage, which literature makes and is, can be performed in two ways. On the one hand, the literary text can transport us into the world of dream, illuminating its wonders, as it were, with the light of wakefulness. Such is the passage of Novalis's *Heinrich von Ofterdingen* or of Proust's *Recherche*, novels which both begin with their protagonist's gradual glide into sleep. These are novels, I want to claim, of oneiric knowledge, novels that reveal beneath the rigid and reified forms of conscious life the flowing—indeed, liquid—shapes of a forgotten past, a forgotten love and loss. On the other hand, the literary passage can be made in the opposite direction, carrying us from dream to wakefulness, but in such a way that the dream lingers on in our waking lives as a kind of opaque and surd remainder, a mystery that blocks us, that we stumble over and obsessively recur to, never fully knowing as a result who this stranger is who, having dreamt so, we have become. This is a literature not of knowledge and discovery, but, rather, of oneiric enigma. Its protagonists are introduced to us not as they drift into sleep, but rather in the rupture of an awakening that is never fully accomplished. "As he awakened one morning out of troubled dreams Gregor Samsa found himself transformed into a monstrous insect"—this the famous first sentence of Kafka's *Metamorphosis*. It is a sentence that conforms exactly to the theory of Kafka's contemporary Freud, for whom the dream is not so much a marvelous landscape as the mystery—fragmented, distorted, and in the last analysis uninterpretable—that haunts the jumbled narratives of his patients. And, of course, it is with Freud that our Cartesian confidence in the thoroughly wakeful subject—our confidence in consciousness—comes to its theoretical end.

Kleist, whose influence on Kafka is well-known, belongs to the second branch of the literary tradition I have sketched here. His is a literature of enigma, and nowhere is this more evident than in the opening scene of *The Broken Jug*. Adam, a small-town judge, awakens. The night has left his physical and ethical integrity damaged; he's as broken as the jug which lends the play its title, and this because, as we shall see, the fractures that split both subject and vessel are one. In his dialogue with Licht, whose name suggests the light of analytical reason, he awkwardly attempts to regain his composure, to mend the fragmentation that has left him a stranger even to himself. But every lie he tells—just like the distortions Freud found in his patients' and in his own narrated dreams—betrays the truth it seeks to hide. "I stumbled and fell, banging my head against the iron goat that ornaments the stove," he tells the probingly skeptical and self-interested clerk. "My pants tore as I grabbed them for support and I smashed my face right there, against the goat's protruding nose." Of course, he's right. The night has been the night of his fall, in every sense of the word, and what he fell against and what wounded him was the sexual desire which that goat, for centuries, has symbolized. That goat which Adam, with his club- and therefore cloven foot, himself is: satyr and satan, pagan and Christian figures for the split condition of desire. No less twistedly true is his claim a little later that the cat has had her litter in his wig: in other words, that the bodily facts of reproduction—of birth and sexuality —have soiled the judicial authority the wig represents. Awake now, Adam continues to live the previous night's dream, a dream in which his own desire has mumbled its confused truth. And his waking language, overdetermined by the oneiric investments of that desire, is as strange to him as the wounded body he can no longer recognize, even in Licht's mirror, as his own. The judicial word—the word that more than any other should be spoken by an agent rational and responsible, by a waking subject—has become club-footed and self-condemnatory. Torn pants, protruding goat's nose . . . indeed.

The scene of the biblical Adam's awakening was well—known to the eighteenth century into which Kleist was born. Buffon's *Histoire naturelle*, in a famous passage, had painted the scene in tones of pristine perfection: the newly created Adam testing in sequence each of the five senses, delighting in the marriage between self and world the senses mediate, dis-

Heinrich von Kleist, from the Bildabteilung, Deutsches Literaturarchiv of the Schiller Nationalmuseum, Marbach, Germany.
Reprinted with permission.

covering then, lying beside him, a being—so Buffon writes—"similar to himself," and therewith the sixth sense of sexuality that will mediate his marriage with Eve. Buffon's is a picture of Enlightenment optimism, of a worldly paradise purified of sin, of a recovered and affirmed sensuality; and it is a picture that rests on the adequacy by similitude that, for the Enlightenment, links world and representation, woman and man. But Kleist's Adam awakens after the night with Eve, after the night Buffon had veiled in discretion, the night of sexuality's darkness, the night of fracture and difference which has split the matinal purity of the Enlightenment paradise. And in this post-lapsarian world, the world of the drama, the light of similarity (think of Licht's mirror) can no longer guarantee the order of nature. Reason has become here a persecutory instrument, cunning, dissimulating, and self-seeking. And Adam will finally be banished from the stage, flogged by the very wig of judicial authority his animality had stained. The old goat becomes a scapegoat; Enlightened reason asserts its rule only by driving divided desire from its administered and artificial garden.

The German word for "administer" is *verwalten*, based on the stem *walten*, "to rule." We hear these terms in the name of Walter, the representative of the district court in Utrecht who has come to Huisom to inspect the files and functioning of Adam's small-town justice. He is an administrator in the strict sense: the representative of an abstract law, the specialist in procedure, the surveyor of accounts. Here we see a second dimension of the complex reversal of the Enlightenment Kleist undertakes in this play, for Enlightenment, in its institutional sense, is precisely that rationalization and centralization of governance and justice of which Walter is the agent. The demise of local justice which the play enacts, in other words, participates in the overriding historical process that, especially across the eighteenth century, replaced tradition and personally instantiated authority with an impersonally regulated procedure grounded in an abstract code. Kleist's drama brings this historical process, in all its dialectical tension, onto the stage. "We have in Huisum," Adam tells Walter at one point, "certain laws peculiar to our village, not written laws I grant you, but rather handed down to us, from generation to generation." Note here that the opposition Adam draws between traditional and modern legal forms is conceived principally as an opposition between orality and literacy. This too is an aspect of the Enlightenment reform: the replacement in trial procedure of the immediacy and unpredictability of oral exchange—the clamorous contention of accuser and accused—with the prescribed canons and meticulous record-keeping of the modern court. Licht, after all, is busily writing throughout the play, and when he's not writing he's reading, detective-like, the traces Adam's deliction of the night before has left behind.

This question of orality and literacy, moreover, allows us to see how the jug itself condenses all the principal dramatic and symbolic elements of the play. As a vessel for drinking, the jug is closely linked to the oral; indeed, Frau Marthe Rull, whose long description of the jug and its history echoes the great oral ekphrasis of Homer, remarks at one point that it is worthy of a lady's mouth. And when Adam says to Walter early on that the oral traditions of his court descend from the time of Charles V, he in fact ties those traditions to the jug whose breakage is at issue in the trial. For on that jug was pictured, as Frau Marthe tells us, that same Charles V as he turned over the Netherlandic provinces to Philip of Spain. The fragmentation of judge and jug are one and the same: the fracture of an oral tradition of legality grounded in the paternal authority of the emperor. Kleist's play stages, in all its ambiguity, the history of legal rationalization, a history that amounts to nothing less than the shattering of the father's law. That law, the judge who inherits its authority, and the jug which represents the scene of its original donation: all of them, at the play's beginning, already lie in shards.

Kleist's engagement with the Enlightenment is also revealed in the play's meticulous exploration of its own generic heritage. Indeed, we have before us a comedy which in so many respects meets the requirements of the comic genre that it can be understood as a reflection on the comic itself. Recall the features of comedy enumerated in the *Tractatus Coislinianus*, that treatise of late antiquity which perhaps stems from the missing portion of Aristotle's *Poetics*. The treatise catalogues the properties of comic language, action, and character: all the jumbled words, confused and surprising events, and hapless and excessive personalities that have peopled the comic stage from the ancients to the present. For example, we find there that perennial pair of characters, the *alazon* and the *eiron*, the boaster and the figure of cunning self-effacement, character types almost perfectly embodied in Adam and Licht. And the overriding action of the play conforms exactly to the classical comic sequence: the couple whose union is blocked by the entrenched unreason of the older male competitor, the play of reversal that finally obliterates this blockage, especially when a *deus ex machina*—here in the person of Walter—arrives to take things in hand. Indeed, since the so-called New Comedy of Plautus, the genre has vacillated between two possibilities of conclusion: either banishment of the comic figure of blockage as a kind of scapegoat or reintegration of that figure into the corrected social order. Kleist delicately holds a balance between these two outcomes, for even as Adam is whipped from the scene Walter sends Licht to bring him back, as if the new society of reason could accommodate him.

The greatest boaster in the history of the comic stage is, of course, Shakespeare's Falstaff, and perhaps this is the place to say that Kleist alone, in the rather thin tradition of German comic dramatists, achieves Shakespearean grandeur. Moreover, he does this precisely because, like Shakespeare, he draws so powerfully on the popular sources of the comic, those sources which alone make our laughter real. Like Falstaff before him, Adam is a man of bulging and rebellious belly, gluttonous and flatulant; his soul, one might say, dwells beneath his belt, close to the functions of sex and digestion. And the laughter he unleashes in us has its locus there too; it's a belly laugh, a corporeal turbulence. This point is important because it was precisely this laughter—deep, trembling, rude—that the comic program and practice of the Enlightenment sought to silence, and succeeded in doing so. The paradigmatic text in this regard is Gottsched's *Critical Poetics* of 1730, which banned the popular figure of sexual-digestive laughter from the comic stage. Can we say that Kleist reverses this Enlightenment reform? I think so. I think, in other words, that Adam, whose predilection for belly-bulging, phallic sausages is documented early on, reincarnates—literally, reincarnates—Hanswurst. But this reincarnation of Hanswurst in Adam is a most ambiguous dramatic deed, for Adam himself, at the play's end, is driven from the stage. In other words, just as Kleist traces in his drama the Enlightenment rationalization of traditional juridical forms, he also sets into scene the Enlightenment cleansing of the comic. He calls Hanswurst, in the character of Adam, back to the theater, but only to rehearse his expulsion. This complex twist in which the genre is made to fold back onto its own history brings this greatest of German comedies into the zone of the tragic.

Of course, the tragedy whose agenda *The Broken Jug* repeats, the same tragedy which Kleist reinterpreted in his novella *The Foundling* and which obsessively echoes through so many of his other works as well, is the *Oedipus Rex* of Sophocles. The brief preface to the play tells us as much. Kleist claims there to have drawn the idea of the drama from an etching he had seen in Switzerland on which was represented a court scene that—jug and all—quite precisely corresponds to the play's array of dramatis personae. Describing that etching, Kleist notes: "the court clerk looked suspiciously across at the judge, much as Creon, on a similar occasion, had looked at Oedipus." The village judge Adam, who is the biblical Adam and Hanswurst in one, is also Oedipus the king, and his story unfolds according to the same analytical structure for which the Sophoclean play is the paradigm case. By the term analytical structure literary critics usually mean a plot in which the decisive event precedes the unfolding of the dramatic sequence and in which the dramatic sequence principally consists in the gradual disclosure of that antecedent happening. It is the pattern of all detective stories, and, as I noted above, our play too, in the person of Licht, has its detective figure. The peculiar twist of Sophocles' tragedy, of course, is that detective and criminal are one and the same: Oedipus, destined to discover that he himself is the agent of the crime he seeks to solve. And this is Adam's situation as well: the judge condemned to preside over a trial that finally demonstrates his own guilt.

A slight modification in the definition of analytical structure, I believe, can bring us closer to the nerve of Kleist's drama. My suggestion is this: rather than conceiving the crux event as thoroughly antecedent and the dramatic sequence itself as a distinct and subsequent phase of cognitive discovery—rather than separating these two components—we should think of their relation as a peculiar and indeed uncanny sort of temporal mixing. The antecedent event, in other words, does not stay comfortably in the past. It returns, brings aftereffects, continues to tremble through and disturb the actions of the dramatic present. Here we approach the Freudian concept of analysis, a concept also profoundly influenced by the Oedipus of Sophocles. Freud's entire teaching and practice rest on this experience: that the traumatic event is not temporally discrete, that it repeats itself in the patient's present suffering, and that this repetition, this dramatic reincarnation, must occur within the analytic labor itself. Kleist, it seems to me, urges this notion of temporal conflation upon us through a miniscule operation he performs on the Sophoclean scenario. I refer to the event of Oedipus's blinding that follows upon his terrible discovery that, yes, he is patricide and husband to his mother. In Kleist's rendition this blinding takes place during the traumatic event itself, as Adam's wounded eye attests. Trauma and discovery are one or, more precisely, *the* trauma around which Kleist's play revolves and which reverberates throughout its structure is a cognitive trauma as well. It is an enigma, it can't be mastered in knowledge, and this precisely because it is the shattering of knowledge and representation. "I am the child of chance," Oedipus cries out in horror, the child, Kleist will say across his entire *oeuvre*, of *Zufall* and the Fall. And it is this chance event—the trauma, the Real—which never ceases never ceasing, the accident of birth, the die-cast of sexuality.

If we are to approach the enigmatic event of the night before, we will do well, I think, to adhere to the insistence of Frau Marthe Rull, the mid-wife mother of Eve, who urges from her first appearance on that just this one thing happened: the jug was broken. The broken jug, *La cruche cassée*: this is the title of the painting by Greuze, copied by Debucourt and reproduced in an etching that hung in the Berne quarters of Kleist's friend Zschokke, where it inspired Kleist and three of his friends to a poetic contest. Each was to write a literary work based on the etching, and it is not surprising that all of them, Kleist included, hit upon the theme of innocence lost, which is the obvious thrust of the Greuze painting as well. Indeed, every painted jug—be it by Greuze or Ingres or Cezanne—suggests the completeness and self-enclosure of the female body, and when that jug is broken it is precisely the pristine innocence of virginity that is lost. But, of course, no excursus through art history is required to understand that what is at stake in the broken jug of Kleist's play is the violation of a girl's virgin innocence. That, after all, is why her destined bridegroom Ruprecht and his father Veit are so upset: they want no part of a marriage if the goods are damaged. "The marriage has a hole in it," the suspicious Veit mutters, and by marriage he also means the god of marriage whose classical name was hymen. Indeed, Kleist goes very far—almost as far as in his *Amphytrion*—in suggesting to us that such a violation might very well have taken place. Eve, after all, admits the blackmailing Adam into what the text refers to as her *abgelegene Kammer*, the sequestered chamber which she, by metonymy, is. Kleist will develop this equation of female body and chamber throughout the play, focusing especially on the apertures through which one enters and leaves the room. Thus, when Frau Marthe arrives on the scene during the fateful night, she finds the door violently broken in, finds the evidence, in other words, of her daughter's violation. And Ruprecht's testimony makes it clear that it is precisely this forced entry that knocks the jug from its resting place on the shelf, leaving it broken on the floor.

Let us note the constellation as precisely as possible. Adam has been together with Eve outside in the garden, exactly where a couple so named ought to be. She allows him into her chamber, into the space of her own intimacy, the contained space symbolized by the jug contained there. This is innocence indeed, not merely that of Eve, but of the biblical pair in their embrace. Here Adam would dream the fulfillment of his desire: to be one with her, to be contained within her unbroken fullness, and thereby himself to be unbroken and full. But immediately Ruprecht shows up, and the scene of Adam's dream is rent asunder by the violence of sexuality. Listen to Ruprecht's speech:

> Honorable Adam, it wells up in me,
> Like a bursting blood vessel. Give me air!
> A button pops on my chest. Air! I tear
> My collar open. Air! Give me air, I say!
> I run, ram, kick and batter, when I find
> The slut's door locked, wedged closed,
> And with a single step I bash it down.
> . . .
>
> And as it gives way,
> That jug falls down from the ledge in the room,
> And—whoosh—someone leaps out of the window.
> (Scene 7)

His entire body turgid, buttons popping, gasping: in this frenzy easily legible as sexual Ruprecht forces his way into Eve's enclosure and drives Adam from the paradise he had sought to recover, the paradise of his oneness with, his similitude (recall Buffon) with Eve. Everything falls: the judge, the jug, and the girl.

Before considering a further detail of this scene, let us return to the jug itself, and in particular to the scene which, as Marthe's ekphrasis tells us, was painted on it. The image is now destroyed, violated by a *Loch* or hole, which, of course, is the same hole Veit sees in the marriage. Or rather doesn't see, for an absence cannot be presented in the fullness of a visual rendering. And this is precisely Marthe's point:

> No, begging your pardon, what you see is nothing.
> The most beautiful of jugs is smashed in two.
> Here right on the hole, where now nothing is,

All the provinces of the Netherlands
Were given over to Philip of Spain.
(Scene 7)

As I mentioned above, this destruction of the jug symbolizes the rupture of the feudal-patriarchal authority whose donation—from father to son—the painted scene depicts. And that authority, of course, is the ultimate source of Adam's judicial legitimacy as well. Indeed, we can go even further here and claim that it was this law of the father which brought Adam to Eve's sequestered chamber; his presumption that Eve's virginity was his to take, in other words, derives from the feudal privilege of the 'first night' which accrued to the local sovereign, a privilege which still haunts the bourgeois mind of the late eighteenth century, as Mozart's *Marriage of Figaro*, another classic comedy of blockage, shows.

But Marthe's description, in its literalist confusion of painted representation and represented event, allows us to grasp more precisely what has torn the paternal law asunder, broken its transmission and tradition, hollowed it out with an internal dehiscence, a kind of active and agitating absence. All the details of destruction she enumerates are instances of a violence directed at the integrity of the male body: Charles, the emperor and paternal source, is severed at the loins; the kneeling Philip remains only as a rump exposed to violation from behind; the swords of Philibert and Maximilian—the signs, that is, of phallic-martial authority—are cut away; the female figures are turned inward in a self-directed lament; and the body of the archbishop—the corporeal representative of God the Father here on earth—is removed altogether, leaving nothing but a shadow, a ghostly shade without a referent.

What are we to make of this double violation which the breaking of the jug enacts? What are we to make of the fact that the broken jug symbolizes at once the loss of virginity and the severance of the male body, which is to say, castration? It seems to me that Kleist's play allows us to think the solidarity of these two lost figures of integrity. What links the phallic authority of paternity and the self-enclosure of virginity, in other words, is their similitude: each is the image of the other, each gives the one back to the other as if in a mirror or painting. Or to put the matter another way: the intact corporeality of virginity is the corporeal schema that guarantees the integrity of patriarchal authority, much as the rounded oneness of the jug supports the drama of the paternal law's transmission. If we return to the night of Adam's deliction, we find this interpretation neatly confirmed. Ruprecht, breaking into Eve's chamber, rips from the door which had sealed her virginal enclosure a phallic instrument: the door handle, a little sword or *Degen*, as Licht calls it, a longish weapon with a *Klumpen* at the end, as if it were a version of Adam's *Klumpffuß*, or clubfoot. And, of course, it is with this detached tool that Ruprecht batters and bashes Adam's head, gashing his eye, as the hapless judge hangs in the trellis that reaches up to Eve's window. The wound of sexuality splits the integrity of the male-female unity, and splits each figure—male and female—within itself. No longer is their adequation to one another possible, no longer are they united in the embrace of an essential similitude. The trauma of the broken jug is the traumatic opening of a sexual difference that resists containment within the schema of the Same. It is this difference out of which and into which Adam—the fallen Adam, the Oedipal Adam, the comic Hanswurst Adam—is born. For there can be no doubt that this night of rupture and severance is also the night of Adam's own birth: battered and bashed by the detached door handle, he falls from the nine-foot-high window of Eve's chamber, falling to the cold earth on which he is condemned to leave the traces of his split and wounded condition.

This difference, which, as Walter recognizes at one point, cannot be resolved through any *Vergleich*—that is, comparison or settlement by equivalence—this difference which opens during the night that is always the night before, the night before any possible experience, this difference cannot be seen. In other words, it takes place, by its very nature, offstage: it is obscenity itself. This is why both characters who confront the event of difference, Adam and Ruprecht, come away from it blinded, that is to say, wounded in the organ of vision which would hold the female body in its gaze and find there the image of its own integrity. Difference is the collapse of ocular power, the collapse of visual representation and its law of similitude. And this means that difference is the undoing of painting, not only the painting on the jug itself, but also the painting of *La cruche cassée* which Kleist and his friends took as the occasion of their poetic competition. Kleist won that competition, to be sure, but not merely due to the immense stature of his drama. His victory stems from the fact that his text, from beginning to end, does nothing but rehearse the inevitability of his and all the poets' defeat. "No, begging your pardon," says Frau Marthe to the judicial subject, "what you see is nothing." And this applies to the drama as well, which enacts the fragmentation of the image in language. For language too, in Kleist's conception, and especially the language of this drama, is broken by the unrepresentable event of the fall: that event which never ceases never ceasing, which repeats itself in every word that Adam stumbles over. The clubfoot of this German Oedipus is the metrical foot that trips through the drama's verse. And this is finally why Adam will never fully awaken from the traumatic dream of the night before and why he will never recover the integrity of his judicial authority: what breaks both jug and judge is the fracture of self-adequation, the event which gives birth to the divided subject of speech, the divided subject of desire. This event, hidden in the obscurity of the night before, is fundamentally enigmatic. It is the enigma of Kleist, in both senses of the genitive, and it cannot be brought to the light of consciousness. But its traces are there, nonetheless, in the text which, as text, is exactly what its title says: *The Broken Jug*. And what my title says as well, if not as well: the play of sexual difference.

THE ENIGMA OF HERMENEUTICS: THE CASE OF KASPAR HAUSER*

GERD GEMÜNDEN

Das Rätsel lösen ist soviel wie den Grund seiner Unlösbarkeit angeben.
To solve the riddle is in effect to give the ground of its insolubility.

—Adorno

Wo wir durch das Fremde der Sprache aufgehalten werden, da freilich forschen wir.
Where we are held up by the strangeness of the language, there we of course do our research.

—Schleiermacher

Ich hatte ja nicht gewußt, daß es eine solche Gestalt giebt, wie ich bin.
I didn't know that there is such a figure as I am.

—Kaspar Hauser

A MYSTERIOUS DOCUMENT: ENTER KASPAR

On Whitmonday 1828 the shoemaker Georg Leonard Weickmann and his colleague Jakob Beck run into, as they later testify, "a funny and foolish"[1] character at the Unschlittplatz in Nuremberg. In the left hand he is holding a letter addressed "Tit. Hr. Wohlgebohner Rittmeister bey der / 4ten Esgataron bey 6ten Schwolische / Regiment / in Nierberg" (Binder, 23). Since this fellow, a lad of about seventeen years, is not able to communicate with the two, but only copies their words like a parrot, they lead him to the address given in the letter. Upon arrival he is brought into the stable to wait for the return of the absent Rittmeister. After he refuses beer and meat with disgust but greedily gulps down bread and water, he falls into a deep sleep. At the return of the Rittmeister he is awakened. The lad is impressed with the richly adorned uniform of the Rittmeister, but unable to answer his questions. When he is not simply repeating the words spoken to

---

*Reprinted with permission from *Die hermeneutische Wende: Disziplin und Sprachlosigkeit nach 1800*, Peter Lang, 1990.

him, his vocabulary is limited to the phrases "don't know" (woiß nit) and "I want to be a rider like my father was once" (ich möchte ein solcher Reiter werden wie mein Vater einer gewesen ist). Since he also has no proof of identity, he is confined to the tower "Luginsland."

The letter in his hands is the only document that could cast a light on the enigmatic darkness of this phantom. The appendix reads: "The / child is already baptized / her name is kaspar / you have to give him a name yourself" ("Das / Kind ist schon getauft / sie Heist Kasper in Schreib / name misen sie im selber / geben") (Binder, 12).[2] Instead of answering the question of his origin and identity, the letter complicates matters even further.[3] These few lines not only refrain from an unambigious answer, but rather display the disseminating semantics of Kaspar Hauser: listing "das Kind," "sie heißt," and "name misen sie *im* selber geben," the note leaves open the question of the gender of the signified. At the same time it invalidates the statement "is already baptized" by immediately adding: "you have to give him a name yourself." The same ambiguity is true for his name: the attributed name Kaspar evokes such different associations as the three Holy Kings and the puppet show; the family name Hauser, on the other hand, seems an ironic allusion to someone—as is later revealed—who has not left his "house" for the last twelve years. The letter claims to be a historic document, which can supplement the identity of its speechless bearer, yet it refuses any concrete statement. It disappoints all those who expected any information about the silent bearer. It refuses any authoritative explanation of the apparent enigma and renders matters even more enigmatic by not naming its own author: "I don't make my name known" (Ich mache mein Namen nicht / Kuntbar) (Binder, 12).

INCIPIT ENIGMA

The short episode of Kaspar's entrance (the letter, the subject only spoken about, not speaking itself but only speaking by corresponding to language) gathers together in striking concentration the themes and topics which are the subject of my essay and which will allow a critique of the philosophy of language that informs Romantic hermeneutics.

The speechless foundling denies any statement about his origin.[4] He monotonously repeats the "parole soufflée"[5] of the speakers; just as he is not the author of his words, the letter also remains without author. The speechless foundling and the authorless letter bring into the arena a philological discipline whose pronounced goals are to make texts speak and to trace speech back to its author: Romantic hermeneutics which was conceived only a few years before Kaspar's appearance by someone by the name of Friedrich Daniel Ernst Schleiermacher.

Probably the most famous desideratum of Schleiermacher's theory of interpretation is "to understand speech at first as good as and then even better than its originator [Urheber].'"[6] Where this originator, i.e., the author, cannot be found, hermeneutics poses the question of the legitimacy, meaningfulness, and truthfulness of a text. Michel Foucault has tried to analyze the significance of the author for a text and its implications for the meaning of a text. For our context it is important to note what happens if the author is missing, since he or she is the guarantee for "a limitation of the cancerous and dangerous proliferation of signification within a world where one is thrifty not only with one's resources and riches, but also with one's discourses and their significations."[7] However, if the author, who restricts meaning and truth and thus guarantees its recovery, is absent

> ... [a]nd if a text should be discovered in a state of anonymity—whether as a consequence of an accident or the

Friedrich Ernst Daniel Schleiermacher, from the Bildabteilung, Deutsches Literaturarchiv of the Schiller Nationalmuseum, Marbach, Germany. Reprinted with permission.

> author's explicit wish—the game becomes one of rediscovering the author. Since literary anonymity is not possible, we can accept it only in the guise of an enigma.[8]

The hermeneuticians surrounding, describing, and inscribing the lad with the letter are forced to make precisely this move. The absence of the name leads to the production of the enigma.

Yet it is not only the absence of the author which turns the letter into a riddle. For to consider the text in its own terms as something strange, incomprehensible or at least not fully understandable on its own is characteristic of Romantic hermeneutics as formulated by Schleiermacher. His basic assumption is that texts are not what they pretend to be and that one has to search for a deeper truth behind superficial statements—hence, "that misunderstanding comes by itself and that at every point understanding has to be wanted and looked for."[9]

The epistemological consequences for philological hermeneutics become more evident if we contrast Schleiermacher's concept with that of the Enlightenment. According to the doctrines of explanation (*Auslegungslehren*) by Johann Martin Chladenius or Georg Friedrich Meier, understanding the text was the normal situation and hermeneutics was a technique or "science of rules" which merely had to apply a fixed canon of rules.

> The criterium for a correct interpretation was not to reconstruct the intention of the authors or their texts but rather the rationality of the matters presented, i.e., the correspondence between the discourse of the interpretandum and the interpreters who base their insight on the eternal statements of a general rationality. . . . Thoughts which are reasonable and composed according to the rules of the soul always designate things as they are, i.e., independent from all individual interpretation.[10]

The author function, just like the historic context, only played a secondary role in determining the truthfulness of a text. The task of this hermeneutics was rather to remove any individual flavor of the author or an era in order to bring to light the truth of the matter.[11] Quite the contrary for Schleiermacher. Nothing is any longer taken for granted and one does not understand anything by itself. Schleiermacher discovers that texts do not simply reveal themselves, but that they hide under a veil. It is therefore important to lift this veil—the task of hermeneutics. The principal attitude of the hermeneutician is therefore a philological skepticism; the hermeneutic will to understand is coupled with "a suspicion a priori."[12] Schleiermacher admits:

> Very often I catch myself in a familiar talk doing hermeneutic operations when I do not content myself with a common degree of understanding. Rather, I try to investigate how my friend concluded from one thought to another, or I try to track down on which assumptions, judgments and intentions it is that my *vis à vis* talks about a certain matter in such and no other way.[13]

Both speech and text—and for Schleiermacher there exists no difference between the two—become subject to a process of deciphering. Dialogue, in the seventeenth century still a witty pleasure, transforms into a hermeneutic effort. "The discourse of the Other is more and more perceived as an enigma that has to be deciphered, a secret that has to be guessed, or a disguise that has to be destroyed."[14] Therefore the enigma begins in the midst of seemingly secured knowledge and conventional understanding. The hermeneutician tries to destroy any familiarity with the world in order to unmask the obvious as mere illusion. The text becomes an enigma, life becomes a book, interpretation becomes an endless task.[15] Hermeneutics, therefore, is fascinated with forms and incidents that further provoke this way of thinking: the sensational, the absurd, the pathological, and of course the incomprehensible stammering of a speechless foundling with an enigmatic letter in hand.

As I intend to show, Kaspar's resistance to the hermeneuticians exposes their belief in the unity of the subject to be a work of fiction; his speech and writing show that one has to search for truth *within* the text and not behind it, and that language does *not* represent. Furthermore, his resistance is symptomatic of someone who is confronted with discipline and disciplinary powers, for these powers intend to classify, regulate, and subjugate every individual. By making understanding the prerequisite for domination, hermeneutics becomes the condition of the possibility of a specifically modern instance of discipline. What is at stake is to make visible the will to dominate or discipline that governs the hermeneutic enterprise; with Kaspar, the grown-up *infans*, an individual enters the arena which personifies the neglect of disciplines, thus forcing them to compensate for the deficiency.

IN THE JUNGLE OF DISCOURSE: A SUBJECT IS BEING PRODUCED

Kaspar's silent appearance in Nuremberg makes him at once the subject of various discourses which all try to take hold of him. Therefore, Kaspar has to be seen as "the intersection of discourses,"[16] i.e., as that point where all these efforts necessarily meet. He is the *medium comparationis* which allows the discourses of history, education, psychology, psychoanalysis, parapsychology, anthroposophy, criminology, biography, law, and literature/fiction to situate themselves in relation to each other.[17] It is necessary therefore to describe how these disciplines work before I can show how they inevitably prompt their object(s). In every instance these discourses are the result of interpretations—interpretation being understood as a practice which reads facts according to their transcendental significance[18]—which they perform by using Kaspar's words and writings. The interpretations share the intention of reducing the polysemy surrounding Kaspar Hauser. Discussing several examples, I analyze the strategies which the participants in these discourses employ and show how Kaspar—implicitly or explicitly, unconsciously or consciously—compromises these strategies.

The *Kemptener Skizze* of 1830 describes Kaspar's first appearance:

> It has sufficiently been publicized that, in May 1828, a young man appeared who, because of stupidity or deceit, was not able to give any information about his origins, his education, or the circumstances of his existence; thus the Nuremberg municipal authorities took care of him.[19]

Kaspar's lack of articulation and his behaviour similar to that of an idiot ("sein einem Blödsinnigen ähnliches Benehmen") were immediately conspicuous. At once the shoemaker Weickmann tried to start up a conversation with him and later "the [*Rittmeister's*] servant tried to possibly interrogate the young man" (Binder, 23). As the *Kemptener Skizze* tells us, both attempts were unsuccessful. When addressed, Kaspar does not react to the approach but only repeats the incomprehensible sentence: "I want to become like my father once was" (ä sechetener möcht ih wähn, wie mei Vottä wähn ist).

The speakers are further provoked by the *infans* because of the letter in his hand. This document pretends to identify its bearer, yet refuses to do so. The letter not only abstains from clear statements about its carrier, it also disappoints the desire to be understandable in itself. Rather, it is the very concept of comprehensibility that is being attacked here. In other words, the letter not only does *not* answer the questions which the people of Nuremberg ask (about) Kaspar, but it renders matters even more enigmatic by immediately retracting the few statements it does make. A few examples will suffice. The letter sets out with the following sentence: "I send you a lad who loyally wants to serve his King"—whereas serving is exactly what Kaspar does not want to do. The writer then claims: "I have raised him as a Christian," but continues "since 1812 I have not let him leave the house," which can hardly be seen as an act of loving one's neighbor. And a further contradiction becomes apparent: the writer claims to be a poor day-laborer yet is conspicuously concerned with the foundling's education. Four times he praises the education of his protégé, although for twelve years Kaspar benefitted from no education whatsoever. Finally, the assertion "you can ask him but he won't be able to say it" (sie derfen ihm schon fragen er kan es aber nicht sagen) can be read as the only coherent remark of the author concerning his *letter*. One can read the letter, but one will not find out anything. Thus the letter produces nothing but an ironic commentary on the process of understanding, a remark that crosses the alleged communicative intention of the letter. It eludes the "critical examination" of the letter which is "the most important document in the entire *Hauser* affair" (Schmidt v. Lübeck, 224) to *understand* the letter as an allegory about incomprehensibility. Instead, one sets out to copy the letter. A facsimile is produced to at least master the text in this way. As a consequence the original is lost.[20]

All this threatens the speakers so much that the municipal authorities decide to take Kaspar into "protective custody" (Verwahr und Pflege), i.e., to put him behind bars. Those threatened by Kaspar's discourse therefore choose the strategy of exclusion; they throw him into jail in order to determine his status as an object of their inquiries and interrogations. "Physicians, teachers, educators, psychologists, police officers, law-court officials, the shrewdest observers of all ranks" are asked to enter his cell; the "police officers have the most urgent duty" (Merker, 215) to get to the bottom of the secret, for it could well be—as argued by Friedrich Karl Merker—that "Caspar Hauser is not unlikely to be a swindler" (214). However, the attempt to get hold of Kaspar Hauser via police interrogations, legal investigations, and hidden observations fails: "The limits of his vocabulary soon determined to abandon the course of formal interrogation" (Binder, 25). As a consequence, not only professionals deal with Kaspar, but solving the riddle becomes the "highest national duty" ([eine] höhere Staatsbürgerpflicht) which involves *all* citizens. This also leads to a significant change of strategy among the discourses surrounding Kaspar. Their primal concern had been to stand up to the threat "Kaspar," this absolute Other, by excluding (i.e., imprisoning) it. In *Madness and Civilization* Foucault describes how rational discourse rejects something that lies outside its boundaries.

> The history of madness would be the history of the Other—of that which for a given culture, is at once interior and foreign, therefore to be excluded (so as to exorcize the interior danger) but by being shut away (in order to reduce its otherness).[21]

The case of Kaspar Hauser does not allow this incarcerating exclusion. Rather, something has to take place that might serve as a complement to Foucault's analysis: a forced assimilation. The citizens of Nuremberg push for a reduction of the strange, for an ordered and orderly assimilation to the status quo with the goal of a frictionless integration into the existing order.

If they at first throw the foundling into the carceral, they now adopt him, making him the son of Nuremberg, and later even the "Child of Europe." Through a rigorous adjustment Kaspar becomes almost "familiar beyond recognition."[22]

KASPAR SPEAKS

Thus one refrains from locking Kaspar up; instead he is to be integrated into society by all possible means (for the release from prison is only without risk if the threat is removed). This undertaking is best described in terms of a coercive subjugation.

This subjugation can only be accomplished via language. For the hermeneuticians, to be a subject essentially means to be able to speak—to say "I". Therefore one has to look at *how*—through which disciplines and what kind of disciplination—Kaspar is made to speak, and what he himself tells us about it. This leads to the question of what relation the signifier and the signified have for the hermeneuticians and for Kaspar.

For the speakers of the late eighteenth and beginning nineteenth century the subject is at once the source and telos of all language. It is the place where self-consciousness originates, since the "I" cannot be seen as a derivative of a function or principle existing prior to it. But it is exactly this which Kaspar denies by talking about himself in the third person singular:

> "Kaspar very good," instead of, I am very good, "Kaspar shall Juli tell," instead of, I shall tell it to Julius (son of the jailer); such were the common modes of expressing himself. . . . Thus also, in speaking to him, if you wished him immediately to understand who you meant, you must not say *you* to him, but Kaspar.[23]

Thus, Kaspar presents himself as the predicate of another subject; his own status as subject is not constituting but rather constituted. The simple fact of how aggravatedly the speakers exorcize this manner of Kaspar's language shows that they find their fiction of the autonomous subject unmasked. Their goal is to make Kaspar believe—as they themselves believe—that language has to be controlled, and that autonomous subjects master their discourse rather than being restricted by language. We therefore need to look at how Kaspar is educated into being a subject and how he undermines and subverts this process.

In his medical certificate from December 30, 1830, Dr. Osterhausen writes: "When Hauser came here his language consisted of hardly 50 words" (50). Others, like the president of the Bavarian Courts of Appeal in Ansbach, Anselm Feuerbach, estimate that his "vocabulary" includes about half a dozen words, among which *Roß* for everything with four legs and *bua* for everything human take up the biggest space. For the most part, however, one finds "tears, moans, and unintelligible sounds," or the words which he frequently repeated: "Reutä wähn, wie mei Vattä wähn is" (Become a rider as my father was) (Feuerbach, 122). The only thing Kaspar is able to describe is his status as being neither a subject nor possessing language: "Woiß nit." This is cause for different reactions among the speakers. For some of them his speechlessness is a sign of stupidity, for others a sign of disguise and deceit. But when the view is accepted that the speechless foundling is "neither crazy nor stupid but apparently has been brutally kept away from any human and social education in the most irredeemable way" (weder verrückt noch blödsinnig, aber offenbar auf die heilloseste Weise von aller menschlichen und gesellschaftlichen Bildung gewaltsam entfernt) the result prescribes the therapy: Kaspar has to learn to speak "correctly" in order to gain a self-consciousness.

The race to recover lost ground is started. The speakers carefully ignore the words that Kaspar actually speaks. Instead they comprehend him as a *tabula rasa* and it is now to be written on this "empty slate of his soul" (leere Tafel seiner Seele) (Feuerbach, 162). Although the different discourses surrounding Kaspar compete on what to write on this board, they share the intention to use it merely as a screen of their projections.[24]

Kaspar already receives the first instruction in language in his "quarters" in the tower from Hiltel, the jailer, and his wife. Hiltel, "perhaps the best teacher Kaspar ever had,"[25] considers Kaspar "a pure child, yes, even less than a child."[26] He lets his own children play with Kaspar, and his son Julius is the first "to instruct him in speaking, to show him letters, and to communicate concepts to him inasmuch as he himself possessed any" (Feuerbach, 130). Kaspar the *infans* (lat.: the one who does not speak), the one "who plays with the materiality of signifiers instead of referring with them intentionally to signifieds"[27] takes his first steps toward becoming, what he is made to believe is an autonomous subject. The eleven-year-old Julius, who has just "mastered" language himself, enjoys being the master of his older pupil. At first he tries to teach Kaspar the names of the different parts of the body.[28] For the concept of the sovereign subject is inseparably connected with the notion that the body is not something strange and exterior to it but rather at its disposal. Contrary to Lacan's theory, according to which the body of the subject undergoes a process of territorialization at birth, for Kaspar identifying his body is supposed to guarantee his unproblematic entry into the symbolic order. Daumer, Kaspar's later "foster"-father, describes how Kaspar remembers this process of learning:

> Initially, his ignorance was so big that he did not even know all the limbs of his body. He told me that one time someone came to familiarize him with them. When they

had him touch his ears with his hands he was very astonished, and he thought that this was something improper that had to be removed from his body. Only when the jailer pulled his ears a little, he became convinced that they were a part of his body.[29]

To teach Kaspar that his body is an inseparable unit is the presupposition for him to recognize the "I," resting in this body, as self-sufficient. But Kaspar refuses to accept this process of differentiation. When Mrs. Hiltel first gives Kaspar a bath a crust of dirt and dust, accumulated in twelve years in his prison, dissolves in the water. Kaspar exclaims in shock: "The skin, the skin!"[30] Kaspar cannot yet draw the line which separates the "I" and the world and which ultimately defines the subject—not because he confuses skin with dirt, but because he does not know where he ends and the world begins.[31] The resistance which he puts up to understand the difference between same and Other is propelled by an insight which the speakers have successfully repressed: that to be a subject means to be alienated from the world qua signification. For it is not true, as the speakers pretend, that the subject is an autonomous entity which situates itself in relation to the world, but the subject is rather, as Lacan has shown, produced within a framework of signification without having the possiblity ever to leave or jump out of this framework in order to gain immediate access to the world of phenomena. This world, which Lacan also calls the real world, is the world of *being*—incompatible with the world of *meaning* in which subjects are constituted.

A scene from Werner Herzog's film *Everyman for Himself and God Against All* depicts Kaspar's language instruction in a way which could well resemble reality:

> Kaspar's corner. He sits in his customary position on the floor beside Julius, serious like an adult. Julius pinches Kaspar's index finger. "Finger," says Kaspar. He taps Kaspar's hand. "Arm," says Kaspar. "No, hand," says Julius, "the arm is the whole part up to here." . . . Julius touches Kaspar's mouth. "Mouth," says Kaspar forthwith, and then "nose," tapping his own nose simultaneously.[32]

According to Julius, every real object as the arm, the mouth, the finger, etc., possesses a linguistic signification through which it is represented. The relationship is established by touching a part of the body and saying its name accordingly. The concept of language informing this praxis belongs, as Kaja Silverman has shown, "to the category of representation rather than that of signification, which implies a system of meaning which excludes the object." Kaspar's difficulties in correctly identifying the parts of his body "result in part from inexperience, but more importantly from the fact that language cannot really be used to represent objects."[33] Once Kaspar enters the symbolic order he has no more access to the real world. Language is a network of reference; words acquire meaning within this network, thus blocking the way for a return to the world of phenomena. Julius is no longer aware of this loss of being in the face of meaning, but Kaspar's resistance suggests that he is not willing to suffer this loss as well.

When Kaspar is moved to the house of the prematurely retired teacher Georg Friedrich Daumer, organized lessons in reading, writing, and mathematics begin. Finally, one succeeds in getting Kaspar to say "I" and "myself"—a proof for the speakers that Kaspar finally considers himself as subject and origin of his discourse with an independent self-consciousness. Yet even this learning process is marked by problems:

> Even when Hauser had learned to say 'I,' he preferred for several months to talk about himself in the third person singular and by adding the name 'Kaspar.' Concerning a drawing of him he said, 'If there wasn't a nose, there would be nothing of Kaspar in this picture.' In the summer of 1828 he said, 'To think myself towards something' instead of, 'To bring forth through my own studies,' and 'it feels to me' as an analogy to 'It feels cold to me,' etc.[34]

Kaspar's language shows the frequent use of infinitives, polysemies, parataxis, and the resistance to form syntagmatic units.[35]

> Many words which signify only a particular species, would be applied by him to the whole genus. Thus, for instance, he would use the word hill or mountain, as if it applied to every protuberance or elevation; and in consequences thereof, he once called a corpulent gentleman, whose name he could not recollect, 'the man with the great mountain.'[36]

His teacher Daumer adds:

> Roots and plaits he called: *tails*, beams he called: *trees*, dancing he called: *running around*, swimming he called: *running*, yawning he called: *to open the mouth*, people who were standing and gathering around he called: *to can*, and so forth.[37]

And Kaspar's initial sentence "I möcht a söchäna Reiter wären, wie mei Vater gwän is" is, as he later describes in his *Lebensbeschreibung*, a polysemically all-describing signifier for complaint, claim, and desire:

> I said: "I want to be such a rider like my father is," which meant to say, one should give me such a shiny and beautiful thing . . . which meant to say, where did the horses go and the water and the bread . . . which meant to say, why aren't the horses coming yet . . . which meant to say, he should not torture me with his speaking, this is hurting me very much.[38]

The speakers have to make Kaspar speak "correctly," i.e., to master language (Preu, 45; Osterhausen, 50). This implies a grammar where paratactic enumeration is replaced by a correct syntax and infinitives are replaced by inflected verbs plus personal pronouns. Furthermore, the most distinguished task of hermeneutics comes into play: the reduction of polysemy. Kaspar's disseminating discourse must be reduced so that matters are expressed *adequately*; as earlier, we are confronted with a philosophy of language which insists on a linguistic representation of extra-linguistic realities. Hence Jochen Hörisch's observation: "Not the proliferation but the reduction of his [Kaspar's] discourse is the ultimate goal of his linguistic socialization."[39] Rather than words themselves, Kaspar is supposed to learn the hermeneutic truth that words signify being, that speech ensues under a coercion of the subject.

There are numerous ways in which Kaspar subverts the speakers' strategies to introduce him into the symbolic order. Rather than interpreting Kaspar, trying to find the 'hidden reasons' for his reaction to these attempts at initiation—which would reproduce the hermeneutics the text struggles against—I shall describe how Kaspar's resistance is provoked.

Kaspar doubles the words of the speakers "like a parrot" (Daumer, 242). If asked to find "the conception corresponding to any new word, or the word corresponding to any new thing" he transforms into a "statue" (*Bildsäule*) (Feuerbach, 152). Though this resistance does not hinder his socialization, it delays the process in a way which makes it possible to describe Kaspar's subversive strategies in more detail. Contrary to the speakers, Kaspar feels that the connection between world and language is established only with violence. The speakers have forgotten this primal truth and believe themselves masters in the house of language. Kaspar, however, seems to understand that entering language will forever alienate him from the immediate access to the realm of things. This feeling, which registers the imperfection of language to represent reality, is expressed in Kaspar's behavior:

> [Kaspar] tried to supplement his speech by strangely moving his arms and hands; the hands were raised, and while turning the inside out he pressed together his thumb and index finger and moved his arms and hands towards the addressed person. While speaking he also liked to knock on the table with the tip of his thumb and his index finger.[40]

The quasi-natural language of gestures is supposed to establish a sort of reference which is not governed by the law of differentiation, and which does not separate but unites signifier and real object. Interestingly, Daumer goes on to say: "If one tried to wean him of these conspicuous movements, he complained that it would be even harder for him to speak."

Just as Kaspar tries to resist becoming a speaking subject, he tries to avoid being defined by gender. He is not willing to identify himself either as a male or as a female subject (although, when forced to make a decision, he would rather be a woman), and he confuses the speakers by understanding masculinity as a cultural construct which can be deliberately modified. Since he likes women's clothes better than men's he expresses the wish "to become a girl" (Feuerbach, 135). And to the question whom he later plans to marry he responds "My cat,"[41] thus bringing his critique of a social identification with *one* gender to a climax. For Kaspar, gender determination, just like language acquisition, is an alienation and separation from self-identical being which he resists giving up.

KASPAR WRITES

Just as from the very beginning Kaspar is able to speak, he is also able to write. An event needs to be noted here which took place almost immediately after Kaspar's arrival in Nuremberg. While interrogating him at the police station, an officer had the idea to check whether Kaspar was able to write.

> [One handed Kaspar] a pen with ink, laid a sheet of paper before him with an intimation that he should write. This appeared to give him pleasure; he took the pen, by no means awkwardly, between his fingers, and wrote, to the astonishment of all who were present, in legible characters, the name *Kaspar Hauser*.[42]

Yet Kaspar is not willing to give any further written information. Being asked "to add also the name whence he came," he moans "his 'Reutä wähn,' etc., his 'hoam weisa,' his 'woas nit' " (Feuerbach, 124). And later, after he has "mastered" reading and writing, he confesses: "I actually wrote the letters and my name without any concept whatsoever" (Vernehmung vom 07.11.1829, 70).

This incidence is remarkable for several reasons. Contrary to other children—with whose level of intelligence he is constantly compared— Kaspar has the ability to write *before* he is able to form syntagmatically correct sentences. However, writing (the signifier) for Kaspar is not required to refer to the described (the signififed). Freed from any coercion of reference, Kaspar can use language as a toy:

> Pretty nearly about the same time, the man once came into his prison, placed a small table over his feet, and spread something white upon it, which he now knows to have been paper; he then came behind him, so as not to be seen by him, took hold of his hand, and moved it backwards and forwards on the paper, with a thing [a lead pencil] which he had stuck between his fingers. He [Hauser] was then ignorant of what it was; but he was mightily pleased, when he saw the black figures which began to appear upon the white paper. When he felt his hand was free, and the man gone from him, he was so much pleased with his new discovery, that he could never grow tired of drawing these figures repeatedly upon the paper.[43]

While painting letters for the sake of pleasure in his cave, Kaspar demonstrates that semantic effects are not only produced at the level of words or sentences but also at the level of letters.[44] The writing of the letter precedes his own words, just like he is first written about, and then spoken of. And writing is still present in the hour of his death. "He seemed to lose his consciousness again, and one could notice that his fingers were moving on the feather-bed as if he wanted to write" (Minutes from December 17, 1833, 82). It is significant that Kaspar's writing is not dependant on consciousness as the speakers define it, i.e., as a sensual reflection of an external, rational world. Kaspar's sentence about writing "ohne allen Begriff" means exactly this: consciousness is not the condition of possibility for writing, but rather the effect of a network of signification.

But instead of reading what Kaspar writes, the speakers interpret his writing: "Kaspar *Hauser*—as the victim of this inhuman treatment calls himself [*sic!*]" (Kaspar *Hauser*—so nennt sich das Opfer unmenschlicher Behandlung) announces Mayor Binder in his proclamation from July 7, 1828, six weeks after Kaspar's appearance. The reflexive pronoun *sich*, which does not exist in Kaspar's vocabulary and against the usage of which he will resist for a long time, represents *in nuce* the misreading by the hermeneuticians which assumes a subject behind sentences and a consciousness behind statements. Yet it is precisely the ability and possibility to refer discourse back to an autonomous *auctoritas* that the case of Kaspar questions. The correspondence of foundling and name does not grow out of the writer's independent consciousness but rather is a projection on the part of the interpreters for whom writer and written possess a quasi-natural link.

It is with this in mind that Kaspar's polysemic *Ursatz* "Ich möchte ein solcher werden, wie mein Vater gewesen ist" has to be read. Different than—and in competition with—other famous "I"-sentences like Descartes' "Cogito ergo sum", Kant's transcendental apperception "Das: *Ich denke* muß alle meine Vorstellungen begleiten können" and Fichte's "Ich bin Ich," Kaspar's "I" is not a meaning and unity constituting "I" but rather an "I" that presents itself as the overdetermined construct of the Other. It names a past (history) ("gewesen ist"), the future ("werden"), as well as a present tense ("ich möchte"), whereby the present is determined by a past which prescribes its doubling for future times. Above all stands a symbolic father who proves the "I" to be a dependent derivative altogether.

One more example might be quoted which further depicts the speakers' belief in an absolute and transcendental subject and Kaspar's subversion of this belief. Still in his prison tower, Kaspar was visited by four clergymen, who tried to explain to him "that God created all things out of nothing" just as Idealist Philosophy claims that the "I" is the condition of possibility of any knowledge. Kaspar does not want to accept this view, and "[when] I told them, All these things I do not yet understand; I must first learn to read and write; they replied, These things must be learned first" (Feuerbach, 178). Kaspar's reference to the primacy of writing is yet again conceived as a threat and rejected.

"THIS STORY OF KASPAR HAUSER I MYSELF WANT TO WRITE"

The described coercive process of subjectivation has to be performed on both levels of language, i.e., written and spoken language. Thus it is only consequential that the speakers demand that Kaspar write down his autobiography in order to push this process. Only six months after Kaspar's first appearance, Daumer, hurried by the police and law officials, asks his protégé to put down in writing his life experience up to the present date.

Kaspar's attempt of a *Lebensbeschreibung* takes up a central place in our analysis because here the different aspects of the problematic of speechlessness and hermeneutics (which earlier were demonstrated with the example of Kaspar's letter) coincide again. The questions developed at the beginning of this essay seem to find their answers here: 1) Kaspar becomes a subject, 2) Kaspar becomes an author, 3) Kaspar himself attempts to solve the enigma which he poses for hermeneutics. "He, who in the beginning had such difficulties to become aware of the existence of his spirit" (Feuerbach, 192) now shines—for the speakers—in the final stage of a successful socialization. "He no longer retains any thing that is extraordinary, but his extraordinary fate, his indescribable goodness, and the exceeding amiableness of his disposition" (Feuerbach, 193). Kaspar has become subject, author, and even a hermeneutician. His *Lebensbeschreibung* documents this sucess as it displays also at the same time—and we might add, for the last time—Kaspar's resistance to the discursive order. For Kaspar seems to be aware of a forced connection between language and world which the speakers have long forgotten. Thus his autobiography is the last rebellion in the face of the order which is about to devour the *infans*. Yet not his failing is important but the gesture. Kaspar's resistance brings attention to an overdue change of philosophizing about language which half a century later Nietzsche will formulate *in extenso* and which only now, in our days, has been taken seriously, mostly by philologists of French provenance.

The oldest version of the autobiography sets out with the sentence: "This story of Kaspar Hauser I myself want to write" (87). Kaspar, now an author, understands himself as the subject and the object of his discourse, which he puts in pronounced dialogue with the discourses about and above him. Whereas so far his history has been written by others, he now plans, having become aware of his potential autonomy, to write his (his)story *himself*. Werner Herzog's "Kaspar Hauser" film portrays this apparent relation of the genesis of a subject and an author; in the film Kaspar is only allowed to tell stories which consist of a beginning, middle, and end—hence a closed form. Kaja Silverman comments:

> *Everyman for Himself and God Against All* is remarkable for posing simultaneously the problems of subjectivity and narrative—for dramatizing subjectivity *as* narrative, and narrative *as* subjectivity. Kaspar learns that the ability to tell a "complete" story is virtually synonymous with being oneself a "coherent" subject.[45]

And Kaspar's autobiography (which he endlessly rewrites and edits and out of which he tears entire pages only to let it stop abruptly) is the narrative of his becoming a subject as well as it portrays subjectivity as a story, i.e., as a form of fiction. Largely repeating Kaspar's earlier statements to the police officers, it describes his life in the cave, his toys, his food, and his writing instructions through "the man," as well as his walk to Nuremberg and his abandonment in the Unschlittplatz. A later version talks about "Hauser's first appearance in Nuremberg": his walk to the police station, to the prison tower, his interrogation with the Rittmeister and the jailer Hiltel, and his stay in the tower. It is therefore quite possible, as Brigitte Peucker argues,[46] to read here a bilingual pun by Herzog, replacing Kaspar's intention "ich möchte ein solcher Reiter [often transcribed as: reider] werden" with the almost homophonic "writer": Kaspar wants to become an author like his father once was. And Herzog's film shows that Kaspar is being taught his first sentence *at the same time* as he is taught to write, thus establishing a direct reference between "reiten" und writing. Just as the hermeneuticians teach him, Kaspar plans to leave behind the status of being described in order to write and to join those who do not belong to the words but who own the words and rule over them.

In his autobiography Kaspar does what he is asked to do: he supplies the proof of identity which the speakers expect from him. At the same time, however, he experiences the demands of subjectivity and narrative such as identity, coherence, and closure as constraints against which he revolts. On a formal level this can be shown in his subversive orthography, his unbroken resistance to grammatically correct sentences, and his refusal to consider his writings a final product, ready to hand away. As for the content, an *Aufsatz* can be quoted which Kaspar wrote for Daumer. It can be read as an allegory of Kaspar's resistance to the symbolic order.

> Several weeks ago I have sown my Name with cress and it thrived nicely and it was a real pleasure that I cannot tell and then someone came into the garden to carry off many pears and trampled on my Name and I wept and the professor told me to do it again so the other morning I did and then the cats stepped on it.[47]

Kaspar tries here to escape from the medium of signification. Being aware of the alienation and isolation which the subject endures when entering the symbolic order, he conjures a system of reference where being and meaning are not separated. The cress, biological entity (it grows!) *as well as* linguistic sign, overcomes this barrier by simultaneously meaning *and* being. The sown signature "Kaspar" thus belongs to both worlds; yet this remains a utopic nostalgia which does not materialize. First "someone" then the cats destroy Kaspar's attempt to transcend syntax[48] and he resigns.

An important role in writing down the autobiography is played by a hermeneutic device to which we so far have devoted very little attention, but which is in fact an implicit guaranty for any successful hermeneutic search for truth—namely memory. Schleiermacher's hermeneutics set out to show how memory fixes "acts of the process of perception"[49] and how it allows for any kind of perception in the first place. The question is therefore how memory comes into existence. Schleiermacher admits "actually no one needs memory for himself,"[50] only to immediately limit the frightening consequences of this insight in the following sentence: "Where needed, the result has to reappear like it appeared for the first time, for the perception is completed in an original production where the transcendental and the empirical become identical."[51] Introducing an "original production" through the back door liberates Schleiermacher from admitting something that would question his entire hermeneutic enterprise, namely that knowledge (*Erkennen*) is based on an order of discourse which must exist *prior* to all memory.[52] With Dilthey's hermeneutics matters are quite similar; according to him, autobiography is the paradigmatic achievement of memory which takes care that harmony and meaning can arise in a life threatened by chaos and dissonance. If Schleiermacher understands memory as the condition for knowledge, Dilthey comprehends it psychologically as a form of remembrance.[53] Even Gadamer, who tries to establish a critical difference between himself and Schleiermacher and Dilthey, describes "the phenomenon of memory . . . as an essential element of the finite historical being of man."[54]

This concept of memory as the guarantor of knowledge, harmonic synthesis of life, and finite historical being of man describes adequately the expectations of the speakers, who demand of Kaspar to employ his memory and formulate his *Lebensbeschreibung*. Hence, Kaspar's autobiography is marked by the effort to inform about the genesis of his memory, as well as it is naturally marked by the failure of the attempt to describe through language that which makes language possible. For memory cannot recall the conditions which constituted it in the first place.[55]

Schmidt von Lübeck describes the problem, representative for other discourse participants, as the following: "While in his first days *Caspar Hauser* was unable to give any explanations due to a lack of words and concepts, this is now just as impossible due to a lack of pure and undistorted recollection."[56] Yet this insight does not lead to the conclusion that the enigma is insoluble, but rather serves as an incentive for even harder hermeneutic efforts. In order to stimulate Kaspar's memory he is taken to castles, palaces, and dungeons, where one suspects he had his secret domicile for many years. He is asked to describe his dreams and to make drawings, and he is introduced to people who are believed to have some relation with his former life.

The rest of the story is well-known. Kaspar Hauser does not solve the riddle which he himself is. Or to be more precise: the hermeneuticians do not decipher the enigmatization which they themselves performed on Kaspar. Instead of listening to the foundling, who in fact speaks from the very beginning, they put their ear on Kaspar's "speechlessness" in order to divine a deeper truth behind his silence.

> This history of the mysterious imprisonment and exposure
> of a young man, presents, not only a fearful, but a most
> singular and obscure enigma, which may indeed give rise
> to innumerable questions and conjectures, but in respect
> to which little can be said with certainty; and which, until
> its solution shall have been found, must continue to retain,

in common with all enigmas, the property of being enigmatical.[57]

As we know, the "solution" was never found. But it seems that this is not really the concern of the hermeneuticians. Because in between Feuerbach's tautological lines one can read a hermeneutic narcissism, a pleasure principle of hide-and-seek. Not the result is important, but the hermeneutic process in itself.[58] It is one of the many ironies of Romanticism, that together with its interest in the enigmatic and the impenetrable it developed the disciplines to overcome this condition. Hermeneutics, psychology (including the interpretation of dreams), archaeology, geology name only a few. The subject of these disciplines and their respective methods rotates in a self-sufficient circle that is unwilling to disclose the hermeneutic truth it seeks to produce.

NOTES

1. Quoted by Jochen Hörisch, ed., *Ich möchte ein solcher werden wie. . . .: Materialien zur Sprachlosigkeit des Kaspar Hauser* (Frankfurt: Suhrkamp, 1979), p. 9. Quotations from this book will be identified by page number in the text plus the name of the respective author. The different texts refered to are: Anselm Feuerbach, "Kaspar Hauser—Verbrechen am Seelenleben des Menschen" (1832); "Mémoire—Wer möchte wohl Kaspar sein?" (1832); "Bekanntmachung" of the Nuremberg Mayor Binder (1828); "Ärztliches Gutachten" by Dr. Preu and Dr. Osterhausen (1830); J. F. K. Merker, "Caspar Hauser, nicht unwahrscheinlich ein Betrüger" (1830); Schmidt v. Lübeck, "Über Caspar Hauser" (1831); G. F. Daumer, "Mittheilungen über Kaspar Hauser" (1832); Anonymous, "Skizze der bis jetzt bekannten Lebensmomente des merkwürdigen Findlings" (1830). Feuerbach's text from 1832 can be found in translation in J. A. L. Singh, Robert M. Zingg, *Wolf-Children and Feral Man* (Archan, 1966), pp. 277–365. Although I have consulted this translation, page numbers always refer to Hörisch's edition.
2. As graphological research showed, this appendix, the so-called "maiden note," stems from the same author as the letter.
3. Cf. J. Hörisch, "Nachwort," *Ich möchte ein solcher werden wie. . .* , pp. 265f. The following remarks to some extent retrace Hörisch's argument.
4. With his bleeding feet the foundling echoes another mythical character with swollen feet who became famous as the paradigm of Aristotle's theory of drama, not to mention Freud's psychoanalysis.
5. For the definition of this term, see Jacques Derrida, "La parole soufflée," in *Writing and Difference*, trans. Alan Bass (Chicago: University of Chicago Press, 1978), pp. 169–95.
6. F. D. E. Schleiermacher, *Hermeneutik und Kritik*, ed. Manfred Frank (Frankfurt: Suhrkamp, 1977), p. 94. Frank notes that this formula is probably a free quotation of Friedrich Schlegel's. Cf. Frank, *Das individuelle Allgemeine* (Frankfurt: Suhrkamp, 1977), p. 358. If not otherwise indicated all translations are my own.
7. Michel Foucault, "What is an Author?" in *The Foucault Reader*, ed. Paul Rabinow (New York: Pantheon, 1984), p. 118.
8. Foucault, "Author," pp. 109f. Foucault is referring here to literary texts; although the letter in Kaspar's hand does not understand itself as literature it does blur the (problematic) distinction between literature and document.
9. Schleiermacher, *Hermeneutik*, p. 92.

10. Frank, "Einleitung," *Hermeneutik und Kritik*, p. 13.
11. The concept of *Sachverständnis* reappears (under somewhat different circumstances) as a central thought in Gadamer's hermeneutics. See Hans-Georg Gadamer, *Wahrheit und Methode: Grundzüge einer philosophischen Hermeneutik* (Tübingen: Mohr, 1960).
12. Norbert Bolz, "Friedrich Schleiermacher: Der Geist der Konversation und der Geist des Geldes," in Ulrich Nassen, ed., *Klassiker der Hermeneutik* (Paderborn: Schöningh, 1982), p. 109.
13. Schleiermacher, *Hermeneutik*, p. 315.
14. Norbert Bolz, "Schleiermacher," p. 110.
15. However, this commonplace existed long before Schleiermacher. Already the Latin Middle Ages knew this metaphor. Tracing the development of this metaphor, Ernst Robert Curtius shows "that the concept of the world or nature as a 'book' originated in pulpit eloquence, was then adopted by medieval mystico-philosophical speculation and finally passed into common usage" (*European Literature and Latin Middle Ages*, trans. Willard R. Trask [New York: Pantheon, 1953], p. 323). Also, Michel Foucault discusses the parallel between Renaissance and Romanticism by pointing out that at the beginning of the nineteenth century "language has resumed the enigmatic density it possessed at the time of the Renaissance." See *The Order of Things* (New York: Vintage, 1973), p. 298. The difference between the enigma of the Renaissance and Schleiermacher's is that the latter, due to the secularizing Enlightenment, has no recourse to God as the final means of explanation. While previously it was possible to assume that the creator possessed a plan unfathomable to humans this answer no longer exists for Schleiermacher.
16. Michel Foucault, ed., *I, Pierre Rivière, having slaughtered my mother, brother, and sister...*, trans. Frank Jellinek (Lincoln: University of Nebraska Press, 1975), p. x.
17. Many of these disciplines are actually a product of Romanticism; the interest in the enigma at the same time brings about the methods to solve it.
18. Cf. Werner Hamacher, "Das Beben der Darstellung," in David E. Wellbery, ed., *Positionen der Literaturwissenschaft* (Munich: Beck, 1984), pp. 149–73.
19. "Es ist bereits durch öffentliche Blätter hinlänglich bekannt, daß im Mai 1828 ein unbekannter junger Mensch erschien, der, sei es aus Blödsinn oder Verstellung, über seine Herkunft, Erziehung und sonstige Lebensverhältnisse durchaus keinen Aufschluß gab, und daher vorerst von dem Magistrat der Stadt Nürnberg in Verwahr und Pflege übernommen ward" (It is already known through public documents that in May, 1828, an unknown young man appeared who—because of idiocy or displacement—could not give any information regarding his origin, his education, or other circumstances, and for that reason was provisionally placed into custody) (Anonymous, 204).
20. Also the other objects Kaspar is carrying seem to mock the attempts of deciphering the riddle rather than contributing to its success: the key (without lock), and the booklet "Kunst die verlorne Zeit und übel zugebrachten Jahre zu ersetzen" forecast the sufferings to come for the just starting Kaspar Hauser research.
21. Foucault, *The Order of Things*, p. xxiv.
22. Hörisch, "Nachwort," p. 217. Tzvetan Todorov has minutely described the relation between repression and assimilation in his book *The Conquest of America*, where he discusses the confrontation of the Conquistadores with the Indians in terms of "comprendre" (understanding) and "prendre" (taking over).
23. " 'Kaspar sehr brav' statt: ich bin sehr brav, 'Kaspar scho Juli sage', statt: ich will es dem Julius (Sohn des Gefangenwärters) sagen, war seine durchgängige Redeweise.... Auch zu ihm mußte man nicht 'Du' sondern 'Kaspar' sagen, wenn er sogleich verstehen sollte, wen man meine" ('Kaspar very brave' instead of: I am very brave, 'Kaspar already tells Juli' instead of: I want to tell Julius [the son of the prison guard] was his normal way of speaking.... Even to Kaspar himself one had to say 'Kaspar' and not 'you' if he was to be able to understand whom one was referring to) (Feuerbach, p. 153).
24. Even the most subtle of Kaspar's interpreters, Anselm Feuerbach, shows these projections: "In these deserted times, when the hearts are shrinking and drying out in the fire

of selfishness" Kaspar seems a "a mirror of pure innocence," his language "a pure expression of the heart" (p. 120).

25. Ulrike Leonhardt, *Prinz von Baden, genannt Kaspar Hauser* (Hamburg: Rowohlt, 1987), p. 22.
26. Hiltel, quoted in Hermann Pies, *Kaspar Hauser: Eine Dokumentation* (Ansbach: Brügel, 1966), p. 20.
27. Hörisch, "Nachwort," p. 284.
28. Lacan's concept of the "mirror stage" describes exactly this: the reflection of the child's body in the mirror possesses a coherence which the subject lacks. For the subject is characterized by an unsurmountable *lack*, which is produced at birth, and later increased by the territorializtion of the body and the entry into the symbolic order. Therefore the subject's reaction to its mirror image is ambiguous: it envies it for a coherence which itself will never achieve, yet it hates it for eternally remaining exterior. (Cf. Silverman, *The Subject of Semiotics*, pp. 149ff.)
29. "Seine Unkunde . . . war Anfangs so groß, daß er nicht einmal alle Glieder seines Leibes kannte. Einmal, erzählte er mir, sey jemand zu ihm gekommen, der sich bemüht habe, ihn damit bekannt zu machen. Als man ihn mit den Händen an seine Ohren langen lassen, sey er sehr verwundert gewesen und habe geglaubt, das sey etwas Ungehöriges, welches von seinem Körper weggeschafft werden müsse. Erst da der Gefängniswärter ihn ein wenig an den Ohren gezogen, habe er sich überzeugt, daß es ein Theil seines Lebens sey" (His ignorance was so extensive at the beginning that he didn't know all of the parts of his body. Once, he told me, someone came to him who attempted to familiarize him with his body. When this person reached his hands to his ears, he was very puzzled and thought that these were something wrong, something that should be cast away from the body. Only after the guard pulled him around a bit by his ears was he able to convince himself that they were actually parts of his body) (Daumer, p. 248).
30. Quoted in Leonhardt, p. 75.
31. Cf. also Kaja Silverman's discussion of the respective scenes in "Kaspar Hauser's 'Terrible Fall' into Narrative," *New German Critique* 24–25 (1981–82), 83.
32. Werner Herzog, *Screenplays*, trans. Alan Greenberg and Martje Herzog (New York: Tanam Press, 1980), p. 123.
33. Silverman, "Terrible Fall," p. 83.
34. "Auch da Hauser 'ich' sagen gelernt hatte, sprach er doch noch mehrere Monate lang von sich selbst gern in der dritten Person und mit Nennung des Namens Kaspar. In der Beziehung auf eine Zeichnung, die von ihm gemacht worden war, sagte er z.B.: 'Wenn die Nase nicht wäre, so wäre gar nichts vom Kaspar in dem Bild.'—'Mich selbst darauf hindenken,' sagte er im Sommer 1828 statt: durch eigenes Studium herausbringen.—'es fühlt mich' nach der Analogie: Es friert mich und so weiter" (Also because Hauser had learned to say "I" he spoke for many months of himself in the third person and by utilzing the name Kaspar. In relation to a drawing that had been made by him, he said, for example: "If it weren't for the nose, there would be nothing of Kaspar in the picture."—"I myself think toward it," he said in the summer of 1828, instead of: bringing it about through one's own study.—"it feels me" according to the analogy: "Es friert mich" and so forth) (Daumer, quoted in Leonhardt, p. 99).
35. Cf. Lucien Malson, Jean Itard, Octave Mannoni, *Les enfants sauvages* (Paris: Union Générale d'Editions, 1964). Comparing the case of the wild boy of Aveyron one can note astonishing parallels within the treatment and documentation by the doctor and pedagogue Jean Itard, and Anselm Feuerbach.
36. "Vieles, bloß eine Spezies bezeichnende Worte gebrauchte er für die ganze Gattung. So z.B. galt ihm das Wort: Berg für jede Wölbung oder Erhebung, weshalb er einen dickbäuchigen Herrn, dessen Name ihm entfallen war, als den 'Mann mit dem großen Berg' bezeichnete" (Many words that simply designate a species he used for the entire genus. In such a manner, the word "mountain" meant for him any elevation or protrusion, and

for this reason he would name a man whose name he had forgotten the "man with the big mountain") (Feuerbach, p. 153).
37. "Wurzeln und Zöpfe nannte er *Schweife*, Balken *Bäume*, Tanzen *Herumlaufen*, Schwimmen *Laufen*, Gähnen den *Mund aufmachen*, das Umringen und Umstehen der Leute *Einmachen*, und so Mehreres" (243).
38. "Ich sagte: 'I möcht a söchana Reiter wern wie Vater is,' womit ich zu verstehen geben wollte, man solle mir ein solches glänzendes, schönes Ding geben . . . womit ich sagen wollte, wo sind die Pferde hin und das Wasser und das Brot . . . womit ich sagen wollte, warum denn meine Pferde so lange nicht kommen . . . womit ich sagen wollte, er solle mich nicht immer mit dem Sprechen so plagen, es tut mir alles sehr wehe" (I said: "I want to become such a rider as my father is," with which I wanted to say "someone should give me such a shiny, beautiful thing," with which I wanted to say "where have the horses gone and the water and the bread," with which I wanted to say "why haven't my horses come for so long," with which I wanted to say "he shouldn't always torment me with speaking, everything hurts me very much") (pp. 107–110).
39. Hörisch, "Nachwort," p. 284.
40. "Er [Kaspar] suchte dem Ausdruck der Rede durch eigentümliche Arm- und Handbewegungen nachzuhelfen; die Hände waren aufgehoben, das Innere derselben nach aussen gekehrt, Daumen und Zeigefinger mit den Fingerspitzen aneinandergeschlossen, und so die Hände und Arme gegen den bewegt, mit dem er sprach. Auch klopfte er mit den geschlossenen Spitzen des Daumen und Zeigefingers im Sprechen gern auf einen Tisch" (He sought to assist the expression of speech with strange arm and hand movements; his hands were raised, the inner arm were turned outward, thumb and index finger clasped together at the tips of the fingers. He would then move his hands and arms in the direction of his addressee. He would also tap his closed fingertips of his thumb and forefinger on the table while he spoke) (Daumer, p. 243).
41. Daumer, quoted in Holger Lakies and Gisela Lakies-Wild, *Das Phänomen: Entwicklungspsychologisch bedeutsame Fakten des Hauser-Mysteriums* (Ansbach: Ansbacher Verlagsanstalt, 1978), p. 163.
42. "[Man] gab ihm eine Feder mit Tinte, legte einen Bogen Papier vor ihm hin und forderte ihn auf, zu schreiben. Er schien darüber Freude zu bezeigen, nahm die Feder nicht weniger als ungeschickt zwischen seine Finger und schrieb, zu aller Anwesenden Erstaunen, in festen, leserlichen Zügen den Namen Kaspar Hauser" ([One] gave him a pen with ink, placed a piece of paper in front of him and challenged him to write. He appeared to show some joy, and took the pen in a slightly awkward fashion between his fingers and wrote, to the astonishment of all of those present, in strong, legible lines the name "Caspar Hauser") (Feuerbach, p. 124). Kurt Kramer, however, argues that he wrote the name "Hauser" with a small "h." See Kurt Kramer, *Kaspar Hauser—Kein Rätsel unserer Zeit* (Ansbach: Ansbacher Verlagsgesellschaft, 1978), p. 22.
43. "Ungefähr gegen dieselbe Zeit habe sich einmal der Mann in seinem Kerker eingefunden, habe ein Tischchen über seine Füße gestellt, habe etwas Weißes, das er jetzt für Papier erkenne, vor ihm ausgebreitet, dann von hinten her, so daß er nicht habe von ihm gesehen werden können, seine Hand ergriffen und sei mit einem Ding, daß er zwischen die Finger gesteckt [Bleistift], auf dem Papier hin und her gefahren. Er [Hauser] habe nicht gewußt, was das sei, habe aber gewaltige Freude empfunden, als er die schwarzen Figuren auf dem weißen Papier entstehen gesehen. Als er seine Hand wieder frei gefühlt und der Mann ihn verlassen, habe er, in der Freude über die neue Entdeckung, nicht satt werden können, diese Figuren immer wieder von neuem auf das Papier zu malen" (About the same time, the man found him in his cell and placed a little table over his feet, and placed in front of him something white that he could recognize as a piece of paper, and then, from behind him, so that he would not be seen by him, he grabbed his hand and, with the thing between his fingers [pencil], moved this way and that on the paper. He didn't know what it was, but he sensed an overwelming joy when he saw the black figures emerge on the white paper. When he felt his hand free once again and the man had left him, he

would draw these figures again and again in the joy of the discovery of not becoming satiated) (Feuerbach, p. 141).
44. Cf. de Man's notion of the play of the signifier in Paul de Man, "Reading and History," in *Resistance to Theory* (Minneapolis: University of Minnesota Press, 1986), pp. 65f.
45. Silverman, "Terrible Fall," p. 74.
46. Brigitte Peucker, "Literature and Writing in Herzog," in Timothy Corrigan, ed., *The Films of Werner Herzog* (New York: Methuen, 1986), p. 112.
47. "Vor etliche wochen habe ich von gartenkreß mein Namen gesähet und dieser ist recht schön gekommen der hat mir ein solche Freude gemacht das ich es nicht sagen kann und da ist einer in Garten hinein gekommen hat viele Birn fortgetragen der hat mir meinen Namen Zertreten da habe ich geweint dann hat der Herr Professor gesagt ich soll ihn wieder machen, ich habe ihn gemacht den andern Morgen haben mir wieder die Katzen Zertreten" (p. 115).
48. Silverman, "Terrible Fall," p. 88.
49. Schleiermacher, *Hermeneutik und Kritik*, p. 381.
50. Ibid.
51. "Ihm muß das Resultat jedesmal, wo er dessen bedarf, ebenso wiederkommen, wie es ihm das erste Mal gekommen ist, insofern nämlich in der ursprünglichen Produktion die Vorstellung vollendet, d.h. zu einer bestimmten Identität des Transzendentalen und Empirischen gelangt war." Ibid.
52. Cf. Friedrich Kittler, "Vergessen," in Ulrich Nassen, ed., *Texthermeneutik* (Paderborn: Schöningh, 1979), pp. 202ff.
53. Wilhelm Dilthey, *Der Aufbau der geschichtlichen Welt in den Geisteswissenschaften*, ed. Manfred Riedel (Frankfurt: Suhrkamp, 1981), p. 248: "Turning back in our recollection we grasp the by-gone links of the course of time under the category of their meaning."
54. Hans-Georg Gadamer, *Wahrheit und Methode*, p. 13.
55. For an interesting discussion of this problem see Alan Bewell, "Wordsworth's Primal Scene: Retrospective Tales of Idiots, Wild Children, and Savages," *English Literary History* 50 (1983), pp. 321-46.
56. "Konnte aber *Caspar Hauser* in den allerersten Tagen keine sicheren Aufschlüsse geben wegen Mangel an Wort und Begriff, so kann er es jetzt eben so wenig wegen Mangel an reiner und unverfälschter Rückerinnerung" (If Caspar Hauser was unable to give any certain information because of his lack of word and concept, he is unable to do it now because of a lack of pure and undistorted memory) (p. 235).
57. "Diese Geschichte der geheimnsisvollen Gefangenhaltung und Aussetzung eines jungen Menschen ist nun fürwahr nicht nur ein grauenhaftes, sondern auch seltsames, dunkles Rätsel, wobei sich außerordentlich vieles fragen und raten, aber wenig mit Gewißheit beantworten läßt, und welches natürlicherweise, solange noch nicht dessen Auflösung gelungen, mit jedem andern Rätsel die Eigenschaft gemein hat, daß es—rätselhaft ist" (This history of the mysterious captivity and displacement of a young man is now really and truly not only a horrible, but also a strange, dark riddle, whereby many questions can be asked and speculations made, but very little can be answered with any certainty and which, naturally, as long as there is no solution, shares with every other enigma the fact that it is—a puzzle) (Feuerbach, p. 143).
58. Still Gadamer admits: "It is our human existence to get entangled while attempting to interprete the polysemy" (Das ist menschliches Sein, sich so im Deuten des Vieldeutigen zu verstricken). Hans-Georg Gadamer, "Dichten und Deuten," in *Kleine Schriften*, vol. II (Tübingen: Mohr, 1967), p. 13.

III

Technologies of the Self

'DIE ERHALTUNG DES GLEICHGEWICHTS': DEFINING AND PRESCRIBING A TECHNOLOGY OF SELF

COURTNEY FEDERLE

Writing in the *Journal des Luxus und der Moden* in the year 1792, Karl August Ragotzky reflects upon a difference between the present and the recent past: "Eine Dame mit dem Siegwart in der Hand und Thränen im Auge, würde jetzt in einer Gesellschaft eine . . . lächerliche Figur machen" (A woman with a copy of *Siegwart* in her hand and tears in her eyes would appear laughable at a social gathering these days). Ragotzky's remark indicates the passing of, in his words, the "weinerliche Epoke, wovon wir jetzt nichts mehr, als jene Bände voll Jammer und Leiden und einige nervenkranke Dulderinnen übrig haben" (the weepy era, from which nothing remains except for those volumes full of tears and a few enervated women).[1] All that remains of a period so recently passed and so intensely lived are the neglected volumes and the "laughable," psychologically and physiologically damaged, feminine casualties of an excessive *Empfindsamkeit* (sentimentality). In that weepy epoch a public debate, ignited in part by such "high cultural" events as Goethe's *Werther* (1774) and Johann Martin Miller's *Siegwart* (1776), to which Ragotzky refers, and fueled further by such "low cultural" events as the blue frock and yellow vest fad, sought to answer two fundamental questions: What is *Empfindsamkeit*? And what degree of *Empfindsamkeit* might be permitted before being deemed excessive? Pedagogues, psychologists, philosophers, physiologists, and literary critics took it upon themselves to delimit the play of emotions and the possibilities of subjectivity. In the 1770s and 1780s the questions and answers that addressed the issue of the essence and proper measure of sentiment mark the first effort in the modern period to define and prescribe, in response to popular cultural modes of self-fashioning, a technology of the self appropriate to a utilitarian vision of society.

With his commentary Ragotzky suggests not only his ability to recognize the ephemeral in social and cultural history but also his willingness to embrace a related ontological notion of being-done-with a recent past: the present has confidently closed itself off from the threatening incursions of that remembered past. What vestiges remain appear, in Ragotzky's terms, laughable, sick, and feminine. Ragotzky represents the transgression of those years as a threat to a masculine economy of the subject. The natural economy was a masculine economy. Ragotzky's female casualties of excess are emblematic of effeminate modernity, of ephemeral, faddish ornament. The imbalance of sentimentality can be understood as a feminine disequilibrium not unlike other imbalances ascribed to women by the authoritative voices of the late eighteenth century. The feminine weakness—the debilitating submission to emotions, the inability to resist sentimental temptation—manifests itself in sentimentality. In the struggle to establish how the subject ought to be constituted as citizen the call for moderation prevailed. Ragotzky lends authority to an apparently triumphant discourse and thereby offers and encourages a sense of having dispatched the excesses of the period just past. The fortified conventions of moderation, its regime of truth, in turn compels the subject to distance itself from the folly of those recent days. Michel Foucault has characterized such compulsion as an "immense labor . . . to produce . . . men's subjugation: their constitution as subjects in both senses of the word."[2] In Ragotzky's image anyone publicly clinging to and exhibiting the sentimentality of those lacrymose years, literally anyone holding a clear sign of sentimentality in their hand, would be subjected to *and* by derision. According to Ragotzky's account of the passing of the fashionableness of the public display of sentimentality, the imbalance of that period's excesses has been successfully countervailed. Enlightened derisive laughter, coupled with the new authoritative knowledge of the pathological consequences of such excess, effectively polices against the return of the transgressions of the tearful period.

The reading of sentimental literature, coupled with the fashioning of a sentimental life-style, gave rise to the first popular cultural phenomenon, indeed to the first fad of the modern period, to be subjected to the rigor of the emerging science of man. As has been the case with all popular crazes that have "infected" the youth of Western societies over the past two centuries, the sentimentality of the 1770s and 1780s compelled fathers to publicly discuss and actively channel the potential dangers to their sons and daughters presented by the passing mode. Pedagogues, psychologists, physiologists, philosophers, and literary critics quickly framed the debate as being concerned with challenges to the order established by the father's techniques of the self. The celebration of sentiment in popular, youthful forms of self-fashioning in the late 1770s and early 1780s seemed to disrupt the project of the fathers. The process of civilization was perceived as having progressed to a point where man had commenced to build a harmonious society founded upon the ability of the subject to govern itself through a process of utilitarian renunciation. It was imperative that each citizen strike a balance among his intellectual, emotional, and corporal faculties. Such an equilibrium would permit the self-governed subject to function effectively both publicly and privately. In accordance with such a prescriptive ontology, proponents of a utilitarian technology of the self problematized faddish sentimentality as a popular life-style which disequilibriates the necessary and natural balance of the faculties.

This problematization receives my attention in the following. I want to consider the ideal formulation of a utilitarian technology of the self as it emerges, *ex negativo,* from the late eighteenth-century discussion of *Empfindsamkeit.* I will look at an instance of the discursive policing of the youthful fad, not as an example of repression, but as an example of how sentiment was subjected to the scrutiny of the emerging "human sciences" and thereby organized as a domain of human activity. Research done in the 1960s and 1970s argued that *Empfindsamkeit,* as a social and cultural phenomenon, formed an integrated element of the Enlightenment.[3] In this scholarship late Enlightenment utilitarianism provides a progressive model in its ability to tolerate, even to assimilate, something which was perceived as threatening when left to develop on its own, as wild growth, uncultivated and ungoverned. This argument contradicted the traditional reading of *Empfindsamkeit* as standing in opposition to the Enlightenment. The old dichotomy of head and heart was dismissed and replaced with a narrative of tolerant union. Rather than pursuing further this attempt to first discover the origins of *Empfindsamkeit* in Enlightenment moral discourse and then correct a tradition of contrasting *Empfindsamkeit* with Enlightenment, I will consider how the late eighteenth-century discussion of *Empfindsamkeit* problematizes the process of constituting the subject as citizen. I argue that the utilitarian call for an equilibrium that would be established by "scientifically" grounded renunciation marks the first broad intervention of the emerging "sciences of man" into the moral sphere in which the modern subject is formed. With rigorous differentiations, definitions, and prescriptions the "human scientists" of late eighteenth-century Germany examine and delimit subjectivity in an attempt to control how each citizen might best be formed so as to serve society.

Before turning to a specific example I want to generally characterize the discussion of *Empfindsamkeit.* The public discussion in late eighteenth-century Germany expressed the common conviction that society was progressing toward a balanced, rational order. The project of Enlightenment committed to achieving this new order can, for the purpose of my study, be broadly defined as the effort to enable reasoned and purposeful public discourse and consequent action, based upon rational moral and aesthetic judgement. All citizens active in the public sphere would engage in such discourse and action. The completion of the project would manifest itself as a harmonious society in which each subject would be rationally assimilated according to its economic and social functions. The assimilation of the subject into the social whole would be achieved after the self had been taught to consciously moderate its own excesses. Clearly, the public discussion contained within the framework of such a project would have to address and channel the "problem" of the emerging culture of sensitivity with all its potential to disturb the balanced, rational development of the citizen and, consequently, the orderly formation of society.

Not surprisingly then, late eighteenth-century attempts to differentiate and define the various degrees of *Empfindsamkeit* can be understood as part of the basic strategy to monitor and steer the untimely emergence in Germany of faddish sentimentality. The discussion inevitably returns to the issue of the proper balance and true relation of things, to the fundamental question of degree. The standard of measure, whether explicit or implicit, is the rationally moderate relation of things. Late eighteenth-century definitions of *Empfindsamkeit* attempt to determine the degree of sensibility which would be reasonably permissible or, *ex negativo,* the degree which would be intolerable. Reasoned action forms a sphere within which all permitted action occurs. Violations of that sphere's boundary are perceived not merely as deviant but as disruptive. Such deviance and disruption are to be held in check by the normative pressures exerted in the reasoned exposition of *Empfindsamkeit's* negative impact upon both individual and society.

I want to emphasize that most of those writing in the last quarter of the eighteenth century did not reject *Empfindsamkeit* outright. The following passage makes clear that the simplifications required by the understanding which isolates enlightenment and sentiment from each other and which perceives them as independent of and in opposition to one another, were recognized as early as 1778:

> Aufklärung bringt Kälte, sagt der Eine—und Gefühlsflamme zeugt Schwärmerey, sagt der Andre, und Beyde sagen wahr und falsch!—wahr! wenn sie Aufklärung und Gefühle isolieren, jedes, vom Andern unabhängig, allein bebauen, und ihren wechselseitigen Einfluß vernichten oder auch nur hemmen;-falsch! wenn sie Aufklärung des Geistes und Erfahrung des Gefühls gegenseitig verbinden, beyde in Einklang stimmen und dadurch einander erweitern, festnen, reinigen.[4]

> Enlightenment brings about coldness, says the one—and the flames of emotion produce wild enthusiasm, says the other, and both speak truly and falsely! Truly if they isolate enlightenment and emotion, when each is developed alone, independent from the other and their reciprocal in-

fluences are destroyed or even just hindered; falsely if enlightenment of the mind and experience of emotions mutually join, both in harmony and thereby enhance, strengthen, and purify one another.

The new science of the heart *(Wissenschaft des Herzens)*[5] attempted to bind intellect and emotion, Enlightenment and sentimentalism, to harmonize the apparently conflicting spheres and thereby subsume the latter within the former. The perceived threat of excessive sentimentality *(Schwärmerei)* would be held in check by the toleration of moderate sentiment as a desirable human quality in balance with other human qualities. A simplistic explanation of *Empfindsamkeit* as emerging in opposition to Aufklärung, it was already argued in the 1770s, fails to account for the multiplicity of the late eighteenth-century differentiations between degrees of *Empfindsamkeit*. We can understand such establishing of difference as part of an attempt to prescribe a mode by which human beings would be made subjects.

Of course, within the wide spectrum of *Empfindsamkeiten* identified, the tolerable, moderate degrees of *Empfindsamkeit* were defined according to the limits determined appropriate by the increasingly authoritative science of the heart. When a definition of the "proper" relationship between reason and emotion was sought, the necessity of containing the latter within a sphere defined by the former was stressed. An essay entitled "Ueber die falsche Empfindsamkeit" (1780) offers an example of such thinking:

> Obgleich warme Empfindsamkeit und zärtliches Gefühl vorzüglich reitzend und liebenswürdig sind, wenn sie von der Natur herrühren, und in das Gebiet der Vernunft und erleuchteter Grundsätze eingeschränkt werden: so ist es doch nichts so widerlich und ungereimt, als wenn selbst die wirklichen nicht von der Vernunft regieret und im Zaum gehalten werden.[6]

> Even though warm sentimentality and gentle feeling are wonderfully exciting and lovable when they are derived from nature and are contained within the sphere of reason and illuminated principles: there is indeed nothing so repulsive and awkward as when even true sentimentality is not governed by reason and held within limits.

The author draws clear boundaries that must not be trespassed. He invokes nature (and here *nature* must be understood according to the Rousseauean model of intellectual, emotional, and bodily economy) as the source, together with reason and law as the sphere that would properly contain appropriately moderate *Empfindsamkeit*. His invocation of nature, reason, and law establishes the difference between real *(wirkliche)* and affected *(affectirte;* 100) sentimentality. Authenticity bears authority; affectation merely corrupts. Affectation serves as a negative signifier in a manner similar to *Mode*. The vocabulary of the discourse of *Empfindsamkeit* shores up the authority of reason by labeling it as the authentic, eternal, and universal while it simultaneously undermines any claim to authenticity that might be made in the name of sentiment by labeling it as the artificial, ephemeral, and local. However, the author goes yet one step further in delineating the hierarchy of authorities when he claims that even real *Empfindsamkeit (selbst die wirkliche)*, even authentic sentimentality, must be governed and fenced in by reason. Real, natural forms of *Empfindsamkeit*, particularly charming and lovable when held in check by reason and law, become repulsive and absurd when they escape containment. Such governing and fencing in of warm sensitivity and gentle feelings would offer an effective means of preventing the transgressions of excessive sentimentality.

Late eighteenth-century authorities in the public debate could only understand *Empfindsamkeit* in terms of the always unstable relationship between reason, law, and emotion. As I pointed out above, late-eighteenth-century "human scientists" did not reject *Empfindsamkeit* outright. However, in their warnings against the potential excesses that they attributed to the culture of feeling, such authors differentiated a broad spectrum of the dangers of disequilibrium and thereby compelled the subject to understand its own feelings in terms of boundaries, order, and balance.[7] In attempting to ameliorate the impact of the popular culture fad of sentimentality by assimilating it into a broad pedagogical vision, late eighteenth-century critics discursively eroded the threat of *Empfindsamkeit's* excessive and potentially unbounded, chaotic, and imbalanced forms.

Here I turn to an exemplary text that was written in response to the emergence of what was perceived as the unruly culture of sentimentality. The author argues for the necessity of balancing the human faculties. The title of the essay reveals the thrust of the argument made in favor of an ascetic technology of the self: "Von der nöthigen Sorge für die Erhaltung des Gleichgewichts unter den menschlichen Kräften. Besondere Warnung vor dem Modefehler die Empfindsamkeit zu überspannen" (On the Necessary Concern for the Maintenance of Balance among the Human Powers. A Special Warning concerning the Fashionable Mistake of Taking Sentimentality Too Far).[8] From the title it can be understood that the author believes that, as a general rule, balance among the human faculties must be maintained in order to assure proper care of the self. With the warning, an addendum to the essay, the author expresses concern for a contemporary, apparently passing, aberrant mode which disrupts the balance prescribed. The author also suggests that his contemporaries are failing to adequately care for themselves. Upon reading the title I am compelled to ask how does the author determine what constitutes equilibrium and when does he know that *Empfindsamkeit* has been stretched too far? In what follows I will try to answer these questions and situate them in the late eighteenth-century German discourse on the technology of the self.

The pedagogue who wrote this essay, Joachim Heinrich Campe, was a central figure in the late eighteenth-century German pedagogical school known as Philanthropism.[9] From the 1770s to the 1790s the philanthropists played a significant role in the public discussion that addressed the issue of how the individual and society might best be formed. The philanthropic project sought to advance German society by cultivating and maximizing the usefulness *(Brauchbarkeit)* of each individual citizen through a system of universal, but highly differentiated, practical education. These educators argued for and implemented a utilitarian pedagogy designed, in part, to restrain the subject from the excesses of sentimentality modeled in popular *Gefühlskultur* (culture of feeling). The philosophical and methodological foundation of the utilitarian pedagogy advocated by the philanthropists is comprehensively presented in a collection of essays solicited and published by Campe in the massive sixteen-volume work: *Allgemeine Revision des gesamten Schul- und Erziehungswesens von einer Gesellschaft practischer Erzieher* (Universal Revision of the Entire School and Educational Systems by a Society of Practical Pedagogues) (1785). Campe wanted his project to be received as an encyclopedia of enlightened pedagogy. With its argument for the establishment and guarding of an equilibrium among the human faculties as the basis for the utilitarian integration of the individual into enlightened society, Campe's essay, "Von der nötigen Sorge für die Erhaltung des Gleichgewichts unter den menschlichen Kräften. Besondere Warnung vor dem Modefehler die Empfindsamkeit zu überspannen" (On the Necessary Concern for the Maintenance of Balance among the Human Powers) mentioned previously represents not only the fundamental position of his encyclopedic undertaking but also that of philanthropism itself.[10]

Campe begins the essay by asking the fundamental question: "Was ist Empfindsamkeit?" (393). This question faintly echoes that famous one, posed two years earlier, which provoked Kant's well-known response. However, when Campe attempts to answer his own question he reverses the spirit of Kant's essay. Whereas Kant's interest lies in describing an attitude necessary to the constituting of an autonomous subject, Campe's lies in defining an attitude necessary to the constituting of a heteronomous subject. Campe replaces Kant's concern for emancipation with his own concern for containment. As we will see below when we consider the rhetoric of Campe's reply to the question that he poses, Campe argues that something like Kant's *sapere aude!* must be held in check because of the threat that this emancipatory call could become an emotionally and sensually excessive *"sentire aude!"* Before answering the question concerning the essence of [*Empfindsamkeit*] Campe follows with a question concerning its limits: "Darf [Empfindsamkeit] geübt werden? Und im bejahenden Falle, bis zu welchem Grade?" (Ought [sentimentality] be practiced? And if so, to what degree?) (393). As we will see below, Campe's cautious interrogative, "bis zu welchem Grade?" points to his desire to define and fix limits that pertain to the formation of the subject.[11] In my reading of his argument I want to look at how he uses a metaphor of equilibrium to express the philanthropic idea that a society must be founded on a harmony of reason and sentiment in each citizen.

Campe argues that excessive, popular forms of sentimental self-fashioning could potentially destabilize the utilitarian order which demands that the subject be constituted according to a model of balance. In effect society as a whole would ideally reflect the harmonious equilibrium among the human faculties (*Gleichgewicht unter den menschlichen Kräften*) of the individual citizen. Campe warns, however, that the business of determining where this necessary balance lies can be perilous:

> Entweder steht die Empfindsamkeit . . . mit allen übrigen Kräften des Menschen, besonders mit seinem Verstande, mit seiner Vernunft und mit seiner Körperkraft in Ebenmaaß, oder nicht. Ist jenes, so ist sie eine schöne und nützliche Kraft des Menschen, welche, solange dieses Ebenmaaß unverrückt bleibt, nie zu stark wirken kann; ist hingegen dieses, ragt die Empfindsamkeit über andere Kräfte des Menschen, besonders über seinen Verstand, über seine Vernunft und über seine Körperkraft ungebührlich hervor: so ist sie das verderblichste Geschenk, welches die Cultur dem Menschen je verleihen kann, verderblich für das Glük des Individuums, verderblich für das Wohl der Gesellschaft. (395–96)

> Either sentimentality exists in proportion . . . with all the other faculties of a person, particularly with his understanding, his reason, and with his physical strengths, or not. If the former is the case, then sentimentality is a beautiful and useful human faculty, which, as long as this proportion remains undisturbed, can never have too powerful an effect; if on the other hand it is the latter, if sentimentality towers disproportionately above the other faculties of a person, particularly over his understanding, over his reason, and over his physical strengths, then sentimentality is the most pernicious gift that culture can ever grant man, pernicious for the individual, pernicious for the welfare of society.

Here Campe charts two possible relations between *Empfindsamkeit*, understanding, reason, and the body. Either balance gently governs and *Empfindsamkeit* functions as that beautiful and useful force, or imbalance tyrannizes and *Empfindsamkeit* becomes the most pernicious gift. Campe characterizes *Empfindsamkeit* as culture's gift to man, though always also potentially the spurious gift of ruinous excess. This civilized, cultivated faculty performs such an essential role in the localized balancing act of each subject's self that, when it is not properly contained, it juts forth *(hervorragt)* with a force that ruins not only the happiness of the individual, but also the welfare of society. With his utilitarian argument Campe posits the dark interior of the subject out of which immoderate, imbalanced *Empfindsamkeit* threatens to emerge as a force capable of destroying both individual and society. The philanthropic pedagogical philosophy that aims to transform society by educating the subject in the art of self-government presupposes a seamless fabric of subjects and society. As a spokesman of this pedagogical program Campe insists that *Empfindsamkeit* be contained by the other faculties so that the balance of both individual and society be preserved. Campe admonishes the subject to install in himself a *de facto* hierarchy of the faculties placing *Empfindsamkeit* under the control of reason, intellect, and physical strength *(Vernunft, Verstand, und Körperkraft)*.

Campe's metaphor of balance permits finer differentiation between the various degrees and types of sentiment which, in turn, allows for a more rigorously argued, utilitarian technique of the self. As part of his effort to define the equilibrium where the human faculties stand in proper proportion *(in richtiger Proportion steht)* to the other faculties Campe distinguishes between what is artificial and genuine, between spurious and natural feelings *(erkünstelte und natürliche Gefühle,* 398). Artificial sentiment is a symptom of the imbalance brought on by excess; genuine sentiment is a manifestation of the balance effected by moderation.

In making his distinction between fabricated and natural feelings Campe proposes a standard for evaluating cultural expressions of subjectivity. His argument clearly privileges the original over the acquired, naturally moderate over disproportionately cultivated sensitivity. Here the pedagogue calls upon the category *authenticity* to argue against an *Empfindsamkeit* which has too strong an effect *(zu stark wirkt)*. Proportional inner strength *(Kraft der Seele)* is natural *(natürlich)*, disproportional *Kraft der Seele* is artificial *(erkünstelt,* 398). Campe bases this distinction on his notion of properly moderate sentiment which reflects, in his phrase, the true relation of things *(wahre Beziehungen der Dinge,* 399). With his definition Campe establishes that authenticity of emotion results from balance grounded in, as we have seen, a hierarchy of the human faculties based on and permeated with reason. It follows from Campe's statements that genuine emotion must be grounded in the economy of reason. Campe's position tolerates *Empfindsamkeit,* in fact promotes it, provided that it is of correct proportion *(richtiger Proportion)*. Where Campe privileges an authenticity that springs from reason he reinforces his argument for the norm of rationally moderated taste *(Geschmack)*. The virtue of moderation in all things is of considerable significance in any eighteenth-century discussion of the individual's relationship to self and society. The assimilation of the individual into the whole, imperative to the formation of an enlightened society of consenting citizens, depends upon the practice of the characteristically bourgeois virtue of moderation. In effect, Campe proposes that sentiment be tamed and then assimilated into the philanthropic project.

By establishing a hierarchy of the faculties *(die Kräfte des Menschen)* in his discourse on sentiment, Campe shores up the philanthropic pedagogical program. However, he simultaneously destablizes and contradicts the language of his own equilibrium metaphor. The rhetorical gesture of equilibrium *(Gleichgewicht)* is thrown out of balance by the weighty presence of reason, intellect, and the body. The notion of balance seems more a necessary fiction for the rational moderation of the subject's sensitivity than a genuine attempt to integrate that sensitiveness into the foundation of both citizen and society. Though Campe recognizes and applauds the ameliorating effect of *Empfindsamkeit* upon an enlightened, rational society and includes it as an element in his model of harmony, the balance that he creates is not the natural, horizontal equilibrium of a scale; rather, it is the coerced, vertical equilibrium of an arbitrary hierarchy. Initially Campe seems to justly permit, or even to champion, balance with his metaphor. However, as he further develops his essay, he shifts the balance, making the human faculties no longer merely a counter-weight, but rather, the standard of measure itself.

The philanthropic goal of creating a rationally constituted society necessarily privileged reason, intellect, and the body over sentiment. The order of the enlightened society would be maintained by the subject's voluntary integration into that order and by the consequent performance of its social obligations. The imperative nature of the social contract was spelled out for the individual. Anything that undermined the subject's capacity or willingness to fulfill his duty to society threatened both to marginalize that individual and to destabilize the foundations of society. Again, Campe warns of the potentially subversive nature of imbalanced *Empfindsamkeit*:

> Aber Empfindlichkeit, d.i. überspannte unverhältniß-mäßig ausgebildete und verstärkte Empfindsamkeit, die ist es, welche den Menschen nicht nur in hohem Grade unbrauchbar zur Erfüllung aller seiner Pflichten als Mensch und Bürger, sondern auch zugleich ausnehmend elend macht. (411)

> But sentimentality, that is, enervated, disproportionately developed and strengthened sentimentality, is that which makes a person not only to a great degree useless to the task of fulfilling all his duties as a human being and citizen, but also at the same time exceptionally miserable.

Campe narrates a story of excess and misery in order to drive home his argument that sentimentality threatens the harmony of the faculties. In differentiating between the various degrees of *Empfindsamkeit* he represents the necessary dissipation of the person, as both citizen and subject, that occurs when sentimentality swells out of all proportion and throws the order of the faculties out of balance. The rhetoric of Campe's tale of over-extended, disproportionately developed, and intensified sentimentality can again be questioned in light of the specific argument of this statement. Campe contends that this imbalanced *Empfindsamkeit* renders the citizen unusable *(unbrauchbar)*. Again Campe defines the equilibrium that must be maintained according to the terms of a utilitarian concept of the individual and society: the utilitarian order permits the individual citizen a degree of sensitivity and defines that degree by the line beyond which the subject is no longer able to fulfill all of its duties as citizen. Campe wants with his model of equilibrium to regulate the subject and citizen so as to achieve an enlightened society in which the individual carries out all its duties *(alle seiner Pflichten)*. Campe's insistence upon an "all or nothing" notion of the subject's obligation, of the virtue of total commitment to achieving the harmonious society, is hardly assuaged by his rhetorical of "nicht nur . . . sondern auch." Not only does the individual become "unusable," which may have sounded frighteningly utilitarian even to the late eighteenth-century reader, but also wretched *(elend)*. Here, fear instructs and polices. The lesson is clear, the priorities are straight: sensitivity must be subordinated to the faculties, must be held in moderation so that the individual citizen can remain useful and happy within the social order.

Campe emphasizes the social threat of an imbalanced *Empfindsamkeit* that no longer recognizes the proper, rational order of the world, and then he ups the ante by claiming that that order is in fact divine. He shifts the level of his argument from the civil to the theological and consequently augments the egregiousness of sentiment's destabilizing transgressions. Campe proclaims that excessively sensitive individuals ignore "die weise und gütige Regierung des Weltbeherrschers" (the wise and benevolent government of the world-ruler) and question "wo sie bewundern, murren, wo sie in Dank und Anbetung zerfließen sollten" (where they should admire, grumble, and dissolve in gratitude and worship) (414). Campe admonishes the subject that has been thrown out of balance by its own overextended, disproportionately developed, and intensified sentiment for failing to appreciate the good in God's reign over this world. The sinful transgressions of self-indulgent doubt *(zweifeln)* and complaint *(murren)* characterize this unappreciative insubordination. At this point in his essay, Campe evokes the divine order so as to shore up his argument for a worldly order in which sentiment must be subordinated to a transcendent balance of the human faculties. Campe compares the "proper" imbalance of the faculties that outweigh sentiment to the divine disequilibrium of the enlightened and absolute dominion of God's government over the world. Campe's initial argument in favor of balance ultimately reveals itself as an argument for a hierarchichal imbalance.

It is not surprising that the rhetorical gesture of Campe's tolerant equilibrium metaphor gradually reveals itself as part of an intolerant effort to shore up a hierarchy of values. The static equilibrium that Campe represents with his image of the absolutely sovereign *Weltbeherrscher,* however, destroys the subtlety of the scale that Campe suggested at the beginning of his essay, where he acknowledges the relation of contending weights. The tension and the fluctuation permitted by the balance between the faculties and sentiment might more closely correspond to the correct proportion *(richtiges Ebenmaaß;* 405) to which Campe refers earlier in his essay. Campe, however, prefers a rigid equilibrium which establishes stability by invoking not only an enlightened, pedagogical idea of subjectivity and citizenship, but also a divine order of things. Each subject/citizen would be compelled to balance its sentiment according to the harmony defined by divine government and civic duty.

Campe weaves the virtue of enduring-through-renunciation, the characteristic virtue of enlightened civilization,[12] into the fabric of his ideal subject. Those who are unable to balance the faculties, those who are now clearly understood to be too weak to subordinate sentiment to reason, intellect, and the body, have veered from the virtuous path of moderation and suffer the consequences of their inability to achieve the proper balance of things. Campe concludes from his assessment of unchecked sensitivity that those who are characterized by such imbalance, that those who "es nicht fassen [können], daß eine Welt, in der sie so viel leiden müssen, die beste sey" ([those who] cannot comprehend that a world in which they must suffer so much is the best world) (413) represent "erklärte Feinde der schönsten Gabe des Himmels, unsers edelsten Vorzuges—der Vernunft" ([represent] declared enemies of the most beautiful gift from heaven, our most noble characteristic—reason) (407). At the beginning of his essay where he attempted to differentiate and delimit from one another acceptable and unacceptable degrees of sentimentality, Campe represented excessive sentimentality as but a minor transgression. Toward the end of his essay he unequivocally labels such excess as a threat that violates divine and civil order. Again, the invocation of the order and administration of a *Weltbeherrscher* lends absolute authority and equilibrium to the model on which Campe bases his argument.

Campe further undermines his metaphor of balance by blending in a metaphor of light, which he then uses to emphasize the implicitly divine source of transparent reason in contrast to the human origins of opaque sentimentality. In mixing his metaphors Campe is cautious not to disturb the figurative hierarchical balance which he had set up. He parallels the hierarchy of reason over sentiment with that of light over darkness. Campe casts the eclipsing of luminous reason, of that most beautiful gift from heaven *(die schönste Gabe des Himmels,* 407), by dark sentimentality, in the dimensions of the Miltonian struggle between the forces of light and dark. The pedagogue grounds the obscure delusion of *Empfindsamkeit*, in its opposition to the clear insight of reason (*deutliche Einsichten der Vernunft*, 406) in dark feelings (*dunkeln Gefühlen*, 406). Campe stablizes the hierarchy of reason by placing the formidable weight of light—the heaviest of all Enlightenment metaphors—on reason's side of the scale.

With his philanthropic argument Campe represents the eighteenth-century attitude which first framed the discussion of the subject in terms of utility and balance and then compelled the subject to think of himself in these terms. Reading Campe's exemplary and, in its time, influential text, one can discern the strategy of discursively assimilating the potentially unruly excesses of human subjectivity into an ideology of utility and moderation. The specific example of *Empfindsamkeit* permits a particularly clear instance of where, when, and how the nascent *human sciences* begin to take on the task of forming the subject for society. The even more specific moment of Campe's admonitory essay provides an example of a late Enlightenment attempt to govern through discourse. Campe locates *authenticity* within the economy of rationally moderated sentiment. The virtue of moderation in all things is of considerable significance in eighteenth-century discussions of the individual's relationship to society. The assimilation of the individual into the whole, imperative to the formation of an enlightened society of consenting citizens, would depend upon the practice of the characteristically bourgeois virtue of moderation.[13] Where Campe discusses *Empfindsamkeit* in terms of taste or judgment, the moderating, normative character of the ascetic imperative is especially clear. When the sentimental subject rejects particular social conventions the charge of bad taste is made. Deviation from the social-cultural norm of moderation represents a violation of the authenticity that has been invented and employed to prevent such trangression. The modern policing of sentiment became effective through the discussion of *Empfindsamkeit,* which differentiated, defined, and prescribed forms of balanced subjectivity. Here the subject, that building block of the system envisioned as the ideal social form by the late eighteenth-century utilitarians, is *subjected* in that it is publicly scrutinized and admonished to care for itself. Campe's argument, representative of philanthropic as well as utilitarian thinking in late eighteenth-century Germany, expresses the convictions of a watershed period in the modern "history of the different modes by which, in our culture, human beings are made subjects."[14]

NOTES

1. I quote from an article entitled "Ueber Mode-Epoken in der Teutschen Lektüre," *Journal des Luxus und der Moden* (Weimar, 1792) pp. 550, 552.
2. Michel Foucault, *The History of Sexuality: Volume I, An Introduction*, trans. Robert Hurley (New York: Vintage, 1980), p. 60.

3. See Georg Jäger, *Empfindsamkeit und Roman* (Stuttgart, 1969); Gerhard Sauder, *Empfindsamkeit: Voraussetzungen und Elemente* (Stuttgart, 1974); Wolfgang Doktor, *Kritik der Empfindsamkeit* (Frankfurt, 1975).
4. Johann Jacob Hottinger and Johann Rudolf Sulzer, *Brelocken ans Allerley der Gros- und Kleinmänner* (Leipzig, 1778), pp. 30f.
5. This term was used in the title of an article that appeared in *Das Deutsche Museum* 2 (1777) 65–76. The full title reads: "Rapsodische Gedanken die Wissenschaft des Herzens betreffend."
6. *Die Feyerstunde der Grazien. Ein Lesebuch*, ed. Johann Georg Heinzmann (Bern, 1780), p. 101. All subsequent references to this work in the text will cite page numbers only.
7. In his book *Kritik der Empfindsamkeit* (1975), Wolfgang Doktor documents the diverse aspects of society considered by late eighteenth-century authors as threatened by sentimental excess. Included are not only the health of the individual (pp. 233f.) but also that of various institutions such as the military (pp. 423f.), the family (pp. 182f.; pp. 415f.) and the judicial system (pp. 352f.).
8. *Allgemeine Revision der gesamten Schul- und Erziehungswesen von einer Gesellschaft praktischer Erzieher*, ed. Joachim Heinrich Campe (Hamburg, 1785), part III, pp. 393–434. In subsequent citations the original text will be cited by page number only. Herwig Blankertz has edited and published the essay "Von der nöthigen Sorge" in his book, Bildung und Brauchbarkeit (Stuttgart: Westermann, 1965), pp. 19f. However, he omits the addendum, "Besondere Warnung" (pp. 393–434). A portion of this part of Campe's essay (pp. 393–417) appears in Doktor and Sauder, *Empfindsamkeit*, pp. 77–91.
9. The term "Philantropism" is derived from the model school called the Philanthropinum founded by J. B. Basedow in 1774 at Dessau. The theoretical and practical position associated with the school came to be called "Philanthropinismus," "Philanthropismus," or "philanthropische Pädagogik." Campe was first a teacher at and later the director the Philanthropinum. For an introduction to Philantropism see Herwig Blankertz, *Berufsbildung und Utilitarismus* (Düsseldorf, 1963) and Blankertz's introduction to his *Bildung und Brauchbarkeit*, pp. 1–17.
10. Though he has remained relatively obscure, Campe (1746–1818) was an influential figure in late eighteenth-century Germany. In addition to being the editor of the *Allgemeine Revision*, which can be considered the culmination of eighteenth-century pedagogy in Germany, Campe was the prolific author of thirty volumes of children's literature. Indeed philantropic pedagogy found its most influential expression in his popular, moral-didactic work, *Robinson der Jüngere* (1779), which was reissued 102 times between 1779 and 1881. He compiled a dictionary of the German language and wrote numerous books concerning childhood and education. In addition to his writing Campe was active as a pedagogue in Potsdam, as director of the Philantropin in Dessau, and as founder of "Erziehungsinstituten" in Hamburg and Braunschweig. He also served as private tutor to Alexander and Wilhelm von Humboldt and accompanied the younger brother on his trip to Paris during the French Revolution. For more on Campe see Jacob Anton Leyser, *J. H. Campe: Ein Lebensbild aus dem Zeitalter der Aufklärung* (Braunschweig, 1896).
11. Numerous attempts to determine and limit appropriate degrees of sentiment were made in response to the emergence of a *Gefühlskultur* in Germany. For examples of texts representative of such efforts see Wolfgang Doktor, *Kritik der Empfindsamkeit* (1975); Gerhard Sauder, *Empfindsamkeit* (1974); and Georg Jäger, *Empfindsamkeit und Roman* (1969), all cited in note 3 above.
12. Horkheimer and Adorno's thesis in *Dialektik der Aufklärung*, in Horkheimer, *Gesammelte Schriften* (Frankfurt, 1987), vol. V, p. 79.
13. In *Dialektik der Aufklärung*, Horkheimer and Adorno criticize the Enlightenment argument for moderation by registering the effect that the rigorous practice of self-denial might have upon the individual. Borrowing from Weber and Freud they elaborate their critique particularly in "Exkurs I: Odysseus oder Mythos und Aufklärung" and "Exkurs II: Juliette oder Aufklärung und Mythos." In the aphoristic style of "Exkurs I" they

state; "Die Geschichte der Zivilization ist die Geschichte der Introversion des Opfers. Mit anderen Worten: die Geschichte der Entsagung." Max Horkheimer *Gesammelte Schriften*, ed. Alfred Schmidt, 14 volumes (Frankfurt: Fischer, 1987) v. V, p. 79. For a contemporary critique of the eighteenth-century virtue of moderation as self-inflicted oppression, see Hartmut and Gernot Böhme, *Das Andere der Vernunft* (Frankfurt: Suhrkamp, 1983).

14. Michel Foucault, "The Subject and Power," in Hubert L. Dreyfus and Paul Rabinow, *Michel Foucault: Beyond Structuralism and Hermeneutics* (Chicago: University of Chicago Press, 1982), p. 208.

Concerning Several Formulae of Communication in Hölderlin[1]

RÜDIGER CAMPE

In Foucault's writings of the sixties two types of reading literature in a discourse-analytical mode can be distinguished. Hölderlin's name is linked to the differentiation between both readings. One type of reading consists of the analysis of *the discourse* (singular) as Foucault practices it in his literary criticism (e.g., in "Le langage à l'infini" or his book on Roussel, *Raymond Roussel*). This kind of analysis also dominates Foucault's concept of literature in the history of madness, *Folie et déraison*. In this context poetry and literature are seen as privileged in the way they represent the law and the historicity of discourse and of representation in general. We find Hölderlin's name among those of writers like de Sade and Nietzsche, Mallarmé and Artaud, Roussel and Bataille. For Foucault, they are authors who push the literary work to an inner limit, a limit where at the same time the question about discourse opens up.

The analysis of *the discourse* is opposed to an analysis of texts that operates on the basic assumption of a multiplicity of discourses, particularly as seen in Foucault's major epistemological work *Les mots et les choses*. The analysis of *discourses* (*plurale tantum*) examines the beginnings and ruptures of the many discourses as well as their interrelations. In this latter kind of analysis, the many discourses are already enclosed in conceptual and institutional frames; the space of the one founding *discourse* remains unoccupied in *Les mots et les choses*. As a consequence, literature loses its privileged position. Literature becomes, at least tendentiously, one of many discourses. With this shift in the status of literature, Hölderlin's name changes sides. In *Les mots et les choses*, Nietzsche and Mallarmé are the writers who specifically perform discursive changes. In this context of a reading where literature is only one of many discourses, the poet Hölderlin, together with the philosophers Marx and Hegel, belongs to the group of writers who only name the rupture of classical thinking but do not perform it.

This simplified sketch of the opposition between the two types of reading literature in a discourse-analytical mode suffices to point out the crucial way in which literature is strikingly affected by the distinction between the analysis of *the discourse* and the analysis of *discourses*. Thus, literary discourse-analysis is bound to offer a way of reading which remains open for both versions of analysis, indeed for a kind of controlled changing between the two opposite versions.

Johann Christian Friedrich Holderlin, from the Bildabteilung, Deutsches Literaturarchiv of the Schiller Nationalmuseum, Marbach, Germany. Reprinted with permission.

In Foucault's oeuvre both kinds of discourse-analysis intersect in an essay on Hölderlin, in his extended review of Laplanche's psychoanalytical study. This is not a simple coincidence; the intersection of the two modes also corresponds to a parallel process in Hölderlin's work, as we shall see. In the Laplanche review, Foucault discusses the relation between aesthetic and psychological commentary on two clearly different levels. First, he comments on the work; his commentaries on the work exclude every psychological explanation and depict Hölderlin's madness, as defined by the work, to be a rupture within the work itself. Foucault also adds an entirely external, historical sketch about the history of authorship, about its connection to the life of the author, and the motive of madness (a line of thought which led to the later lecture "Qu'est ce qu'un auteur?"). Foucault's interest does not lie in the harmonic interplay between 'technical' and 'historical' interpretation as we see it in the foundation of modern hermeneutics with Schleiermacher. Foucault places literary discourse, which is one discursive practice and one institution among others, clearly separate from the work, which opens itself up to *the discourse* which precedes all individual practices and institutions.[2]

This essay focuses on the *act of speaking* in Hölderlin. The act of speaking is a much smaller unit of analysis in comparison to the categories of work and authorship. Nevertheless, in the act of speaking, the relationship between discourse and institution is already entirely at stake. The speech-acts as defined and named in Austin's speech-act theory can be understood as the smallest institutional units of speech. This interpretation becomes particularly evident when one assumes with Bourdieu that purely linguistic means can never arrive at a full definition of a speech-act. Social categories or terms of the theological and juridical tradition constantly come into play in conscious or unconscious ways (e.g., theologians speak of the language of creation and the language of law; jurists ask how one makes a promise, or how one gives testimony, etc.).[3]

Several individual observations in the reading of Hölderlin are significant for the context of our discussion. Hölderlin pays special attention[4] to the procedure and the names of the acts of speaking. His care can be found in reflections on the status of giving testimony in religious practices. We see it in the composition of the letters in the epistolary novel *Hyperion*, as well as in his private letters, especially the late ones from the period when Hölderlin lived under supervision. His care is also evident in the hymns at certain places, where the status of speaking is at stake.[5]

Hölderlin's care for the acts of speaking can also be seen as historically determined. It is not a mere coincidence that the speech-act became a concept only in the twentieth century. In the context of this study on Hölderlin, we can only point out one concrete historical connection which pertains to the historical genesis of the speech-act: the contemporary debate about epistolary style and a consideration of the real historical circumstances of the postal dispatch of messages.

Hölderlin's care for the speech-act belongs to the work *and* it belongs to the history of communicative practices. Both ways of reading Hölderlin's care for the speech-act cannot be traced back to a common denominator; in many ways the two versions exclude and contradict each other. It is precisely for this reason that we are interested in the following question, especially as it regards Hölderlin: where does the institution originate in speaking? Does the institution of speaking originate in speaking itself or from external practices? Does speech in the work produce the status of its speaking from itself or does it rely on already existing practices?

We will discuss these questions from four different standpoints: (I) In Hölderlin's early works, his private letters and epistolary novel *Hyperion*, the speech-act is thematized whenever ritual acts are criticized and what one could call 'free' institutions are sketched out. (II) The external and historical preconditions for this can be found in the style of the sentimental letter and in the undisturbed freedom of a communicative exchange[6] (*Nachrichtenverkehr*), whose ideal resurfaces in the epistolary novel *Hyperion*. (III) Underlying the thematization of the speech-act and the corresponding utopian program of communication one sees Hölderlin's insistence on the conventional formulae of communication, particularly in his very late letters. These letters are part of the case history regarding Hölderlin's madness; what can be detected in these letters is a discursive practice which simultaneously performs and obstructs the program of the new epistolary style in a very particular way. (IV) In an inquiry methodologically distinct from the preceding point, we will look at one of Hölderlin's great poems from his later period. The conventionality of communicative sequences (e.g., requesting and thanking, asking and answering) as the precondition of the linguistic institution in general and of the work in particular is placed into question: does Hölderlin create or explore a 'non-circumventable" space for the defined discursive practices within *the discourse*, which opens up in the work?

The observations which apply to the late letters (III) and the theses on the poem (IV) will be kept clearly separate from one another. But each one of the two parts relates separately to the care for the speech-act, the meaning of which will be sketched out in the first two sections.

I. SPEECH-ACTS

Hölderlin's care or uneasiness concerning the acts of speaking is a reflection on two aspects of what we today call the speech-act. The one aspect may be called the institutional or communicative role of a certain linguistic unit, the other aspect concerns sequential patterns of linguistic units in the process of communication.

In particular, we find the uneasiness about the institutional role of speech-acts at points when religious practices or familial rites are concerned. In a letter from Frankfurt to his brother-in-law, Hölderlin comments about his becoming a godfather and the rite of baptism that took place in his absence:

> Glauben Sie, es heißt mir recht viel, mich den Pathen Ihres lieben Kindes nennen zu dürfen. . . . Ich betrachte auch seine Taufe als ein Zeugniß unseres Glaubens an die künftige Menschenwürde des Kindes.[7]
>
> Believe me, it means very much to me to be allowed to call myself the godfather of your dear child . . . . I also regard his baptism as a testimony of our belief in the future dignity of the child.

Hölderlin does not state directly that the child receives a name. Explicitly he states that as the witness of the naming he can now call himself godfather. Even more striking is the fact that the baptism is not seen as the sacramental act of the priest. Hölderlin interprets the sacrament as a testimony of the faith of those who witness the sacramental act. It seems that the witnesses are not there for the sake of the sacramental act. Instead, the sacrament exists for the sake of the witnesses. The testimony does not really serve the fulfillment of the act by the priest. For the witnesses do not primarily testify to the institutional act; rather, they perform a speech-act that testifies or bears witness to their inner beliefs. If one takes literally this passing remark made by Hölderlin, a young theologian, then it appears to be a continuation of the Protestant critique of the sacrament. This rather insignificant example already indicates the connection of the interest in the speech-act to the critique and reinterpretation of the traditional (religious) institution.

The critique of law and institution which Hölderlin shares, for example, with the young Hegel, his companion in the Tübinger Stift, is in Hölderlin tightly bound up with the notion of testimony and witnessing, in its Christian as well as in its juridical meaning. Bearing witness often seems to reformulate or even replace the act or event which is to be attested. Among other examples in Hölderlin's oeuvre, there is a particularly striking one in his novel *Hyperion*. The period of composition for this narrative passage is the same as for the letter quoted above. Here, however, we are not concerned with a baptism, but with the institution of engagement or marriage. Before Hyperion leaves Diotima to participate in the war of liberation he demands an engagement or rather a kind of provisional marriage. Hyperion asks Diotima's mother to perform the rite by an act of blessing which substitutes for the proper ritual act. This act of blessing, however, is again linked with bearing witness or is even identified with a mere bearing witness.

> Sie soll uns segnen, diese theure Mutter, soll mit euch uns zeugen—komm Diotima! unsern Bund soll deine Mutter

heiligen, bis die schöne Gemeinde, die wir hoffen, uns vermählt.[8]

She shall bless us, this dear mother, she shall bear witness for us with you all—come, Diotima, your mother shall bless our union, until the beautiful society for which we hope joins us in marriage.

Also the future, utopian ceremony of marriage shall not be performed by a priest, but rather by the "beautiful society." For Hyperion, this beautiful community is the liberated society which shall exist at the end of the war for which he is now departing. A "beautiful society" however, like the "beautiful soul," needs no law and no appointed mediator in order to perform the nuptials. In this way, the blessing mother (at the engagement) comes closer to the future and free institution (of marriage) than the father or priest would, whom she replaces here. This also becomes clear as the mother only fulfills the second of the two demands: " 'She shall bless us . . . she shall bear witness for us.' " Hyperion and Diotima confirm their love for each other in a kind of duet which they direct to Nature. The mother and the others bear witness to this speech-act, which is in a way a veiling of the institution and of the law. " 'I bear witness to it,'' her mother said. 'We bear witness to it,'' cried the others.''[9] The act of "bearing witness" replaces the institutional act and is performed as the act of the mother (and "the others"), who replaces the father (and the institution of law).

In this context, one may notice the double meaning of the German *zeugen*, which means "to bear witness" as well as "to generate."[10] Hyperion's request: "Sie soll . . . uns zeugen" (She shall bear witness for us) could also be translated "she shall generate us." So it could be argued that, at this place in *Hyperion*, the replacement of the institutional act also means the veiling of the paternal act. One could show that, with the replacement of the institutional act by the maternal speech-act, we are at a crucial point where the philosophical critique illustrated by the novel and the psychological frame of the narrative are closely linked to each other.

Instead of following this trace we shift our attention to the other aspect of the speech-act, which again will lead us to an important point in the composition of *Hyperion*. This aspect involves sequencing or tying into communication, especially in initiating communicative practices.

The usual place of this uneasiness is the formulaic beginning of a letter. Thus Hölderlin begins: "Sie erlaubten mir, theuerster Herr Schwager! Ihnen zuweilen von mir Nachricht zu geben" (You allowed me, dearest brother-in-law, to give news of myself from time to time).[11] This worry is, in contrast to the theoretical critique of institution and convention, itself a conventional element in letter writing. But it seems that in Hölderlin there is a very particular uneasiness about how to begin to speak or write , especially when it was a matter of "giving news of himself."

Hyperion begins to narrate his life to the addressee of his letters in the following way: "Ich danke dir, daß du mich bittest, dir von mir zu erzählen, daß du die vorigen Zeiten mir in's Gedächtniß bringst" (I thank you for asking me to tell you of myself, for making me remember earlier days).[12] The narration of Hyperion's life does not start abruptly. It occurs as an act of thanking for a preceding request. However, this earlier request is not mentioned in the preceding letters (we also read only Hyperion's letters in the novel). This makes the formula of thanking for the request stand out that much more. One can find another similar introduction when Hyperion tells his life story to Diotima in the context of an epistolary report.

"Wovon sprechen wir doch geschwind?" konnt' ich rufen, "man hat oft seine Mühe, man kann den Stoff nicht finden, die Gedanken daran festzuhalten. . . ."

"Du hast schon mehr, als einmal," sagte sie, "versprochen, mir zu erzählen, wie du gelebt hast, ehe wir uns kannten, möchtest du jetzt nicht?"

"Das ist wahr," erwiedert' ich.

"What shall we talk about, I wonder?" I would cry. "It is often difficult, finding a subject from which one's thoughts will not stray." . . .

"You have more than once promised," she said, "to tell me of your life before we came to know each other—will you not do it now?"

"True," I said.[13]

Also in this case there has been no previous mention of Hyperion's—repeated—earlier promises to Diotima. The problem the partners in the dialogue, especially Hyperion, have in beginning communication is thus solved at the expense of the novel *Hyperion*. Both times, Hyperion's attempts to narrate his life are traced back to communicative sequences that are presupposed but not narrated.

The act of narrating one's life appears at first as an expression of thanks for a request, then as the keeping of a promise. This act is always already the second step in a sequence. In its origin, Hyperion's life-story refers to those to whom it is narrated: the addressee of the letters has asked for the narration, Diotima requests what has been repeatedly promised to her. The relationship to the friend and to the beloved woman precede the narration. These observations lead us far into the theoretical and psychological construction of the novel: autobiographical narration as a psychological representation of self-reflection does not start outside a contextual frame. It represents itself as mediated through a connection (to a friend) and an obligation (already assumed regarding the woman). The theoretical moment of an already existing connection or obligation of each beginning and self-constitution, however, is narrated psychologically in *Hyperion*: this moment appears as Hyperion's care for communication. One may generalize and say that communicative acts only exist because communication has always already begun. Each beginning is already the second step in a sequence which has already started before the beginning. The attention given to communication seems (as if by itself) to dissolve—on the level of the narration—the problem which theory constructs in the logic of self-reflection.

For Hölderlin the attention to the acts of speaking and their roles in communication is connected to the themes of philosophical questions. Once he criticizes the institutions of law and the conventionality of the rite, he is confronted with the description and naming of speech-acts. Communicative acts realize, so to speak, the utopian framework for noninstitutionalized institutions by means of language. On the other hand, one encounters interest in the speech-act whenever the beginning of autobiographical narration is at stake. The beginning of self-reflection is now embedded in a prior convention (to request—to thank; to promise—to fulfill). The sequential structure of communication plays the role of the medium which precedes self-reflection. In the careful naming and sequencing of speech-acts we can see the solution to theoretical tasks by linguistic means. The mentioned speech-acts in *Hyperion* are quasi-institutions of speech which the literary work brings forth. They function as poetical figures in the place of certain theoretical problems.[14]

II. EPISTOLARY STYLE AND THE CIRCULATION OF LETTERS

The care for the speech-act occurs in certain places in Hölderlin's oeuvre and refers to definite theoretical problems. However, we may also say that the care for the speech-act is the result of a historical discursive change. We refer specifically to the innovations propagated by the representatives of the sentimental epistolary style. The epistolary style in *Hyperion* can be traced back to Goethe's *Werther* and further to the discursive reforms of Richardson or Gellert, even though Hölderlin's Classicism goes well beyond this tradition. The demand for the new or true "naturalness" of the letter since the mid-eighteenth century meant at the same time a criticism of the old performative formulae and it meant a narrative performance of the (written) speech-act. In this case, the criticism of style proves to be part of a larger politics of discourse.[15]

In order to illustrate this thesis, we can simply take the first example from Gellert's "Gedanken von einem guten deutschen Briefe" (Reflections on a well-done German letter) (1742). This small text was at the origin of the reform of style in German letter writing. At the beginning of his text, Gellert opposes the new letter to the old. An invitation to a sentimental circle of friends, where a dialogue between friendship and love is read, is given as the example of the new, "free" letter:

A group of six ladies awaits you here to demand that you read the conversation between friendship and love with my aunt. Some of us believed that my aunt would perform the role of friendship very well, yet the voice of love would speak most pleasantly from your mouth. However do not believe that I made this remark. I am nothing but the secretary of the society which awaits you.

The old, "forced" letter reads:

Upon the occasion that a society of six ladies wish for you to read the conversation between love and friendship. Friendship *however* would let itself be heard best from the mouth of my aunt and love from the mouth of yours truly. *Therefore* we entreat you to fulfill our wishes and join us. (My own emphasis, R. C.)[16]

Gellert refers to the first letter as "free" because it is "lively." "Liveliness"—a term used very often in the eighteenth century against traditional rhetoric—in connection with metaphorics points to personification and, in connection with style in general, points to pictorial presencing. How is this relevant in the case of the letter?

The coherence of the "old" letter is found obviously on the surface of the argumentation ("upon the occasion that"—"however"—"therefore"). The "new" letter does not possess this kind of coherence. In this context Gellert uses the term "beautiful chaos" for the "new" letter, a term which in verse-form traditionally was ascribed to the ode. In the critique of rhetoric in the eighteenth century, itself formulated rhetorically, the letter plays a comparable role for prose which the ode plays for poetry. The "new" letter refers to an image which in turn tells a little story: the *descriptio* of the impatiently waiting society and the little story of their waiting.

In the old letter, the performative expression "we entreat you" concludes the argumentation; in fact, the expression is on the same level as the argumentation itself. In the new letter, the performance is part of the image ("the society awaits you") and the story which is added to the *descriptio* then specifies the speech-act indirectly ("some of us believed"). Finally, the expression of the speech-act and its difference from the act of writing itself is shown *ante oculos* ("I am nothing but a secretary").

In the "old" letter, the performative expression is named directly. In the "new" letter it is doubly inscribed. First in the introductory displacement, "One awaits you here, in order to ask of you, when you get here" and then in the concluding negation, "Others have expressed this invitation, not I the one who is writing." Thus, "beautiful chaos" and "liveliness" coincide. Both of these inscriptions share the *deictica* "I" and "here" which are typical for the "new" epistolary style. These performative *deic-*

tica produce the "new" narrative and figurative coherence instead of the "old" surface coherence.

To generalize these observations one may say that the referential or fictional *deixis* in the "new" letter allows the entire text to appear as an arc around the center of an often by no means explicit performance, which in this way becomes itself an object of representation. The entire text, one could say, becomes the *descriptio* or *prosopopoeia* of a concealed, subdivided performative act. The critical avoidance of the performative in the modern letter only intensifies the power of performance and gives it the status of an act. It is the deictic coherence which produces the identity and unity of the act. Traditionally the letter was defined as *sermo absentis cum absente*. Sender and recipient were seen as being equally absent to one another as well as to the letter as a thing and as a discourse. As it was shown in Gellert's example of an "old" letter, the performative formula was part of this epistolary neutrality. With the *descriptio* of the speech-act and the coherence of the *deixis* in the "new" letter, we have a double asymmetry between the sender and the recipient which could be described as follows: I, in the position of the sender, from the point of my self-presence, see you as absent and indeed see you, as you see me, in my self-presence, as absent. The speech-act as it is evoked and represented in the *deixis* of the "new" letter is the focus of this new asymmetry of communication.

The speech-act, as it was introduced by the "free" letter, as discursive practice in writing, is not a juridical institution. It does not show the direct and argumentative style of the performative formulae of the "old" letter, which stands in the tradition of humanist epistolography and was first and foremost a diplomatic or business letter. The speech-act represents itself by an image or a minimal story and makes this image into an asymmetry between "I" and "you"; the asymmetry is in turn made into the constitutive part of the image. Such a speech-act shows the paradox of a private institution.

The epistolary style of *Hyperion* is certainly not the sentimental style of Gellert's reforms, although it uses its innovations. Even more, Hölderlin's text goes beyond the reforms of the epistolary style which determine certain linguistic patterns: in *Hyperion* as well, the sending and receiving of the letters plays a role in the action. A certain mode of operation of the postal system, however, is the juridico-technical precondition of such a communication which presents itself linguistically as a "private institution."

Communication understood in this way is not yet assured by any courier service which makes it probable that a message arrives rather than not. More than that, a private communication requires a regular and generally available, accessible circuit. Up until the dissolution of the Holy Roman Empire at the beginning of the nineteenth century, the opposition between the Reich mail of Thurn and Taxis and the municipal and guild courier institutions, and the posts of the territorial states, determined the juridical debate.[17] From Frankfurt,[18] where Hölderlin's particular epistolary style and the style of the letters in *Hyperion* undergo the final development, Hölderlin writes in the first letter to his mother: "Ich könnte von hieraus alle Tage schreiben. Die Post geht alle Tage" (From here I could write every day. The mail goes every day).[19]

The novel *Hyperion*, written for the most part in Frankfurt, reflects upon the question of the system of communication in its negative sense, that is, in the catastrophe: Diotima literally passes away upon reading the letter in which Hyperion announces his death to her. The letter and the effect it has are determined in various ways through the mishaps of sending and receiving. Here we can see that, as in other epistolary novels of the time, the modern postal service is the precondition of the epistolary fiction in the novel, regardless of how the delivery of mail is depicted in the narrative.

In a letter, Hyperion announces that he is seeking his death in the war of liberation after his previous letters to Diotima went unanswered for a long period of time. Having already dispatched the letter where he announces his death, Hyperion receives a letter from Diotima where she presumes that three of her letters were lost. Now Hyperion tries to revoke the announcement in his last letter. But the revocation comes too late. Or as Diotima puts it in her last letter to Hyperion, the letter of the announcement came to her "früher als du nachher wünschtest" ('sooner than you afterward wished').[20] The catastrophe lies in the fact that the speech-act of the announcement cannot be revoked. He who announces his death brings it upon the recipient.

More important still is the fact that Hyperion's announcement already had its cause in a failure of the distribution of messages. The point is not if and when a single letter reaches its recipient, but precisely the regularity and calculability of the distribution of messages. Notably, Hyperion announces his death after the regular rhythm of correspondence between Diotima and himself was disrupted. For the reader of the novel, this "rhythm" is concealed by the fact that Hyperion's fifth and Diotima's first letter crossed paths.[21] If one arranges the letters according to the chronology of their dispatch, one observes a repeated rhythm of four letters from Hyperion followed by one responding letter from Diotima. A third series begins again with four letters from Hyperion—but Diotima's expected response fails to occur, even though she for her part has already sent three letters. Hyperion does not announce his death because Diotima's letters fail to arrive for a long period of time. Rather, the rhythm of their communication is disrupted, a rhythm whose decisive significance comes to light only in this disruption and its consequences. Even more, this rhythm is not simply the precondition for communication; it seems to be part of the communication itself. Such a rhythm in communication, which is itself a constitutive part of communication, however, requires the existence of a postal system.

The rhythm of the letters and its disruption in the novel point to yet another premise of its historical discursive conditions. The communication which could make use of the innovations in the sentimental style of letters relies on the calculability of the system for the exchange of messages. This technical side of communication has a fully different status in Hölderlin's novel than the thematization of the speech-act. While this thematization is linked to the theoretical questions in Hölderlin's earlier writings and pertains to the utopian dimension of the work, the technical system for the exchange of messages functions as the merely pragmatic circumstance of the catastrophe. Therefore, the postal catastrophe has a special meaning for the reading of the novel which inquires about the history of discursive practices.

III. EXAMPLES FROM THE LATER LETTERS: CONVENTIONAL FORMULAE

We have gained a first overview of Hölderlin's care for the speech-act in *Hyperion*. This care stands at first within the context of theoretical questions: the critique of the juridical institution leads to the names of the speech-acts, and self-reflection receives a preliminary medium in communicative sequences. Speech-acts appear as noninstitutionalized institutions, as a free and previously given sphere of certain acts. Especially here the work shows itself to be determined by discursive innovations recognizable in the history of epistolary style. The novel even attests indirectly to the postal service as the technical precondition of the new style. However the technical aspects serve only as the pure pragmatics of the catastrophe.

The "positive turn" toward the sphere of communication (and the "turn against" its technical preconditions) is certainly a typical development for Hölderlin's age. Yet once we look at Hölderlin's later writings, we may ask whether his insistence on the formulae of communication puts the idea of the "free," poetical institution of communication into question. We can see a return of convention into communication. In order to show this, two examples with completely different status will be analyzed; these examples question the idea of a free institution of communication in two very different ways. The first example consists of some of Hölderlin's very late letters which apparently contain only "successful" acts of communication and fail precisely for that reason. The second example consists of some verses of the hymn "To Mother Earth," where the question is raised about the conventional sequentiality of communication and about a first speech-act which at the same time founds its own lawfulness. There is no commonality between what the later letters do and the hymnic verses say except that both can be read in reference to the project of free communication laid out in *Hyperion*.

Hölderlin wrote his late letters to his mother and sister while he was living under supervision. Chosen are three letters which consist almost entirely of performative expressions. The pictorial fictional speech-acts discussed previously in context of the "new," "free" letter are not pertinent at this point in our discussion. In these letters, it is through the accumulation and assemblage of conventional performative formulae that a letter becomes one single performative act.[22] The emphasis on the communicative level in the late letters makes this level dominant and at the same time, as we shall see, leads to the obstruction of communication.

The commentaries following the examples do not interpret, they only point out the construction of the performative.

[#1]
Theuerste Mutter!
　　　Wenn Sie es nicht ungütig nehmen, schreibe ich wieder an Sie einen Brief. Ich befleißige mich, es an Bezeugung meiner Ihnen gebürigen Ergebenheit nicht fehlen zu lassen. Ich muß schon wieder abbrechen. Ich bin mit Bezeugung meiner gehörigen Empfindung
　　　　　　Ihr / gehorsamster Sohn / Hölderlin.

Dearest Mother!
(1) If you do not take it ill of me, I write another letter to you.
(2) I strive not to fail in evidence of my proper devotion to you.
(3) I must already break off again.
I am, with evidence of my proper feeling, / your / most obedient son / Hölderlin.[23]

The letter has a symmetrical shape. Both the first and the third sentences—not including the salutation and the signature—both refer exclusively to the acts of beginning or ending the writing. The middle sentence, which by its position represents the *narratio* of the letter, contains a phrase recognizable as the formula of beginning or ending a conventional letter. The repetition of the phrase "evidence of" (*Bezeugung von*) in the sentence which leads up to the signature clarifies this point.

The minimal exposition of the conventional letter can be recognized in these short lines: performative form of the beginning; narration of the message; performative form of the closing. However, in this letter, the narrated message is itself nothing but a performative which can stand at the beginning or the end. Another possible way of reading sentences (1) and (3) is to read them not only as performatives of beginning and closing but also as constative assertions that the writer will now begin or cease writing. The differentiation between the performative production of communication and of the communicated content becomes difficult to ascertain. Communication itself is in danger.

[#2]
Verehrungswürdigste Frau Mutter!
　　　Ich schreibe Ihnen schon wieder einen Brief. Ich habe Ihnen immer vieles Gute zu wünschen. Die Empfin-

dungen, mit denen ich dieses wünsche, sollen diesem gemäß sein. Das Gute und das Wohlbefinden sind wichtige Gegenstände, die man nicht gern entbehrt, wenn man auf das sieht, was den Menschen das beste ist. Ich nehme mir die Freiheit, schon wieder abzubrechen. Ich nenne mich
      Ihren / gehorsamsten Sohn / Hölderlin.

Most praiseworthy Madam Mother!
(1) I am already writing you another letter.
(2) I always have so much good to wish you.
(3) The feelings with which I wish this, should be appropriate to this.
(4) The good and well-being are important things, which one doesn't like to do without, when one considers what is the best for people.
(5) I take the liberty of breaking off again already.
I call myself / your / most obedient son / Hölderlin.[24]

 The first and last sentences of the letter perform beginnings and endings, the second and fourth make statements regarding the speech-act "wishing someone well." The third and middle sentence makes a statement regarding the duty of "wishing someone well."
 The middle sentence contains a proposition that, in Searle's terminology, could be called the condition of sincerity for the speech-act of "wishing someone well." The *narratio* in the letter, sentences two through four, thematize or even "analyze" the speech-act of "wishing someone well." Yet the speech-act itself is not carried out. One may argue that the third sentence performs a wish. However in that interpretation the wish would be the wish of being willing or able to carry out the speech-act of "wishing someone well."
 The letter is a lucid statement on wishing well. That is exactly the reason why it does not perform the speech-act "wishing well." Perhaps it performs the wish for performing the wishing someone well. As in the first letter, the symmetry, which in this case consists of five sentences, gives an even stronger impression of the emptiness of the communication, since in the symmetrical center where one would expect the narrative message (*Mitteilung*), only the act of giving a message is relayed.

[#3]
Theuerste Mutter!
 Ich muß Sie bitten, daß Sie das, was ich Ihnen sagen mußte, auf sich nehmen, und sich darüber befragen. Ich habe Ihnen einiges in der von Ihnen befohlenen Erklärbarkeit sagen müssen, das Sie mir zustellen wollten. Ich

muß Ihnen sagen, daß es nicht möglich ist, die Empfindung über sich zu nehmen, die das, was Sie verstehen, erfordert. Ich bin
> Ihr / gehorsamster Sohn / Hölderlin

Dearest Mother!
(1) I must beg you to take on yourself that which I had to tell you and to question yourself about it.
(2) I had to tell you some things in that explainability you commanded, which you wanted to deliver to me.
(3) I must tell you, that it is not possible to take on the feeling which that which you understand requires.
I am / your / most obedient son / Hölderlin.[25]

The letter once again has the mirror shape of three sentences. Each sentence is a cluster of hierarchical performatives. If one underlines the like or similar expressions, one sees that the symmetry extends to each detail.

First, between the first and third sentences there are the correspondences in the performative phrases "I must beg you" (1) and "I must tell you, that it is not possible" (3); and in the propositional phrases "to take on yourself that which . . ." (1) and "to take on the feeling" (3). Then, there is one parallel between (1) and (2) where performative acts are reported: "that which I had to tell you" (1) and "I had to tell you some things" (2). We also find one similar parallel between (2) and (3): "in that explainability which you commanded" (2) and "(the feeling which) that which you understand requires" (3). If one excludes the phrase "to question yourself about it" in the first sentence, which reformulates the phrase "to take on yourself" in (1) and (3), each discursive part in the sentences (1) and (3) has its symmetrical counterpart in the letter. Even when the semantic references change, the symmetry, which is carried through to the last detail, has the effect of erasing the message (*Mitteilung*).

There is a phrase in this letter which even performs the erasure. One expression in the second sentence—the only one in this letter—remains without a corresponding expression in the otherwise symmetrical letter: "which you wanted to deliver to me" (*mir zustellen*) (2). The primary usage of *zustellen* according to Fischer's Swabian Dictionary is "to grant someone credibility" (*jemandem Glauben zustellen*). According to Campe's Dictionary, it has both this older, dialect usage and also the newer, High German one of sending and delivering letters. The new meaning of *zustellen* which belongs to the terminology of the postal service emerges in the place where, in the center of a mirror structure, the question of the communicative relation is posed.

Hölderlin's usage, however, oscillates not only between these two correlated meanings, but at the same time within a semantic opposition.

Zustellen can mean "to grant credibility" and "to deliver letters" on the one hand, and "to obstruct" or "to hinder" on the other. The total accessibility of communication is at the same time the obstruction of communication: this could be an attempt to formulate the double meaning of *zustellen*.[26]

The late letters are not part of the work. They are not interpretable. However, they have a place within the examination which asks about the fundamental relationship between discourse and institution. In a certain way they are pure discursive practice itself. As the program of the "new" epistolary style demands, they place the speech-act into the center of the letter. Yet they do this precisely with the conventional means of the "old" style, with the conventional performative formulae. Thus, the success of the speech-act becomes a catastrophe.

IV. FOUR VERSES FROM THE HYMN "TO MOTHER EARTH": THE LAW, THE SPEECH-ACT

Wer will auch danken, eh' er empfängt,
Und Antwort geben, eh' er gehört hat?
Ni   indeß ein Höherer spricht,
zu fallen in die tönende Rede.[27]

Who wants to thank, before he receives,
And to give answer, before he has heard?
N   while a higher one speaks,
To break into resounding speech.

These four verses of a late (fragmentary) hymn apparently speak of a conventional "order of discourse." It is evident that the posing of the question whether these verses thematize a specific discursive convention would be fruitless. Nevertheless one can ask how the poetical work, the "song" of the hymn, relates to the category or institution of discursively ordered speaking. In this way, the question of the elemental relationship between discourse and institution arises *within* the work.

At first, an attempt shall be made to read the four verses isolated from the entire hymn, as if the question of communication and speech-act were directly thematic within them. Consequently the achieved results have to be reconsidered once the four verses are placed back into the context of the entire hymn. One must then ask whether these four verses make a statement about ordered discourse or whether or not thanking and answering are to be interpreted differently.

We can use the aspects of "act" and "sequence" which we gained from the analysis of *Hyperion* as a point of departure to approach these questions. Act and sequence are immediately related to one another in the four verses: one can only wish to give thanks if one has received (otherwise the act has no meaning, or it is forced); one can only answer if one has heard (otherwise the name "answer" is logically incorrect, or, the person who thinks he is answering is insane). Units like "thanking" and "answering" exist in language only insofar as the sequences "to give—to receive—to thank" or "to hear—to answer" exist. The sequences realize themselves linguistically, but they are not linguistic units. They exist logically before language, but they do not exist without language. The linguistic act is bound to the sequence of communicating, and the sequential structure of communication inserts itself into language in distinct acts. The communicative sequence is the structural ground for defining conventional acts, but there would not be any act without the work of language. The relation differs once again in both sequences: one can conceive of the sequence "to give—to receive—to thank" as being realized without language. However, that is not the case with the sequence "to hear—to answer."

Thus, the four verses show that the law, in which the conventionality of the speech-act has its origin, exists in the fact that communication occurs linguistically in a prelinguistically ordered sequence. The law that legislates this prelinguistic order, though, has its origin in a primary, noncircumventable form of speech that, for its part, is exclusively and essentially bound to language. However one fills in the signifier of the negation "Ni"/"N" ("nicht," "nie"/"not," "never"), both of the following questions clearly state the ban against interrupting the speech of a "higher one." This statement can be understood in two ways: either one *may not* interrupt the speech because it is the speech of a "higher one," that is, of the L/lord. Or, one *cannot* interrupt the speech insofar as it always already sounds or always continues to sound like the speech of a parent addressing a child. The speech of the "higher one" is the privileged speech of the lord and the always already resounding speech of father and mother. In any case, the law which the resounding voice of the "higher one" *gives* is not the content of any sentence he *says*. The law lies solely in the resounding of speech, that is, in the first sequence defined by its sounding: as long as this speech resounds, it may not be interrupted.

The structural ground of the delimitation of individual speech-acts is the sequentiality of communication. This sequentiality, however, has its first and law-giving example in the pure act of speech: in its resounding. Resounding speech is the law which establishes convention, a law which stands prior to every substantial law which defines speech-acts. Resounding speech linguistically institutes every institution. The privileged or prior resounding is an event in which speech, solely in its occurring, unremittingly becomes an institution.

One can attempt to formulate the isolated interpretation of the four verses by referring back to the methodical differentiation proposed at the beginning. The first two verses deal with the relationship between discourse and institution; whereas the following two verses bring together both sides of the relationship, discourse and institution; In effect, they perform the event of speech becoming an institution. *The discourse* becomes a single *discourse* in the second sense referred to above in its own sheer performance. *The discourse* defines single discourses while at the same time *the discourse* itself is already one specific discourse. Only the work testifies to that.

At this point we should ask whether it is legitimate to arrive at such an interpretation? Posing this question is in fact asking whether the four quoted verses deal with speech, or whether speech is the example, analogy, or model for something else, in particular, whether it is the example or model of a specific action. What is ultimately meant by the point of intersection between speech and institution—speech or act? Is the act of speaking which grounds all speech-acts ultimately a speaking or an act?

The question of the speech-act leads us deeply into the interpretation of Hölderlin's works. Hölderlin's understanding of the Logos of John, for instance in the hymn "Patmos," is crucial; also the relationship between language, reflection, and action; and finally also how the work perceives itself as a work.

Continuing this line of argumentation we will formulate some theses regarding the poem "To Mother Earth." The quoted verses introduce the last of three triadic strophes, each of which is allotted a different singer. The three singers—three brothers with the names Ottmar, Hom, and Tello—direct their hymn to Mother Earth.[28]

The three singers respectively characterize in each of their three strophes the song and the singing in different ways. At the beginning of each one of the triads the singer thematizes his own position as the singer of the song.

The first brother begins: "Statt offner Gemeine sing' ich Gesang" (Instead of open congregation, I sing song) (v.1). "Instead of" has two meanings which are unfolded in the subsequent verses. A double play is at work: "instead of" refers to the fact that the singer represents the community in his song and at the same time means that the singer initiates the song which later becomes "[d]er Chor des Volks" (the choir of the people) (v.14). His representative solo anticipates the future song of the whole, the choir and the people. Thus representation is necessary only for the beginning; it precedes and leads up to the historical state when those represented will sing themselves. The phrase "instead of" at the beginning of the hymn defines a social and at the same time historical dimension of the song. In this way, the first verse functions as a performative phrase that names and performs the social and historical character of the song for the first singer: the first institution of speech is representation.

The second singer begins his three strophes with:

> Indessen schon', o Mächtiger deß
> Der einsam singt, und gieb uns Lieder genug,

> Bis ausgesprochen ist, wie wir
> Es meinen unserer Seele Geheimniß.²⁹
>
> Meanwhile spare, o mighty one, of him,
> who lonely sings, and give us songs enough
> until it has been declared, how we
> mean it, our souls' secret.

Once again the first verses define the status of the song and its historical level. The second singer includes himself in a "we" that is, however, an additive plural of individual "I"'s, and not yet the whole of the choir and the people. The singer, as opposed to the people referred to in verses 31ff., is clearly not the singer of this second triad. The additive "we"'s, to which the second singer includes himself as a member, can be considered only as the audience of the first singer. The song during this intermediary time is not opposed to the song of the many nor does it any longer represent their future choir. This strophe is the song of the many single individuals that hear the one and first singer who represents the people. The social and historical status of representation appears to them and to the second singer in a private, almost psychologized fashion: they name the one singer to be "lonely" and plead for mercy for him.

With the speech-act of the request, the second singer places himself between the lonely singer, the future people and the mighty one ("Meanwhile spare, o mighty one"). While the first singer defines and performs the act of his singing himself in the first verse, the second uses already defined roles of speaking and speech-acts. He stands in the already instituted sequence of speaking.

The third singer joins in with the four verses already quoted which sing of thanking and answering and the ban against interrupting the resounding speech:

> Who wants to thank, before he receives,
> And to give answer, before he has heard?
> N   while a higher one speaks,
> To break into resounding speech.

With the expression of thanks and response, the third singer clearly takes up and continues the situation of the second singer. For instance, the second singer already reported of *hearing*: "Denn öfters hört" ich / Des alten Priesters Gesänge" (For often I heard / The songs of the old priest) (v. 35f.). And in the following fragmentary verses he apparently pled for the readiness to *thank* (v. 37f.).³⁰ Yet the third singer does not name himself at the beginning of his verses, nor does he name an individual singer at all, not even a "we." (At least that is the way it appears to be in the third triad. However the second strophe is incomplete and the third is missing.) In the four beginning verses, the third singer speaks of a general law which manifests and realizes itself in the anonymous instance of the "speech of the higher one," that is, "the resounding speech." The third singer radicalizes the gesture of stepping back in the face of other speech, as was already the case with the second singer. In his anonymity and generality, which is the consequence of his stepping back, the third singer subordinates himself to the law of speech itself. By doing so he defines and performs a beginning like the first singer. But with the third singer, the act of beginning is not the definition and performance of representation; instead it is the explanation and performance of the law of speech itself.

Like the beginning verses of both of the earlier triads, the beginning verses of the third explain the status of the speaking of the singer. Thus far one can say that truly the law of speech itself is thematic in the four verses.

Nevertheless, the lines which follow the four verses persistently call into question whether the "speech of the higher one," in its abstractness and authoritative lawfulness, really can mean "only speech itself":

> Viel hat er zu sagen und anders Recht,
> Und Einer ist, der endet in Stunden nicht,
> Und die Zeiten des Schaffenden sind,
> Wie Gebirg, /. . . .   (v. 65–67)

> Much has he to say and right otherwise,
> And there is One who does not end in hours,
> And the times of the creating one are,
> Like a mountain-chain, /. . . .

Once we recall the verses quoted at the beginning of this section, we note a shift in Tello's strophe from speech to creation. At this point we must ask what type of connection or division between speech and act exists when that shift happens.

It is indisputable that v. 65 ("Much has he to say") pertains to the speech of the "higher one." One could continue to understand the "higher one" to be the subject in the following verses (65ff.). The saying and the creating, the speech and the act would then be directly identical. The divine act of creation would already be speech, the divine speech of the law would already be creation. In his commentary, Beißner decided emphatically against establishing such a correspondence. He emphasizes that in verse 66 ("And there is One . . .") a new beginning is made, a new persona introduced. Beißner adds that the speaking "higher one" is subordinate to the "creative God" of verses 66ff.[31] For the sake of theological orthodoxy, speech and act are kept separate from one another to the extent that not even the question of their relation remains. The supporting argument which claims the "subordination" of the "higher one" to the "one" indicates that Beißner's decision cannot be made without violence.

Certainly verse 66 begins from a new angle. Whether one can assume different "personae" remains questionable. Nothing could be said about their relationship. Nevertheless the "higher one" and the "one" appear to be connected in the verbal phrases in which time and power correspond: "much has he to say"[32] (v. 65) and "does not end in hours" (v. 66). In regard to their respective *structural precedence*, and only in this, the act of creation and the speech of the law collapse into one another. And the positing power of the law is attributed to speech and act only in the *temporal-structural sense* in which they are brought together. The collapse is an extreme, structural point (in the correspondence of the verbs); speech and creation remain otherwise apart (in the possible difference of subjects). The law-giving speech-act happens in the resounding of a speech with changing or uncertain subjects of utterance.

This third reading gives structure to the opposition of the first two versions. It shows the third singer being confronted with the (theological) question of the speech-act. The text brings together speech and act precisely in the founding act of law and thereby of conventions (that in return can define further rules of speech). At the same time, however, speaking and act remain separate when outside of this clearly demarcated, law-founding sphere.

In such places in the work, the theme of the speech-act leads to central linguistic and theological questions. In contrast to *Hyperion*, in the example of "Mother Earth" the thematization of the speech-act is not connected with a utopia of communication. Communication is here not the realm of quasi-institutional acts that would be widely accessible and freely available. The consideration of convention and law halts the success of the speech-act. That is, according to the thesis here adopted, the other side of Hölderlin's care for the speech-act.

In this sense of separateness, the late letters, which are pure discursive practice, remain separate from the work, which opens itself up to *the discourse. Within* the work the contact between speech and act is on the one hand precisely limited, yet on the other hand is proven to be the institutionalizing instance of every institution. These two defining characteristics of speech/act halt the catastrophic success of "free communication."

NOTES

1. This essay was translated by Ruth Krekeler and Regina Marz.
2. Michel Foucault, "The 'No' of the Father," in *Language, Counter-Memory, Practice: Selected Essays and Interviews*, ed. Donald F. Bouchard (Ithaca: Cornell University Press, 1977). For more extensive commentary on Foucault's interpretations of Hölderlin,

see my commentary on the German translation of this text by Foucault in *Pauvre Holterling* 8 (1988), 73–92.

3. "Le discours juridique est une parole créatrice, qui fait exister ce qu'elle énonce. Elle est la limite vers laquelle prétendent tous les énoncés performatifs, bénédictions, malédictions, ordres, souhaits ou insultes: c'est-á-dire la parole divine, de droit divin" (Juridical discourse is a creative speech which places into existence that which it enunciates. It is the limit in terms of which all of the enunciative speech-acts, benedictions, maledictions, orders, desires and insults are intended: that is to say, it is a divine speech, of divine right). Pierre Bourdieu, *Ce que parler veut dire. L'économie des échanges linguistiques* (Paris: Fayard, 1982), p. 21.

4. Translator's note: The German word *Sorge* can be translated as care, concern, worry, uneasiness. In this essay, *Sorge um* refers to the particular attention given to the status of acts of speaking and speech-acts, specifically to the naming and defining of speech acts.

5. At this time there is a first, larger analysis of the topics of speaking and communicating; see Brigitte Haberer, *Sprechen, Schweigen, Schauen. Rede und Blick in Hölderlins 'Der Tod des Empedokles' und 'Hyperion'* (Bonn, Berlin: Bouvier, 1991). Haberer begins immediately to expand upon the interpretation of the texts with observations on speaking and communicating. My essay, however, addresses the preliminary question which has not yet been discussed: at which points and in which ways do Hölderlin's texts encounter what we today call the 'speech act' and the 'process of communication'?

6. Translator's note: "Communicative exchange" is a translation for the German term *Nachrichtenverkehr*, which carries both the technical meaning of a "circulation of messages (or letters)" (i.e., the postal system) and the more general meaning referring to a "communicative exchange" or "correspondence."

7. StA 6.1, 260f.; # 151. StA refers to Friedrich Hölderlin, *Große Stuttgarter Ausgabe*, ed. Friedrich Beißner (Stuttgart: Kohlhammer, 1946 ff.). The first number refers to the volume, the second to the page, the third to the letter.

8. StA 3, 100f; T 112. English translations of *Hyperion* are from *Hyperion or the Hermit in Greece*, translated by Willard R. Trask (New York: Frederick Ungar Press, 1959). Subsequent citations from this translation will be indicated in the text by a "T."

9. StA 3, 101; T 113.

10. In "As on a Holiday" one reads: "kindled by a holy ray, / The fruit born in love, work of gods and men / The song, so that it bears witness to both [damit er beiden zeuge], succeeds" (V. 47–49; StA 2, 119).

11. StA 6.1, 120; #81.

12. StA 3, 10; T 24.

13. StA 3, 66; T 78f.

14. Linguistic action is central in the dramatic fragment *Empedokles*: the speech acts of cursing (of the priest, but also of Empedokles) and of blessing (of Empedokles) determine the drama; the act of Empedokles to call himself a god is seen as his guilt. Cf. Haberer's detailed description in *Sprechen, Schweigen, Schauen*, pp. 89–178. However, a reading of *Empedokles* would have to confront the question about the interrelation of communication and the critique of institution. Such an inquiry is not discussed in this essay since the drama requires an approach that takes into account the specificity of the genre.

15. For questions regarding the history of letter and epistolary style, see Georg Steinhausen, *Geschichte des deutschen Briefes* (Berlin, 1891); Eric A. Blackall, *The Emergence of German as a Literary Language 1700–1775*, 2nd ed. (Ithaca: Cornell University Press, 1978) pp. 178–210; Reinhard Nickisch, *Die Stilprinzipien in den deutschen Briefstellern des 17. und 18. Jahrhunderts* (Göttingen: Vandenhoeck & Ruprecht, 1969); and Wilhelm Voßkamp, "Dialogische Vergegenwärtigung beim Schreiben und Lesen," *Deutsche Vierteljahresschrift* 45 (1971): 80–116. About Hölderlin's letters, see Paul Raabe, *Die Briefe Hölderlins. Studien zur Entwicklung und Persönlichkeit des Dichters* (Stuttgart: Metzler, 1963); Rolf Zuberbühler, *Die Sprache des Herzens. Hölderlins Widmungsdichtung* (Göttingen: Vandenhoeck & Ruprecht, 1982).

16. Christian Fürchtegott Gellert, "Gedanken von einem guten deutschen Briefe," in *Die Epistolographischen Schriften*, reprint (Stuttgart: Metzler und Poeschel, 1971), pp. 180f.
17. The confrontation between the continuous and calculable postal service which would work on the territory of the empire with the municipal and guild courier institutions characterizes the postal history of the Holy Roman Empire of German nations between 1500 and 1800. Götz Herrmann, "Der Streit der Thurn und Taxischen Reichspost und der reichsstädischen 'Post' um das Postregal im 16. und 17. Jahrhundert," Diss. Erlangen, 1958.
18. From 1610 on, Frankfurt is the main office of the postal service of the empire. Throughout the seventeenth century there are half-a-dozen municipal courier institutions in the city. Around the middle of the eighteenth century most of these institutions are dissolved; others have to be sold to the Thurn and Taxis postal service. Bernd Faulhaber, *Geschichte der Post in Frankfurt a.M.* (Frankfurt/Main: Völcker, 1883).
19. StA 6.1, 195; #112.
20. StA 3, 144; T 154.
21. StA 3, 108f.
22. In the late letters the phrases that precede the signature alone point to the return of conventional performative formulae. With two exceptions, there appear only the two variants "I call myself (e.g., your son)" (Ich nenne mich [z.B., Ihren Sohn]) and "I am (e.g., your son)" (Ich bin [z.B., ihr Sohn]). The two formulae which are performative or constative speech acts that exclusively affirm the position toward the addressee have a very peculiar history in Hölderlin's letter-writing. The first, by far a more frequent performative formula, does not occur in any earlier letter. The second, apparently constative, can be found in letters from his youth on until the beginning of 1791, mostly addressed to his mother. After that period we find it only in two more letters to his mother from Homburg (1799), and in some letters to Schiller as well as to the publishers Cotta and Wilmans.
23. StA 6.1, 463; #297.
24. StA 6.1, 466; #303.
25. StA 6.1, 463; #296.
26. See '*zustellen*' in Herrmann Fischer, *Schwäbisches Wörterbuch* (Tübingen: Laupp'sche Buchhandlung, 1904ff.); Johann Heinrich Campe, *Wörterbuch der deutschen Sprache* (Braunschweig, 1807-11; reprint Hildesheim, New York: Olms, 1969).
27. "Der Mutter Erde," v. 61-64 in StA 2.1, 125.
28. A further fragmentary complex of texts is connected with "To Mother Earth." The publisher Beißner suspects that it records "ideas" for a "presumed continuation of the hymn" (StA 2, 683). In his comments on "To Mother Earth" Hans-Georg Gadamer clearly doubts Beißner's claim of a possible continuation of the hymn. See "Hölderlin und George," *Hölderlin Jahrbuch* (1967/78), pp. 75-91, 87-91. Reasons related to form and content appear to support Gadamer's position.
29. StA 2.1, 124; v. 31-34.
30. The speech act of 'thanking' in Hölderlin often has a strong relationship to the sacrament. So in the eighth strophe of "Bread and Wine," bread and wine appear as 'signs' in the interval of "gifts" and "thanks" (v. 112, 121, 123; StA 2, 93 f.).

    Both sequences "to receive—to thank" and "to hear—to answer" can be found united in the verses of the "Rhein" hymn dedicated to Rousseau. In this hymn *hearing* is a *gift* (Gabe) that Rousseau receives; and in exchange he *gives language*: "Und süße Gabe zu hören, / Zu reden so, daß er aus heiliger Fülle / Wie der Weingott, thörig göttlich / Und gesezlos sie die Sprache der Reinesten giebt" (v. 143-46; StA 2, 146).
31. StA 2.2, 686.
32. The phrase "having much to say" (v. 65) evidently means "speaking for a long time because there is so much to tell." In a rather colloquial understanding the German phrase "viel zu sagen haben" also means "having high authority and power." In these two interpretations of the phrase the two aspects, as analyzed above, of the "sounding speech" and the authoritative speech are interwoven.

AUTOBIOGRAPHICAL HYPERBOLE: SCHILLER'S *NAIVE AND SENTIMENTAL POETRY*

LINDA M. BROOKS

*I am I, and settle myself—and if I settle
Nothing to be, well and good—nonentity formed.*[1]

—Schiller

I am thinking of those today who would try to reconstruct a discourse around a subject . . . that would no longer include the figure of mastery of self, of adequation to self, center and origin of the world, etc. . . . but which would define the subject rather as the finite experience of nonidentity to self, . . . with all the paradoxes or the aporia of being before the law.[2]

—Derrida

[W]hat is proper to a culture is not to be identical with itself. *Not to not have an identity, but not to be able to identify itself, to be able to say 'me' or 'we'; to be able to take the form of a subject only in the nonidentity to itself. . . . This can be said of all identity.*[3]

—Derrida

On the opening page of *The Society of the Spectacle*, Guy Debord introduces postmodernism's autofigurational extravagance by quoting the Romantic philosopher G. W. F. Hegel: " 'In the case where the self is merely represented and ideally presented, there it is not actual: where it is by proxy, it *is not.*' "[4] For the postmodern era, the substitution of a "proxy," negated identity for the empirical self has become commonplace.[5] Yet the melodramatic idea of the self re- or de-structured as a nonentity has its roots in the aesthetic and cultural shift we've come to call "Romanticism," particularly in the philosophical essays of Friedrich von Schiller.[6]

THE SENTIMENTAL QUEST FOR SELF

Grounding the "sentimental," or "modern," individual's identity on the illusory freedom given by the play drive (*Spieltrieb*),[7] Schiller's *Naive and Sentimental Poetry* (1797) dramatizes the hyperaestheticism of Romantic self-construction.[8] Schiller complains at length in *Aesthetic Education* (1795) that sentimental identity has been "mutilated,"[9] anatomized into meaninglessness by a hyperrational neglect of man's sensible and imaginative nature. "We"—as Schiller constitutes the fragmented subjectivity of the modern or Romantic era—have lost the unified selfhood enjoyed by Grecian antiquity: "At that first fair awakening of the power of the mind, sense and intellect did not as yet rule over strictly separate domains. . . . How different with us Moderns! With us . . . the image of the human species is projected . . . as fragments" (*AE*, 6, #3, 33). The naive unity of the Classical self given by an "all-unifying nature" has been "torn to pieces" by "the all-dividing intellect" (*AE*, 6, #5, 33), leaving an automaton, "an ingenious clock-work, in which, out of the piecing together of innumerous but lifeless parts, a mechanical kind of collective life ensue[s]" (*AE*, 6, #3, 35). To

Johann Christoph Friedrich von Schiller, from the Bildabteilung, Deutsches Literaturarchiv of the Schiller Nationalmuseum, Marbach, Germany. Reprinted with permission.

Schiller, sentimental or modern identity has become a divided and unreal phenomenon. As modern individuals, "we" are no longer whole, no longer our selves.

Naive and Sentimental Poetry, published two years later, documents the modern individual's loss of self and proposes a plan for its recovery. Though the Sentimental has three "modes of perception"—the "satiric," the "elegaic," and the "idyllic" (*N&SP*, 145n)—the elegaic dominates.[10] Satire may express her "burning indignation" (*N&SP*, 119), but only elegy expresses her fundamental lament and sense of absence. The Sentimental's occasional forays into the idyllic, which occur as s/he[11] attempts to recapture the naive, unified selfhood of pastoral poetry, are always signals of a dangerous lapse into nostalgia.[12] This is because the Sentimental project must be a struggle toward the discovery of "something [that has] existed and [is] now lost"—the self, now signified by the object it desires, an objective which in its absence initiates the self as an act of self-engendering (*N&SP*, 127).

Schiller's rejection of the idyll uncovers the hyperbole beneath the Sentimental's projected self-recovery. By turning to the idyll, the sentimental poet obscures modern man's proper goal: "Let him not lead us backwards into our childhood . . . but rather lead us forward into our maturity" (*N&SP*, 153). This maturity, however, entails falling into a meaninglessness that destroys the conventional self. All men, says Schiller, "without exception, must fall away from Nature by the abuse of Reason before they can return to her by the use of Reason" (*AE*, 6, #1, 31). With this and similar statements,[13] Schiller offers a 1795 version of postmodernism's "fall" into self-doubt and its hyperbolic "leap," as Schiller calls it, into a projected, "proxy" self (*N&SP*, 121). Prefiguring Hegel and Debord, Schiller consciously prescribes the destruction of the conventional self as part of the sentimental individual's autobiographical task: "I readily concede," he writes, "that, little as individuals might benefit from this fragmentation of their being, there was no other way in which the species as a whole could have progressed" (*AE*, 6, #11, 39).

The desultory "falling" and "leaping" of the Sentimental's hyperbolic attempts at self-recovery mark him as intrinsically sublime. While the naive tragic poet is "supported by his theme, the comic poet . . . must raise his [theme] to aesthetic height through his own person." The tragic poet is "already . . . there"; but the sentimental comic poet must "make a leap," and indeed, "cannot attain without a starting leap": "It is precisely in this way," Schiller writes,

> that the beautiful character is distinguished from the sublime. In the first, all the dimensions are already contained, flowing unconstrainedly and effortlessly by its nature . . . ; the other can elevate and exert itself to any dimension, by

the power of its will it can tear itself out of any state of limitation. The latter is, then, only intermittently and with effort free, the former with facility and always. (*N&SP*, 121)

Suggestive in terms of our own postmodern sublime,[14] the desultory sublimity (versus effortless beauty) of the sentimental character is simultaneously comic and ironic, in the profoundest sense of these words:

> Even if tragedy proceeds from a more significant point . . . comedy proceeds toward a more significant purpose and it would, were it to attain it, render all tragedy superfluous and impossible. Its purpose is uniform with the highest after which man has to struggle, to be free of passion, always clear, to look serenely about and within himself, to find everywhere more coincidence than fate, and rather to laugh at absurdity than to rage or weep at malice. (*N&SP*, 123)

Accomplished with clarity and serenity, the Sentimental's sublime leap reveals the basis of Schiller's *Freiheit in der Erscheinung* (freedom in appearance) in the notion of *style*—style as a process of ironic self-creation. Style in this sense would be a *panache* of the first order, in which *panache* were the sole remedy for despair. Its leap would not be "upward" toward an ideal but a conscious hurling of oneself into the banal incomprehensibility of existence, a "*salto mortale*" in which all that is "human" is fiction, all that is "real" is unreality, and all that is "meaningful" is artifice.

Based on such style, the Sentimental's autofiguration becomes hyperbolic in the Greek sense, a *hyper ballein* or conscious "throwing beyond" of an unreal "self." The Sentimental must posit a fictive "whole of himself" (*N&SP*, 155), a whole in which "the naive character would be united with the sentimental" (*N&SP*, 175). The resultant proxy would "collect his whole nature" (*N&SP*, 171), would be the "complete expression [of] the humanity within himself," his "human nature in its absolute capacity" (*N&SP*, 164). Accomplishing this, he would literally become a transcendent "other," since under his proxy identity, he would pass "from a limited condition . . . over into an infinite one" (*N&SP*, 154).

Paralleling Paul de Man's characterization of autobiography's hyperbolic "prolepsis" or anticipatory character,[15] the Sentimental's proxy self would be discovered at some point within a temporal sequence or pseudo-history. Like Hegel, Schiller postulates a "truth" to be proven in time, a self which can be recognized at the end of a progress. But while it is our "real" self, Schiller writes, the issue of "whether . . . it actually does exist . . . is another question" (*N&SP*, 175). Its existence must simply be assumed, or postulated as an eventuality, an "approximation . . . possessing degrees and display[ing] a progress" (*N&SP*, 113), a "self" toward which we "approach in endless progress" (*N&SP*, 85).

The Sentimental's future self is thus necessarily and permanently indeterminate.[16] Anticipating de Man's question of how a self can be recognized at the end if it has already been "erased and forgotten,"[17] Schiller admits that the "whole" self of "this fine accord between feeling and thinking . . . [is] only an idea that is never entirely attained in actuality," "an infinitude which [the individual] never attains," a goal of identity before which "he must fall infinitely short" (*N&SP*, 159, 113). In the Sentimental's dilemma, "the first," the empirical self, will always be "treated as lost," "and the second," the fictive unified self, will always remain "as unattained" (*N&SP*, 125).

THE FUTILITY OF SENTIMENTAL SELF-WRITING

The impossibility of the Sentimental's autobiographical task resides in his self-reflexiveness, a quality absent in the Naive character: "I have called naive poetry a *favor of nature*," Schiller writes, "to underscore that reflection has no part in it" (*N&SP*, 156). The Sentimental enjoys no such favor; he "*reflects* upon the impressions that objects make upon him, and only in that reflection is the emotion grounded which he himself experiences" (*N&SP*, 116). Thanks to the "assistance" that the naive poet receives from his external surroundings—surroundings unmediated by the Sentimental's awareness that its apparent order stems from his own perceptions—the naive poet eludes the Sentimental's nagging sense of meaninglessness: "If, however, this assistance is not forthcoming," if the naive poet "finds himself surrounded by a spiritless matter" [sheer materiality], then he "becomes sentimental only to remain poetic"; once struck by such self-consciousness, in other words, even the naive succumbs to the sentimental (*N&SP*, 158). He too "finds his cognitions and motives [only] in himself. . . . His character draws everything out of itself, and to itself, it refers everything" (*N&SP*, 180–81).[18]

The mode of escape from such specularity directly prefigures the postmodern self noted by Debord. The Sentimental's trick becomes a feigned negation, a dissimulative forgetting of the fragmented reflective self in order to clear the way for the postulation of a whole, unreflective identity. Because the Sentimental "sees in his own existence only a limitation, and as is reasonable, tears this down in order to penetrate to the true reality" (*N&SP*, 137), he can "by the power of [his] will, . . . tear [himself] out of any limitation" (*N&SP*, 121), forget himself "in order simply to be rid of the conflict within" (*N&SP*, 129).[19] In Schiller, therefore, as in de Man's characterization of Heidegger, "Being is in the act of its self-hiding and, as conscious subjects, we are necessarily caught up in this movement of dissolution and forgetting."[20]

However, though the Sentimental must forget—"I" must erase I in order to postulate an unconscious unified self—he can do so only through a reflective process which, ironically, aborts the sequential narrative required for the fiction of a unified self. "The opposite of naive perception," Schiller writes, "is . . . reflective understanding, and the sentimental mind is the result of the effort, *even under the conditions of reflection*, to restore naive feeling according to its content" (*N&SP*, 154–55, my italics). Thus, despite his efforts, the conditions of reflection produce not the Naive's fluid unconsciousness but the desultory, ever-expanding reflexivity he has attempted to forget.[21] The Sentimental's ideal self must be recognized in time, must achieve closure or final identity at the end of some history or temporal sequence. But the self-reflexiveness of his project subverts the sequentiality required to complete it. As Paul de Man has accurately observed, the specularity characteristic of autobiography "is not primarily a situation or an event that can be located in a history," since its constant self-referral subverts history's requisite narrative movement.[22] The Sentimental's fiction of an unreflective self evolving in time, therefore, dissolves its own narration. Since the Ideal self can neither come into being through the continuity which characterizes what Schiller calls the "flow" of naive beauty, or through the abortive wrenchings characteristic of the sublime, the Sentimental poet must always fall back into specular fragmentation (*N&SP*, 121): "The interest of autobiography," de Man remarks, "is not that it reveals reliable self-knowledge—it does not—but that it demonstrates in a striking way the impossibility of closure and of totalization (that is, the impossibility of coming into being)."[23]

The specularity of the Sentimentals' endeavor is a philosophical dilemma: "tearing down" a limited empirical existence, he "seek[s] . . . the true reality" of [his] identity beyond such limits (*N&SP*, 137). However, the project's theoretical nature, its metadiscursive character, disrupts not only the imagination which makes them poets, but the imagination by which they conceive and postulate the fiction of a unified self. "Philosophy and art," Schiller writes to Goethe, "have not penetrated one another, and we are more than ever conscious of the want of an organ to act as a medium between the two."[24] This divisiveness is exacerbated by philosophy's tendency to stifle creativity: "I have for long not felt so prosaic as during these last days," Schiller writes, "and it is high time that I should close my philosophy book for a while. My heart pines for some tangible object."[25] Like Schiller, the sentimental poet will always pine for the tangible, for it is his "nature" to labor under "the excess of thought that lays shackles upon his imagination" (*N&SP*, 128). Thus Schiller's complaints about philosophy to Körner: "I am studying Kant's 'Powers of Judgment.' . . . I am now quite impatient to commence some poetical work . . . criticism has spoiled me. I feel, that . . . I have lost that boldness and living fire I formerly possessed. I now see what I create and form. I watch the progress of the fruits of inspiration, and my imagination is less free, since it is aware that it is being watched."[26]

SENTIMENTAL LANGUAGE: THE REPRESENTATION OF NOTHING

Caught in the reflexivity of his quest, the Sentimental prefigures the postmodern crisis of representation. All reference to objective meaning—meaning beyond the Sentimental's own fictions—dissolves, and with this disappearance language, as naive representation, disintegrates as well. The Sentimental's sense of his own fragmentation excludes him from traditional forms of expression—that "imitation of actuality" by which the Naive remains unaware of representational disjunction. Should the Sentimental attempt the mimetic in his art, "that opposition is still within his heart and will betray itself . . . even against his will. For the very language which he must employ, because it bears the spirit of the age . . . would serve to remind us of actuality and its limitations" (*N&SP*, 126). Throughout the ten-year period of his aesthetic essays, Schiller realizes increasingly that the correspondence between language and meaning, between myself and what I *say* is myself or between I and saying "I," had only existed (if ever) in a naive or ancient time; in his own "modern" period, it has long since disappeared.[27] In the naive expression of classical Greece, "language springs as by some inner necessity out of thought, and is so at one with it that even beneath the corporeal frame the spirit appears as if laid bare. It is precisely this mode of expression in which the sign disappears completely in the thing signified" (*N&SP*, 98). "Modern" expression, however, enjoys no such fate. In the language of the Sentimental, Schiller writes, "the sign remains forever heterogeneous to the thing signified" (*N&SP*, 98). Such heterogeneity appears in Schiller's poem, "Language":

> Warum kann der lebendige Geist dem Geist nicht erscheinen? Spricht die Seele, so spricht, ach! schon die Seele nicht mehr.
>
> Why can't living spirit appear to the mind?
> If the soul speaks, then, alas! what speaks is no longer the soul.

To suggest, as Schiller does, that the "soul" or meaning has fallen away from language, is to acknowledge—whether or not Schiller would approve the term—the tropological structure on which traditional or naive meaning is based. With naive meaning thus discredited, sentimental language falls into "emptiness," as Schiller describes it (*N&SP*, 181); proceeding out of the meaninglessness of "actuality," language becomes "the formless play of chance, [and the Sentimental's] thought the empty play of representation."[28]

Schiller observes that it is the sublime and not the beautiful that guides the sentimental or modern age: "Beauty is for a happy race," he writes; "an unhappy one has to be moved by sublimity."[29] Thus, in his questioning of the sentimental poet's "empty play of representation," Schiller is grappling with and attempting to formulate the problematic character of sentimental representation, the "as if" representation of the sublime. The very process of sentimental representation reflects the problem of sublimity. It pervades the sentimental artist's activity, which "is always involved with two conflicting representations . . . with actuality as a limit and with his ideas as infinitude" (*N&SP*, 116). The object of sentimental poetry is equally sublime. Whereas the naive is "*Nachahmung des Wirklichen*"[30] (the imitation of actuality [*N&SP*, 111]), the sentimental is "*Darstellung des Ideals*"[31] (representation of the ideal [*N&SP*, 112]). Schiller specifically defines naive figuration as an "imitation" (*Nachahmung*), a Neoclassical mimesis or mirror reflection of nature which assures a sign/meaning identity. Sentimental figuration, on the other hand, is a "representation" (*Darstellung*), a Romantic approximation characterized by its disparity with the thing or idea it signifies. This is not a "*Vorstellung*" or "placing before," as if it were possible—as in mimesis—to aesthetically present the object perceived. It is a "*Darstellung*," a repetition or re-presentation which in its temporal belatedness can never achieve identity with its object.

Reflecting the sublime's assault on conceptual closure, the subject matter of the sentimental is precisely that which is unrepresentable, incapable of totalization or of coming into being. Sentimental art, says Schiller, is the "art of the infinite" (*N&SP*, 114), of "whatever is insusceptible of representation and ineffable" (*N&SP*, 115). Because naive art is a mimesis or an imitation of actuality, "we always rejoice . . . in the living presence of the object . . . ; whereas with the sentimental we have to reconcile the representation of imagination with an idea of reason and hence always fluctuate between two different conditions" (*N&SP*, 116n). The "object" does not obtain in sentimental poetry; it is not there, or else it is other than what we experience in the natural, the traditional order of meaning. While the lost ideal, the naive, had offered a poetics of presence, the sentimental has slipped into a poetics of absence. Sentimental representation becomes a representation of nothingness, or of "other."

Given the "empty play" of sentimental art, Schiller admits that his era faces the emergence of an aesthetics that defies conventional categories. He calls for new poetic categories that might account for it, asserting that if

> one is inclined to take sentimental poetry, as . . . a genuine order (and not simply as a degenerate species) and as an

extension of true poetic art, then some attention must be paid to it in the determination of poetic types . . . which is still one-sidedly based on the observances of the ancient and naive poets. The sentimental poet deviates too radically from the naive for those forms . . . to accommodate him. . . . [This] much we learn from experience, that in the hands of sentimental poets, . . . often very new types have been executed. (*N&SP*, 147n)

Yet, he had also said that a poetry that goes beyond the human is overstrained, "provided that it has declared itself as representable and poetic" (*N&SP*, 165). This provision, combined with his call for poetic categories reveal a basic ambiguity: Schiller knowingly confronts an aesthetic phenomenon that may well *not* declare itself as either "representable" or "poetic." Aware that the new aesthetics deviates radically from naive orders, and calling for new types which might define it or might admit it into the aesthetically legitimate, Schiller is clearly attempting to come to terms with a sensibility and an art in which traditional representational structures no longer function.

DAIMONIAS HYPERBOLE: CONSTRUCTING THE SENTIMENTAL'S DEMONIC SELF

What Schiller discovers in the Sentimental's autobiographical project is the absence of all that could be called "natural." Though the Sentimental is more intensely attached to nature than is the Naive, it is "not in [his] greater *accord with nature*, but quite the contrary, the unnaturalness of [his] situation" (*N&SP*, 103). Even the presence of naive nature, such as the sight of a child, merely foregrounds nature's unattainability, "revealing more closely the unnatural in [the Sentimental]" (*N&SP*, 86). This "contranatural" quality, as Coleridge would later call it, becomes the informing characteristic of the Sentimental's proxy self. Barred by her specularity from the use of natural categories, the Sentimental fabricates a unified self from the unnatural, "suppressing human nature altogether" (*N&SP*, 164). Like Mary Shelley's Victor Frankenstein, the Sentimental's project cannot "remain within the conditions that are entailed in the concept of human nature" (*N&SP*, 164), but must "totally abandon" that nature (*N&SP*, 165). Even the feelings associated with the endeavor are inhuman: "Since [the sentimental poet's] subject is not drawn from nature . . . the feeling is therefore not purely human. It is not an illusion that . . . [he] feel[s] for [his] ideal. The feeling is true but its object is artificial and lies outside human nature" (*N&SP*, 167).

If, as Harold Bloom writes perceptively, "the program of Romanticism demands something more than a natural man to carry it through,"[32] the successful perpetrator of that program is a character of marked emotional unbalance. Embodying de Man's statement that there "is no longer anything natural about [Romanticism's] supernaturalism,"[33] the Sentimental is obsessed with insanity and death; the sublime is the material of his art, and as Schiller discovered in his earlier aesthetic essay "Of the Sublime,"[34] death is the ground of sublimity, the foundation of the utterly incomprehensible.[35] In his final aesthetic essay "On the Sublime,"[36] Schiller would emphasize the inevitability of this ground:

> There is a cure for everything except for death. But this single exception . . . would destroy the whole concept of humanity. . . . This single terror, which he simply must do and does not will, will haunt [man] like a spectre and . . . will deliver him up to the blind terrors of the imagination."[37]

As Schiller well knew, however, the Sentimental rarely seeks a cure; on the contrary, what attracts her is "this single exception": "While the naive is the child of life, and to life it leads us back," he writes, "the Sentimental will always for a few moments disaffect us for actual life"—in the spell of her art, "we fall back, lost in our thoughts" (N&SP, 156).[38]

Though Schiller's own art tends toward such a spell, he warns against such poets as Klopstock and the English death-poet Edward Young, whose "fantast" despondency poses a threat to the Sentimental's equilibrium:[39] "The path from experience to the ideal is long," he cautions, "and in between lies fantasy with unbridled fortuitousness" (N&SP, 168). More than its morbidness, the "dangerous freedom" of the Sentimental project, the "lawless" imagination required to bring it off, imperils the poet himself (N&SP, 168). This lawlessness is endemic not merely to the sentimental poet's sublime metier,[40] but to the contranaturalness of his character—to the fact that his goal of an ideal identity involves the abandonment of the human. While it is "only for the ideal [that the sentimental] may . . . abandon actuality . . . [,] if he leaves nature through caprice, then he will remain without a law and is thus rendered up a prey to the fantastic" (N&SP, 168). A typical Romantic paradox, the chief threat to the sentimental character is also the trait that produces it.

Often, Schiller writes, the poet who wishes to be the "portrayer" of his times becomes its grotesque "creature and its caricature," and his "unbridled" productions either approach madness or succumb to it (N&SP, 163). Friedrich Schlegel is such a caricature: "A few hours after reading Schlegel's *Lucinde*," Schiller tells Goethe, "my head felt so giddy, that I still feel the effects of it. You must read the work if only for the sake of the astonishment you will feel. . . . Here also we have things everlastingly formless and fragmentary."[41] But the formless and fragmentary astonish Schiller less than the tendency to the grotesque, the fact that the Sentimental "will reconcile himself even with the extravagant and the monstrous if it only testifies to a great potentiality" (*N&SP*, 184)—undoubtedly because the grotesque attracts Schiller himself. It is no accident that a penchant for the monstrous initiates the "*Spieltrieb*" or "play impulse," Schiller's panacea for human woe in *Aesthetic Education*; the play drive starts when man "seiz[es] on what is new and startling—. . . the fantastic, and bizarre, the violent and the savage. . . grotesque shapes" (*AE*, 27, #4, 211). Indeed, though reluctant to admit it, Schiller frequently slips into the monstrous in his own work. In a note to his play *Don Carlos* on the character of Philip, the cruel and insane father of Carlos, Schiller writes: "I do not know what kind of monster one expects when Philip is mentioned. My drama collapses when such a monster is found in it."[42] But when an awestruck Coleridge exclaims after reading Schiller's *Die Räuber* (*The Robbers*) that "Schiller has the material sublime," he refers not to some cerebral moment in Schiller's play but to the scene in which "mothers and babes alike [are] thrown into the flames."[43] Far from collapsing, Schiller's work frequently achieves its power through such monstrousness.

Schiller's own slide into the lawlessness of which he warns demonstrates the problem of sublimity that underpins sentimental representation. On the one hand, the only way to present the abstractions of sublimity is to release the imagination. For the sublime, as Lyotard aptly explains, "What is required of the imagination, for this abstract presentation which presents nothingness, is that it should 'unlimit' itself . . . It is even a dementia, a *Wahnsinn*, in which the imagination is 'unleashed.' "[44] In order to reach the human ideal of sublimity, in other words, the Sentimental must take a few steps into the lawless and the inhuman. On the other hand, says Schiller, in order to control these peregrinations into the other, the sentimental poet must cling to the "ideal." The difficulty of such a check, as Schiller becomes aware, is the task of distinguishing the ideal. As he writes:

> Because the genuine sentimental impulse must . . . pass beyond the limits of actual nature, the inauthetic goes beyond every limit . . . and persuades himself that mere wild play of imagination is all that makes for poetic inspiration. To the true poetic genius, who abandons actuality only for the sake of the idea, this can never happen, or *only in those moments in which he has lost himself;* yet he, on the other hand can be seduced by his own nature into an *exaggerated mode of perception*. (*N&SP*, 168; italics mine)

Even the "true" genius can be seduced by the Sentimental's autobiographical project, wrenched out of the *Wahnsinn*, or "acceptable" freedom of sublime imagination and hurled into the insanity of *Wahnwitz*. Lyotard's discussion of Kant's similar fear is instructive here. The *Wahnsinn* or *dementia* which normally attends the imagination confronted with sublimity is nevertheless, Lyotard writes,

> preferable to the *Schwärmerei*, to the tumult of exaltation, which is a *Wahnwitz*, an *insanitas*, a "disorder" of the imagination, an "illness deep-rooted in the soul." . . . The *Schwärmerei* gives rise to an illusion, to "seeing something beyond all limits of sensibility," i.e., to thinking that there is a presentation when there is not. It makes a non-critical transition which is comparable to the transcendental illusion (the illusion of knowing something beyond all the limits of knowledge). ("Philosophy," 17)

Like the potential *Schwärmerei* or *insanitas* of the sublime, the Sentimental's "as if" representations "seduce" and even "possess" him, as Coleridge would later describe it.

Schiller frequently worries about the Sentimental's desire to see beyond all limits of sensibility: such "withdrawal from life" "will not only remove from his vision the accidental limitations of mankind—it will often remove the necessary and unsurmountable limitations, and in seeking the pure form he stands in danger of losing the entire meaning" (*N&SP*, 174). The seductiveness of such a quest lies beyond the control of reason or the ideal, indeed, beyond meaning altogether: "Wanting to be what we are not," Nietzche writes, "we come to believe ourselves something else than we really are, and this is how we become mad." The Sentimental's goal is precisely to become something other, as well as the very likely possibility that he might come to believe it. As Schiller writes ominously at the conclusion of *Naive and Sentimental Poetry*:

> If . . . true idealism is insecure and often dangerous in its effects, false idealism is appalling in its effects . . . the fantast . . . is completely lawless, hence nothing in himself and fit for nothing. But for the very reason that his phantasmagoria is not a deviation from nature but from freedom, and this develops out of a capacity in itself estimable and infinitely perfectible, it leads likewise to an infinite fall into a bottomless abyss and can only terminate in complete destruction. (*N&SP*, 121)

The peril of the Sentimental's search for identity lies in the fact that the ideal self she desires must ground itself on her own empty play of representation, and thus on the "as if" representation of the negative sublime. The poet is left, in the last analysis, with the phantom self noted by Hölderlin in "Mnemosyne": *"Ein Zeichen sind wir—Deutungslos"*—such as a sign are we—meaningless.

With this dilemma, Schiller approaches the nonrational basis of thought itself. Grown tentative from his concessions to the materialist rigor of Kant's aesthetic theory, Schiller writes: "Be not afraid of the confusion around you, only of the confusion within you" (*N&SP*, 101). His caveat speaks to an issue that is prevalent in our own time. For the Sentimental as for the Postmodern, to reach for absolute meaning is to invite the abandonment of meaning itself: "the evil," Schiller writes, "is that [the Sentimental] can scarcely elevate himself to the true ideal of human ennoblement without in any case taking a few steps beyond it" (*N&SP*, 173). But a few steps beyond the human also leads to a "bottomless abyss," Schiller writes, or, more precisely, to the abyssal awareness that it is such incomprehensibility alone that grounds meaning. "Evil," perhaps, from a conventional or logical perspective, the Sentimental's confrontation and acknowlegement of this abyssal ground is also, Schiller writes, "a capacity" that is "in itself estimable and infinitely perfectible" (*N&SP*, 190). The madness produced by such a confrontation, he admits, is the source not only of insanity but of wisdom: "Thus the very same produces the fanatic that was solely able to engender the sage, and the advantage of the latter may perhaps subsist less in that he did not become the former than that he did not remain so" (*N&SP*, 174). The sage and the madman, in other words, are one. Both rise out of the abyss. Their only distinction, and a fine one at that, is that the sage can, for a time, forget his origin.

With this remark, an insight possible only to the sentimental or modern mind, Schiller acknowledges the ground of postmodern philosophy, the *Abgrund* of the negative sublime. Stated differently, Schiller's insight prefigures what Phillip Lacoue-Labarthe has called philosophy's predestination to madness: "Might philosophy not move more towards its end," he writes, "if, pushed to its limit, exhausted, unsettled . . . it were forced . . . to bear witness to the hypothesis that there is . . . some philosophical predetermination of madness?"[45]

To call a sage a willfully amnesiac madman, as does Schiller, participates in the same "hyperbolic audacity," the same confrontation with the abyss that Derrida discerns in the Cartesian *Cogito*, and with the same striking implications for the intrinsic postmodernity of sentimental autofiguration. Derrida writes:

> The hyperbolic audacity of the Cartesian Cogito, its mad audacity . . . would consist in the return to an original point which no longer belongs either to a determined reason or a determined unreason. . . . It is the point at which

the thinking of this totality by escaping it: i.e., by exceeding the totality, which—within existence—is possible only in the direction of infinity or nothingness; . . . This is why . . . this project is mad, and acknowledges madness as a liberty and its very possibility. This is why it is not human, in the sense of anthropological factuality, but is rather metaphysical and demonic: it first awakens itself in its war with the demon, the evil genius of non-meaning, by pitting itself against the strength of the evil genius, and by resisting him through reduction of the natural man within itself. In this sense, nothing is less reassuring than the Cogito at its proper and inaugural moment. The project of exceeding the totality of the world, as the totality of what I can think in general, . . . plants in us the light of a hidden sun which is epekeina tes ousias. And Glaucon was not mistaken when he cried out: 'Lord! what demonic hyperbole? *daimonia hyperboles*'[46]

Though tentative, Schiller's project of a contranatural self that exceeds the the thinkable totality reflects the postmodern invitation to unmeaning through a "reduction of the natural man."[47] To reach this infinite point requires a few steps into the meaningless; it requires one to become other, or demonic, in order to return to "humanity" with one's "knowledge" authenticated by an awareness of its fictive character. When such knowledge has itself deadened, falsified into hyperrational dogma as it had in Schiller's era—and perhaps in today's—the Sentimental (read Postmodern) returns again to the insanitas of the negative sublime. As in 1797, the leap that produces the madman produces the sage. Perhaps Schiller's equation of lunatic and philosopher reflects his own demonism: "The higher a man is," Goethe remarked to Eckermann, "the more he lives under the influence of demons, and he must be careful not to let the guiding will be led astray. In my acquaintance with Schiller, something demonic was clearly at work."[48] To stray from the Goethean "naive," to think the totality by exceeding it, by abandoning the figures of mastery of self, of adequation to self, is precisely Schiller's sentimental direction, the movement toward the concept of self before the law. By acknowledging the madness of this quest, Schiller marks the beginnings of the postmodern sensibility, in which the absence of identity is both the crisis of the postmodern self and the condition of its possibility.

NOTES

1. Schiller, "The Philosophers," 1. 143.
2. Jacques Derrida, "Eating Well," in *Who Comes After the Subject*, eds. Eduardo Cadava, Peter Conner and Jean-Luc Nancy (New York: Routledge, 1991), p. 103.

3. Jacques Derrida, "The Other Heading: Memories, Responses, and Responsibilities," *PMLA*, vol. 108, no. 1 (January 1993), 89–93; 90.
4. G. W. F. Hegel, quoted in Greil Marcus, *Lipstick Traces: A Secret History of the Twentieth Century* (Cambridge: Harvard University Press, 1989), pp. 98–99.
5. Cf. Paul Jay's discussion of Roland Barthe's *Roland Barthes* in Paul Jay, *Being in the Text: Self-Representation from Wordsworth to Roland Barthes* (Ithaca: Cornell University Press, 1984), pp. 161–85.
6. My discussion of Schiller's concept of "sentimental" identity as a precursor to postmodern selfhood refers only to Western concepts of the self. The incomprehensibility of the Western idea of one's "real" self, and the use of manifold proxy identities have been commonplace in Eastern cultures for millennia.
7. For a discussion of Schiller's play drive (*Spieltrieb*) and the heautonomy (*Heautonomie*) or illusory freedom (*Freiheit in der Erscheinung*) it provides, see Schiller, *Kallias, oder über die Schönheit*, ed. Klaus Berghahn (Stuttgart: Reclam, 1972), pp. 3–67; Schiller, *Aesthetic Education*, trans. E. Wilkinson (Oxford: Oxford University Press, 1967); and J. M. Ellis, *Schiller's 'Kalliasbriefe' and the Study of His Aesthetic Theory* (The Hague and Paris: Mouton, 1969).
8. Schiller, *Naive and Sentimental Poetry* in *Friedrich von Schiller: Naive and Sentimental Poetry and "On the Sublime"*, trans. Julias A. Elias (New York: Frederick Ungar Publishing Co., 1966), pp. 83–190; 168. Hereafter *N&SP*.
9. Schiller, *On the Aesthetic Education of Man: In a Series of Letters*, trans. E. Wilkinson (Oxford: Clarendon Press, 1967), Letter 6, #3, p. 31. Hereafter *AE*.
10. The elegiac also dominates Schiller's discussion of sentimental perception, comprising twenty pages, in contrast to ten pages on the idyll and seven on satire.
11. Since Schiller championed the sentimental female, as his plays *Mary Stuart*, *The Maid of Orleans*, and *The Bride of Messina* show, I have tried to intersperse masculine and feminine pronouns where it does not interfere with the argument.
12. The least effective of the sentimental or modern genres, the idyll is a futile and delusive endeavor, which "imbue[s] us only with a sad feeling of loss" (*N&SP*, 149). Schiller's vacillation with regard to the idyll is worth note. He says first that there are only two sentimental modes, the satiric and the elegaic—appropriately expressing the anger and the sorrow of loss. As an apparent afterthought, he adds a third mode, the "idyll." The idyll's incompatability with the sentimental system emerges in Schiller's cursory introduction of the genre: "There are a few more words for me to say about this third species of sentimental poetry, a few words only, because a more detailed development . . . is reserved for another occasion" (*N&SP*, 145). This "more detailed development" was never written (cf. *N&SP*, p. 219, n.33).
13. Cf. Schiller's exhortation to "kill ourselves morally before nature does it for us" in "On the Sublime."
14. For the postmodern sublime see J. S. Librett ed., *Of the Sublime: Presence in Question* (Albany: SUNY Press, 1993); L. Brooks, "Sublimity and Theatricality: Romantic Pre-Postmodernism," 1990.
15. Cf. prolepsis in de Man, "Time and History in Wordsworth," in *Romanticism and Contemporary Criticism* (Baltimore: Johns Hopkins University Press, 1993), p. 81; "Sign and Symbol in Hegel's Aesthetics," *Critical Enquiry*, 8 (Summer 1982), 761–77, 770. Hereafter, "Hegel's Aesthetics."
16. This indeterminacy is, as Jean-François Courtine notes, the crux of Schiller's, and later Schelling's, concepts of the sublime. According to Schiller, Courtine writes: "The one who, in the face of the world as it is, wishes that all were organized in accordance with a wise economy . . . has no hope of seeing his desire satisfied . . . : inversely 'if he renounces willingly [*gutwillig*] the claim to submit the chaos of phenomena, rebellious against all law, to the unity of knowledge, he thereby gains on another side more than all he has lost.' " This renunciation, as Courtine accurately observes, constitutes the crucial refocus upon the chaotic that Schelling was to adopt for his own theory: to Schiller, one

must judge not in terms of the comprehensible but of the incomprehensible; not in terms of the conceivable but of the inconceivable. However, Schiller's discernment of chaos as the *Urgrund* of a "higher" knowledge formed the basis not only of Schelling's theory of sublimity but of the sublime that underpins contemporary postmodernism. Cf. Jean-François Courtine, "Tragedy and Sublimity," in *Of the Sublime: Presence in Question*, trans. Jeffrey S. Librett (New York: SUNY Press, 1993), pp. 157–174; 170–71.

17. de Man writes: "The mind has to recognize at the end of its trajectory—in this case at the end of the text—what was posited at the beginning. It has to recognize itself as itself, that is to say, as I. But how are we to recognize what will necessarily be erased and forgotten, since 'I' is, per definition, what I can never say?" Cf. "Hegel's Aesthetics," p. 770.
18. Indeed, such reflection becomes itself the topic of cogitation, in which the "mind cannot tolerate any impression without at once observing its own activity and reflection. In this mood we are never given the subject, only what the reflective understanding has made of it, and even when the poet is himself the subject . . . we never learn of his condition directly and at first hand but rather how he has reflected in his own mind what he has thought about it as an observer of himself" (*N&SP*, p. 130).
19. Unlike the naive character, Schiller writes, "*we*, not at one with ourselves and unhappy in our experience of mankind, possess no more urgent interest than to escape from it and cast from our view so unsuccessful a form" (*N&SP*, p. 104).
20. de Man, "Impersonality in Blanchot," in *Blindness and Insight: Essays in the Rhetoric of Contemporary Criticism, Theory and History of Literature*, No. 7 (1971; rev. Minneapolis: University of Minnesota Press, 1983), pp. 60–79; 76. Hereafter, *Blindness*.
21. Cf. de Man on Peter Szondi in *Blindness*, p. 219.
22. de Man, "Autobiography as De-facement," in *The Rhetoric of Romanticism* (New York: Columbia University Press, 1984), p. 70. Hereafter, "Autobiography."
23. "Autobiography," p. 71.
24. Schiller, Letter to Goethe, January 20, 1802.
25. Schiller, Letter to Goethe, December 17, 1795.
26. Schiller, Letter to Körner, May 23, 1792.
27. Schiller's despair for his own time of a classical consubstantiality of sign and thing signified is summarized in the contrast between his early poem "Words of Faith," and its later pendant poem, "Words of Illusion." In "Words of Faith" the praise of freedom, virtue, and God is couched in a paean to the ideal of ancient Greece. In "Words of Illusion," Schiller attacks the superstition of a belief in the golden age or in any modern realization of the ideals of that age.
28. "*Das formlose Spiel des Zufalls, seine Gedanken . . . das gehaltlose Spiel der Vorstellungskraft.*" Cf. Schiller, *Werke* (Weimar, 1962), XX, 437.
29. Schiller, Letter to Prof. Suvern, July 26, 1800.
30. *Werke*, Wiese, Berlin, XX, 437.
31. *Werke*, XX, 437
32. Harold Bloom, *Anxiety of Influence: A Theory of Poetry* (New York: Oxford University Press, 1973), p. 271.
33. de Man, "Ludwig Binswanger and the Sublimation of the Self," in *Blindness*, pp. 36–50; 43. Hereafter, "Sublimation."
34. Schiller, "Vom Erhabenen," in *Werke*, XX, 170–95. Hereafter, "Of the Sublime."
35. Cf. L. Brooks, "Sublime Suicide: The End of Schiller's Aesthetics," in *Friedrich von Schiller and the Drama of Human Existence*, ed. A. Ugrinsky (New York: Greenwood Press, 1988), pp. 91–103; 94–95.
36. Schiller, "On the Sublime."
37. Schiller, "On the Sublime," pp. 191–213.
38. Kant had warned of this self-reflexive "monomania" in his *Anthropology*. Not surprisingly, Kierkegaard's *Either/Or* engages the same question. In the later work's debate between "aesthetics" and "ethics," the defender of aesthetics, reflecting the sentimental's aestheticized identity, exhibits what Schiller had already suspected was the modern

character's fatal solipsism: "He has not chosen himself," writes Kierkegaard; "like Narcissus he has fallen in love with himself. Such a situation has certainly ended not infrequently in suicide."

39. While Schiller laments the fact that the sentimental characteristically "disaffects us for actual life," it is Klopstock (along with the English death-poet Edward Young), "who always leads us only away from life" (*N&SP*, p. 135).
40. With the sublime, Jean-François Lyotard writes, "what is regulated is the fact that there is no rule," the fact that its only "rule" is a "rule of non-regulation." Cf. J.-F. Lyotard, "The Philosophy of Phrases," trans. Geoff Bennington, n.d., n.p., 17. Hereafter, Lyotard, "Philosophy."
41. Schiller, letter to Goethe, July 19, 1799.
42. Schiller, *Don Carlos*, in *The Classic Theater: Five German Plays*, ed. Eric Bentley 2 vols. (Garden City, New York: Doubleday, 1959), II, 94.
43. Coleridge, January 6, 1823, in *Table Talk*, ed. Carl Woodring, (Princeton: Princeton University Press), I; 26. In a letter written immediately after reading Schiller's *Die Räuber*, Coleridge exclaimed: "My God! Southey! Who is this Schiller?! This convulser of the Heart. Did he write his Tragedy amid the yelling of Fiends?" *Collected Letters*, ed. E. L. Griggs, 6 vols. (Oxford: Clarendon Press, 1956-), I, 122.
44. Lyotard, "Philosophy," p. 17.
45. Philippe Lacoue-Labarthe, "Typography," trans. Eduardo Cadava, in *Typography: Mimesis, Philosophy, Politics*, ed. C. Fynske, ed. cons. Linda M. Brooks (Cambridge: Harvard University Press, 1989), pp. 43–139; 45. I use Cadava's original translation as closer to Lacoue-Labarthe's meaning than Fynsk's later revision.
46. Jacques Derrida, "Cogito and the History of Madness," in *Writing and Difference*, trans. Alan Bass (Chicago: University of Chicago Press, 1978), pp. 31–64; 56–57.
47. Cf. Donna Haraway, *Simians, Cyborgs, and Women* (London: Routledge, 1991).
48. Goethe, *Conversations with Eckermann* (San Francisco: North Point, 1984), letter of March 24, 1829.

THE ROMANTIC ARCHAEOLOGY OF THE PSYCHE: NOVALIS'S *HEINRICH VON OFTERDINGEN**

KENNETH CALHOON

The usefulness of archaeology as a metaphor describing the recovery of hidden or forgotten associations is apparent to those familiar with the work of Sigmund Freud and Michel Foucault, both of whom found in that discipline a means of conceptualizing the stratified and contiguous arrangements that structure mental life. Archaeology suggested to Freud an interplay of surface and depth that corresponded to that between consciousness and the unconscious, promising further a prehistorical substratum at which the ontogenetic and phylogenetic origins of neurosis would coincide.[1] What archaeology offered Foucault was access to, in his (translator's) words, "a *positive unconscious* of knowledge,"[2] a body of rules that, though never formulated in the mind of the practitioner, conditioned the discourse of a wide range of disciplines. Foucault's definition of the library—the site of his excavations—as a space that collapses temporal distance by rendering all historical epochs copresent,[3] is not unlike Freud's account of the process whereby sense perceptions, as they work their way into the more complex folds of the psychic apparatus, proceed from temporal to spatial configurations.[4]

A departure is marked by Foucault's juxtaposition of the *archive* and the *archaic;* the former he understood as an inescapable interior of language that refuses all access to origins. Yet by characterizing language as

---

*Reprinted from *Fatherland: Novalis, Freud, and the Discipline of Romance*, Wayne State University Press, 1992.

"the locus . . . of what lies hidden in a people's mind,"[5] and by thus privileging philology as the means of penetrating the deeper layers of discourse. Foucault not only recalls how Freud probed the surface of a patient's speech for traces of the unconscious, but he also points to an implication of that practice made explicit by Lacan, who held that the unconscious is linguistic in structure.[6] The post-Freudian focus on language, by modifying Freud largely from within, revives certain impulses that as part of Freud's intellectual heritage may have contributed to the possibility of psychoanalysis. A dissociation of language from the realm of conscious intention was crucial to the work of Wilhelm von Humboldt, who regarded language not as the product of consciousness, but as its formative agent.[7] His concept of linguistic relativity built upon the historicist view that language, rather than being an analogue of universal human reason (as the Enlightenment believed), was part of the cultural-geographical matrix within which the thinking of a particular people took its unique shape. Hence Jacob Grimm's equation of language and history: "Unsere Sprache ist auch unsere Geschichte" (Our language is also our history).[8] Grimm conceived of Germanic philology as a form of historical self-analysis, a means of recovering origins that the historical process had obscured (*getrübt*).[9] A parallel emerges between Foucault's emphasis on the library and its idiom of proximity and the shift in attention, marked by Grimm, away from Oriental tongues to older German languages that were exotic by virtue of time alone, not space.

This literal reorientation brings to light a second spatial extension performed by the metaphor of archaeology, for in addition to providing an architectonics based on depth, it also isolates, as a virtual necessity, the element of distance: the archaeological site is one that must be gained by journey, the more arduous the better.[10] The suggestion of an enduring impulse to travel fosters the proposal that archaeology did not simply *become* a metaphor for disciplines that appeared later, but was metaphorical at its very inception, an attempt by a nostalgic era to preserve a role for quest in the face of its social and institutional obsolescence. Archaeology shows that Romanticism did more to compensate for the loss of adventure than merely exalt that pseudo-nomadic survivor of a less sedentary age, the traveling merchant. The "fernhinsinnender Kaufmann," the "tradesman in thought far-wandering" blessed by the gods in Hölderlin's *Archipelagus*,[11] found his modern incarnation in Heinrich Schliemann, whose explorations so captivated Freud that he likened his own discovery of the Oedipus complex to the former's excavation of Troy.[12] Schliemann's "conversion" from magnate to explorer is emblematic of how the advent of archaeology in effect replaced commercial venture, the modern form of romance, with adventure proper. Freud himself identified the importance of that substitution when he wrote that Schliemann achieved through archaeology a happiness wealth alone would have denied him.[13] Freud generalized elsewhere that money lacks the power to bring true happiness because it does not satisfy a childhood wish.[14] By placing Schliemann's discovery of Priam's treasure within a basic economics of wish fulfillment, Freud prepares the ground for the hypothesis that archaeology constitutes a formal imitation of regression and as such represents the desire to return to primary positions long since abandoned.

THE ROMANCE OF PHILOLOGY

That Germanic philology too was inspired by a nostalgia for quest is suggested by the imagery Jacob Grimm used when he located the birth of that discipline in the library of his teacher, the legal scholar Friedrich Carl von Savigny, where as a young law student he caught his first glimpse of medieval German poetry. At a ceremony honoring Savigny years later, Grimm recalled how the sight of the strange language instilled in him a fascination that presaged his eventual commitment to the study of older German texts. What distinguishes Grimm's account is its stylization; the visit to Savigny's home is represented as a meanderous pilgrimage through the medieval city of Marburg, where narrow streets and winding stairways take him through churchyards and towers to heights that afford Romantic vistas of the surrounding countryside. His immediate destination is the house in which the professor leads a reclusive existence, and once inside the visitor continues inward to the sanctum of the library. Grimm's prose, halting and winding, pausing for detail before continuing upward, recreates the breathlessness the "climb" itself must have produced:

> Zu Marburg muss man seine Beine rühren und Treppe auf, Treppe ab steigen. Aus einem kleinen Hause der Barfüsser Strasse führte mich durch ein schmales Gässchen und den Wendelstieg eines alten Turms der tägliche Weg auf den Kirchhof, von dem sichs über die Dächer und Blütenbäume sehnsüchtig in die Weite schaut, da war gut auf und ab wandeln, dann stieg man an der Mauerwand wieder in eine höherliegende Gasse vorwärts zum Forsthoff. . . . Zwischen dessen Bereich und dem Hoftor unten, mitten an der Treppe, klebte wie ein Nest ein Nebenhaus, in dem Sie Ihr heiteres, sorgenfreies und nur der Wissenschaft gewidmetes Leben lebten. Ein Diener . . . öffnete und man trat in ein nicht grosses Zimmer, von dem eine Tür in ein noch kleineres Gemach mit Sopha führte. Hell und sonnig waren die Räume, . . . die Fenster gaben ins Giesser Tal, auf Wiesen, Lahn und Gebirg duftige Aussicht, die sich zauberhafter Wirkung näherte, in den Fensterecken hingen eingerahmt Kupferstiche . . . , an denen ich mich nicht satt sehen konnte, so freute ich mich deren scharfe und zarte Sauberkeit.

In Marburg one must really move one's legs, climbing up stairs and down stairs. From a small house in the Barfüsser Strasse, my daily walk led me along a narrow alley and up the spiral staircase of an old tower to the churchyard, from which one gazed longingly beyond roof tops and flowering trees into the distance, that was quite an up-and-down hike, then one climbed along the wall up to an even higher lane and onward to the Forsthof. . . . Between its realm and the gate below, perched midway on the stairs like a nest, was the side house in which you led a happy and carefree life devoted only to learning. A servant . . . answered, and one stepped into a small room, from which a door led to an even smaller chamber with sofa. The rooms were bright and sunny, . . . and the fragrant view that the windows afforded of meadows, the river Lahn, and the mountains beyond bordered on magic; in the windows hung framed copper engravings . . . on which I could not feast my eyes enough, so did I delight in their sharp and delicate clarity.

The copper engravings, intelligible to the eye and placed in full view of the natural landscape, are monuments to the Enlightenment cult of visibility, an attitude interrupted when Grimm's attention is diverted by old books altogether lacking in the clarity of those pictures. Replacing intelligibility with mystery, Grimm's discovery demarcates an historical watershed, sealing once and for all the end of the Enlightenment.

Doch noch viel grösseren Reiz für mich hatten die im Zimmer aufstrebenden Schränke und in ihnen aufgestellten Bücher. . . . Ich entsinne mich, von der Tür eintretend an der Wand zur rechten Hand ganz hinten fand sich auch ein Quartant, Bodmers Sammlung der Minnelieder . . . mit Gedichten in seltsamem, halb unverständlichem Deutsch, das erfüllte mich mit eigner Ahnung. . . . Solche Anblicke hielten die grösste Lust in mir wach, unsere alten Dichter genau zu lesen und verstehen zu lernen.[15]

Yet I found an even greater attraction in the room's towering cabinets and the books displayed in them. . . . I remember how on the right hand side in the back as one entered there lay a quarto, Bodmer's anthology of medieval songs . . . with poems in strange, half incomprehensible German, and I was filled with a peculiar premonition.

> ... Such impressions kept awake in me the tremendous desire to study and understand our older poets.

One reader of this tale, pointing out the intentional arrangement of Grimm's narrative, has discussed this account as the "primal scene" of German philology, that is, as an attempt to locate the origins of that discipline in a single apocryphal moment.[16] But if Grimm's tale seems contrived, it is as much an imitation as an invention. His trek to the private center of his teacher's monastic world retraces the steps of the poet-hero in Novalis's *Heinrich von Ofterdingen,* whose quest leads him deep into the cave of Friedrich von Hohenzollern, a former crusader now pursuing scholastic interests in subterranean isolation. The journey to the cave bears a topical similarity to the route Grimm followed to Savigny's house, and like Grimm, Heinrich ends up in a library, a veritable archive of illuminated manuscripts:

> Der Einsiedler zeigte ihnen seine Bücher. Es waren alte Historien und Gedichte. Heinrich blätterte in den grossen, schöngemahlten Schriften; die kurzen Zeilen der Verse, die Überschriften, einzelne Stellen, und die saubern Bilder ... reizten mächtig seine Neugierde.[17]
>
> The hermit showed them his books. They were old histories and poems. Heinrich leafed through the large, beautifully painted writings; the short verse lines, the titles, individual passages, and the clear pictures ... greatly aroused his curiosity.

The essential similarity between these two experiences is that the desire to understand the books is fostered by their strangeness and incomprehensibility. Grimm's discovery of poems in difficult medieval German ("in seltsamen, halb unverständlichem Deutsch") kindles in him the desire to study older German poets. Heinrich finds himself likewise drawn to a manuscript whose language, Provençal, is completely unfamiliar to him: "Er hätte sehnlichst gewünscht, die Sprache zu kennen, denn das Buch gefiel ihm vorzüglich ohne dass er eine Sylbe davon verstand" (He yearned to know the language, for the book pleased him immensely even though he understood not a single syllable, 264).

Heinrich's descent into the cave mirrors the dream at the beginning of the novel in which he enters an opening in a mountainside and follows a dark passageway to a luminescent fountain. But his discovery of the old manuscript, described by Hohenzollern as a romance about the life and adventures of a poet (265)—and as such a mirror-image of the novel itself—replays a philological find responsible in part for the genesis of *Ofterdingen*.

In 1799, Novalis explored a historian friend's library where he discovered a manuscript of Johannes Rothe's fifteenth-century chronicle of Thuringia (*Düringsche Chronik*). In this work Novalis encountered the historical Heinrich von Ofterdingen, a courtly poet none of whose works survive, though some Romantics wrongly thought him the author of the *Nibelungenlied*. Rothe's history tells of how in the year 1206, Heinrich won the Wartburg song-competition, an event in which Novalis's novel would, if completed, have culminated.

In pointing out this library experience, my aim is not to reduce Novalis's work to a particular historical antecedent. Instead, I want to argue that the novel in question attests to a functional affinity between philology and romance. Philology appears in *Ofterdingen* disguised as romance, and the quest becomes an expression of the same needs and desires that cause

Novalis (Friedrich Freiherr von Hardenberg), from the Bildabteilung, Deutsches Literaturarchiv of the Schiller Nationalmuseum, Marbach, Germany. Reprinted with permission.

one to delve into old and strange texts. Grimm's apparent fashioning of his conversion to philology on a literary model suggests a science born of poetry, and his characterization of his new interest as the fascination for the unfamiliar exposes the Romantic aspect of that discipline. Heinrich's pilgrimage, as a quest for the self in the unknown, constitutes the narrative spatialization of philological inquiry. As an undertaking Novalis could only know vicariously, the journey is an attempt to supersede philology—to substitute the text with a more immediate experience. In representing Rothe's history as the Provençal romance, the novel introjects its own source; yet at the same time it subordinates that find to another, more primal event. The structural counterpart of the manuscript in Hohenzollern's cave is the spring at the heart of Heinrich's dream-cave; both are sources (*Quellen*), and the association of written text and dream contradicts Heinrich's skeptical father, who declares that old texts are the only "sources" of true revelation: "Die alten Geschichten und Schriften sind jetzt die einzigen Quellen, durch die uns eine Kenntniss von der überirdischen Welt . . . zu Theil wird" (Old histories and manuscripts are now the only sources through which we may gain knowledge of the spiritual world, 198).

The same opposition of natural and verbal sources pervades no less influential a work than Goethe's *Faust,* the action of which proceeds from the hero's desire to abandon the enclosure of his library in favor of a more immediate experience of nature and society. Goethe represents this tension repeatedly as that between text and spring or beast, as illustrated in a rhetorical question Faust puts to the bibliophile Wagner: "Das Pergament, ist das der heil'ge Bronnen, / Woraus ein Trunk den Durst auf ewig stillt?" (The parchment, is that the sacred fount, / a drink from which would still this thirst forever?).[18] Faust's drama begins as a search for a privileged kind of text that, rather than confining him to his library, would lead him out of it. His lament of being "confined by this heap of books" (Beschränkt von diesem Bücherhauf, 21) represents the modern condition Foucault attributed to the loss of faith in the revelatory sign and the ensuing realization that, ultimately, language can only represent itself.[19] This nascent understanding of language as nonmimetic would necessitate the advent of a science that studies language as an object unto itself, namely philology. The awareness that our knowledge of the world is indissociable from the texts that represent it makes philology the dominant mode of discourse, and the library, as the space in which texts are gathered and organized, defines the outer limits of human vision.[20] This lesson is lost on Wagner, whose faith in the revelatory power of texts is unshaken: "entrollst du gar ein würdig Pergamen, / so steigt der ganze Himmel zu dir nieder!" (if you just unroll a worthy parchment, / all the heavens will descend to you, *HA* III:40). This is a far cry from the elder Ofterdingen's assertion that, in an age in which the gods no longer speak to man, the most we can do is read ancient accounts of the revelatory experiences of others. His claim that revelation is available only through texts *as history* represents a modernist insight that Romanticism at once acknowledges and resists. And it is worth considering whether Novalis, by giving Heinrich's dream chronological priority over Hohenzollern's manuscript, is not attempting to reinstate the primacy of vision by literally burying the philological origins of his novel.

The presence of history is felt throughout *Ofterdingen*—so much so that even the fairy-tale world, described elsewhere by Novalis as a state of natural anarchy thoroughly opposed to the world of history (III:281), contains various harbingers of historicism. The most conspicuous of these is Sylvester, whose house Heinrich's father had visited in Rome and who appeared in the dream the father recounts for Heinrich. While the novel is set in the Middle Ages, Sylvester's "parlor" (*Stube*) resembles that of the middle-class professor of history who transforms his private dwelling into a reflection of his antiquarian fancies—a monument to what Nietzsche called the pious historian's "fanaticism for collecting" ("Sammelwut").[21] "Die Stube war voll Bücher und Alterthümer . . . ; er erzählte mir viel von alten Zeiten, von Mahlern, Bildhauern und Dichtern. . . . Er wies mir Siegelsteine und andre alte Kunstarbeiten" (200) (The parlor was full of books and antiquities . . . ; he told me much about ancient times, of painters, sculptors and poets. . . . He showed me seals and other antique works of art). Sylvester appears in the dream as a guide, leading Heinrich's father by the hand through long corridors and into an open space where, like his son twenty years later, he is enchanted by the sight of a blue flower. It is striking that the dream entails the agency of its own analysis: Sylvester tells Heinrich's dreaming father that a great fortune will be his if he returns within the year and bids God reveal to him the meaning of his dream ("wenn du . . . Gott herzlich um das Verständniss dieses Traumes bittest," 202). The problem of understanding dreams is a recurrent theme in this novel; Heinrich and his father have already debated the meaning and function of dreams, and at several stations in his journey the youth is faced with making sense of his own dream-imagery. What makes Sylvester crucial is the relation between his role as dream-patron and his other pursuits. As a doctor, ardent lover of literature, and collector of antique figures he reminds us of Freud, who was all of these—reminds us, in other words, that Freud's investigation of the human psyche in general and of dreams in particular was at base an excavation of prehistory. Freud's overriding view that the meaning of the present was informed by the past finds ample representation here, and Sylvester's nostalgia, which his numerous collectibles are meant to satisfy, suggests the historicism of a Grimm or Ranke: "[er] sehnte sich mit unglaublicher Inbrunst in dies graue Alterthum zurück" (he yearned with incredible fervor to return to that grey antiquity, 200; *PH* 21).

ARCHAEOLOGY, GEOLOGY, AND THE IMAGES OF KNOWLEDGE

That Sylvester's various interests in old texts, archaeological finds, history, and art converge on the site of the father's dream and recommend themselves to its interpretation exemplifies how Novalis's novel, by concocting a kind of *allgemeines Brouillon* of the sciences, uses existing disciplines metaphorically to ground others that had yet to emerge. The thesis here is that Heinrich's quest is a scientific fable and that the places he visits or dreams and hears about—caves, old archives, mythic landscapes, ancient civilization, the Orient—are *topoi* of the fields of natural history, philology, comparative religion, archaeology, and Orientalism. To the extent that metaphor has the power to transform what it transfigures, the metaphorical grounding of one discipline in another effects certain important transfers; for example, the relocation of an exotic culture in an underground dream-text suggests the hidden presence of the past and with it the possibility of an archaeology of the mind. Hence the prophecy of a science that would not appear for many years, but the need for which was being produced by a new understanding of dreams and myths.

Freud's most vivid application of the archaeological metaphor occurs in his controversial treatise on the sexual aetiology of hysteria that, when delivered as a lecture to colleagues in 1896, was ill-received, characterized by one of the more distinguished auditors as "a scientific fairy tale" (ein wissenschaftliches Märchen, SA VI:52). The label betrays what the user did not intend: namely, Freudian theory is part of a post-Enlightenment discourse that redeemed the folk tale by exposing the reason at the core of what was manifestly irrational; beyond that, Freud's reliance on the imagery of romance bears witness to his inability to detach himself from the narratives, epic or otherwise, of which psychoanalysis is a retelling. The passage in which Freud compares his method with the uncovering and deciphering of ancient inscriptions is, like Grimm's account discussed earlier, striking in its attempt at sustained narration. One is left with a sense of generic, if not novelistic, purpose, as both texts are retarded by an unexpected opulence of minor detail—particulars which in turn are transfigured by the unifying trajectory of quest.[22] Freud's paragraph is here reproduced in full:

> Nehmen Sie an, ein reisender Forscher käme in eine wenig bekannte Gegend, in welcher ein Trümmerfeld mit Mauerresten, Bruchstücken von Säulen, von Tafeln mit verwischten und unlesbaren Schriftzeichen sein Interesse erweckte. Er kann sich damit begnügen zu beschauen, was frei zutage liegt, dann die in der Nähe hausenden, etwa halbbarbarischen Einwohner ausfragen, was ihnen die Tradition über die Geschichte und Bedeutung jener monumentalen Reste kundgegeben hat, ihre Auskünfte aufzeichnen und—weiterreisen. Er kann aber auch anders vorgehen; er kann Hacken, Schaufeln und Spaten mitgebracht haben, die Anwohner für die Arbeit mit diesen Werkzeugen bestimmen, mit ihnen das Trümmerfeld in

Angriff nehmen, den Schutt wegschaffen und von den sichtbaren Resten aus das Vergrabene aufdecken. Lohnt der Erfolg seine Arbeit, so erläutern die Funde sich selbst; die Mauerreste gehören zur Umwallung eines Palastes oder Schatzhauses, aus den Säulentrümmern ergänzt sich ein Tempel, die zahlreich gefundenen, im glücklichen Falle bilinguen Inschriften enthüllen ein Alphabet und eine Sprache, und deren Entzifferung und Übersetzung ergibt ungeahnte Aufschlüsse über die Ereignisse der Vorzeit, zu deren Gedächtnis jene Monumente erbaut worden sind. *Saxa loquuntur!* (*SA* VI:54)

Imagine that a traveling explorer came to a little-known region where his interest is aroused by an expanse of ruins, with remains of walls, fragments of columns, and tablets with faded and illegible inscriptions. He may content himself with examining what is already visible, then interrogate the semi-barbaric inhabitants dwelling nearby about what tradition has told them regarding the history and meaning of those monumental remains, record the information and—journey onward. But he can also proceed differently. He may have brought picks, shovels, and spades with him, and he may set the inhabitants to work with these implements, together with them start upon the ruins, remove the rubble and from the visible remains uncover what is buried. Should this work meet with success, then the findings will clarify themselves; the fallen walls belong to the fortification of a palace or a treasure-trove, out of the column-fragments a temple is constructed, the numerous inscriptions, which, if fortune prevails, are bilingual, reveal an alphabet and a language, whose decipherment and translation yields unsuspected clues of events from the remote past, in commemoration of which these monuments were built. *The stones speak!*

The Latin exclamation with which Freud concludes his story becomes one of the found inscriptions, performing the same *ekphrasis* or "speaking out" it proclaims and awakening multiple resonances, one of which is the opening line of Goethe's *Roman Elegies:* "Saget, Steine, mir an, o sprecht, ihr hohen Paläste!" (Declare to me, stones, speak ye tall palaces!" *HA* I:57) The allusion to the elegiac supplies an intimation of death that reinforces the formal closure the epigram provides, suggesting further a connection, theorized by Walter Benjamin, between mortality and "The End" of narrative.[23]

While Freud's reference to "bilingual" inscriptions shadows the concept of overdetermination developed in *The Interpretation of Dreams*, it also invokes what for Romanticism became the essence of indecipherability—the Egyptian hieroglyphs. The hieroglyphs of Isis and the complex of theoretical problems they represent are central to Norvalis's novel-fragment of 1798, *Die Lehrlinge zu Sais*. The following passage, describing travelers who have come from afar to learn about the forgotten language and the people who spoke it, contributes to the impression that Freud, as well as Grimm, was subject to the dictates of a Romantic genre:

> Die Trümmer dieser Sprache, wenigstens alle Nachrichten von ihr, aufzusuchen, war ein Hauptzweck ihrer Reise gewesen, und der Ruf des Alterthums hatte sie auch nach Sais gezogen. Sie hofften hier von den erfahrnen Vorstehern des Tempelarchivs wichtige Nachrichten zu erhalten, und vielleicht in den grossen Sammlungen aller Art Aufschlüsse Selbst zu finden. (I:107)

> To search for the remains of this language, or at least word of it, had been the principal purpose of their journey, and the call of antiquity had drawn them to Isis. They hoped to get important information from the experienced custodians of the temple archive and perhaps to find clues of all kinds in the large collections.

This hieroglyphic language, as the object of an archaeological expedition, is a metaphor representing the language of nature, a "script of ciphers" (Chiffernschrift, I:79) that was everywhere legible, yet that had become unintelligible to a society grown alienated from the natural world. Underscoring the metaphorical role of archaeology is the ease with which Novalis, in the course of his writing, replaces it with geology, the discipline he practiced professionally during the last four years of his life, and which, as a natural science which is also an archaeology, casts the study of language as a form of natural history.

That the study of nature becomes a kind of source-work through language is apparent in the case of the old miner Heinrich meets whose boyhood interest in mineralogy is characterized as a search for hidden origins: "Von Jugend auf habe er eine heftige Neugierde gehabt zu wissen, . . . wo das Wasser in den Quellen herkomme" (From the days of his youth he had felt a powerful curiosity to know . . . where the water in the springs came from, 239). This describes a program already realized by Heinrich in his first dream in which he follows a stream from its source deep within the earth to a spring above ground. Much as Heinrich seeks the words that would help him understand his dreams, so too did the miner wish as a boy that the glittering stones he collected could speak so as to reveal their secret origin:

"Er habe . . . nur gewünscht, dass sie zu ihm reden könnten, um ihm von ihrer geheimnissvollen Herkunft zu erzählen" (He only wished they could speak to him and reveal their mysterious provenance, 239–40). Novalis's novel thus makes the earth into a *tertium comparationis* of manifold relevance, and geology appears as a sibling to those humanistic disciplines that seek to uncover the archaic strata of consciousness that have disappeared from view. It is significant in this context that Novalis's mentor, Abraham Gottlob Werner, a preeminent geologist who saw his field as a foundational science in which other disciplines could be grounded, was also planning a universal etymological encyclopedia in accordance with classificatory principles he had developed for mineralogy.[24]

The analogy by which the study of the earth becomes a discipline of memory is compressed brilliantly into a few lines in the Tale of Atlantis, one of the shorter narratives embedded in *Ofterdingen,* when a love-struck youth finds a ruby engraved with "incomprehensible ciphers" (unverständliche Chiffern, 218). Believing the gem to belong to his new beloved, he spontaneously scribbles down a poem, the meaning of which evades even him, and wraps it around the tiny treasure. The image of a precious stone bearing mysterious inscriptions enfolded by a cryptic poem poses the problematic nature of writing that has other writing as its subject—that is, translation in the broad sense. The poem itself describes a parallel between sign (*Zeichen*) and image (*Bild*), invoking the familiar Romantic distinction between a script of letters and one of visual images, between *Buchstabenschrift* and *Bilderschrift,*[25] and making writing in stone an analogue of memory:

> Es ist dem Stein ein räthselhaftes Zeichen
> Tief eingegraben in sein glühend Blut,
> Er ist mit einem Herzen zu vergleichen,
> In dem das Bild der Unbekannten ruht. (218–19)

> There is engraved an enigmatic token
> Full deep into the jewel's glowing blood;
> Of likeness to a heart may well be spoken
> Which holds the stranger's image like a bud. (*PH* 41)

The poem has certain methodological implications in that it suggests, through its analogy, that the study of cryptic languages might have something to teach us about how the psyche represents itself. Freud once offered that psychoanalysis could benefit from an understanding of the philologist's procedure; he maintained that dreams, like the Egyptian hieroglyphs, were not informed by a universal grammar but had to be understood in terms of their own internal syntax, that certain elements of dreams determined other elements but themselves possessed no translatable content. Here the possibility of always finding a verbal equivalent of the image is denied. The object of psychoanalysis is not the dream-image, nor is it the narrative told by the analysand about the dream; rather it is the juncture at which the narrative falters to reveal a resistance—the trace of a repression.[26]

The problem of translating dream-imagery into a verbal narrative becomes explicit when Heinrich finds the mysterious Provençal manuscript in Hohenzollern's underground library. Not only does the old romance correspond topographically to the fountain at the center of the original dream-cave, but it also contains figures from that dream, which appear at the point where the images are the most obscure. Heinrich's reaction to the book is as to a dream:

> [Einige Bilder] dünkten ihm ganz wunderbar bekannt, und wie er recht zusah entdeckte er seine eigene Gestalt ziemlich kenntlich unter den Figuren. Er erschrak und glaubte zu träumen. . . . Die letzten Bilder waren dunkel und unverständlich; doch überraschten ihn einige Gestalten seines Traumes mit dem innigsten Entzücken. (264–65)

> Some of the pictures seemed oddly familiar to him, and as he looked closely he discovered his own form rather distinct among the figures. He started and thought he was dreaming. . . . The final pictures were dark and incomprehensible; yet several shapes from his dream surprised him with the innermost delight.

Heinrich's longing to know the language of the manuscript is premised on the belief that a narrative would lend the imagery coherence and intelligibility, a premise Heinrich voices at the outset of the novel when, estranged by his own excited emotional state, he asserts that a greater command of words would give him a better grasp of things: "Dass ich auch nicht einmal von meinem wunderlichen Zustande reden kann! . . . wüsste ich mehr [Worte], so könnte ich viel besser alles begreifen" (That I can't even speak about my peculiar condition! . . . If I knew more words, I could grasp everything much better, 195). This is the assumption the poem interrogates; enshrouding the inscribed talisman, it is little more than a commentary on the incomprehensibility of those inscriptions, and the analogy the poem constructs merely uses one form of puzzlement to represent another.

A kind of dream-book, the manuscript represents the dream as a text of words that defy comprehension. The resistance dreams pose to translation is exemplified by Heinrich's second dream (Chap. 7), which foretells the death by drowning of Mathilde, his future fiancée. After reuniting in an aquatic underworld reminiscent of the waterscape in which he first saw the blue flower, Heinrich and Mathilde share a lingering kiss during which she imparts a mysterious word directly to his soul—a word he cannot recollect upon awakening:

> Sie sagte ihm ein wunderbares geheimes Wort in den Mund, was sein ganzes Wesen durchklang. Er wollte es wiederholen, als sein Grossvater rief und er aufwachte. Er hätte sein Leben darum geben mögen, das Wort noch zu wissen. (279)
>
> She spoke a wonderful, secret word into his mouth which resonated through his whole being. He wanted to repeat it just as his grandfather called, and he awoke. He would have given his life to remember that word.

The kerygmatic word of the second dream corresponds to the elusive blue flower of the first, and Heinrich's quest for self-knowledge is clarified as a search for a lost word. The claim that Heinrich would have sacrificed his very life to exhume that word makes death the condition of full understanding, and the equation of life with the absence of clarity places interpretation itself within a curious relationship with human mortality. Aesthetics, which the Englightenment had opposed to philosophy and designated as the "science of confused perception,"[27] now begins to acquire the function of sustaining life by confounding clarity. Incomplete almost by definition, the German Romantic novel is shaped by the wish to exclude that moment at which things become irreducibly clear, and *The Arabian Nights,* for Novalis and others a standard for narrative, describes the perpetual delay of an ending equal to the desire to stay alive.[28]

THE DEATH-INSTINCT AND THE HERMENEUTICS OF STIMULUS

The structure of Novalis's novel would thus indicate that death is more than an ending that confers meaning on all that has come before: death is the inevitable end of which even the beginning is an anticipation and of which every intermediate station is but a deferral. Upon awakening from a dream that simulates his own birth, Heinrich defines life itself as a "pilgrimage to the holy grave" (Wallfahrt zum heiligen Grab, 199), thus casting death as the *telos* of life, the result of internal momentum rather than external circumstance. The "grave" Heinrich mentions refers simultaneously to what is to become his geographical destination, the Holy Sepulchre of Jerusalem, and this double reference establishes a parallel between instinct and quest, identifying the economy of *Todestrieb* (death instinct) as a narrative economy.[29] Indeed quest romance, as the tale of an epic hero who is by nature *fey* ("feig")—that is, fated to die ("dem Tode bestimmt")[30]—now becomes a paradigm for a development in which death is the object of tireless striving. The journey charts a temporal expanse between two moments of undifferentiation: the latter is death; the former is the unity of self and world known to the infant at the mother's breast. In between lies a state of excitation, a general experience of nonidentity, and the movement toward death is conceived as a drive to eliminate stimulus. As the pertinent myth reveals, the death instinct satisfies a narcissistic aim, and Heinrich's path can readily be described in terms of narcissism. The narrative is replete with images of inundation and orality, as the youth wavers between a gradual separation from his mother and a lingering attachment to her. Equally interesting, however, is the way Novalis represents the middle ground of that development in terms of its epistemological counterpart: incomprehensibility. Novalis would elsewhere characterize philosophy itself as an odyssey of instinct, as the "drive to be at home everywhere" (Trieb überall zu Hause zu seyn, III:434). That the enigmatic word of Heinrich's second dream is delivered with a deep kiss suggests a connection between mystery and desire, and just as his journey amounts to the repeated encounter with the incomprehensible, so might one define his movement toward epiphany as a periodic deferral of understanding. Consider in this context that the only inscription Heinrich sees is at once both immanently legible and literally cryptic: the epitaph of the hermit's wife, who lies buried within the cave.

The equation of stimulus with incomprehensibility is apparent in Grimm's narrative as well as Novalis's. In either case, the relative opacity of the language engenders the desire to understand it, an act that would in turn neutralize the incitement. So defined, understanding constitutes a kind of stimulus-reduction, the quelling of the disturbance that attends any contact between a life-form and its environment. In a fragment that restates a familiar philosophical problem in anthropological, if not biological, terms, Novalis argues that the elimination of stimulus is the basis of all mediation between subject and object: "Der Geist strebt den Reitz zu absorbiren. Ihn reizt das Fremdartige. Verwandlungen des *Fremden* in ein *Eignes*. . . . Einst soll kein *Reitz* und nichts *Fremdes* mehr seyn" (The mind strives to absorb stimulus. It is stimulated by strangeness. Transformations of the *strange* into the *familiar*. . . . Eventually there shall be no more *stimulus* and no more *strangeness,* II:646). The transformation described here is commensurate with the reduction of stimulus Freud held to be the originary function of the unconscious and the principal task of living organisms. Organic life resulted from the disturbance of inorganic matter, an event that instilled in the organism the drive to restore the original hypostasis. Freud defined "drive" as the impulse on the part of the organism to recover the state of inertia or nonlife that external stimuli had interrupted (*SA* III:246). Put differently, the goal of a drive is the satisfaction that can be attained only by undoing the stimulus at the source of that drive.[31] This notion of *Trieb* seems an elaboration of *Bildungstrieb,* a morphological concept introduced by the anthropologist Johann Blumenbach and adopted by Goethe, the latter of whom described organic development as the progressive manifestation of previously latent stages leading ultimately to the reproduction of the original stage. It seems only appropriate that Novalis's *Bildungsroman*, which was developing toward its own elegiac culmination in "Das Lied der Toten" (The Song of the Dead), should spring to life through excitation from without: "Du hast in mir den edlen Trieb erregt" (You have aroused in me the noble drive, 193)—so reads the first line of the novel's dedication, a moment soon to be repeated when Heinrich encounters a stranger whose uncanny tales activate in him an "inner drive" (inniges Treiben, 195).

The notes for the continuation of this novel indicate that Heinrich's route to Jerusalem was to be anything but direct, a circuitous journey leading first to Loreto and Rome, then to North Africa, Egypt, and Greece, each of these the setting of an adventure, insubordinate as it were—a sojourn in its own right (I:335–48). In light of the above discussion of the death instinct, it will seem less paradoxical that a journey should have the purpose of forestalling arrival instead of accelerating it: the journey as end in itself, as opposed to the end of the journey. The "pilgrimage to the Holy Grave" is a veritable allegory of instinctual gratification, the deferral of which is the ground whereupon Novalis founds his aesthetics. The so-called "Orient-chapter" of *Ofterdingen* (Chap. 4) presents two versions of that pilgrimmage: one is aligned with the Christian crusades, the other with the mystery and beauty of the Middle East. At the beginning of this chapter, Heinrich and his companions are received for the night by an aging nobleman who that same evening is hosting a feast for his fellow crusaders—men of whom it is said that they knew no other pastime than "the full [wine-]tumbler" (den gefüllten Becher, 230). Heinrich is allowed to attend the drunken affair and is there encouraged to participate in the next campaign, and the warriors promise more libation at the other end of the journey, predicting that within the year they would meet in Jerusalem to celebrate victory "with wine from the fatherland" (bey vaterländischem Wein, 231). They represent the goal of their quest as the expeditious return to an earlier state of minimal excitability, and the assimilatory aims of their military mission are reproduced at a more basic level by the desire to suspend any difference between the self and the world around it.[32] Zulima, the young Saracen captive Heinrich meets after leaving the crusaders to their pleasures, characterizes the murderous zeal of her captors (they have slain her husband) in terms of a "dark impulse," activated by the experience of strange surroundings, to return to ancestral origins:

> und vielleicht ist es dieser dunkle Zug, der die Menschen aus neuen Gegenden, sobald eine gewisse Zeit ihres Erwachens kömmt, mit so zerstörender Ungeduld nach der

alten Heymath ihres Geschlechts *treibt*. (237, my emphasis)

and it is perhaps this dark impulse which, with the coming of an age of awakening, *drives* men with destructive impatience from new regions back to the homeland of their ancestors.

The crusaders' instinctual urge to forge an identity out of difference is close to what Freud defined as secondary narcissism, the desire to recover the undifferentiation of infancy (*SA* III:329). Novalis's text emphasizes that the narcissistic tendency to avert or absorb stimulus runs contrary to aesthetic experience. Music itself is described as the mediation of *Reize*—the plucking of the strings of a lute and the receptivity of the ear to those vibrations[33]— and it is Zulima's song that transforms the German countryside into a fantastic Oriental landscape (in contrast to the crusaders' alcohol, which transforms the Other into the Same).

The organological model of stimulus furnishes Novalis with a framework for describing an aesthetics that opposes, not necessarily the natural propensities of the organism, but certainly a notion of philosophy that follows that model. The deferral of understanding mentioned earlier defines the space of aesthetics as the domain of *Reiz*; the "anaesthetic" tendency is embodied by the heavy drinking crusaders and their inability to tolerate stimulus (and the difference it represents) or, less crudely, their subordination of stimulus as an instrument of its own undoing. They appeal to Heinrich's sense of the exotic to enlist him in their cause, and his momentary enthusiasm corresponds to a sexual awakening. His host presents him with a sword, which he takes in his hand and kisses passionately (231), an onanistic gesture later replicated in even greater caricature by the Scribe of Klingsohr's tale—an act of self-stimulation that underscores the narcissistic character of his endeavor: "Er kitzelte sich, um zu lachen" (He tickled himself in order to laugh, 304). In analogy to the hermeneutic principle discussed earlier according to which "enigma does not block understanding but provokes it,"[34] it can be said that radical cultural difference does not deter assimilation but ensures it. Stimulus becomes incompatible with the end to which it is the means, and the context of colonialism shades Novalis's fragment with an ominous hue: "Einst soll kein *Reitz* und nichts *Fremdes* mehr seyn." The narcissistic aversion to prolonged excitation provides the counterpoint to Heinrich's poetic apprenticeship, which entails the cultivation of a stance toward the world that allows the world free play. The critique of narcissism is pronounced in a passage contrasting poets to "men of action" who devour earthly fruits instead of contenting themselves with their fragrance (267). The aesthetic experience for Novalis is one of *sustained difference*, as becomes explicit in a fragment defining Romantic poetics as "the art of making an object foreign and yet familiar and compelling" (die Kunst . . . , einen Gegenstand fremd zu machen und doch bekannt und anziehend, III:685). What is most damning in Zulima's characterization of the crusaders is the impatience with which they seek to nullify the difference that is the source of excitation and thus to collapse the distance wherein narrative takes shape. Zulima's legacy to Heinrich is, most appropriately, a hair-band bearing her name in "unfamiliar letters" (unbekannten Buchstaben, 239).

One might conclude by reconsidering Freud's observation that Schliemann, through his discovery of the lost city of Troy, fulfilled a wish born in childhood when his father told him stories from the *Iliad*.[35] It now seems possible to read Novalis's novel as a commentary on that interpretation, at least to the extent that Heinrich, whose own longing to travel is induced by a stranger's tales of afar, and whose initial journey is tethered to the enterprise of the merchants he and his mother accompany to Augsburg, articulates a distinction crucial to psychoanalysis generally and underlying Freud's remarks on Schliemann. Freud's implicit denial that the large cache of gold the archaeologist found was anything more than an indirect source of gratification echoes Heinrich's own disavowal of greed; his first utterance of the novel, contrasting the legendary riches with the inauspicious blue flower, expresses surprise at a bewildering cathexis: "Nicht die Schätze sind es, die ein so unaussprechliches Verlangen in mir geweckt haben . . . , aber die blaue Blume sehn' ich mich zu erblicken" (Tis not the treasures which have awakened in me such unpronounceable desire . . . , but I yearn to glimpse the blue flower, 195). Heinrich betrays an awareness that the flower, unlike the precious metals and gems, is not self-representing—that is, not a symbol in the idealist vein, but a metonymy that facilitates connections between the hero and the various love-objects he encounters, himself included. The flower's attraction (*Reiz*) lies in its nonidentity; inscribed in its very color is the "romantic distance" (romantische Ferne) that adorns the commonplace with an aura of mystery by transforming even the most mundane household utensils into "sacred relics" (geweihten Pfändern, 203).[36] The journey, that essential component of the archaeological venture, is the spatial extension of this nonidentity. Heinrich's words warn against the confusion of value that is intrinsic with that imputed on the basis of contiguity.

In a paper from 1899 entitled "Screen-Memories" (*Deckerinnerungen*), Freud discusses the role of contiguous associations in such confusion, and his analogy seems tailored for Schliemann: he declares that a particular childhood memory may acquire a certain value because of its proximity to another, more deeply submerged experience; that is, "not because it is itself gold, but because it has lain next to gold" (nicht etwa weil es selbst Gold ist, sondern weil es bei Gold gelegen ist).[37] The same distinction informs Freud's analysis of the sexual fetish, and the importance of gold for the Schliemann episode only makes it easier to relate Freud's concept of fetishism to that of Marx. Both describe a similar logic of displacement, and both borrow their metaphor from the theological domain, Marx to emphasize the mechanism of mystification, Freud to implicate the very origins of religion. But the analogy itself implicates these respective disciplines as part of an archaeology, a search for not only sacred objects and their modern surrogates, but also what lies beneath the historical sedimentation of language. This new sensitivity to the "enigmatic density" of language made philology the modern form of criticism—this according to Foucault, who characterized the first book of *Das Kapital* as an "exegesis of 'value.' "[38] The following passage from that book (indeed, from the discussion of commodity fetishism) suggests that Marx, contemporary of Grimm and successor to Novalis, found in the archaeology of language a metaphorical foundation for his own critical project.[39]

> Der Wert verwandelt vielmehr jedes Arbeitsprodukt in eine gesellschaftliche Hieroglyphe. Später suchen die Menschen den Sinn der Hieroglyphe zu entziffern, hinter das Geheimnis ihres eigenen gesellschaftlichen Produktes zu kommen; denn die Bestimmung der Gebrauchsgegenstände *als* Werte ist *ihr* gesellschaftliches Produkt so gut wie die Sprache.
>
> Value actually transforms every product of labor into a social hieroglyph. People try later to decipher the meaning of the hieroglyph, to penetrate the mystery of their own social product; for the determination of use-objects *as* values is *their* social product just as much as language.

By the time Marx had written his chapter on fetishism and certainly by the time Freud began interpreting dreams, the recalcitrant hieroglyphs of the famous Rosetta stone had been decoded, and the feat well publicized; the stone had spoken, and the powers of philology had been confirmed. This meant that the discourse of Marxism, as well as of psychoanalysis, is predicated on the ultimate possibility of decipherment. By contrast, Novalis lived and died in an age that had come to accept the apparent indecipherability of the hieroglyphs. In a lecture Novalis probably attended, Schiller speculated that the first Egyptian priests of monotheism, in an effort "to employ this device of deception to the advantage of truth" (von diesem Kunstgriffe des Betrugs auch zum Vorteil der Wahrheit Gebrauch zu machen), developed a system of highly codified pictograms to disguise and thereby preserve their forbidden teachings while simultaneously through the appeal of their imagery to fire the imagination of the novices and make them receptive to truths they would only later comprehend.[40] Schiller suggested that the key to the code had been lost, and the images themselves became mistaken for the truths they were meant to veil.[41]

This account is stark in its anticipation of the link, of great concern to the later Freud, between the censorial mechanism of preconsciousness and the calculations of an ancient monotheistic priesthood (*Der Mann Moses und die monotheistische Religion*). It also reveals a tension between psychoanalysis and Romantic aesthetics. Schiller's account of how the hieroglyphs assumed an attraction independent of their meaning describes an untranslatability that conditions this aesthetics.[42] This same condition is what psychoanalysis undertakes to relieve. Romanticism had made the lure of the untranslatable the basis for a quest not subordinate to its destination but extant for the sake of the journey, an allegorical pilgrimage as it were,[43] and it is worth considering whether archaeology, once associated with a realizable goal (once the possibility of translation was secured), did not become dislodged from its metaphorical beginnings. In any case, the Romantic narrative of deferred arrival is resituated, inscribed by Freud as a process that portends death for anyone who succeeds in lifting the veil of Isis.[44]

NOTES

1. Peter Gay, introduction to Edmund Engelmann, *Berggasse 19: Sigmund Freud's Home and Offices* (New York: Basic Books, 1976).
2. Michel Foucault, *The Order of Things: An Archaeology of the Human Sciences* (New York: Vintage Books, 1973), p. xi.
3. Michel Foucault, "Language to Infinity," in his *Language, Counter-Memory, Practice*, ed. Donald Bouchard (Ithaca: Cornell University Press, 1977), pp. 53–67.
4. Sigmund Freud, *Studienausgabe*, ed. Alexander Mitscherlich, Angela Richards, James Strachey (Frankfurt: Fischer, 1973), vol. II, p. 515 (my translation). Henceforth cited in text as *SA*.
5. Foucault, *The Order of Things*, p. 297. See also Edward Said, *Beginnings: Intention and Method* (Baltimore: Johns Hopkins University Press, 1975), p. 302.
6. Jonathan Culler, *The Pursuit of Signs* (Ithaca: Cornell University Press, 1981), pp. 33–34.
7. Wilhelm von Humboldt, *Gesammelte Schriften*, ed. Berlin Academy of the Sciences (Berlin: De Gruyter, 1968), vol. III, pp. 167–70.
8. Jacob Grimm, *Reden an der Akademie*, ed. Werner Neumann and Hartmut Schmidt (Berlin, GDR: Akademie-Verlag, 1984), p. 93.
9. See Helmut Jendreiek, *Hegel und Jacob Grimm* (Berlin: Erich Schmidt, 1975), p. 21.
10. That the vocabulary of archaeology continues to be informed by the metaphor of questromance is apparent in the title of Bruce Norman's recent popularization, *Footsteps: Nine Archaeological Journeys of Romance and Discovery* (Topsfield, Mass.: Salem House, 1987). See below, note 44.
11. Friedrich Hölderlin, *Sämtliche Werke und Briefe*, ed. Günter Mieth (Munich: Carl Hanser Verlag, 1978), vol. I, p. 272.
12. Freud, *Briefe an Wilhelm Fliess*, ed. Jeffrey M. Masson (Frankfurt: Fischer, 1986), p. 430.
13. Ibid., p. 387.
14. Ibid, p. 320. See Steven Marcus, *Freud and the Culture of Psycho-Analysis* (New York: Norton, 1984), pp. 18–19.
15. Jacob Grimm, *Kleinere Schriften*, ed. Karl Müllenhoff (Berlin: Dümmler, 1864–71), vol. I, pp. 115–16.
16. Ulrich Wyss, *Die wilde Philologie: Jacob Grimm und der Historismus* (Munich: Fink, 1978), p. 51.

17. Novalis [Hardenberg, Friedrich von], *Schriften,* ed. Paul Kluckhohn, Richard Samuel, Gerhard Schulz, Hans-Joachim Mähl. 3rd edition (Stuttgart: Kohlhammer, 1977–84), vol. I, p. 264. Henceforth cited in text by volume and page number (page number only if vol. I). I have had the benefit of consulting Palmer Hilty's English rendering of Novalis's novel (*Henry von Ofterdingen.* New York: Ungar, 1964), and though my translations generally deviate from his, I have cited him (as *PH*) whenever I have modified my version in light of his.
18. Johann Wolfgang von Goethe, *Werke: Hamburger Ausgabe,* ed. Erich Trunz (Munich: C. H. Beck, 1976), vol. III, p. 25. Henceforth cited in text as *HA.*
19. Friedrich Kittler, *Aufschreibesysteme 1800/1900* (Munich: Fink, 1985), pp. 11 ff.; Neil M. Flax, "The Presence of the sign of Goethe's *Faust,*" *PMLA* 98 (1983); 183–203.
20. Foucault, "Language to Infinity."
21. Friedrich Nietzsche, *Werke,* ed. Karl Schlechta (Frankfurt: Ullstein, 1969), vol. I, p. 228.
22. In an unpublished manuscript (Fables of the Subject), Ashish Roy discusses the *Bildungsroman,* of which quest is a more ancient counterpart, as an allegory of what he calls the "normative economy of increase in narrative," a "hegemony of *recit*" that "demands that narrative kernels be developed through an increasingly meaningful series of events." As a modernist indictment of this structural movement, Roy offers the work of Kafka, which "contests the principle that the trials and tribulations of adventure be simply an agency of quest, a carrier of preordained meaning." If the point is to situate a convention of credibility within a matrix of self-transcending detail, then the "scientific fables" of Grimm and Freud may be testimonies to the holding power of that convention.
23. Walter Benjamin, *Illuminations* (Frankfurt: Suhrkamp, 1977), pp. 395–96.
24. Raymond Schwab, *The Oriental Renaissance* (New York: Cornell University Press, 1984), p. 173. See also Hartmut Böhme, *Natur und Subjekt* (Frankfurt: Suhrkamp, 1988), pp. 67ff.
25. See Jean Paul, *Vorschule der Ästhetik,* in *Werke,* ed. Norbert Miller (Munich: Carl Hanser Verlag, 1973), vol. V, p. 33.
26. Jacques Derrida, "Freud and the Scene of Writing," in his *Writing and Difference,* trans. Alan Bass (Chicago: University of Chicago Press, 1978), p. 220.
27. Alexander Baumgarten, *Reflections on Poetry,* translated (from Latin) and introduced by Karl Aschenbrenner and William B. Holther (Berkeley: University of California Press, 1954), p. 39.
28. Peter Brooks, *Reading for the Plot: Design and Intention in Narrative* (New York: Vintage, 1984), pp. 60–61; Alice Kuzniar, *Delayed Endings: Nonclosure in Novalis and Hölderin* (Athens: University of Georgia Press, 1987).
29. Brooks, *Reading for the Plot,* pp. 96ff.; Derrida, "Freud," p. 202.
30. Friedrich Kluge, *Etymologisches Wörterbuch der deutschen Sprache* (Berlin: De Gruyter, 1960), p. 189.
31. Paul Ricoeur, *Freud and Philosophy,* trans. Dennis Savage (New Haven: Yale University Press, 1970), p. 123.
32. Ulrich Stadler, *"Die Theuren Dinge": Studien zu Bunyan, Jung-Stilling und Novalis* (Bern: Francke, 1980), p. 207.
33. Ibid., pp. 130ff., esp. 134.
34. Ricoeur, p. 18. In a similar vein, Hans-George Gadamer asserts that the locus of hermeneutic understanding lies "between strangeness and familiarity" (zwischen Fremdheit und Vertrautheit). *Wahrheit und Methode,* 5th ed. (Tübingen: J. C. B. Mohr, 1986), p. 300.
35. Heinrich Schliemann, *Ilios: The City and Country of the Trojans* (New York: Benjamin Blom, 1881; reprint, 1968), p. 3. Schliemann has, like Freud, fallen prey to the accusation of having written "scientific fairy-tales" where scholars invoke historicist premises to indict the veracity of his accounts. William M. Calder III, who impugns Schliemann with considerable vituperation, not only points to individual inaccuracies in the latter's writings, but also to the literary strategy with which particular misrepresentations are

incorporated into narrative: "The entry remains a masterpiece of its genre, the narration of outrageous untruth within the setting of accurate details. We have the precision of train times, traveling companions, hotels, oysters." "A New Picture of Heinrich Schliemann," in *Myth, Scandal, and History: The Henrich Schliemann Controversy*, ed. William M. Calder III and David A. Traill (Detroit: Wayne State University Press, 1986), p. 24. See note 22 above.

36. In a passage that invokes the imagery of Romanticism, Walter Benjamin describes the aura as a "distance" (Ferne) inscribed in the object, however close it may be; to bring something closer, which is the effect of technical reproducibility, is to destroy its aura. *Illuminations*, p. 142.
37. Freud, *Gesammelte Werke*, ed. Anna Freud with Marie Bonaparte (London: Imago Publishing Co., 1940–52), vol. II, p. 537. (The essay "Deckerinnerungen" is not contained in the *Studienausgabe*.)
38. Foucault, *The Order of Things*, p. 298.
39. Karl Marx, *Werke*, ed. Hans-Joachim Lieber and Peter Furth (Darmstadt: Wissenschaftliche Buchgesellschaft, 1975), vol. IV, p. 50.
40. Friedrich Schiller, *Sämtliche Werke*, ed. Jost Perfahl (Munich: Winkler, 1972), vol. IV, p. 744.
41. Ibid., p. 747.
42. Regarding the impossibility of translation that the Romantics asserted, Kittler (*Aufschreibesysteme*) discusses the meaning in terms of general equivalency, which came to be of crucial importance to Marx (pp. 76ff.).
43. Stadler, p. 11.
44. A postscript to this discussion is furnished by the French anthropologist Claude Lévi-Strauss in his autobiography, *Tristes Tropiques*, trans. John and Doreen Weightman (New York: Athenaeum, 1984). Lévi-Strauss implicates his own discipline in a nostalgia for romance when he states: "I wished I had lived in the days of *real journeys*" (p. 43); "Journeys, those magic caskets full of dreamlike promises" (p. 37). He recalls a boyhood fascination for geology much like that of the old miner in *Ofterdingen*, and he describes it as "a quest . . . which I took upon as the very image of knowledge" (p. 56). Indeed, he uses the geologist's excavations as a metaphor for both Marxism and psychoanalysis (p. 57).

WRITING AFTER MURDER (AND BEFORE SUICIDE): THE CONFESSIONS OF WERTHER AND RIVIÈRE*

JOEL BLACK

"It looks obvious, sir, murder followed by suicide. The classic pattern of self-inflicted wounds . . ."

—P. D. James, *A Taste for Death*

BETWEEN TWO DEATHS

If thou didst ever hold me in thy heart,
Absent thee from felicity awhile,
And in this harsh world draw thy breath in pain,
To tell my story.

Such are the dying words of Prince Hamlet as he enjoins his friend Horatio not to die along with him, like "an antique Roman," by drinking from the poisoned cup prepared by his murderous uncle. Hamlet beseeches Horatio to live on in order to "Report me and my cause aright / To the unsatisfied," and to clear the prince's "wounded name." In other words, Hamlet's final speech-act is to appoint Horatio as his biographer, or more precisely, as his surrogate autobiographer. Unable to offer his own autobiography, Hamlet arranges for someone else to do so in his place.

By suggesting that autobiographies are not told by "oneself" but by someone else, Hamlet's dying speech seems to question the authority, integrity, and capability of the autobiographical subject. On the one hand, dramatic logic dictates that Hamlet's history cannot be told, his (auto)biography cannot be written, until his own death. On the other hand, the same

---

*This is a revision of the Afterword from Joel Black's *The Aesthetics of Murder*, The Johns Hopkins University Press, Baltimore/London, 1992.

logic requires that Horatio survive, even against his own will, to serve as the dead prince's autobiographical surrogate who can tell the truth about the prince that he is unable to tell. Hamlet cannot stop Horatio from eventually taking his life; in asking his friend to be his voice beyond the grave, Hamlet can only postpone Horatio's suicide—"Absent thee from felicity *awhile*," he tells him—much as Scheherazade defers her death through the tales she tells the sultan. In order to rehearse his dead friend's misfortunes, Horatio is compelled to "draw [his] breath in pain," to draw out his agony by putting off his suicide until, having fulfilled his commission, he can at last play the "antique Roman." While Horatio's task as a surrogate autobiographer—his obligation to tell Hamlet's story in his absence—may defer his own suicide, this same obligation can also be seen as a deliberate, protracted suicidal gesture in its own right.

This connection between autobiography and suicide is not as strange as it sounds. It is only a specific instance of the general relation between narrative and death that has been addressed by writers like Sartre and Benjamin. In his psychoanalytic adaptation of this insight, Peter Brooks has described what he calls the "Freudian masterplot" in which "narrative must tend toward its end, seek illumination in its own death. Yet," Brooks adds, "this must be the right death, the correct end. The complication of the detour is related to the danger of short-circuit: the danger of reaching the end too quickly, of achieving an improper death."[1] Brooks's observation readily applies to *Hamlet*. Had the prince taken his life before carrying out his mission of killing his uncle, his death would have been improper; by the same token, if Horatio takes his life before reporting Hamlet's story, *his* death will be improper. But it can also be the case in certain narratives that death may be "im-proper," not because it comes too soon but because it comes too late. Instead of following the Scheherazadean strategy of delaying death, such suicidal narratives are a means of hastening the narrator's end. Horatio's obligation to tell Hamlet's story will defer his death for a time, but the act of telling that story will make it possible for him to then go on to die a proper death at his own hand, thereby avoiding a life he no longer considers worth living.

Both strategies—delaying and hastening the end of the subject's life—are pertinent to autobiography, which, of all the diverse narrative genres, bears the most personal and intimate relation to death. Autobiographical narrative is shadowed by—and is read and interpreted in light of—the imminent demise not of a fictional character, but of the real-life protagonist who is also the narrating subject. Although the death of the narrator/protagonist cannot be incorporated into the autobiographical narrative, it is the narrative's logical and inevitable culmination. This explains why some writers have explicitly viewed autobiography as a suicidal gesture. Henry Adams described his autobiographical work *The Education of Henry Adams* (1906) to Henry James as a salutary form of suicide that offers a "shield of protection in the grave," and Adams "advise[d]" James "to take

[his] own life in the same way."[2] (The fact that Adams's *Education* is in the third person also questions the self's capacity to narrate its own history, as do such works as Stendhal's [Henri Beyle's] *Life of Henry Brulard*, Gertrude Stein's *Autobiography of Alice B. Toklas*, and, more recently, Louis Wolfson's *Le Schizo et les langues*.) Far from being an act of self-creation, autobiography may on the contrary be a way of killing off the self. Both Adams and Hamlet reveal an equivalence between the activity of narrating either one's own or someone's else's life story and the act of taking one's life. Adams and Hamlet offer James and Horatio respectively the same message: if you're going to kill yourself, at least do it by telling the story of your (or my) life.

But suicide in the case of *Hamlet* is only part of the "story"—a story that can only be understood in relation to a prior act of murder. The motivating agent in the play, of course, is the slain king, Hamlet's father. Slavoj Zizek has suggestively described the Lacanian predicament of this ghostly apparition as a being who is caught between two deaths—the real death he has suffered at the hands of his brother, and the symbolic death that he will only experience when his murder is avenged and his accounts finally settled.[3] After he hears the ghost's narration of the actual circumstances of his father's death, Prince Hamlet is assailed by suicidal thoughts. He begins to experience his own existence as being framed between two deaths: his father's murder and his own suicide, which he contemplates as a way of avoiding his appointed task of murderous revenge. When he finally does slay his uncle and is himself dying at the end of the play, he adjures his closest companion not to take *his* life, at least for the time being, and instead assigns him the task of "telling my story." In this way, Hamlet will not have to suffer his father's fate of a purgatorial existence between two deaths, but—by having his story told and retold—will be able to die a symbolic as well as a real death. As Hamlet had allowed his father's ghost to die a symbolic death by avenging his actual murder, so Horatio's narration of Hamlet's story will enable the prince to die a second, symbolic death. Every performance of *Hamlet* is a posthumous retelling of Hamlet's story by Horatio. The story reenacted in every performance of the tragedy unfolds in the interval opened at the end of each prior performance between acts of murder and suicide—between the murders of Hamlet and Claudius that have always already taken place and Horatio's suicide which is always about to occur.

In the following remarks, I will offer some parallels to the narrative subject's predicament as a being caught between the two deaths of murder and suicide, suggesting that such a position is not at all arbitrary, but is indicative of an important feature of autobiographical discourse in general. The fictional and nonfictional texts that I take as my examples will be discussed not on the basis of their formal, textual features, but with the aim of examining their relation to the sensational extratextual events that both precede and follow them. In the case of these autobiographical texts, we ignore at our peril the author/narrator/protagonist's extratextual experiences of murder and suicide. These experiences are bound to play a decisive role both in our reception of the texts and in our very conceptions about what kind of texts they are.

THE SUICIDE NOTE AND THE MURDER MEMOIR

Autobiographical narratives are situated chronologically between two deaths. In the future is the author's own imminent demise, which provides the authorial subject with perhaps the most powerful motive for creating a self in and as discourse, and which can be considered autobiography's final cause. But prior to the act of writing there is another death—the death of someone in the author's past—and this death often functions as autobiography's efficient cause. This dead Other may be an actual person with whom the author has had a close bond and whose passing the author may either mourn or exult over in his narrative.[4] Alternately, the Other may have a figurative existence as an earlier phase of the author's life, a former self who has "died" or whom the author has decided to "kill off" in the act of writing about him or her. The particular kind of autobiography the reader encounters will in large part be determined by the reader's perception of the authorial subject's relation to his or her absent Other.

The fact that autobiographical narrative unfolds in the interval between two deaths—the author's and his Other's—is most apparent, and can be studied most readily, in the case of certain marginal autobiographical forms in which the deaths of self and Other play a direct, constitutive role in the text. I refer to the extreme, and therefore revealing, autobiographical subgenres of the suicide note and the murder memoir—literary forms in which the deaths of self and Other are literalized as violent events, and in which the subject's ostensible narrative activity of self-creation is conditioned by a prior act of (self-)destruction.

Ian Hacking has suggested that as types of deviant behavior that only began to be statistically quantified and classified in the nineteenth century, murder and suicide are as much moral categories and cultural fictions as social realities: "Even the unmaking of people has been made up."[5] With respect to literary autobiography, however, the reverse formulation is more accurate: life histories are made up from the unmaking of individuals. Murder and suicide are the two most powerful expressions of selfhood, or rather, the two non-discursive occasions that seem most urgently to call forth a discursive creation, a narrative account, of self. Even when the autobiographical subject does not actually commit murder or suicide, it often contemplates these acts as possibilities and strives to "confess" them—to come to terms with and to justify them, even to flaunt and display them. Considered as a discourse of self-creation composed between two deaths—real death and symbolic death, death of self and death of other—the autobiographical text pivots between the extratextual extremes of murder and suicide as the two crisis-points between which the subject generates the narrative of its own history as a self. We need to keep in mind, however, that text and action are reflexive, and if the murder *memoir* is a "postscript" or "con-fession" written after a homicidal act, it may also serve as a *memorandum*, a "pre-script" or "pro-fession," of subsequent acts of violence to be taken against others or against the self. Similarly, while the suicide note functions as a textual act that precedes and even brings about the author's death, in many cases it also provides the author with the opportunity to confess some aspect of his or her life. In short, autobiographical writing alternates between prescriptive and postscriptive modes according to the insight of the author and the hindsight of the reader.

As subjects who typically have the most pressing need to confess, murderers are logically most suited to become autobiographers.[6] The killer who has been apprehended, and who either awaits his trial or execution or simply waits out his prison sentence, has a strong reason to tell his story or to have it told.[7] He has a strong reason, that is, to produce a text with a "confessional intent" as Stanley Corngold calls it, a text that carries "the illocutionary force of a demand for exculpation."[8] But it is more often the case that the individual accused of murder has a compelling reason *not* to tell his story as he knows it to have happened; if anything, he will be inclined to distort the facts of the case to his advantage. In such instances, we have to do not with autobiographical confession—the purest form of autobiography, in Corngold's view, in that it conveys a sense of "the virtue, wholeness, or intactness of the self at the order of experience"[9]—but rather with autobiographical fiction in which the author intentionally plays with various personas of the self. The individual accused of murder may knowingly lie in his self-presentation in order to persuade a judge or jury of his innocence. There is also the case of killers—like the nineteenth-century poet-assassin Pierre-François Lacenaire—who write memoirs[10] in which they freely admit their crimes and make no attempt to deny them, and yet cannot be said to have written "confessions" in the strict sense, because they are so obviously adopting a fictional persona[11] and making a point of "displaying" their crimes. And yet even in such self-serving fictions, one hears a Rousseau-like protestation of innocence on the part of the speaker, an appeal to future readers to exculpate and vindicate the speaker by understanding him. Whether the accused subject seeks to conceal or reveal his crimes, he writes out of a belief that *tout comprendre, c'est tout pardonner*.

Similarly, the writer of a suicide note frequently feels the need to "confess" the state of mind that has led him to his irrevocable act. The principal difference between the murderer's memoir and the note left by the suicide is, of course, that the murderer usually makes his "confession" after his crime, while the suicide must make his confessional statement before taking his life.[12] Questions of motivation and timing become particularly pertinent in the case of the specific autobiographical confessions I wish to consider, which situate themselves in relation to both murder *and* suicide—after a murder committed by the authorial subject or a surrogate, and before the subject or surrogate's own suicide.

THE BIRTH OF THE AUTHOR: *WERTHER* AS A MURDER STORY

> In all languages derived from Latin, the word 'reason' (*ratio, raison, ragione*) has a double meaning: first, it designates the ability to think, and only second, the cause. Therefore reason in the sense of a cause is always understood as something rational. A reason the rationality of which is not transparent would seem to be incapable of causing an effect. But in German, a reason in the sense of a cause is called *Grund*, a word having nothing to do with the Latin *ratio*. . . . Such a *Grund* is inscribed deep in all of us, it is the ever-present cause of our actions, it is the soil from which our fate grows. I am trying to grasp the *Grund* hidden at the bottom of each of my characters.
> —Milan Kundera, *Immortality*

The suicide note is a curious literary genre in that it only becomes what it is retrospectively, after an act external to it.[13] Inversely, it is possible to read *any* text written by a suicide before his death for the light it sheds on the author's reasons for taking his life.[14] Thus, a fictional text like Goethe's *Die Leiden des jungen Werthers* (1774, revised 1787), which consists of a posthumously edited series of letters composed by a sentimental youth who resolves his hopeless passion for an engaged woman by killing himself, can be read both as an autobiography of sorts culminating in the narrator's suicide note and as an autobiographical narrative that is, in its entirety, a suicide note in its own right—the record of a subject's self-creation through its own annihilation.

A study of *Werther* as a discourse of suicidal self-formation must refer to the highly relevant circumstances of Goethe's life at the time of the work's composition. It is well known that the novel is based on the author's experiences while he was an intern at the Imperial Chamber of Justice in Wetzlar in 1772; indeed, *Werther* is arguably the most autobiographical of all Goethe's fictional works. By his own admission, it enabled him to put his frustrated passion for Charlotte Buff, the fiancée of his colleague Kestner, into perspective. Goethe succeeded in resolving his own youthful crisis by imaginatively projecting his sufferings onto another acquaintance, the young legal attaché Jerusalem, whose own longing for the wife of a friend ended with his shooting himself in October of that year. "Jerusalems Tod," Goethe confided years later,

Johann Wolfgang von Goethe, from the Bildabteilung, Deutsches Literaturarchiv of the Schiller Nationalmuseum, Marbach, Germany. Reprinted with permission.

schüttelte mich aus dem Traum, und weil ich nicht bloß mit Beschaulichkeit das, was ihm und mir begegnet, betrachtete, sondern das Ähnliche, was mir im Augenblicke selbst widerfuhr, mich in leidenschaftliche Bewegung setze; so konnte es nicht fehlen, daß ich jener Produktion, die ich eben unternahm, alle die Glut einhauchte, welche keine Unterscheidung zwischen dem Dichterischen und dem Wirklichen zuläßt.

Jerusalem's death . . . shook me out of my dream, and since I did not consider what had happened to him and me with disinterest, but was profoundly affected by the similarity to my own experience at that time, I found myself infusing into the work I now undertook all the passion that admits no distinction between the poetic and the real.[15]

Jerusalem's death provided Goethe with the occasion to purge himself once and for all of his own youthful obsession with suicide so that he could carry out his decision to live: "Um dies aber mit Heiterkeit tun zu können, mußte ich eine dichterische Aufgabe zur Ausführung bringen, wo alles, was ich über diesen wichtigen Punkt empfunden, gedacht und gewähnt, zur Sprache kommen sollte" (So as to live with enthusiasm, I had to bring to completion a poetic work in which I could articulate everything I had felt, thought and fancied about this important subject) (9:585). Finding that he could exploit the parallel between Jerusalem's situation and his own, Goethe was able "nach so langen und vielen geheimen Vorbereitungen" (after long and much secret preparation) to write *Werther* in a white heat, "in vier Wochen, ohne daß ein Schema des Ganzen, oder die Behandlung eines Teils irgend vorher wäre zu Papier gebracht gewesen" (in four weeks, without ever putting down on paper beforehand either a plan of the whole or the draft of any part) (9:587).

Such a sudden creative outpouring—so much at odds with the laborious process of composition of Goethe's subsequent writings—signals the cathartic nature of this early work. The purgation that the young author achieved by writing *Werther*, however, was less his infatuation with Charlotte Buff than his infatuation with the act of suicide itself. In his nonfictional autobiographical work *Dichtung und Wahrheit*, Goethe reveals his youthful obsession with suicide and his extensive research "über die verschiedenen Todesarten, die man wählen könnte" (into the various forms of death that one might choose) (9:584). It was this morbid, misanthropic obsession with death that attracted him to, and later repelled him from, the melancholic tradition in English poetry that would be epitomized in Keats's Romantic sentiment of being "half in love with easeful death." Goethe describes his composition of Werther's tragedy as a therapeutic act whereby he managed to overcome the impulse to take his own life by sacrificing his lovesick hero instead:

[I]ch hatte mich durch diese Komposition, mehr als durch jede andere, aus einem stürmischen Elemente gerettet. . . . Ich fühlte mich, wie nach einer Generalbeichte, wieder froh und frei, und zu einem neuen Leben berechtigt. Das alte Hausmittel war mir diesmal vortrefflich zustatten gekommen

[B]y means of this composition, more than any other, I had saved myself from a tempestuous element. . . . I felt like a man after absolute confession—happy and free again, and entitled to a new life. This time the old household cure had worked for me like a charm. (9:588)

This was not the only time that an artist claimed to have avoided self-destruction through artistic creation. Sixty years later, Hector Berlioz channeled his murderous and suicidal rage upon learning of his fiancée Camille Moke's betrothal to a piano manufacturer into the composition of the *King Lear* overture. An even closer parallel to the circumstances of *Werther*'s composition is provided by Jack London's novel *Martin Eden*. As described by Leo Braudy, the novel represents London's "1909 attempt to purge some extreme of [his own obsession] by staging the suicide of" his fictional surrogate.[16] (It remains unclear whether London's death at age forty, seven years after the publication of *Martin Eden*, was a case of suicide.) It should be noted that the nature of London's artistic catharsis differed significantly from that of Goethe. The specific obsession which the immensely successful American author attempted to purge through the suicide of his hero was "the excess of his own desire for fame and recognition";[17] this was hardly a problem for the young Goethe, whose obsession was of an amorous nature, and who in fact laid the basis for the most successful of literary careers with the publication of *Werther*.

The history of *Werther*'s composition offers a particularly interesting illustration of "the singular relationship that holds between an author and a text, the manner in which a text apparently points to this figure who is outside and precedes it," that Foucault explored in his famous 1969 essay "What is an Author?"[18] By writing his novel, Goethe not only saved himself from possible destruction, he established himself as an author and laid the basis for his artistic immortality. He did this, moreover, by projecting his actual suicidal impulse onto a fictional character—or, what amounts to much the same thing, by appropriating another man's suicide as his own. *Werther* may be Goethe's *Generalbeichte*, his "absolute confession," but it is also his own suicide note which made his suicide unnecessary and altogether superfluous. Like Horatio's posthumous "report" of Hamlet's "story," it can be seen as a suicide note written by Goethe for someone else, the confession Jerusalem might have made before his death. By writing someone else's suicide note, Goethe established himself as an (immortal) author rather than as a (mortal) writer.

Goethe's "use" of Jerusalem's suicide in the creation of the fictional character Werther need not have been so successful. Had Goethe been of a more impressionable disposition, Jerusalem's example might only have reinforced his own suicidal impulses. This is in fact what happens to Werther himself in his chance encounter with a minor but significant character in the revised version of the novel. This character is a servant who has had the misfortune to fall in love with his widowed mistress, and who has been discharged by the widow's brother for having made advances to her. The widow has since taken on another servant whom she has decided to marry in spite of her brother's opposition. The discharged servant is "fest entschlossen, das nicht zu erleben" (determined not to live to see it) (6:78). Instead of resolving this untenable situation through suicide, however, he murders his replacement. " 'Keiner wird sie haben, sie wird keinen haben' " ('No one shall have her, and she shall have no one') (6:95), he explains after his arrest to Werther, who identifies completely with the young peasant in his plight:

> unüberwindlich bemächtigte sich die Teilnehmung seiner, und es ergriff ihn eine unsägliche Begierde, den Menschen zu retten. Er fühlte ihn so unglücklich, er fand ihn als Verbrecher selbst so schuldlos, er setzte sich so tief in seine Lage, daß er gewiß glaubte, auch andere davon zu überzeugen. Schon wünschte er für ihn sprechen zu können, schon drängte sich der lebhafteste Vortrag nach seinen Lippen. (6:96)
>
> he was overcome by an irresistible sympathy for him, and he was seized by an indescribable urge to save the fellow. He felt him to be wretched, he found him—even as a criminal—to be so innocent, and he put himself so profoundly in his place, that he was convinced others could be persuaded as well. He was already wishing for a chance to speak on his behalf; the most forceful argument had already leapt to his lips.

Of course, Werther's efforts to persuade others of his conviction of the peasant's innocence are futile. When the judge tells him "Nein, er ist nicht zu retten!" (No, he cannot be saved) (6:96), Werther takes this as his own death sentence, writing in a note "Du bist nicht zu retten, Unglücklicher! ich sehe wohl, daß wir nicht zu retten sind" (You cannot be saved, poor fellow! I plainly see that we cannot be saved) (6:97).

The incident concerning the servant-murderer has a critical function in the novel's revised version. It is Werther's last straw, his final disillusionment with life. In the original version of 1774, Werther's letters break off somewhat inexplicably, at which point an editor steps in and claims to give an objective report based on eyewitness accounts of the protagonist's final days. In the 1787 version, Werther's correspondence ends abruptly with his crusade to defend the servant.[19] Well before he decided to take his life, he had vigorously defended suicide to Charlotte's fiancée Albert. However, his identification with the servant-murderer and his personal involvement in the case make him resolve to take his life. As the editor reports:

> Der vergebliche Versuch, den Werther zur Rettung des Unglücklichen gemacht hatte, war das letzte Auflodern der Flamme eines verlöschenden Lichtes; er versank nur desto tiefer in Schmerz und Untätigkeit; besonders kam er fast außer sich, als er hörte, daß man ihn vielleicht gar zum Zeugen gegen den Menschen, der sich nun aufs Leugnen legte, auffordern könnte.
>
> Werther's vain effort to save the unfortunate man was the last flicker in the flame of a dying light, after which he only sank ever deeper into pain and inertia. He was nearly beside himself when he heard that he might be called upon to testify against the man, who now denied any guilt. (6:98)

Far from helping the servant, Werther has set a disastrous example for him. Instead of displaying an attitude of abject humility that might have won the court's sympathy and worked in his favor, the unfortunate servant has taken his cue from Werther and arrogantly protested his innocence. To make matters worse, Werther has himself become a dupe of the legal process: instead of becoming the accused man's defender and savior, he has been set up by the court to bear witness against him, thereby hastening his conviction and execution. Werther's impulse to take up the servant's cause as if it were his own only escalates the violence initiated by the murderer's deed. The murderer's suicidal prophecy "nicht zu erleben," not to live to see his beloved's marriage to another, will indeed come to pass: his murderous deed has sealed his fate as certainly as if he had taken his own life. And Werther's grim forecast—"ich sehe wohl, daß wir nicht zu retten sind"—is similarly borne out: society's decision to condemn to death a man who has committed a *crime passionnel* leads directly to Werther's decision to take his own life.

The virtual equivalence of suicide and murder in the novel's revised version is apparent in the equivocal responses of the servant and Werther to their respective frustrated passions. Why didn't the servant kill himself straight off, rather than commit murder and be condemned to death? Why didn't Werther kill his rival Albert instead of killing himself? In his actual suicide note, which he addresses to Charlotte, Werther raises the possibility of murder: "O meine Beste! in diesem zerrissenen Herzen ist es wütend herumgeschlichen, oft—deinen Mann zu ermordern!—dich!—mich!" (Oh, my dearest one, slinking around this tattered heart the thought often rages—to murder your husband!—you!—myself!) (6:104). But murder isn't a solution, because Werther has already made up his mind to die. Just before he confesses his murderous impulse he has written:

> ich will sterben!—Ich legte mich nieder, und morgens, in der Ruhe des Erwachens, steht er noch fest, noch ganz

> stark in meinem Herzen: ich will sterben!—Es ist nicht Verzweiflung, es ist Gewißheit, daß ich ausgetragen habe, und daß ich mich opfere für dich. Ja, Lotte! warum sollte ich es verschweigen? Eins von uns dreien muß hinweg, und das will ich sein!
>
> I want to die! I went to bed, and in the morning, in the calm of awakening, it remains firm and strong in my heart: I want to die! It is not out of despair, but out of certitude that I have made my decision, and that I sacrifice myself for you. Yes, Lotte, why should I hide it? One of us three must go, and I want it to be me!(6:104)

Why does Werther settle on suicide rather than murder as a response to his thwarted passion when, in a similar situation, the servant resorts to murder, even after contemplating suicide? The principal difference between the servant's situation and Werther's/Goethe's is that the servant was *succeeded* by another in his mistress's affections, while Werther was *preceded* by Albert in his love for Charlotte, and Goethe was *preceded* in his love for Charlotte Buff by her fiancé Kestner. It is as if a vestigial code of male honor dictates the response of murder in cases where the rival replaces the subject in his role of lover, and the response of suicide in cases where the subject himself plays the role of the would-be replacement, "[d]er neue Ankömmling" (the new arrival) (9:543) as Goethe describes himself in his autobiographical account of the Wetzlar idyll with Charlotte and Kestner.

Whatever his motive for committing suicide—rather than murder—may be, Werther responds to his own failure to plead the servant's (and his own) cause by resolving to take his own life, and to offer himself as a sacrifice to Charlotte. He begins to write the letter to her that will become his suicide note within a week or two of learning of the servant's deed. But since Werther by this time has virtually identified himself with the servant, the suicide note is also a kind of murder memoir in which Werther professes/confesses his desire to murder Charlotte and her husband. Through the servant's actual slaying of his rival, Werther acts out the fantasy of murdering *his* rival, and proceeds to write his suicide-note/murder-memoir in preparation for his own self-sacrificial act.

Where Werther's suicide-note/murder-memoir is composed between the servant's act of homicide and his own suicide, Goethe's composition of the novel *Werther* took place before, as well as after, actual suicidal events. Goethe responded to Jerusalem's suicide by creating the fictional character of Werther as a scapegoat who allowed the author to "save" himself from a possible episode of mimetic violence. If the confessional text of *Werther* had been a kind of drug or *pharmakon* (Hausmittel) that enabled Goethe to get through a crisis-period in his life and be "wieder froh und frei'' (9:588), it proved to be a lethal poison for many of its youthful readers, who succumbed to an epidemic of mimetic identification with the suicidal protagonist and actually emulated Werther's dress and demeanor, even his unhappy end. Goethe describes this virtually unique event in literary history:

> Das alte Hausmittel war mir diesmal vortrefflich zustatten gekommen. Wie ich mich nun aber dadurch erleichtert und aufgeklärt fühlte, die Wirklichkeit in Poesie verwandelt zu haben, so verwirrten sich meine Freunde daran, indem sie glaubten, man müsse die Poesie in Wirklichkeit verwandeln, einen solchen Roman nachspielen und sich allenfalls selbst erschießen; und was hier im Anfang unter wenigen vorging, ereignete sich nachher im großen Publikum und dieses Büchlein, was mir so viel genützt hatte, ward als höchst schädlich verrufen.
>
> This time the old household cure had worked for me like a charm. But while it made me feel relieved and enlightened to have transformed reality into poetry, my friends deluded themselves into believing that they had to turn poetry into reality, to enact such a novel, and actually shoot themselves. What happened at first among a few occurred later among the general public, and this booklet that had been so useful to me was denounced as being extremely harmful! (9:588)

Because actual instances of suicide haunt both its conception and reception, *Werther* would seem to demand an extrinsic, as opposed to an exclusively intrinsic, critical approach. Rather than study Goethe's text "in itself," one needs to examine the shifting relation that subsists between this text and the extratextual suicidal behavior that preceded its composition and succeeded its publication. If Goethe wrote *Werther* as an imaginative, posthumous suicide note for Jerusalem, as a published work it became an actual, public suicide note for all the sentimental youths who took their lives in imitation of the work's protagonist. As a text framed by extratextual acts of suicide, *Werther* replicates its own sub-text—its protagonist's suicide note—which in the novel's revised version is itself framed by the intratextual events of the servant's murderous deed and Werther's own death.[20]

THE (SELF-)EXECUTIONER'S SONG: RIVIÈRE'S MEMOIR AS SUICIDE NOTE

> "Murder is the one crime for which there can't be any reparation for the victim. We're all conditioned to regard

it with particular abhorrence. So murderers, unless they're psychopaths, have to come to terms with what they've done."

—P. D. James, *Innocent Blood*

We can better appreciate the relation between autobiographical confession and the extratextual acts of murder and suicide if we turn to a nonfictional, but nevertheless "literary," text—the nineteenth-century murder memoir of Pierre Rivière. This autobiographical text was written by a young peasant from Aunay, France, a month after his arrest for killing his mother, his sister, and his brother on June 3, 1835. Despite their atrocity, these acts of parricide and mass murder were overshadowed by Joseph Fieschi's attempted regicide on July 28 (King Louis-Philippe survived, but eighteen persons were killed by Fieschi's "infernal machine," which consisted of twenty-five rifles rigged to fire at once), and Lacenaire's sensational trial, memoir, and execution the following year. Nearly a century-and-a-half later, the sensational circumstances of Rivière's crime were brought to the public's attention when, in 1973, Michel Foucault and his seminar students at the Collège de France published a "dossier" consisting of the available documents pertaining to the case, along with their own "notes" and Rivière's memoir concerning the "Particulars and explanation of the occurrence." As the centerpiece of the published volume, Rivière's memoir provided Foucault and his research team with a unique opportunity to study the confessional discourse of the assailant in a case of parricide and mass murder, and to situate this text in the context of the legal and medical discourses of the time.

Because they were attracted to Rivière's text as a murder memoir, Foucault and his fellow researchers ignored the possibility that, like *Werther*, Rivière's text can also be read as an example of the confessional genre of the suicide note: although convicted and sentenced to death as a parricide, Rivière was reprieved by the king and sent to prison where he hanged himself five years later. Rivière presents himself in his memoir as one who fully expects to die, who is preparing to die, and who even considers himself already dead. He presents the slaughter of his mother, sister, and brother not as acts of murder, but as acts in a *self-sacrificial ritual*. As Werther described his death in his suicide note to Charlotte as a sacrifice to her—confessing at the same time that the thought of murder has often occurred to him (deinen Mann zu ermorden!—dich!—mich!)—Rivière repeatedly characterizes his triple-murder as a sacrifice to his father. Through the deaths of his mother, sister and brother—but, more significantly, through his *own* death—he will deliver his father from his many persecutions.[21] Citing as many examples of sacrificial deaths as he can recall from his reading, including that of Christ Himself, Rivière concludes that "I can deliver my father only by dying for him" (106). "I should immortalize myself by dying for my father" (105). When the neighbors came upon him immediately after his slaughter, he told them to look after his father and grandmother, and to "see to it" that they "do not do themselves a mischief, I die to restore them peace and quiet" (112). At his trial, when he was presented with the blood-stained pruning bill that he had used to slay his victims, he reportedly responded that "I am in haste to die" (140). After his death sentence was commuted to life imprisonment, it was left to Rivière to confirm his statement that his murders had been a sacrificial act in which he had died for his father. The announcement of the suicide in a local newspaper suggests the degree to which he had been obsessed with dying.

> Rivière believed himself to be dead and refused to take any sort of care of his body; he said he wanted his head cut off, which would not hurt him at all because he was dead; and if they would not comply with this wish, he threatened to kill everybody. Because of this threat he had to be isolated from all the other prisoners, and he took advantage of this isolation to commit suicide.[22]

Given Rivière's longstanding obsession with suicide, it is surprising that Foucault and his students have virtually nothing to say about his death or, more to the point, about his description in the memoir of the murders as a sacrificial act that prefigured his death. Only four years before in "What is an Author?" Foucault had referred to "the kinship between writing and death," asserting that writing entails "a sacrifice, an actual sacrifice of life, a voluntary obliteration that does not have to be presented in books because it takes place in the very existence of the writer."[23] Yet it was not to Rivière's self-sacrificial suicide but to his murders that Foucault and his research team turned their attention; they were interested in the memoir not as a personal suicide note but as a public statement that was inextricably interwoven with other discourses of the period. Rather than approaching Rivière's memoir as a nonfictional, autobiographical confession, Foucault reads it as an example of the early nineteenth-century fictional sub-genre of "sorrowful lamentations" or "songs of murder." This popular literary form portrays the criminal in the act of calling "for both memory and execration," "speaking up when the punishment is imminent; in the very moment before death," and "rais[ing] his voice to summon the justice which is about to engulf him." In the act of "confessing," Foucault seems to say, the subject takes up a place in a highly artificial fictional form — a first-person lyrical form which anyone can "sing" as if he were the lyrical subject himself.

Such a "literary" reading of Rivière's memoir no doubt stems from Foucault's penchant for French "avant-garde thinkers, and the surrealists in particular, [who] sang the virtues of crime and all that bourgeois society deemed other."[24] Foucault's reading fails to do justice to Rivière's memoir, which is not merely an impersonal, fictional "song . . . placed between two deaths—murder and execution" (207–08), but a poignant, nonfictional confession written between the two deaths of murder and suicide. As a highly personal document that presents his murders as an act of devotion to his father, and that can be read in hindsight as his own suicide note, Rivière's memoir is worlds apart from his contemporary Lacenaire's brazen self-dramatizing presentation of his murders as his revenge on society. It is Lacenaire, rather than Rivière, who would seem to belong to the nonconfessional genre of "fictional lyricism" described by Foucault in which the "speaker displays his murder for all to see, isolates himself in it, summons the law, and calls for both memory and execration" (208). In contrast, Rivière doesn't revel in his crimes, but writes his memoir as a personal, confessional, textual act that finds its ultimate resolution not in the public event of execution but in the private gesture of suicide.[25]

Foucault admits at the outset to having been seduced by Rivière's memoir. His interest in it is aesthetically motivated: "Its beauty alone is sufficient justification for it today" (199). Even more than the legal and medical controversy surrounding the case, it was "simply the beauty of Rivière's memoir" that led Foucault and his students "to spend more than a year in these documents." "The utter astonishment" that Rivière's memoir "produced in us was the starting point": "We were captivated by the parricide with reddish-brown eyes" (x, xiii).

In his study *Seductions of Crime*, Jack Katz has pointed out that Rivière's memoir only appears "beautiful" because its author "was motivated to construct an account that would make his viciously cruel, extremely messy act neatly reappear as a self-sacrificial, efficient blow for justice." Rivière accomplished this by devoting "less than a sentence" to what he himself calls the "particulars of the occurrence"—the actual slaughter itself—and reserving "the sixty-seven pages his 'memoir' covers" for "the background of his family biography." (Small wonder that Foucault hailed the memoir as a discourse that was even more "extraordinary" than the crime that it ostensibly described, with the result that the crime "ended up ceasing to exist."[26]) "By glossing over the homicidal event itself," Katz argues, Rivière "continued the attack on his mother before a new, larger audience." That audience—which, besides Rivière's contemporaries, eventually came to include Foucault and his students as well as their readers—has tended to respond favorably to the simple peasant's account. (Although Rivière's jury found him guilty, it "petitioned the King to commute the sentence."[27]) Katz summarizes his remarks with the observation that "many of the interpreters sought to exploit too much from the murder to dwell on its gruesome lived reality." And with an oblique reference to Foucault, he writes that while "Rivière's account was elaborately inculpating in substance, in style, it bespoke a sophisticated rationality, which in many eyes was exculpating. (Some even labeled it 'beautiful.')"[28]

Katz is undoubtedly right to put readers on guard against the seductive "beauty" of Rivière's account to which Foucault himself was not immune. But Katz even goes beyond Foucault in reading the memoir as a fiction rather than as a confession—as a cannily crafted artifice whereby the "simple" peasant sought to transform his ghastly deed into an act of beauty and justice. Like Foucault, Katz ignores the fact of Rivière's subsequent suicide. Even if Rivière deliberately misrepresented "his viciously cruel, extremely messy act" as "a self-sacrificial, efficient blow for justice," his subsequent act of taking his life nevertheless had the effect of validating his version of the murders *as* a self-sacrificial act. If the state was unwilling to execute him, he would execute himself. If his text could not be situated between the deaths of murder and execution, then by taking his life, even after a five-year delay, Rivière would re-position it between the deaths of murder and suicide. In so doing, he retroactively, and indeed posthumously, recast his autobiographical fiction as a nonfictional confession. This explains why Rivière was so enraged in prison, insisting that he was dead and threatening "to kill everybody" if his jailers did not cut off his head. Having composed what was effectively a suicide note as well as a murder memoir, he had committed himself to death and could not authenticate his identity until his self-sacrificial scenario was fulfilled and his impersonal "song" validated as his personal confession.

Foucault's case study is most credible when it turns away from Rivière's seductive narrative about his crime and concerns itself instead with the relation between the narrative and the actual crime. Curiously, Rivière's contemporaries and judges were not particularly struck by this relation. As Foucault notes, "no one seemed really surprised that a humble Norman peasant 'barely able to read and write' should have been able to couple his crime with a narrative of this sort, that this triple murder should have been interwoven with the discourse of the murder, or that when Rivière undertook to kill half his family he should have conceived of writing a text which was neither confession nor defense, but rather a factor in the crime" (200–1). It is with respect to this highly problematic relation between text and murder, discourse and deed, that the parallel between the confessions/suicide notes of the historical figure Rivière and the fictional character Werther are most in evidence.

Foucault implies that Rivière's memoir (published in 1836 in the *Annales d'hygiene publique et de médecine légale*) failed to arouse anything approaching the sensation caused by the publication of Lacenaire's *Mémoires* in the same year because his contemporaries were incapable of giving it a proper reading. For Rivière's contemporaries, "the fact of killing and the fact of writing, the deeds done and the things narrated, coincided since they were elements of a like nature. . . . The murder and the narrative of the murder were consubstantial" (200). Memoir and murder were regarded as products of the same author, and as such, the memoir was read as evidence, as a sign either of Rivière's sanity (and hence his guilt) or his madness (and hence his "innocence"). Foucault insists, however, that Rivière's text cannot be read as a sign of the "author's" state of mind at the time of his crime. The relation between memoir and murder cannot be reduced to a simple "chronological sequence—crime and then narrative. The text does not relate directly to the deed" (201). For as Rivière reveals in his narrative, he originally undertook to write about his deed *before* actually doing it. Moreover, the "memoir" he envisioned writing was not so much an account of his own life as a history of his parents' lives, since it was his mother's unremitting persecution of his father that Rivière claimed had induced him to kill her as a way of "delivering" his father from his tribulation.

> I intended at first to write down the whole life of my father and my mother practically as it is written here, to put an announcement of the deed at the beginning and my reasons for committing it at the end, and the way I intended to flout the law, that I was defying it, that I was immortalizing myself and so forth; then to commit my deed, to take my letter to the post, and then to take a gun I would hide beforehand and kill myself. (107)

Rivière was obliged to change his writing plans because his sister Aimée became inquisitive and "wanted to see what there was that had already been written." Rivière claims that he "took great care not to show her, for it was the announcement of the beginning." When Aimée persisted in asking her brother to show her what he was writing, he became fearful "that someone might read this announcement," and so he adopted what Foucault called his "second project" (201). He allegedly burned the announcement and planned to compose two texts: a memoir about his parents' life that he would write "without hiding from anyone," and a text in which "I would secretly put in the reasons of the end and the beginning" (107). According to this new plan, as Foucault says, the "murder would no longer be interwoven with the text; it would be shifted from the center, placed outside, at the culminating point, and at the same time moved to the far end of the text, and would, so to speak, be finally produced by it" (201).

But this plan also failed, this time because Rivière, in his own words, "got up to write a night or two but I almost always went to sleep and I could only write a little." It was then that Rivière made his final decision, which he ultimately put into effect: "I gave up writing, and I thought that after the murder I would come to Vire and give myself up to the district prosecutor or the police inspector; then I would make my declarations that I would die for my father" (107). Although Rivière did not give himself up immediately after his crime but wandered about aimlessly for a month, and although he gave a distorted account of his actions during his initial interrogation after his arrest, he insisted in the memoir he eventually wrote for the judge presiding over his case that he "had intended to write this history before the crime and had considered most of the words that I would put in it" (107).

Commenting on "all these transformations" in which "the text and the murder kept changing places, or, to put it more precisely, moved one another around," Foucault notes that the murder itself

> has been reversed and has gradually become disengaged from the memoir; from the original intention that it should happen after the memoir was written and simply for the purpose of triggering its dispatch it has broken free and has at length arisen to stand alone and to happen first, propelled by a decision which had determined the narrating of it, word for word, but without being written down.

The murderer's confession is an *énoncé* that cannot be spoken or written beforehand, but only after the murder itself—the true act of *énonciation*—has first been performed. Although he planned the very wording of his discourse before his crime, he could not write it down and fix it in narrative form until after he had actually committed the murders, at which point his threatening pro-fession to avenge his father became a retrospective con-fession, his inarticulate *histoire* became a written *mémoire* claiming authorship for past events.[29] Yet as Foucault suggests, although the murders were a precondition for the writing of the memoir, they could not take place until the memoir had been conceived in Rivière's mind as a program that he could enact. We must, however, add the further crucial point that Rivière could not have composed his memoir in the form he did without the firm expectation of his imminent death, if not by execution then by suicide. If he was only able to write his history-as-memoir after the murders, he could only validate the memoir-as-suicide-note with his own death. Having presented his murders in the memoir as a sacrificial act—not of his mother, brother, and sister, but of himself—Rivière was in effect writing his own death sentence which no monarch could commute, a suicide note which would only become readable as such through his death.

SEDUCTIVE FICTIONS

> "Fu Manchu is more real than Nathan the Wise, and History is closer to what Sue narrates than to what Hegel projects. Shakespeare, Melville, Balzac, and Dostoyevski all wrote sensational fiction. What has taken place in the real world was predicted in penny dreadfuls."
> —Umberto Eco, *Foucault's Pendulum*

Werther is ostensibly a fictional autobiographical narrative about suicide, while Rivière's memoir is a nonfictional autobiographical confession about a sensational murder. By calling attention in the case of Goethe's novel to the significance of the murder incident, and in the case of Rivière's memoir to the author's characterization of his crimes as a sacrificial act as well as to his subsequent suicide, I have suggested a closer relation between these works than one might initially suspect. Both texts are situated in the gap between two deaths—mass murder and individual suicide in the case of Rivière's memoir, individual and mass suicide in the case of Goethe's novel. Moreover, the subtext of Werther's suicide note within Goethe's novel is itself framed between fictional acts of murder and suicide. How we read these assorted texts depends upon our classification of their specific autobiographical mode (fiction or confession) and sub-genre (murder memoir or suicide note). This will in turn depend on how we as readers (re-)construct the deaths that frame the narratives themselves.

Whatever Goethe's intention in writing *Werther*, and whatever effect its composition had on him, the work was read by many of its original readers as a suicidal "script" that they themselves proceeded to enact. These readers adopted Werther's suicide note as their own, provoking the novel's censure by Pastor Goeze, Nicolai, and other moralists. As a murderous text that mediated a number of its readers' deaths, *Werther* played a role similar to that of Eugéne Sue's novel *Le Juif errant* in the case of the Alsatian journeyman Jean-Baptiste Troppmann, whose obsession with this work inspired his 1869 slaughter of a family of eight.[30] One is reminded more recently of the role of J. D. Salinger's *The Catcher in the Rye* in Mark David Chapman's assassination of John Lennon in December 1980, or of Martin Scorsese and Paul Schrader's film *Taxi Driver* in John Hinckley, Jr.'s, attempted assassination of President Reagan less than four months later.[31] Whether such media-mediated violence culminates in suicide or murder ultimately seems arbitrary. (It is noteworthy that both Chapman and Hinckley had attempted suicide before their respective murderous assaults on public figures.) The key point is that a fictional story becomes a "script" for nonfictional violence.

The reason that texts like *Werther* and *The Catcher in the Rye* exert such a compelling and seductive effect on their readers surely has a great deal to do with the fact that they are autobiographical fictions written in the first person and featuring young, sensitive, alienated protagonists. Texts of this kind lend themselves to the identification fantasies of impressionable, noncritical readers who, unable to produce any artistic fiction of their own, emulate a fiction provided by the media. Himself an aspiring artist who is unable to give expression to his feelings in a pictorial form, Werther is drawn into the dramas of the other characters he encounters—Albert's courtship of Charlotte, the servant-murderer's defense. While Goethe countered his dangerous identification with the suicide Jerusalem by writing *Werther*, his blocked hero can only react to his identification with the servant-murderer (unüberwindlich bemächtigte sich die Teilnehmung seiner, er setzte sich so tief in seine Lage) by accepting the unhappy man's fate as his own: "ich sehe wohl, daß wir nicht zu retten sind." One may suppose that the suicidal readers of Goethe's novel, failing to respond to their identification with Werther by producing a counterfiction of their own, became inextricably implicated in his fatal narrative.

Pierre Rivière seems to have suffered from a similar case of writer's block. He tried to write down the circumstances behind his decision to kill his mother, sister, and brother *before* committing the deed, but for one reason or another he was unable to do so. As Goethe could only write *Werther* after Jerusalem's suicide—and as it only occurred to him to write the murder episode *in Werther* after the suicide epidemic among readers of the original work, and as Werther himself was only motivated to write *his* suicide note in the revised version of the novel after the murder episode—so Rivière was only able to write about his slayings *after* the fact, when he was asked to do so by the judge presiding at his trial.

As texts that exist in the space between two deaths, Goethe's fictional novel and Rivière's nonfictional memoir originated in acts of violence, and in turn gave rise to violent acts. It took nothing less than murder or suicide (either the suicides of others or the prospect of their own) for Werther and Rivière as blocked artists to find it within themselves to write, and to achieve the Romantic goal of "self-expression." We can thus qualify our earlier observation about literary fictions functioning as scripts for real acts of violence by noting that this type of story typically deals with a youth's frustrated attempts to express his feelings; such stories are most likely to provoke violent reactions in young readers who themselves aspire to, but are incapable of, artistic self-expression.

In this respect, the late eighteenth- and early nineteenth-century texts of *Werther* and Rivière's memoir invite comparison with two recent films: the Cohen brothers' 1991 picture *Barton Fink* and David Cronenberg's 1992 adaptation of William Burroughs's *Naked Lunch*. These films deal with writers who become unblocked, and even inspired, either after killing someone (as in *Naked Lunch*, based on Burroughs's actual killing of his wife), or after being exposed to and implicated in murderous mayhem (as in *Barton Fink*). The artistic crises depicted in these films suggest an alternative approach to Rivière's memoir than that of Foucault, who, succumbing to the memoir's artistic seductions, reads it in the literary tradition of the song of murder in which the "use of the first person" made it possible for "everyone . . . to sing [the murderer's song] as his own crime, by a lyrical fiction" (207–08). We need instead to recognize that Rivière's ability to produce his extraordinary memoir was a consequence of his *inability*, as a literalist, to participate in the cultural game of singing criminal songs about legendary figures as if they were his own. Had he joined everyone else in singing (or writing) fictional songs of murder, he may never have felt compelled to commit his crime. Instead, he slaughtered half his family, an act that made it possible for him to compose his own original autobiographical "song."

Our reading of an autobiographical text like Rivière's memoir changes dramatically depending upon how we situate it in relation to the extratextual acts of murder and suicide. In Foucault's reading, Rivière's text is a free-floating fiction that lacks a precise relation to these external events. It readily assumes the conventional form of the murder song or memoir, and it is indistinguishable from the public and publishable performance of Lacenaire or any other legendary criminal on the eve of his execution. Considered as a text composed in the interval between the extratextual acts of murder and suicide, however, Rivière's "confession" appears as the textual equivalent of a speech-act in which the speaker demands his own death. Having played the role of the young Hamlet, who undertook to end his father's tribulations and who feigned madness as a religious maniac immediately after his arrest,[32] Rivière proceeded to assume the complementary role of Horatio, confessing the "true" motive behind his deed with the knowledge firmly in mind that he would shortly die, if he was not already dead.

My sense that Rivière's memoir should be considered a personal, nonfictional confession rather than as an impersonal, artistic fiction stems not only from the relation this text bears to a murderous act in the past and a suicidal act in the future—both of which it "announces" in a disturbingly matter of fact way—but also from a basic difference in the popular reception of the two autobiographical forms. Both types of first-person narrative are written down, not as scripts to be enacted or performed, but simply as texts to be recited or read. Nevertheless, readers have shown a surprising readiness to identify with the made-up narrators of autobiographical fictions, more so than with the real-life narrators of nonfictional memoirs. Hence the appeal of the first-person narrators in fictional narratives like *Werther*, *The Catcher in the Rye*, and *Taxi Driver* to young readers who have been led to commit acts of violence as a direct result of their identification fantasies. Literary masterworks ranging from the *Inferno* (the Paolo and Francesca episode) to *Don Quixote* to *Madame Bovary* to *Notes from Underground* have thematized this mimetic tendency of readers of fiction and its disastrous consequences.[33]

Something about fictional discourse seems to invite readers and moviegoers to identify more closely with its narrators and characters than with those of nonfiction. Consumers of literature and film, in turn, are able to read themselves into fictional characters and situations more readily than they are in the case of real-life personalities and events.[34] It is hard to think of someone enacting Rivière's own first-person memoir, or even the much-publicized *Mémoires* of Lacenaire. The fact that Foucault admits to being so captivated by Rivière's discourse is interesting in this regard; I would argue that his fascination is a direct result of his idiosyncratic, if not perverse, reading of Rivière's nonfictional text as a literary fiction. And if one accepts the thesis recently suggested by Foucault's American biographer James Miller—namely, that "death, and its significance, was one of Foucault's lifelong obsessions," and that, by the time of his sojourn in San Francisco where he appears to have contracted AIDS, he "had long placed death—and the preparation for suicide—at the heart of his concerns"—Rivière would appear to be one of the models upon which the French philosopher's own transformative/transgressive life and quasi-suicidal death were patterned.[35]

The Romantic era provides one of the most striking examples of an episode of murder and suicide publicized in such a sensational manner that it resulted in numerous imitative deaths. In 1811, Goethe's literary rival Heinrich von Kleist carefully planned his suicide with Henriette Vogel. The couple prepared for death by composing letters in which they took their leave of the world; then Kleist shot his companion, after which he took his own life. The highly sensationalized and often fictionalized coverage of this incident triggered a second wave of suicides after the earlier devastation caused by *Werther's* publication. But Kleist had already anticipated his dramatic end in his own fiction. In his 1808 play *Penthesilea*—dedicated to a revolted Goethe "on the knees of my heart"—he had "scripted" the Amazon queen's orgiastic slaughter of Achilles followed by her own suicide upon realizing what she had done. And in the tale *Die Verlobung in San Domingo* (1811), Kleist again presented a lover who takes his own life after slaying his beloved, whom he mistakenly believed had betrayed him. As Werther composed his final letter to Charlotte after the murder committed by the servant and before his own suicide (with a copy of Lessing's play *Emilia Galotti*, in which another senseless murder occurs, lying open on his desk), and as Rivière wrote his autobiographical statement after committing murder and before committing suicide, so Kleist rehearsed his own end in his art, writing works that dramatically prefigured his combined acts of murder and suicide. (One article about the Kleist scandal was called "Public Beatification and Deification of Murder and Suicide in Germany."[36])

Because of their mediated and mediating nature, autobiographical fictions are more seductive than their nonfictional counterparts, even though the latter are based on fact and would thus seem to offer the more compelling model to follow. This is why it is really unjustified to contrast Goethe's "strengths" as the artist-author of *Werther* with the "weaknesses" of the novel's protagonist or of the novel's readers who imitated him by taking their lives. Werther and his imitators may have been blocked artists who, unable to produce any fictions of their own, enacted a ready-made script provided by someone else; Goethe, in contrast, was the true artist, who, rather than succumb to Jerusalem's example, went on to write the script that the young suicide might have followed—and that *Werther's* suicidal readers did follow. But then Goethe had only to contend with the straightforward circumstances of Jerusalem's actual fate, while his readers had to face the far more seductive prospect offered by a fictional character's demise.

NOTES

1. Peter Brooks, *Reading for the Plot: Design and Intention in Narrative* (New York: Knopf, 1984), pp. 103–4.
2. Henry Adams, *The Education of Henry Adams*, ed. Ernest Samuels (Boston: Houghton Mifflin, 1973), pp. 512–13. Paul Jay discusses Adams's conception of *The Education* "as a putting to death of its author" in *Being in the Text: Self-Representation from Wordsworth to Roland Barthes* (Ithaca and London: Cornell University Press, 1984), pp. 158–59. Adams's wry tag echoes a line in Wilde's *The Importance of Being Earnest* (1895), when the character Jack speaks of killing off his fictitious brother Ernest. "And I strongly advise you to do the same," he tells Algernon, referring to *his* fictional counterpart Bunbury.
3. Slavoj Zizek, *Looking Awry: An Introduction to Jacques Lacan through Popular Culture* (Cambridge and London: MIT Press, 1991), pp. 21–23; see also the section "Between the Two Deaths" in *The Sublime Object of Ideology* (London and New York: Verso, 1989), pp. 131–36, esp. 135. The likely source for the title "Between the Two Deaths" is Pierre Boileau and Thomas Narcejac's 1956 novel *D'entre les morts*, upon which Hitchcock's film *Vertigo* is based.
4. Nancy K. Miller has written very perceptive analyses of autobiographical narratives that focus on the writer's dead or dying parent. See her article "Autobiographical Deaths" in *Massachusetts Review* (Spring 1992) and her paper "Representing Others" (presented May 11, 1993, at the University of Georgia) in which she argues that St. Augustine's portrayal of his mother Monica's death in the *Confessions* is quite literally a self-serving act.
5. Ian Hacking, "Making Up People," in *Reconstructing Individualism: Autonomy, Individuality, and the Self in Western Thought*, eds. Thomas C. Heller, Morton Sosna, and David E. Wellbery (Stanford University Press, 1986), p. 235.
6. The confessional impulse of the murderer is evident in the logical progression from Thomas De Quincey's *Confessions of an English Opium-Eater* to his projected sequel, which he planned to call *Confessions of a Murderer* (see Grevel Lindop, *The Opium-Eater: A Life of Thomas De Quincey* [New York: Taplinger, 1981], p. 258). The fact that De Quincey never wrote this work may be explained by the fact that although he was an opium-eater, he was not a murderer and therefore lacked the authority required to write the authentic autobiographical "confession" of a killer.

    In chapter 6 of *The Self and its Pleasures: Bataille, Lacan, and the History of the Decentered Subject* (Ithaca and London: Cornell University Press, 1992), Carolyn J. Dean explores the connection between "writing and crime," but focuses her inquiry on the tradition of the French avant-garde, and on writers who are not themselves criminals (e.g., André Breton), and on criminals who are not themselves writers (e.g., Henri Landru).
7. The problems that may arise when a professional writer undertakes to narrate the story of a convicted murderer can be seen from the examples of Truman Capote's "non-fiction novel" *In Cold Blood*, where Capote was censured by some critics for exploiting the story of his condemned subjects instead of working to avert their death sentence, and most recently in the case of Joe McGinnis's book *Fatal Vision*, in which the author's subject Jeff MacDonald, who is serving a life sentence for murdering his wife and children, sued McGinnis for betraying his trust by presenting him as his family's killer instead of a wrongly accused victim. (See Janet Malcolm, *The Journalist and the Murderer* [New York: Knopf, 1990].)
8. Stanley Corngold, *The Fate of the Self: German Writers and French Theory* (New York: Columbia University Press, 1986), p. 222.
9. Corngold, p. 226. One needs to bear in mind, however, that what Corngold calls "intactness of the self" is itself often made possible by the scandalous misdeed or misdeeds that

compel the subject to confess, and that give the subject its unique sovereignty and enable it to establish its selfhood in the first place.
10. Pierre-François Lacenaire, *Mémoires de Lacenaire avec ses poèmes et ses lettres*, ed. Monique Labailly (Paris, 1968).
11. As Laurence Senelick shows, Lacenaire carefully crafted his persona on the Romantic image of the Byronic hero (*The Prestige of Evil: The Murderer as Romantic Hero from Sade to Lacenaire* [New York and London: Garland, 1987]). Senelick suggests that Lacenaire may have taken Julien Sorel, the hero of Stendhal's *Le Rouge et le noir*, as his literary model in his *Mémoires* (pp. 319–20); Lacenaire was himself the model for the character Valbayre in Stendhal's final, unfinished novel, *Lamiel* (pp. 320–23).
12. It may be objected that the "note" left by a suicide can hardly be considered a confession, first, because unlike the murderer, the suicide has not committed a crime for which he must be punished, and secondly, because its customary brevity prevents it from fulfilling any autobiographical function. We should remember, however, that in Christian culture suicide is considered a sin for which the suicide may well ask forgiveness or demand exculpation. Even in the non-Christian, warrior cultures of ancient Rome and feudal Japan suicide was honorable only because it often was a means of avoiding *dishonor*; thus the act of suicide was itself an affirmative or defensive statement of the virtuous, intact self. If suicide has ceased to be considered a crime in the modern era, this is only because it has come to be diagnosed by the medical profession as a form of mental illness (Hacking, p. 234). As for the brevity of the suicide note, I argue below that the extended autobiographical narrative written by the protagonist in Goethe's novel *Werther* can be considered a suicide "note" that the suicide may have composed even before determining to kill himself.
13. According to Hacking (p. 235), the suicide note is "an art form that . . . was virtually unknown" before the nineteenth century, when the new "systems of reporting positively created an entire ethos of suicide, right down to the suicide note."
14. Thus, when no note was immediately found after the unexplained apparent suicide in 1993 of President Clinton's close friend and aide Vincent Foster, Jr., the press turned to a commencement speech that Foster had given shortly before his death for clues to his state of mind. See David Shribman, "Death Alters View of Clinton's Aide's Words," *Boston Globe* (July 23, 1993), pp. 1, 10.
15. *Goethes Werke* (Hamburg: Christian Wegner, 1967), 9:587; translation mine. Subsequent citations from Goethe's writings will be followed in parentheses by the volume and page numbers from this edition.
16. Leo Braudy, *The Frenzy of Renown: Fame and Its History* (New York and Oxford: Oxford University Press, 1986), p. 535.
17. Braudy, p. 524.
18. Michel Foucault, "What is an Author?" in *Language, Counter-Memory, Practice: Selected Essays and Interviews*, ed. Donald F. Bouchard, trans. Donald F. Bouchard and Sherry Simon (Ithaca: Cornell University Press, 1977).
19. As Eric A. Blackall has shown, the editor who resumes the narrative in the later version is concerned less with distancing himself from his subject than with imaginatively trying to reconstruct Werther's disturbed state of mind from his final letter (*Goethe and the Novel* [Ithaca and London: Cornell University Press, 1976], ch. 3, esp. pp. 50–53).
20. Goethe's principal revision of the novel concerned the story of the servant-murderer and the concluding narrative by the fictional editor (see Blackall, p. 50). In contrast to the editor of the first version, the editor in the revised version "reveals that Werther's situation springs only from inside himself." Blackall suggests that "Goethe is most anxious, in this second version of his novel, that we shall see the sickness of Werther and not identify him with his author, nor ourselves with him *totally*" (p. 53). In the wake of the suicide epidemic that followed the initial publication of the novel, Goethe no doubt found it desirable to lessen the reader's identification with Werther in the revised version.
21. The slaying of his brother, who had not taken sides against his father as his mother and

sister had, underscores Rivière's sense of his murders as an act of self-sacrifice: "I determined to kill all three of them, the first two because they were leagued to make my father suffer, as to the little boy I had two reasons, one because he loved my mother and my sister, the other because I feared that if I only killed the other two, my father though greatly horrified by it might yet regret me when he knew that I was dying for him, I knew that he loved that child who was very intelligent, I thought to myself he will hold me in such abhorrence that he will rejoice in my death, and so he will live happier being free from regrets" (Michel Foucault, ed., *I, Pierre Rivière, Having Slaughtered My Mother, My Sister, and My Brother . . . : A Case of Parricide in the Nineteenth Century*, trans. Frank Jellinek [New York: Pantheon, 1975], p. 106). Subsequent references will be followed by the page number in parentheses.

22. *Pilote du Calvados*, October 22, 1840, cited in *I, Pierre Rivière*, p. 171.
23. Foucault, "What is an Author?," p. 117.
24. Dean, *The Self and its Pleasures*, p. 207.
25. In a later interview, Foucault did in fact differentiate Lacenaire from Rivière, describing the former as "the very artist of criminality," a "rather poor type" of criminal whose "very shoddy and ignoble" acts only acquired "consistency" through "the splendor and intelligence of his writing." Rivière's case "is something altogether different: a really extraordinary crime which was revived by such an even more extraordinary discourse that the crime ended up ceasing to exist . . ." ("I, Pierre Rivière . . . ," interview by Pascal Kane in *Cahiers du cinéma* (November 1976); translated by John Johnston in *Foucault Live (Interviews, 1966–84)*, ed. Sylvère Lotringer [Semiotext(e), 1989], p. 133). But if Rivière's discourse had the effect, as Foucault claims, of erasing the crime that preceded it, it was also a statement announcing his resolve to die.
26. Ibid.
27. *Annales d'hygiène publique et de médicine légale*, 1836; cited in *I, Pierre Rivière*, p. 212.
28. Jack Katz, *Seductions of Crime* (New York: Basic Books, 1988), pp. 310–11.
29. I make use here of Louis Marin's adaptation of Benveniste's distinction between *histoire* and *discours* ("The Autobiographical Interruption: About Stendhal's *Life of Henry Brulard*," *MLN*, 93 [1978], p. 599); since Rivière's narrative (*histoire*) could not be written until after his crime, it is necessary to make an additional distinction between *histoire* and *mémoire*, between narrative fictions and narrative confessions.
30. Troppmann made the statement, "He who reads many novels, and has them in his head, falls asleep. But he who reads only one, has a fixed idea" (cited in William Bolitho's *Murder for Profit* [1926; reprint; New York: Time, Inc., 1964], p. 63). As the title of Bolitho's study indicates, Troppmann killed the Kinck family for his own benefit, while Rivière presents his slaughter of half his own family as an act of self-sacrifice.
31. See chapter 4 of *The Aesthetics of Murder* for an extensive analysis of these events and their interrelation.
32. The parallel between Hamlet and Rivière is supported by the latter's confession in his memoir of his mortal fear of incest with his mother and sisters.
33. See René Girard, "The Mimetic Desire of Paolo and Francesca," chapter 1 of *'To Double Business Bound': Essays on Literature, Mimesis, and Anthropology* (Baltimore: Johns Hopkins University Press, 1978).
34. Cf. Leo Braudy's observation (*The Frenzy of Renown*, p. 567) concerning "Reagan's experience as an actor," which "allowed him to project a much more complicated character than he may have actually possessed." Reagan was far more successful than his presidential predecessor because "[l]ittle could be read into Carter, while Reagan, like any good performer, suggested a host of possibilities and 'personal' messages that could be read as desired by any fan."
35. James Miller, *The Passion of Michel Foucault* (New York and London: Simon and Schuster, 1993), pp. 20, 28. According to Miller, Rivière was one of a series of "dangerous individuals" to whom Foucault was drawn, individuals "whose motives were unfathom-

able and whose deeds seemed unforgivable" (p. 225). Foucault regarded Rivière in the same way he regarded Sade, Artaud, or Roussel—namely, as a tragic hero (p. 228).

36. Joachim Maass, *Kleist: A Biography*, trans. Ralph Manheim (New York: Farrar, Straus and Giroux, 1983), p. 295.

NOTES ON THE CONTRIBUTORS

Joel Black is Associate Professor in the Department of Comparative Literature at the University of Georgia, Athens. He is the author of *The Aesthetics of Murder: A Study in Romantic Literature and Contemporary Culture* (Johns Hopkins, 1991), and has written articles on the postmodern fiction of Thomas Pynchon, William Gaddis, Carlos Fuentes; the Romantic tradition; and the intersections between literature and science. He is currently working on the topic of seduction in literature, psychoanalysis, and pornography.

Linda M. Brooks is Assistant Professor of Comparative Literature at the University of Georgia. She has written *The Negative Sublime: Autobiography and Self-Annihilation in Schiller and Coleridge* (forthcoming at University of Edinburgh Press) and edited *Alternative Identities: The Self in Literature, History, Theory* (Garland, 1994). She has also written articles on Schiller and Coleridge, including "Sublimity and Theatricality: Romantic 'Pre-Postmodernism' in Schiller and Coleridge" in *MLN* (1990). She has also been editorial consultant for the publication of two volumes of Phillipe Lacoue-Labarthe's works into English—*Typography: Mimesis, Philosophy, Politics* (Harvard, 1989), and *Literature and Philosophy* (Minnesota, 1993).

Kenneth Calhoon is Associate Professor of German at the University of Oregon, Eugene. He is the author of *Fatherland* (1991), and has published work on Romanticism, Lessing, and Freud ("The Education of the Human Race: Lessing, Freud, and the Savage Mind," *The German Quarterly* [1991]), Kleist ("Sacrifice and the Semiotics of Power," *Comparative Literature* [1989]) and is currently working on the topic of detection.

Rüdiger Campe is Professor of German at the Universität Gesamthochschule Essen. He is the author of *Affekt und Ausdruck: Zur Umwandlung der literarischen Rede im 17. und 18. Jahrhundert* (1991), as well as many articles on the historical transformations of the concept of style, rhetoric, noise, and other topics in the history of discursive practices, among them "Pathos cum Figura, Frage: Sprechakt" in *MLN* (1990).

Courtney Federle is Assistant Professor of German at the University of Chicago. He has edited the volume *Rethinking Germanistik* (Lang, 1991), and wrote his dissertation entitled "Authenticities: Gardens, Bodies, and Pedagogy in Late Eighteenth Century Germany." He has also written "KuchenmesserDADA: Hannah Höch's Intervention in the Discourse of Visuality," which appeared in *Qui Parle* (1992). He is currently working on imagining the street in Weimar architecture, film, and literature.

Franz Futterknecht is Professor of German at the University of Florida, Gainesville. He is the author of *Das Dritte Reich im deutschen Roman der Nachkriegszeit* (1975) and *Heinrich Heine. Ein Versuch* (1985), as well as numerous articles on such figures as Mörike, Herder, Günter Kunert, Friedrich Schlegel, and Alfred Andersch.

Gerd Gemünden is Associate Professor of German at Dartmouth. His book *Die hermeneutische Wende: Disziplin und Sprachlosigkeit nach 1800* was published at Peter Lang in 1990. He has also written on Wim Wenders, Werner Herzog, hermeneutics, and deconstruction.

Ian Hacking is a Professor at the Institute for the History and Philosophy of Technology and Science at the University of Toronto. He is the author of many articles and books on topics in the history and philosophy of science and language study, among them *The Emergence of Probability* (1975), *The Logic of Statistical Inference* (1965), *Why Does Language Matter to Philosophy?* (1975), *Representing and Intervening* (1983) and, most recently, *The Taming of Chance* (1990). He has also edited the volume *Scientific Revolutions* (1981).

Friedrich Kittler is Professor of Media Science and Aesthetics at the Humboldt Universität in Berlin. He is the author of *Grammaphon, Film, Typewriter* (1987) and *Aufschreibesysteme 1800/1900* (1985), which has been translated into English as *Discourse Networks 1800/1900* (1991). He is widely known for his work in German literature of the eighteenth and nineteenth centuries, his studies of media and psychoanalysis, and has edited, with Gerhard Kaiser, *Dichtung als Sozialisationsspiel: Studien zu Goethe und Gottfried Keller* (1978) as well as *Austreibung des Geistes aus den Geisteswissenschaften* (1977), and with Horst Turk, *Urszenen: Literaturwissenschaft als Diskursanalyse* (1979).

Robert S. Leventhal is Assistant Professor of German at the University of Virginia. He is the author of articles on Vico, Lessing, Herder, Friedrich Schlegel, Kant, Heidegger, Thomas Bernhard, Kafka, and, with Volker Kaiser, Wim Wenders. His book *The Disciplines of Interpretation: The Emergence of the Hermeneutic Order in Germany, 1750–1800* is forthcoming in 1994.

Dorothea E. von Mücke is Associate Professor of German at Columbia University. She is the author of *Virtue and the Veil of Illusion: Generic Innovation and the Pedagogical Project in Eighteenth-Century Literature*

(1991), as well as articles on German and comparative literature of the eighteenth century.

David E. Wellbery is Professor of German at the Johns Hopkins University. He is the author of *Lessing's Laocoon: Aesthetics and Semiotics in the Age of Reason* (Cambridge, 1984), and has written articles on contingency, Nietzsche, Foucault, E. T. A. Hoffmann, Kleist, and Friedrich Schlegel. He has edited *Positionen der Literaturwissenschaft* (1985), and, with John Bender, *The Ends of Rhetoric* (1990). He is also co-editor of the volume *Reconstructing Individualism: Autonomy, Individuality and the Self in Western Thought* (1986).

INDEX

A
Aarsleff, Hans, 38
Abitur, 71; and the interpretation of poets, 71–72
Adorno, Theodor W., 127, 166n.12
Aesthetics, 200, 224; in Reinhold, 71; in Hegel, 71; poetry exceeding the region of, 72; classical, 93; education, 96; Kant and, 205
Allgemeines Preussisches Landrecht (1794), 16
Anthropology, 53
Archaeology, 10, 211–12, 221
Archive, 211
Aristotle, 121
Author: function, 16, 130; emergence of in the eighteenth century, 16; Heinrich Bosse's work on the history of, 17; Romantic theory of, 17
Authority: of the sovereign, 102; judicial, 118; of the speech-act, 184–89

B
Benjamin, Walter, 42, 220, 234
Berlin Academy of Sciences, 20, 38, 76, 78; the discourse of reciprocity within, 77; Adolf Harnack's history of, 81; the genre of the prize-essay, 81; J.G. Herder and, 88
Berlin, Isaiah, 37
Berlin, University of, 78, 88; Hegel and, 71
Bildung, 53
Bildungsroman, 53–54, 112, 226
Bloom, Harold, 201
Bloomfield, Leonard: reading of Wilhelm von Humboldt's *Über die Verschiedenheit des menschlichen Sprachbaus*, 36
Blumenbach, Johann, 226
Bodmer, Johann Jakob, 214
Bopp, Franz, 35
Bosse, Heinrich, 17
Bourdieu, Pierre, 171
Brooks, Peter: *Reading for the Plot*, 231n.28, 234
Buchstabe, 1

Buchstabenschrift, 222
Buffon, Georges-Louis Leclerc: *Histoire naturelle*, 119–20

C
Campe, Johann Heinrich, 21, 159–65
Canguilhem, Georges: *The Normal and the Pathological*, 7
Chladenius, Johann Martin, 130
Chomsky, Noam, 36
Coleridge, Samuel, 201–3
Condillac, Étienne Bonnot, Abbé de, 38
Corngold, Stanley, 237

D
Darstellung, 200
Debord, Guy, 193, 197
De Man, Paul, 196–97
Derrida, Jacques, 80; "Rhétorique de la drogue," 79; *Limited inc*, 89n.22, 205
Descartes, René, 31; *Discourse on Method*, 7, 117; the "cogito," 141
Dilthey, Wilhelm, 144
Discipline: the discourse of, 14; that cannot be reduced to 'rule' and 'law', 14; and the forms of normalization, 14; into individuals, 112
Disciplines, human scientific, 131, 155, 219, 221, 222
Drugs: as antidote to the "disease" of scholars, 69; opium, poppy juice, tobacco, 69; as the dangerous figure of the "third," 79; the "rhetoric" of, 79; as they appear in Herder's prize-essay of 1780, 85; alchohol, 227; *pharmakon*, 240, 245; the confessional text as, 244

E
Empfindsamkeit, 153–67; research on in the 1960s and 70s, 155
Enlightenment, 21; semiotic system characteristic of, 1; the flip-side of, 6; and the new forms of punishment, 8; debate between Foucault and Habermas on, 18; and analytic philosophy, 32; Kant and,

43; rationalist philosophies in, 52; centralization of governance and justice, 120

F

Fetish, 228
Feyerabend, Paul, 6, 12
Fichte, Johann Gottlieb: "intellectual intuition," 141; lecturing in Jena on Sunday, 67; *Science of Knowledge*, 67; *Vocation of Man*, 117
Foucault, Michel: on philology as the modern form of criticism, 3–5, 217, 229; theory of epistémès, 8; on "normalization," 14; and literary criticism and theory, 14–17; theory of statements, 15; the dispositive of discourse, 52; on subjugation and the constitution of subjects, 154. Works: *The Archaeology of Knowledge*, 15; *The Birth of the Clinic*, 7; *Discipline and Punish*, 8, 12, 77, 107; *The History of Sexuality*, 12–13; *I, Pierre Rivière. . .* , 23, 246–55; *Les mots et les choses* (*The Order of Things*), 2, 3, 8, 35, 169; *Madness and Civilization*, 6, 133, 169; "Nietzsche, Genealogy, History," 12; "What is an Author?," 16, 241, 247; "What is Enlightenment?," 18
Frederick II, King of Prussia, 38
Frege, Gottlob, 31, 33
Freud, Sigmund: relation to Romanticism, 22, 211–30; "screen memories," 228; theory of dream, 118, 218; concept of analysis, 123; archaeology as a metaphor, 211; overdetermination, 221; and the procedure of philology, 222; *Todestrieb* (death instinct), 224; definition of "drive," 225; narcissism, 227. Works: *Interpretation of Dreams*, 73; *Moses and Monotheism*, 230

G

Gadamer, Hans-Georg, 144
Gellert, Christian Fürchtegott: and the new letter, 177; *Gedanken von einem guten deutschen Briefe*, 176
German Tragedy, Classical, 21, 112
Goethe, Johann Wolfgang von: infatuation with the act of suicide, 240. Works: *Conversations with Eckermann*, 206; *Dichtung und Wahrheit*, 240; *Faust*, 217; "Roman Elegies," 220; *Sorrows of Young Werther*, 23, 153, 176, 238–45; *Wahlverwandtschaften*, 1–2, 6, 17–18
Göttingen, University of: and the founding of the philological seminar (1761), 35, 46
Gottsched, Johann Christoph: *Critical Poetics*, 122
Grammar, general, 2, 36, 37
Grimm, Jacob, 212

H

Habermas, Jürgen, 18, 77
Hacking, Ian, 13, 19, 24; and the theory of sentences, 6; and the categorization of mental illness, 7; on the genre of the suicide note, 236; "Making Up People," 9, 236
Hamann, Johann Georg, 61; as public linguist, 32; Hegel's review of, 42; and Kant, 42; *Socratic Memorabilia*, 44; *Metacritique of the Purism of Reason*, 45
Harnack, Adolf, 89n.2
Hegel, Georg Wilhelm Friedrich: language as self-consciousness, 33; on the labor of the concept, 71, 85; and Hölderlin, 173; on the merely represented self, 193, 196; *Phenomenology of Spirit*, 33, 37; *Vorlesungen zur Ästhetik*, 71–72
Heidegger, Martin, 5
Herder, Johann Gottfried: Isaiah Berlin's reading of, 37; *Treatise on the Origin of Language*, 9, 39, 79; "On the Reciprocal Influence of Science and the Government," 20, 75–88; *Auch eine Philosophie der Geschichte zur Bildung der Menschheit*, 61, 84; *Über die neuere deutsche Literatur. Fragmente*, 24n.3, 75
Hermeneutics: Foucault's reading of, 3; Renaissance, 4; Romantic, 4, 16, 128, 130, 221; and philology, 4, 217–21; modern, 83; as an instance of discipline, 131
Hertz, Neil, 116n.24
Herzog, Werner, 142
Historicism, 218
Hobbes, Thomas: theory of language, 32; *Leviathan*, 11
Hölderlin, Friedrich: and the speech-act, 22, 172–76; communication in, 169; *Hyperion*, 22, 173–76; *Archipelagus*, 212; "Mnemosyne," 205
Hörisch, Jochen, 138

INDEX

Humboldt, Alexander von: and the Prussian educational system, 35
Humboldt, Wilhelm von, 35–36, 212
Hume, David, 31; and Hamann, 41; on Berkeley's argument against abstract ideas, 45

I

Incomprehensibility, 132, 225
Information, 77
Institution: the family, 20, 51–63; the University, 35, 46, 65, 88; religious, 173–74; of marriage, 174; of law, 174, 176; replacement of by a maternal speech-act, 174; juridical, 178–80; the letter and the postal system, 178–80; of communication, 180; discourse and, 184; of discursively ordered speaking, 184; the linguistic institution of, 185; speech becoming an, 186. *See also* Berlin Academy of Sciences; Berlin, University of; Göttingen, University of; Jena, University of

J

Jena, University of: Schiller's inaugural address at, 65

K

Kafka, Franz, 118
Kant, Immanuel: constitution of the subject, 9–10, 43; and Foucault, 10; and Hamann, 42–44; and the private language argument, 45. Works: *Anthropologie*, 40, 43; *Critique of Judgment*, 11; *Foundations of the Metaphysics of Morals*, 10; *Logik*, 4
Katz, Jack, 248–49
Kierkegaard, Soren, 49
Kittler, Friedrich, 25, 26, 116n.25
Kleist, Heinrich von, 117–26, 255
Kojéve, Alexander, 5
Koselleck, Reinhard, 16, 26n.50, 75, 77, 88n.1
Krafft-Ebing, Baron Richard von, 7
Kuhn, Thomas, 6

L

Lacan, Jacques, 4, 5; and the reinterpretation of Freud, 5; production of the subject, 136; the linguistic structure of the unconscious, 212
LaCapra, Dominick, 16
Lacenaire, Pierre-François, 237

Lacoue-Labarthe, Phillip: *The Literary Absolute*, 24; on philosophy's predestination for madness, 205
Language, theory of: in Frege, 6, 33; in Peirce, 32; and Husserl, 6; Port Royal's *Grammaire générale et raisonée*, 36; representational, 138
Leibniz, Gottfried Wilhelm von, 31; *Nouveaux Essais*, 35; and Chinese language and writing, 34
Lévi-Strauss, Claude, 232n.44
Locke, John, 31, 34
Lyotard, Jean-François, 203, 204

M

McCluhan, Marshall, 85
Marx, Karl, 229
Marxism, 5, 229
Masculine subjectivity, 106
Medusa: the oriental version of (basilisk), 100; as a sight of violence and horror, 101
Michaelis, Johann David, 75, 85
Miller, Johann Martin, 153
Minsky, Marvin, 31

N

Nancy, Jean-Luc, 24n.4
Narcissism: and fantasy, 56
Nietzsche, Friedrich: genealogy, 10; thought-, writing-, and discourse-machines, 23; on language, 142, 204, 218; *Homers Wettkampf*, 83
Novalis (Hardenberg, Friedrich von): *Heinrich von Ofterdingen*, 215–30; *Die Lehrlinge zu Sais*, 221

O

Orality, 120
Orientalism, 219, 226
Origin: as a category of eighteenth century thought, 9, 75; Rousseau (*Discourse on the Origin of Inequality*), 9; Herder (*Treatise on the Origin of Language*), 9, 39

P

Pathology: in the work of Canguilhem, 7; the emergence of, 7; and sexual psychopathology, 7; and the sublimation of desire, 57
Pedagogy, 159
Peirce, Charles Sanders: and the theory of the external sign, 32; the interpretant, 79

INDEX

Performatives. *See* Speech-Acts
Peucker, Brigitte, 142
Phenomenology: Foucault's critique of, 5
Philology: Friedrich Schlegel's notebooks *Zur Philologie*, 2; in Foucault's work, 4; the emergence in Germany of, 35–37; Hamann's, 48n.6; Germanic, 212; as romance, 213–20; narrative spatialization of, 217
Polizeiwissenschaft, 81, 133
Power: as a system of surveillance and control, 8; critique of Foucault's notion of, 11–12; and the establishment of knowledge techniques, 12; in *The History of Sexuality*, 12–13; in *Discipline and Punish*, 12; and sovereignty, 11–12; shift from law to institutions and disciplinary measures, 13; distribution of in performatives, 15
Prison; 88; function and architecture of, 106; as an institution of examination and reform, 106; the body as, 109–11
Prussia, 58
Psychoanalysis, 5, 112, 118, 122, 131, 211–12. *See also* Freud, Sigmund

R

Ragotzky, Karl August, 153
Reinhold, Karl Leonard: the interpretation of C.M. Wieland's *Oberon*, 67
Rhetoric: classical, 82; formal, 94; as the power-technology of the scholarly servants of sovereigns, 71
Romanticism, 22; as the entwinement of infantilism and idealism, 2; and the development of human scientific disciplines, 21, 193; philology as one strand of, 37; and the "culture-concept," 38; revelation through texts as history, 218
Rorty, Richard: critique of Foucault, 11–12
Rousseau, Jean-Jacques, 75; pedagogical theories, 55, *Discourse on the Origin of Inequality*, 9; *Emile*, 53
Russell, Bertrand, 31–32

S

Sartre, Jean-Paul, 234
Savigny, Friedrich Carl von, 213
Schiller, Friedrich, 230; inaugural lecture at Jena, 66; review of the poems of Gottfried August Bürger, 69. Works: *Maria Stuart*, 93–112; *Über Naive und Sentimentalische Dichtung*, 193–206; *On the Sublime*, 202; *Letters on the Aesthetic Education of Man*, 96, 194, 203; "Spaziergang," 70; *Don Carlos*, 203; *Die Räuber*, 203
Schlegel, Friedrich: theory of the novel, 4; reading of Lessing, 71; Schiller's response to *Lucinde*, 202; *Gespräch über die Poesie*, 2; the notebooks entitled *Zur Philologie* (1797), 2
Schleiermacher, Friedrich Daniel Ernst, 128–29
Schliemann, Heinrich, 212, 228
Science: Foucault and the history and philosophy of, 6; of the heart, 157. *See also* Disciplines, human scientific
Semiotics: characteristic of the Enlightenment, 1; within the discursive system of literature, 1; the sign and the signified, 8, 199
Serres, Michel, 79, 80, 88
Sexuality: Hamann and, 42; female desire, 93–112; in Kleist's *The Broken Jug*, 118; the violence of, 124
Signs. *See* Semiotics
Silverman, Kaja, 136, 142
Skinner, Quentin, 15
Sophocles, 122
Spectacle: of disciplinary practices, 8; of *Maria Stuart's* imprisonment, 21; of the battle, 77; the scene of, 98; in German Classical Tragedy and its function, 112
Speech-Acts, 15, 78, 171, 172, 182, 233, 254
Spiess, Christian Heinrich, 6
Sublime, 195–96, 198, 200
Sulzer, Johann Georg, 75

T

Taylor, Charles, 25
Tissot, Simon André: *On the Health of Scholars*, 67

W

Weber, Samuel, 89n.18
Weimar, Klaus, 71, 73n.15
Wellbery, David, 23
Werner, Abraham Gottlob, 222
Wezel, Johann Karl: and the history of science, 51; and the concept of *Bildung*, 53; *Herrmann und Ulrike*, 51–63
Wieland, Christoph Martin, 65

INDEX

Wissenschaft: discourse as, 75–76, 80, 83; abuses of, 80, 87–88; Nietzsche and, 83; transmission of, 85

Wittgenstein, Ludwig, 19; *Philosophical Investigations*, 32; *Tractatus*, 46

Writing: and the written text, 1–2; and the distinction to oral communication, 1, 120; the simple act of, 3; the power of, 97

Y

Young, Edward: and Hamann, 44; on language as the organon and criterion of reason, 46; Schiller's response to, 202

Z

Zizek, Slavoj, 235